Reading Ethics

Reading Philosophy

Reading Philosophy is a series of textbooks offering interactive commentaries on selected readings, and covering the major sub-disciplines of the field. Each volume contains a number of topical chapters each containing primary readings, accompanied by an introduction to the topic, introductions to the readings as well as the commentary. Edited by leading scholars, the aim of the books is to encourage the practice of philosophy in the process of engagement with philosophical texts.

Reading Philosophy
Samuel Guttenplan, Jennifer Hornsby and Christopher Janaway

Reading Philosophy of Language
Jennifer Hornsby and Guy Longworth

Reading Aesthetics and Philosophy of Art
Christopher Janaway

Reading Epistemology
Sven Bernecker

Reading Metaphysics
Helen Beebee and Julian Dodd

Reading Ethics
Miranda Fricker and Samuel Guttenplan

Reading Ethics

Selected Texts with Interactive Commentary

Miranda Fricker
and
Samuel Guttenplan

A John Wiley & Sons, Ltd., Publication

This edition first published 2009
© 2009 Blackwell Publishing Ltd

Blackwell Publishing was acquired by John Wiley & Sons in February 2007. Blackwell's publishing program has been merged with Wiley's global Scientific, Technical, and Medical business to form Wiley-Blackwell.

Registered Office
John Wiley & Sons Ltd, The Atrium, Southern Gate, Chichester, West Sussex, PO19 8SQ, United Kingdom

Editorial Offices
350 Main Street, Malden, MA 02148-5020, USA
9600 Garsington Road, Oxford, OX4 2DQ, UK
The Atrium, Southern Gate, Chichester, West Sussex, PO19 8SQ, UK

For details of our global editorial offices, for customer services, and for information about how to apply for permission to reuse the copyright material in this book please see our website at www.wiley.com/wiley-blackwell.

The right of Miranda Fricker and Samuel Guttenplan to be identified as the authors of the editorial material in this work has been asserted in accordance with the Copyright, Designs and Patents Act 1988.

Library of Congress Cataloging-in-Publication Data

Reading ethics : selected texts with interactive commentary / [edited by] Miranda Fricker and Samuel Guttenplan.
    p. cm. – (Reading philosophy)
    Includes bibliographical references (p.   ) and index.
    ISBN 978-1-4051-2473-7 (hardcover : alk. paper) – ISBN 978-1-4051-2474-4 (pbk. : alk. paper) 1. Ethics–Textbooks. I. Fricker, Miranda. II. Guttenplan, Samuel D.
    BJ1012.R355 2009
    170–dc22

                                                            2008020126

A catalogue record for this book is available from the British Library.

Set in 10.5/12.5pt Sabon
by SPi Publisher Services, Pondicherry, India

1   2009

Contents

Sources and Acknowledgements

The editor and publisher gratefully acknowledge the permission granted to reproduce the copyright material in this book:

Philippa Foot, 'Utilitarianism and the Virtues', pp. 196–209 from *Mind* 94 (1985). © 1985 by The Mind Association. Reprinted with permission from Oxford University Press.

Raimond Gaita, 'Remorse and Its Lessons', pp. 43–58 from *Good and Evil: An Absolute Conception*, 2nd edn. (Routledge, 2004). © 2004 by Raimond Gaita. Reprinted with permission from Taylor & Francis Books UK.

D. Hume, pp. 413–17, 456–9, from *A Treatise of Human Nature*, ed. Selby-Bigge (Oxford University Press 1978). © 1978 by Oxford University Press. Reprinted with permission from Oxford University Press.

Immanuel Kant, pp. 24–47 from *Groundwork of the Metaphysics of Morals*, trans. and ed. by Mary Gregor, Introduction by Christine M. Korsgaard (Cambridge University Press, 1997). © 1997 by Cambridge University Press. Reprinted with permission from the Estate of M. J. Gregor and Cambridge University Press.

John McDowell, 'Are Moral Requirements Hypothetical Imperatives?', pp. 13–29 from *Proceedings of the Aristotelian Society*, Supplementary Volume 52 (1978). © 1978. Reprinted by courtesy of the Editor of the Aristotelian Society.

J. L. Mackie, 'The Subjectivity of Values', pp. 15–16, 19–27, 31–7, 38–9, 40, 41, 42–4, 45–6, from *Ethics: Inventing Right and Wrong* (Harmondsworth: Penguin Books, 1977). © 1977 by J. L. Mackie. Reprinted with permission from Penguin Books Ltd.

Thomas Nagel, pp. 138–49, 152–5, 156–63, from *The View From Nowhere* (New York/Oxford: Oxford University Press, 1986). © 1986 by Thomas Nagel. Reprinted with permission from Oxford University Press, Inc.

Martha Nussbaum, 'Flawed Crystals: James's *The Golden Bowl* and Literature as Moral Philosophy', pp. 125–47, from *Love's Knowledge: Essays on Philosophy and Literature* (New York/Oxford: Oxford University Press, 1990). © 1990 by Martha Nussbaum. Reprinted with permission from Oxford University Press, Inc.

Plato, extracts from *The Republic*, pp. 605–9, 614–19, 660–87, from *The Collected Dialogue of Plato*, eds Edith Hamilton and Huntingdon Cairns, trans. Paul Shorey (Princeton University Press, 1973).

John Rawls, pp. 3–23 from *A Theory of Justice*. © 1971, 1999 by the President and Fellows of Harvard College (Harvard University Press, 1973). Reprinted with permission from Harvard University Press.

Bernard Williams, 'Morality, the Peculiar Institution', pp. 174–96, from *Ethics and the Limits of Philosophy* (London: Fontana, 1985). © 1985 by Bernard Williams. Reprinted with permission from Taylor & Francis Books UK.

Every effort has been made to trace copyright holders and to obtain their permission for the use of copyright material. The publisher apologizes for any errors or omissions in the above list and would be grateful if notified of any corrections that should be incorporated in future reprints or editions of this book.

Introduction

It is a distinguishing mark of human beings that we have the capacity to be puzzled by many different aspects of the world and our place in it. Sometimes our puzzlement has a distinctively philosophical character – when we stare at the night sky and wonder how it is possible that, in the midst of an indefinite expanse of space and matter, there can be meaning, or reason, or consciousness, or values. These sorts of question, and the attempts to answer them, define in a general way much of the subject matter of philosophy. But when our puzzlement is focused specifically on issues of value, and the significance of the manifold ways in which human beings can respect each other, treasure each other, or betray and abuse each other, we are in the territory of moral philosophy.

Moral philosophy grows from a desire to make sense of how human beings find value and disvalue in the things that people do, and in the character traits from which those actions spring. There are ways of acting which we regard as *right* or as *wrong*, features of character which we regard as *virtues* or as *vices*, and life choices seen as *admirable* or as *contemptible*. Moreover, opinions about these matters – opinions about the specific things which are of value – are not simply observations made to satisfy some kind of curiosity. These opinions guide our actions, figure in the shaping of our social institutions, and contribute to programmes of education we provide for future generations.

No other creature finds value in things the way we do, or is swayed in one or other direction by these findings. Nor is it simply that we alone have words for these values. It is certainly true that a cat, for example, will pursue courses of action that, by our lights, count as valuable for its survival, and, as with many animals, including ourselves, the desire not to be hungry can lead it in one direction rather than another. But, in our case, what we find valuable does not simply coincide with what we desire; indeed, it may even oppose it. That there should be such things as values, and that they should play a prominent part in what we do, and how we choose, can seem deeply puzzling.

The range of questions in moral philosophy is vast, as are the contents and styles of the answers that make up its subject matter. No single volume can adequately cover all of this material, but comprehensiveness is in any case not our aim. As with other volumes in the series, *Reading Ethics* is intended to encourage you to *do* philosophy. Rather than simply presenting you with a mass of material, we have chosen some central interconnected issues, introduced the broad questions that arise, and provided detailed commentaries on excerpted texts that we think combine to present the issues in a philosophically intriguing but lucid and accessible way. These texts come from both historical and contemporary sources – indeed we often juxtapose the two – and they tend to be in implicit, or sometimes explicit, dialogue with one another. Additionally, the commentaries come as close to being interactive as any written material can be: markers in the margins of the texts (of the form 'a $\mapsto$') not only focus attention on particular passages, but are typically an occasion for you to break off and do some thinking on your own, as prompted by the questions and comments enclosed in grey-shaded boxes.

Even though we do not aim at blanket coverage, we have selected topics so that, while doing some moral philosophy, you will also end up with a good idea of central issues that shape the subject. Chapters 1–3 are by S. G.; chapters 4–6 are by M. F. The first two chapters look at two fundamental moral concepts – goodness and justice. No one doubts that these concepts pick out two crucial values figuring in human choices, characters and lives. But this does not mean we have a full understanding of them. In chapter 1 we see that, upon closer examination, the basis for regarding goodness as a value at all is far from clear; and in chapter 2 the question is raised whether there is any such thing as a single, unified concept of justice.

Whatever is said about which things come to count as values, there are interesting and delicate issues surrounding the connection between our finding something valuable and our being motivated to act on that evaluation. In its concern with the notion of a reason, chapter 3 confronts these issues, examining our understanding of how values might actually translate into the kinds of reason to choose and live in the ways that we consider characteristic of a moral life.

The general question of how far moral values and judgements are subjective and how far they are objective is the subject matter of chapter 4. This is one of the most basic underlying questions in ethics, and while it is as old as moral philosophy itself, it still remains a locus of keen debate today. The subjectivity/objectivity opposition can be posed in relation to two different models of objectivity: an idea of moral values as metaphysically real (persisting 'out there', wholly independently of human sensibility); or an idea of moral rationality as absolute. Chapter 4 sees the issue unfold in relation to metaphysical realism, and chapter 5 in relation to rationality.

Finally, we move in chapter 6 to the question of the boundaries of moral philosophy as such. Any introduction to ethics, and especially anything that includes some classic texts, cannot help but implicitly present something like a canon. But any presentation of a canon should include the means to de-stabilize it somewhat, indicating ways in which the discipline is self-questioning, and dynamic. This is part of the purpose of the last chapter – to open out your conception of the possible styles of moral philosophy, and to place traditional moral philosophical approaches in some critical perspective.

Philosophy is always an internally diverse and critical enterprise, and we have tried to present texts that tell that story of ongoing critical discussion, discussion about issues within the subject area, and about the very nature of the subject area itself. All this being said, the main ambition of *Reading Ethics* is something open-ended. Its aim is to make these texts, and the issues they raise, open to your own interpretive and critical contribution, and to encourage you to go on to read further in ethics, better practised and better equipped to gain intellectually from that reading and to enjoy the philosophy.

1

Goodness

Introduction

It would be easy to get people to agree to the idea that goodness plays a central role in morality. When thought of as a quality of persons, it is something moralists teach us to admire in others, and to cultivate in ourselves. However, for all that these opinions about the role of goodness in morality are common, there are difficulties. There is the obvious difficulty of deciding which specific quality of a person counts as goodness – what the content of this notion is. And there is the distracting further fact that goodness can be spoken of in wholly non-moral ways, as when one speaks of the goodness in the food we are about to eat. But these are only a part of the story, and the real difficulty starts further back.

The place to begin is with the adjective 'good' which is after all the place from which much of our talk of goodness arises. Like many other adjectives, 'good' has a special affinity with, and dependence on, the nouns it qualifies. Thus, consider expressions like 'good knife', 'good computer', 'good athlete', or, to put it more generally, 'good X'. First, notice that from the claim, for example, that John is a good athlete we don't infer *both* that John is an athlete *and* that John is good. That he is an athlete does follow, thus showing how good differs from adjectives such as 'fake' or 'alleged'. (When something is described as a 'fake diamond', we most certainly cannot infer that it is a diamond.) But it would take a very strange view of athletic prowess to justify the move from John is a good athlete to John is good. In short, in the ordinary run of cases, the adjective 'good' cannot intelligibly be separated from the noun it qualifies.

The second thing to notice arises from this inseparability, and perhaps partly explains it. In claims of the form, 'O is a good X', we have to look to what replaces X to give us some grounds for deciding whether what is claimed is true or false. To be a good knife is, presumably, to do whatever it is that knives do, and do it well; to be a good computer is to do well whatever is wanted in a computer, and to be a good athlete is to be an athlete who, for example, wins, or breaks records, or has certain outstanding physical characteristics. Clearly, it can be a matter of dispute what it takes in each case to count as a good X, but in every case we look to features of whatever X is to guide that discussion.

These features of the adjective 'good', lead directly to problems for the idea of goodness as an independent property which might figure in claims about morality. Taking 'goodness' to be the nominalization of the adjective 'good', we would expect it to retain, in some form, the features of the adjective, as this is pretty much what we find in the case of other nominalized adjectives. Thus, when Brown insists on her ecological credentials by claiming that she owns a *small* car, we have no trouble in understanding this as interchangeable with the claim that *smallness* is a property of the car. But just as the adjective 'small' requires its noun 'car' to give us some idea of the relevant standard of size, we must understand 'smallness' here as related to cars, and not as a self-standing property. If *smallness* were self-standing, then by choosing a different reference class – perhaps 'possession' – since the car is a large possession, we would end up saying that the car had the self-standing properties both of *smallness* and *largeness*, a conclusion that is surely unacceptable.

Taking 'good' to follow the model of 'small', the aptness in a specific case of the description 'good human being' cannot be understood as making reference to some independent property – goodness – which this human being happens to have. That is, from the claim that 'X is a good human being', we can infer that 'X is a human being', but not that 'X is good', i.e. has a self-standing property of goodness.

Why does this matter? Don't we think that the kind of goodness we are interested in is anyway a property of human beings? It is at this point that the second feature of the adjective 'good' comes into play. A good knife is one which does well – or to some high standard – what knives do. Similarly, then, a good human being must be one which does well – or to some high standard – what human beings do. Obviously, trying to say what it is that human beings do is not going to be as easy as it is for knives, but that is only part of the problem. Given that we are interested in the ways in which goodness might help us understand morality, there are two more pressing and interconnected issues. First, there are ways in which one might judge a human life as conducted well, or to some high standard, that have little directly to do with morality. Second, insofar as we restrict our interest in standards to those that have moral relevance, we will in effect be defining goodness in terms of a prior conception of morality, and this undermines the thought that we can get some kind of leverage on the moral by appealing to a notion of goodness. Both of these points are worth further comment.

Leaving moral issues on one side for the moment, we surely recognize that human lives can take many forms: some people set out to gain the recognition of others, either by the things they do, or by the things they produce; some aim at the accumulation of wealth; some seek power, whether political or economic; and some aim to acquire knowledge. In respect of each of these ways of life, it is possible to imagine standards of achievement: some lives of these kinds fulfil these standards to a high degree, and, with respect to the relevant aims, these lives would be judged good. Thus, we find it natural to speak of good artists, writers, actors, politicians, entrepreneurs, scientists, and, not least, good philosophers. Moreover, though we might think that pursuing one of these to the exclusion of any other is unreasonable, it is difficult to deny that some combination of these activities might well constitute a good human life. Yet there is so far no explicit mention of what we might call 'moral goodness', and this might well make one doubt that the notion of human goodness is going to tell us much about morality.

To assuage this doubt, an obvious next move would be to insist that the above descriptions of a good human life are incomplete: in addition to achieving some high standard in one or more of those activities, there must be some kind of moral engagement. Thus, one might insist that to be a good human being one has also to possess virtues such as justice, benevolence and kindness, or generally know what is right, and do it. This would then constitute a composite account of what goes to make up human good.

This move certainly seems sensible enough, but it is just here that the second of the above points comes into play. The intuition that we can understand moral assessment by deploying a conception of human good requires that we start with some idea of what constitutes that goodness. One idea would be, for example, that we could use goodness to define rightness: an action is right if it leads to more good than any other available action. But if the only way we can spell out a plausible conception of human goodness is to build into it, from the start, some kind of moral assessment, this project won't work. In using human good to define right, but having already needed the notion of right to define the good, any such proposal would be unhelpfully circular.

Aside from this problem of circularity, the composite conception of human good might be thought problematic on its own. When people speak of someone as a good person, this assessment tends to be understood as a moral one: a person can be judged good, even if that person's life is not marked by high achievement in the arts, politics, business, education, science or in any other non-moral sphere. Yet if we follow the trail suggested by the adjective 'good', it does take us to something like the composite view. In finding the standard needed to make sense of 'good', we must make reference to human beings' lives, and the things they pursue, so goodness is bound to include more than a merely moral dimension of assessment.

Faced with these problems, someone might just refuse to follow the adjectival trail: though in many ordinary contexts 'good' seems to require a noun to give it some determinate sense, perhaps things are just different when the subject matter is morality. Perhaps 'goodness' is simply a self-standing property that some human beings have, and others lack, so that when we say 'X is a good person' – and intend the moral sense of 'good' – it does follow both that X is a person and X is good. Such a view might also help to explain something you may have already noticed: there is a certain awkwardness in speaking sometimes about a 'good human life' and sometimes about just plain 'goodness'. As we saw, a good human life includes some degree of achievement in activities that are not directly relevant to morality, but human goodness, even if it often seems in short supply, is most often understood as a singularly moral notion. Of course, 'good' does function adjectivally. So, any refusal to accept the consequences of this must be accompanied by an account explaining why 'goodness' does not derive its sense directly from adjectival uses of 'good'.

Whether we insist on understanding 'good' in a way which sweeps up all of its uses, as well as our use of 'goodness', or whether we think there is a kind of ambiguity in this adjective, an ambiguity that might well be brought out by the different ways in which the nominal 'goodness' is sometimes used, or whether the truth goes beyond either of these, each of these will have consequences for the role that goodness can play in moral thought. For, as we have seen, goodness certainly seems to have a close relationship with rightness and the virtues, and there can be no doubt that this trio of notions, and their inter-relationships, would be central to any account of morality.

Introduction to Aristotle

Aristotle was born (384 BCE) in Stagira in the Chalcidicean peninsula of Macedon – now northern Greece – but his philosophical career is firmly associated with Athens. Arriving there when he was eighteen, he was a distinguished pupil of Plato's at the Academy for nearly twenty years, until the latter's death. On being passed over for the position of head of the Academy, Aristotle left Athens and was eventually summoned to the court of Philip II of Macedon to serve as the tutor to his son, the thirteen-year-old Alexander. When the latter embarked on the military campaigns that, as it were, transformed him into the young Alexander the Great, Aristotle returned to Athens (in 335 BCE) and founded his own institution, the Lyceum. Alexander was not popular in Athens, and when news of his death in 323 BCE reached that city, Aristotle thought it prudent to leave, reputedly insisting that in doing so he would avoid Socrates' fate, and therefore prevent Athens from 'sinning twice against philosophy'. He himself died the following year.

Further details about his life are matters of speculation. Much has been written both about what some regard as the strained relationship between

Plato and Aristotle, and about the extent of Aristotle's influence on Alexander the Great. But the one thing we can be sure of is that, together with Plato, Aristotle transformed the Greek philosophical scene, and, as a result, the whole of philosophy up to the present. His work covered what today would be regarded as natural and social science, as well as the more conventional philosophical topics of logic, metaphysics, ethics, the philosophy of mind and the philosophy of art. Very unfortunately, we seem to have only about a fifth of the writings he was known to have produced, and much of what we do have seems to be notes for lectures given in the Lyceum, perhaps even lecture notes taken by students.

The text below is taken from the work known as the *Nicomachean Ethics*, a treatise probably dedicated to his son Nicomachus (who was himself named after Aristotle's father). As you will see, the selection is very brief. It is intended to get us started asking a certain kind of question about goodness, but you are very strongly encouraged to read the whole of this work, one still regarded as a central work in moral philosophy.

Aristotle, *Nicomachean Ethics* (extracts from Book I)

[a] → **1.** Every art and every inquiry, and similarly every action and pursuit, is thought to aim at some good; and for this reason the good has rightly been declared to be that at which all things aim. But a certain difference is found among ends; some are activities, others are products apart from the activities that produce them. Where there are ends apart from the actions, it is the nature of the products to be better than the activities. Now, as there are many actions, arts, and sciences, their ends also are many; the end of the medical art is health, that of shipbuilding a vessel, that of strategy victory, that of economics wealth. But where such arts fall under a single capacity – as bridle-making and the other arts concerned with the equipment of horses fall under the art of riding, and this and every military action under strategy, in the same way other arts fall under yet others – in all of these the ends of the master arts are to be preferred to all the subordinate ends; for it is for the sake of the former that the latter are pursued. It makes no difference whether the activities themselves are the ends of the actions, or something else apart from the activities, as in the case of the sciences just mentioned.

[b] → **2.** If, then, there is some end of the things we do, which we desire for its own sake (everything else being desired for the sake of this),

and if we do not choose everything for the sake of something else (for at that rate the process would go on to infinity, so that our desire would be empty and vain), clearly this must be the good and the chief good. Will not the knowledge of it, then, have a great influence on life? Shall we not, like archers who have a mark to aim at, be more likely to hit upon what is right? If so, we must try, in outline at least, to determine what it is, and of which of the sciences or capacities it is the object. It would seem to belong to the most authoritative art and that which is most truly the master art. And politics appears to be of this nature; for it is this that ordains which of the sciences should be studied in a state, and which each class of citizens should learn and up to what point they should learn them; and we see even the most highly esteemed of capacities to fall under this, e.g. strategy, economics, rhetoric; now, since politics uses the rest of the sciences, and since, again, it legislates as to what we are to do and what we are to abstain from, the end of this science must include those of the others, so that this end must be the good for man. For even if the end is the same for a single man and for a state, that of the state seems at all events something greater and more complete whether to attain or to preserve; though it is worth while to attain the end merely for one man, it is finer and more god like to attain it for a nation or for city-states. These, then, are the ends at which our inquiry aims, since it is political science, in one sense of that term.

[...]

4. Let us resume our inquiry and state, in view of the fact that all knowledge and every pursuit aims at some good, what it is that we say political science aims at and what is the highest of all goods achievable by action. Verbally there is very general agreement; for both the general run of men and people of superior refinement say that it is happiness, and identify living well and doing well with being happy; but with regard to what happiness is they differ, and the many do not give the same account as the wise. For the former think it is some plain and obvious thing, like pleasure, wealth, or honour; they differ, however, from one another – and often even the same man identifies it with different things, with health when he is ill, with wealth when he is poor; but, conscious of their ignorance, they admire those who proclaim some great ideal that is above their comprehension. Now some thought that apart from these many goods there is another which is self-subsistent and causes the goodness of all these as well. To examine all the opinions that have been held were perhaps somewhat fruitless; enough to examine those that are most prevalent or that seem to be arguable.

5. Let us, however, resume our discussion from the point at which we digressed. To judge from the lives that men lead, most men, and men of

the most vulgar type, seem (not without some ground) to identify the
good, or happiness, with pleasure; which is the reason why they love
the life of enjoyment. For there are, we may say, three prominent types
of life – that just mentioned, the political, and thirdly the contemplative
life. Now the mass of mankind are evidently quite slavish in their tastes,
preferring a life suitable to beasts, but they get some ground for their
view from the fact that many of those in high places share the tastes of
Sardanapallus. A consideration of the prominent types of life shows
that people of superior refinement and of active disposition identify
happiness with honour; for this is, roughly speaking, the end of the
political life. But it seems too superficial to be what we are looking for,
since it is thought to depend on those who bestow honour rather than
on him who receives it, but the good we divine to be something proper
to a man and not easily taken from him. Further, men seem to pursue
honour in order that they may be assured of their goodness; at least it
is by men of practical wisdom that they seek to be honoured, and
among those who know them, and on the ground of their virtue; clearly,
then, according to them, at any rate, virtue is better. And perhaps one
might even suppose this to be, rather than honour, the end of the political life. But even this appears somewhat incomplete; for possession of
virtue seems actually compatible with being asleep, or with lifelong in-
activity, and, further, with the greatest sufferings and misfortunes; but
a man who was living so no one would call happy, unless he were
maintaining a thesis at all costs. But enough of this; for the subject has
been sufficiently treated even in the current discussions. Third comes
the contemplative life, which we shall consider later.

[…]

7. Let us again return to the good we are seeking, and ask what it can
be. It seems different in different actions and arts; it is different in
medicine, in strategy, and in the other arts likewise. What then is the
good of each? Surely that for whose sake everything else is done. In
medicine this is health, in strategy victory, in architecture a house,
in any other sphere something else, and in every action and pursuit
the end; for it is for the sake of this that all men do whatever else they
do. Therefore, if there is an end for all that we do, this will be the
good achievable by action, and if there are more than one, these will
be the goods achievable by action.

So the argument has by a different course reached the same point;
but we must try to state this even more clearly. Since there are evidently
more than one end, and we choose some of these (e.g. wealth, flutes,
and in general instruments) for the sake of something else, clearly not
all ends are final ends; but the chief good is evidently something final.
Therefore, if there is only one final end, this will be what we are seeking, and if there are more than one, the most final of these will be

what we are seeking. Now we call that which is in itself worthy of pursuit more final than that which is worthy of pursuit for the sake of something else, and that which is never desirable for the sake of something else more final than the things that are desirable both in themselves and for the sake of that other thing, and therefore we call final without qualification that which is always desirable in itself and never for the sake of something else.

Now such a thing happiness, above all else, is held to be; for this we choose always for itself and never for the sake of something else, but honour, pleasure, reason, and every virtue we choose indeed for themselves (for if nothing resulted from them we should still choose each of them), but we choose them also for the sake of happiness, judging that by means of them we shall be happy. Happiness, on the other hand, no one chooses for the sake of these, nor, in general, for anything other than itself.

From the point of view of self-sufficiency the same result seems to follow; for the final good is thought to be self-sufficient. Now by self-sufficient we do not mean that which is sufficient for a man by himself, for one who lives a solitary life, but also for parents, children, wife, and in general for his friends and fellow citizens, since man is born for citizenship. But some limit must be set to this; for if we extend our requirement to ancestors and descendants and friends' friends we are in for an infinite series. Let us examine this question, however, on another occasion; the self-sufficient we now define as that which when isolated makes life desirable and lacking in nothing; and such we think happiness to be; and further we think it most desirable of all things, without being counted as one good thing among others – if it were so counted it would clearly be made more desirable by the addition of even the least of goods; for that which is added becomes an excess of goods, and of goods the greater is always more desirable. Happiness, then, is something final and self-sufficient, and is the end of action.

$\boxed{\text{h}} \mapsto$ Presumably, however, to say that happiness is the chief good seems a platitude, and a clearer account of what it is is still desired. This might perhaps be given, if we could first ascertain the function of man. For just as for a flute-player, a sculptor, or an artist, and, in general, for all things that have a function or activity, the good and the 'well' is thought to reside in the function, so would it seem to be for man, if he has a function. Have the carpenter, then, and the tanner certain functions or activities, and has man none? Is he born without a function? Or as eye, hand, foot, and in general each of the parts evidently has a function, may one lay it down that man similarly has a function apart from all these? What then can this be? Life seems to be common even to plants, but we are seeking what is peculiar to man. Let us exclude, therefore, the life of nutrition and growth. Next there would be a life of perception, but it also seems to be common even to the horse, the ox, and every animal. There remains, then, an active life of the element that has a rational principle; of this, one part has such a principle in the sense of being obedient to one, the other in the sense of possessing one and exercising thought. And, as 'life of the rational element' also has two meanings, we must state that life in the sense of activity is what we mean; for this seems to be the more proper sense of the term. Now if the function of man is an activity of soul which follows or implies a rational principle, and if we say 'so-and-so' and 'a good so-and-so' have a function which is the same in kind, e.g. a lyre, and a good lyre-player, and so without qualification in all cases, eminence in respect of goodness being added to the name of the function (for the function of a lyre-player is to play the lyre, and that of a good lyre-player is to do so well): if this is the case, and we state the function of man to be a certain kind of life, and this to be an activity or actions of the soul implying a rational principle, and the function of a good man to be the good and noble performance of these, and if any action is well performed when it is per-

[i]→ formed in accordance with the appropriate excellence: if this is the case, human good turns out to be activity of soul in accordance with virtue, and if there are more than one virtue, in accordance with the best and most complete.

[j]→   But we must add 'in a complete life'. For one swallow does not make a summer, nor does one day; and so too one day, or a short time, does not make a man blessed and happy.

Commentary on Aristotle

The *Nicomachean Ethics* is divided into ten books, and our text consists of only a few of the numbered sections of Book I. Taking the first step in laying the groundwork for what follows, and to a large extent laying the groundwork for much of moral philosophy, Aristotle, at [a]→, makes what seems a straightforward enough claim.

While Aristotle's claim in the sentence at [a]→ can seem uncontentious, can you think of any way in which it might be challenged?

It might be thought that Aristotle is here making the very strong claim that there is some single thing – the good – at which everything we do aims. However, while there is more to say about this interpretation, it doesn't seem to be what Aristotle has in mind at $\boxed{a}\!\mapsto$. For, only a couple of sentences later, he insists that there are as many ends – things we aim at – as there are actions, arts and sciences. So, at least initially, it is more plausible to treat his opening sentence as the claim that every art, inquiry and action has something or other it aims at, and that for each of these, we can understand that as the good appropriate to that activity. But even under this weaker reading what he claims might be challenged. Is it really the case that everything we do aims at some good or other? Might we not sometimes just do things without any thought about what we are aiming to achieve? Obviously, these are difficult questions, but the fact that Aristotle's claim invites them suggests that his claim is a substantial one. It gives the notion of the good a clear and central place in understanding human endeavour.

Aristotle then takes an important further step. Between $\boxed{a}\!\mapsto$ and $\boxed{b}\!\mapsto$ he prepares the ground for this step by asking us to recognize that the good we aim at in some of our activities (e.g. bridle-making) is subordinate to the good of those more general activities which encompass the former (e.g. riding, and ultimately military strategy). Thus, faced with an activity and the good we expect in pursuing it, it is always possible to ask after the point of that good, and to get an answer in terms of some further activity which subsumes the original one. However, at $\boxed{b}\!\mapsto$ he claims that there is indeed a 'chief good', a good which stops the potentially infinite regress that the questions lead to. Such a chief good is the one which we pursue without it being necessary to ask what it is itself good for; it is something good for itself and the good of everything else is ultimately to be explained by reference to it. Speaking metaphorically, he notes (at $\boxed{c}\!\mapsto$) that knowing such a good will makes us like archers who have a mark to aim at. Or, less metaphorically, we can say that someone who knows what constitutes the good – that for the sake of which everything we do is done – will be in a strong position to live a fulfilled life.

Aristotle goes on to claim that politics is the science which is most likely to be concerned with this kind of goodness; he describes it as the 'master art'. We won't stop here to consider why, given the Aristotelian notion of politics, this is more plausible than it might seem now, familiar as we are with the often unedifying nature of political discourse.

> Can you imagine a conception of politics and its aims which would have encouraged Aristotle to have regarded it as the master art? (Hint: read carefully what Aristotle says between $\boxed{c}\!\mapsto$ and $\boxed{d}\!\mapsto$.)

At $\boxed{d}\!\mapsto$, Aristotle, returning from a digression, begins the next stage of his account of goodness. Having, as he thinks, established that the good is to be understood as that for the sake of which we do everything, he sets out to give some content to this notion. For up to this point the notion of the good has only been a kind of place-holder: using Aristotle's metaphor, we can say that 'good' labels the fact that we aim at some target or other, though it doesn't yet tell us what the target is like.

Aristotle begins to flesh out his account (at $\boxed{e}\!\rightarrow$) by noting something that he believes would command almost universal assent: the good for human beings is happiness. And, with this apparently simple move, he opens up a Pandora's box of philosophical and interpretative issues.

> Can you imagine anyone who would not go along with Aristotle's claim about happiness being the good at which we aim in everything we do?

It is very difficult to resist taking our word 'happiness' as the label for some psychological state, something we experience in reaction to, for example, some success or piece of good news. However, taken in this way, it is easy to imagine someone challenging Aristotle's claim by insisting that there are more important things in life than happiness – that, for example, devoting oneself to a cause, or to knowledge, or to one's family count more than happiness. So, given that Aristotle regards his claim as one which commands general agreement, the suspicion must be that he is not speaking about happiness in the merely psychological sense. Moreover, given that this suspicion is well and truly borne out by all the things that Aristotle says about it in the *Nicomachean Ethics*, one might wonder whether 'happiness' is the best translation of Aristotle's notion of *eudaimonia*. The problem is that, on the one hand, there seems no better alternative (we will discuss this shortly); and, on the other hand, our notion of happiness can in fact be used in ways that are closer to Aristotle's intent.

Some have suggested 'living well' as a translation – and it works well enough when understood as an almost technical term by Aristotelian commentators – but in ordinary use this phrase conjures up images of a life of ease and plenty that is far removed from Aristotle's *eudaimonia*. The English word 'happiness' can mislead in respect of Aristotle, but at least there is a use of this term which fits some of the things that Aristotle intends. When, at the very end of our text (at $\boxed{j}\!\rightarrow$), Aristotle notes that a complete human life can be judged as good or happy, we find no difficulty in what he says, even though he clearly does not have in mind a kind of feeling that comes and goes depending on our emotional state at any particular moment. As he often says, happiness for a human being consists in leading a certain kind of life, and there is no guarantee that such a life will be one of continuous happiness in the narrower psychological sense. Indeed, when one might think one is challenging Aristotle's identification of the good with happiness by pointing out the 'other things' in life that matter, one is in fact agreeing with him. For when he leaves behind his verbal point – when he sets out to find out what human happiness is – he makes very clear that it is much more than the kind of psychological state often described as 'pleasure' or 'contentment'.

Just after the point marked $\boxed{f}\!\rightarrow$, Aristotle identifies three kinds of life, each of which might be regarded by some as happy and as cases in which a human being lives well. One is a life spent in the pursuit of pleasure, and he dismisses this as a life suitable to beasts, even though he also notes that one can sometimes find those who should know better devoting themselves to such a pursuit. The second suggestion is that of a life spent in the pursuit of honour and the third is a contemplative life, one spent in pursuit of knowledge.

> ## What do you think Aristotle means by a life spent in pursuit of honour?

Aristotle describes honour as the end of political life, and this might suggest to us a life spent pursuing honour as one spent in trying to achieve public office, and everything that goes with it. However, while this is not simply wrong, it narrows the conception of honour to one that makes it difficult to understand why it figures so centrally in Aristotle's list. But if one thinks of the pursuit of honour as more general – as the pursuit of recognition for one's achievements including those in the arts, sciences, or in public life generally – this provides a better idea of what Aristotle has in mind. And we will be able to understand why he thinks such a pursuit is at most second best. For, as he says, what one is doing in seeking such recognition is looking to others to judge one's abilities, and accepting their verdict as a way of ensuring that one is worthy. But he notes (at g→) that finding our merits in the judgements of others is superficial, and that the good should be 'something proper to a man and not easily taken from him'.

> ## Say what you think Aristotle means by claiming this.

You can get an idea of what he has in mind by looking further ahead to h→. In the passages between g→ and h→, Aristotle offers a number of interesting further considerations for his conclusion that happiness is what we aim at in everything we do. These arguments seek to establish that happiness is 'final and self-sufficient'; it is something which we choose not for the sake of something else, but for itself, and which is itself most desirable, rather than being one good among a number of others. However, having done this, he returns to the question of how to fill out our account of what actually constitutes happiness. And at h→ he offers a new approach: he says that we could better answer our question if we could 'first ascertain the function of man'.

As we have seen, it is not always easy to find good translations for Aristotle's terms, and this is especially true in the present instance. Using 'function' as a translation of Aristotle's *ergon* can be justified, but can also be highly misleading. In certain contexts, we tend to think of the function of a thing as the purpose for which it was designed, or is employed: the function of a telephone is to allow us to speak across distances; that of a car is to travel those distances. Against this kind of background it is all too easy to think that Aristotle's thought is something like this: human beings are in some sense designed to do, or achieve, certain things, and once we have worked out what we are designed to do or achieve – something we are supposed to be able to work out independently of knowing what human goodness or excellence is – we can understand a good human being as one who fulfils that function most successfully. On this understanding, what Aristotle offers at $\boxed{h}\!\!\rightarrow$ is a way to fill in what he had so far left blank, namely, a specific understanding of the good for humankind.

Tempting though this picture might be, there is reason to think that it is not what Aristotle had in mind in using *ergon* in the way he does. Look at the passage beginning at $\boxed{h}\!\!\rightarrow$ and going to $\boxed{i}\!\!\rightarrow$. There is no suggestion here that 'function of human beings' means the specific purpose that human beings were designed to fulfil. More importantly, Aristotle does not use the so-called 'function argument' to give us a detailed picture of the good (for human beings). He does say that human life is distinctive in involving the exercise of rational activity. This is what distinguishes us from plants and other animals. And he does go on to say that human goodness therefore consists in the 'good and noble' performance of the rational activity that is definitive of our nature. But nowhere does he indicate exactly what this rational activity involves; whether, that is, it involves living one's life in one kind of way or another.

> Aristotle concludes the function argument by saying that 'human good turns out to be activity of soul in accordance with virtue'. Does this give us any guidance about what it is that we do or should pursue in aiming at the good?

It is difficult to see that it does. Given that 'activity of the soul' here refers to the rational activity that makes us what we are, and, given that 'virtue' could as well be translated here by 'excellence', this claim repeats the point discussed above. Human good consists in achieving a kind of excellence in the exercise of our rational natures. But nothing is said, at any rate here, about what makes up the exercise of these faculties. So, while the discussion has been moved along, it hasn't reached any very definite conclusion.

At $\boxed{j}\!\!\rightarrow$, he does add that we cannot judge a person to have been happy except in relation to a complete life, and this certainly shows why it is wrong to treat 'happiness' as the ephemeral psychological notion it is sometimes taken to be. But it also shows why this English word is not simply a mistranslation of Aristotle's *eudaimonia*. For, while we do describe people as happy (or not) on a day-to-day basis, we also recognize the wisdom in Aristotle's metaphorical insistence that one swallow does not make a summer.

Where does this leave us? Well, in spite of the controversy that surrounds the interpretation of the *Nicomachean Ethics*, it is perhaps fair to say two things. First, in treating the notion of the good in the way he did, Aristotle has made that notion central to what we might now describe as the project of morality. Second, he has given us some idea of where to look for an understanding of the good. It is, for example, not to be found in a kind of life we share with plants – namely growth – nor in the appetitive nature of animals. It has, therefore, an intrinsic connection with what is rational, since this is something that marks off human nature from that of other beings. But there are many different kinds of life that could be judged consistent with this requirement, and, at least in Book I, Aristotle has said very little about choosing between them.

Introduction to Mill

John Stuart Mill was born in London in 1806 and died in Avignon in 1873. His Scottish father, James Mill, was a distinguished writer and civil servant who, with Jeremy Bentham, was deeply involved in the political reform movement of the 1830s. James Mill and Bentham arranged for John Stuart Mill to be carefully educated, without what they saw as distracting contact with companions of his own age, so as to carry on the work of this movement. In his *Autobiography*, John Stuart Mill described his education – which most would regard as extraordinarily intensive – as one suitable for any normal child. That said, he also records a period of extreme depression that he suffered as a young man, and many now regard that depression as the direct result of his lack of anything one would count as a childhood. (Aside from its relevance to Mill's thought, the *Autobiography* is an interesting account of his political and social context. Moreover, not counting very recent philosophers, proper autobiographies are rather rare in philosophy.)

A central philosophical view of the reformist movement of James Mill and Bentham was known as 'utilitarianism', and John Stuart Mill made a major contribution to this doctrine as well as to politics, economics, women's rights, philosophy and logic. He was by any standards a prolific writer and had an enormous influence on social and political life in nineteenth-century Britain and on the European continent.

Utilitarianism was originally published over three issues of the monthly *Fraser's Magazine* in 1861, and then collected together as a short book in 1863. It should be noted that Mill's aim in *Utilitarianism* was to expound and defend the doctrine of utilitarianism for the more general public, rather than to construct arguments for narrowly philosophic purposes. And it should be remembered that, whatever view one comes to about its philosophical content, in its time the doctrine was, and was seen to be, radical and utopian by both its adherents and its detractors.

J. S. Mill, *Utilitarianism* (extracts from Ch. 2, 'What Utilitarianism Is')

[...]

a⊢→   The creed which accepts as the foundation of morals, Utility, or the Greatest Happiness Principle, holds that actions are right in proportion as they tend to promote happiness, wrong as they tend to produce the reverse of happiness. By happiness is intended pleasure, and the absence of pain; by unhappiness, pain, and the privation of pleasure. To give a clear view of the moral standard set up by the theory, much more requires to be said; in particular, what things it includes in the ideas of pain and pleasure; and to what extent this is left an open question. But these supplementary explanations do not affect the theory of life on which this theory of morality is grounded – namely, that pleasure, and freedom from pain, are the only things desirable as ends; and that all desirable things (which are as numerous in the utilitarian as in any other scheme) are desirable either for the pleasure inherent in themselves, or as means to the promotion of pleasure and the prevention of pain.

 Now, such a theory of life excites in many minds, and among them in some of the most estimable in feeling and purpose, inveterate dislike. To suppose that life has (as they express it) no higher end than pleasure – no better and nobler object of desire and pursuit – they designate as utterly mean and grovelling; as a doctrine worthy only of swine, to whom the followers of Epicurus were, at a very early period, contemptuously likened; and modern holders of the doctrine are occasionally made the subject of equally polite comparisons by its German, French, and English assailants.

When thus attacked, the Epicureans have always answered, that it is not they, but their accusers, who represent human nature in a degrading light; since the accusation supposes human beings to be capable of no pleasures except those of which swine are capable. If this supposition were true, the charge could not be gainsaid, but would then be no longer an imputation; for if the sources of pleasure were precisely the same to human beings and to swine, the rule of life which is good enough for the one would be good enough for the other. The comparison of the Epicurean life to that of beasts is felt as degrading, precisely because a beast's pleasures do not satisfy a human being's conceptions of happiness. Human beings have faculties more elevated than the animal appetites, and when once made conscious of them, do not regard anything as happiness which does not include their gratification. I do not, indeed, consider the Epicureans to have been by any means faultless in drawing out their scheme of consequences from the utilitarian principle. To do this in any sufficient manner, many Stoic, as well as Christian elements require to be included. But there is no known Epicurean theory of life which does not assign to the pleasures of the intellect, of the feelings and imagination, and of the moral sentiments, a much higher value as pleasures than to those of mere sensation. It must be admitted, however, that utilitarian writers in general have placed the superiority of mental over bodily pleasures chiefly in the greater permanency, safety, uncostliness, etc., of the former – that is, in their circumstantial advantages rather than in their intrinsic nature. And on all these points utilitarians have fully proved their case; but they might have taken the other, and, as it may be called, higher ground, with entire consistency. It is quite compatible with the principle of utility to recognize the fact, that some kinds of pleasure are more desirable and more valuable than others. It would be absurd that while, in estimating all other things, quality is considered as well as quantity, the estimation of pleasures should be supposed to depend on quantity alone.

d→ If I am asked, what I mean by difference of quality in pleasures, or what makes one pleasure more valuable than another, merely as a pleasure, except its being greater in amount, there is but one possible answer. Of two pleasures, if there be one to which all or almost all who have experience of both give a decided preference, irrespective of any feeling of moral obligation to prefer it, that is the more desirable pleasure. If one of the two is, by those who are competently acquainted with both, placed so far above the other that they prefer it, even though knowing it to be attended with a greater amount of discontent, and would not resign it for any quantity of the other pleasure which their nature is capable of, we are justified in ascribing to the preferred enjoyment a superiority in quality, so far outweighing quantity as to render it, in comparison, of small account.

Now it is an unquestionable fact that those who are equally acquainted with, and equally capable of appreciating and enjoying, both, do give a most marked preference to the manner of existence which employs their higher faculties. Few human creatures would consent to be changed into any of the lower animals, for a promise of the fullest allowance of a beast's pleasures; no intelligent human being would consent to be a fool, no instructed person would be an ignoramus, no person of feeling and conscience would be selfish and base, even though they should be persuaded that the fool, the dunce, or the rascal is better satisfied with his lot than they are with theirs. They would not resign what they possess more than he for the most complete satisfaction of all the desires which they have in common with him. If they ever fancy they would, it is only in cases of unhappiness so extreme, that to escape from it they would exchange their lot for almost any other, however undesirable in their own eyes. A being of higher faculties requires more to make him happy, is capable probably of more acute suffering, and certainly accessible to it at more points, than one of an inferior type; but in spite of these liabilities, he can never really wish to sink into what he feels to be a lower grade of existence. We may give what explanation we please of this unwillingness; we may attribute it to pride, a name which is given indiscriminately to some of the most and to some of the least estimable feelings of which mankind are capable: we may refer it to the love of liberty and personal independence, an appeal to which was with the Stoics one of the most effective means for the inculcation of it; to the love of power, or to the love of excitement, both of which do really enter into and contribute to it: but its most appropriate appellation is a sense of dignity, which all human beings possess in one form or other, and in some, though by no means in exact, proportion to their higher faculties, and which is so essential a part of the happiness of those in whom it is strong, that nothing which conflicts with it could be, otherwise than momentarily, an object of desire to them.

Whoever supposes that this preference takes place at a sacrifice of happiness – that the superior being, in anything like equal circumstances, is not happier than the inferior – confounds the two very different ideas, of happiness, and content. It is indisputable that the being whose capacities of enjoyment are low, has the greatest chance of having them fully satisfied; and a highly endowed being will always feel that any happiness which he can look for, as the world is constituted, is imperfect. But he can learn to bear its imperfections, if they are at all bearable; and they will not make him envy the being who is indeed unconscious of the imperfections, but only because he feels not at all the good which those imperfections qualify. It is better to be a human being dissatisfied than a pig satisfied; better to be Socrates dissatisfied than a fool satisfied. And if the fool, or the pig, are a different opinion, it is because they only know their own side of the question. The other party to the comparison knows both sides.

[...]

I have dwelt on this point, as being a necessary part of a perfectly just conception of Utility or Happiness, considered as the directive rule of human conduct. But it is by no means an indispensable condition to the acceptance of the utilitarian standard; for that standard is not the agent's own greatest happiness, but the greatest amount of happiness altogether; and if it may possibly be doubted whether a noble character is always the happier for its nobleness, there can be no doubt that it makes other people happier, and that the world in general is immensely a gainer by it. Utilitarianism, therefore, could only attain its end by the general cultivation of nobleness of character, even if each individual were only benefited by the nobleness of others, and his own, so far as happiness is concerned, were a sheer deduction from the benefit. But the bare enunciation of such an absurdity as this last, renders refutation superfluous.

g⟶　According to the Greatest Happiness Principle, as above explained, the ultimate end, with reference to and for the sake of which all other things are desirable (whether we are considering our own good or that of other people), is an existence exempt as far as possible from pain, and as rich as possible in enjoyments, both in point of quantity and quality; the test of quality, and the rule for measuring it against quantity, being the preference felt by those who in their opportunities of experience, to which must be added their habits of self-consciousness and self-observation, are best furnished with the means of comparison. This, being, according to the utilitarian opinion, the end of human action, is necessarily also the standard of morality; which may accordingly be defined, the rules and precepts for human conduct, by the observance of which an existence such as has been described might be, to the greatest extent possible, secured to all mankind; and not to them only, but, so far as the nature of things admits, to the whole sentient creation.

h⟶　Against this doctrine, however, arises another class of objectors, who say that happiness, in any form, cannot be the rational purpose of human life and action; because, in the first place, it is unattainable: and they contemptuously ask, what right hast thou to be happy? a question which Mr Carlyle clenches by the addition, What right, a short time ago, hadst thou even to be? Next, they say, that men can do without happiness; that all noble human beings have felt this, and could not have become noble but by learning the lesson of Entsagen, or renunciation; which lesson, thoroughly learnt and submitted to, they affirm to be the beginning and necessary condition of all virtue.

The first of these objections would go to the root of the matter were it well founded; for if no happiness is to be had at all by human beings, the attainment of it cannot be the end of morality, or of any rational conduct. Though, even in that case, something might still be said for the utilitarian theory; since utility includes not solely the pursuit of happiness, but the prevention or mitigation of unhappiness; and if the former aim be chimerical, there will be all the greater scope and more imperative need for the latter, so long at least as mankind think fit to live, and do not take refuge in the simultaneous act of suicide recommended under certain conditions by Novalis. When, however, it is thus positively asserted to be impossible that human life should be happy, the assertion, if not something like a verbal quibble, is at least an exaggeration. If by happiness be meant a continuity of highly pleasurable excitement, it is evident enough that this is impossible. A state of exalted pleasure lasts only moments, or in some cases, and with some intermissions, hours or days, and is the occasional brilliant flash of enjoyment, not its permanent and steady flame. Of this the philosophers who have taught that happiness is the end of life were as fully aware as those who taunt them. The happiness which they meant was not a life of rapture; but moments of such, in an existence made up of few and transitory pains, many and various pleasures, with a decided predominance of the active over the passive, and having as the foundation of the whole, not to expect more from life than it is capable of bestowing. A life thus composed, to those who have been fortunate enough to obtain it, has always appeared worthy of the name of happiness. And such an existence is even now the lot of many, during some considerable portion of their lives. The present wretched education, and wretched social arrangements, are the only real hindrance to its being attainable by almost all.

The objectors perhaps may doubt whether human beings, if taught to consider happiness as the end of life, would be satisfied with such a moderate share of it. But great numbers of mankind have been satisfied with much less. The main constituents of a satisfied life appear to be two, either of which by itself is often found sufficient for the purpose: tranquillity, and excitement. With much tranquillity, many find that they can be content with very little pleasure: with much excitement, many can reconcile themselves to a considerable quantity of pain. There is assuredly no inherent impossibility in enabling even the mass of mankind to unite both; since the two are so far from being incompatible that they are in natural alliance, the prolongation of either being a preparation for, and exciting a wish for, the other. It is only those in whom indolence amounts to a vice, that do not desire excitement after an interval of repose: it is only those in whom the need of excitement is a disease, that feel the tranquillity which follows excitement dull and insipid, instead of pleasurable in direct proportion to the excitement which preceded it. When people who are tolerably fortunate in their outward lot do not find in life sufficient enjoyment to make it valuable to them, the cause generally is, caring for nobody but themselves. To those who have neither public nor private affections, the excitements of life are much curtailed, and in any case dwindle in value as the time approaches when all selfish interests must be terminated by death: while those who leave after them objects of personal affection, and especially those who have also cultivated a fellow-feeling with the collective interests of mankind, retain as lively an interest in life on the eve of death as in the vigour of youth and health. Next to selfishness, the principal cause which makes life unsatisfactory is want of mental cultivation. A cultivated mind – I do not mean that of a philosopher, but any mind to which the fountains of knowledge have been opened, and which has been taught, in any tolerable degree, to exercise its faculties – finds sources of inexhaustible interest in all that surrounds it; in the objects of nature, the achievements of art, the imaginations of poetry, the incidents of history, the ways of mankind, past and present, and their prospects in the future. It is possible, indeed, to become indifferent to all this, and that too without having exhausted a thousandth part of it; but only when one has had from the beginning no moral or human interest in these things, and has sought in them only the gratification of curiosity.

Now there is absolutely no reason in the nature of things why an amount of mental culture sufficient to give an intelligent interest in these objects of contemplation, should not be the inheritance of every one born in a civilized country. As little is there an inherent necessity that any human being should be a selfish egotist, devoid of every feeling or care but those which centre in his own miserable individuality. Something far superior to this is sufficiently common even now, to give ample earnest of what the human species may be made. Genuine private affections and a sincere interest in the public good, are possible, though in unequal degrees, to every rightly brought up human being. In a world in which there is so much to interest, so much to enjoy, and so much also to correct and improve, every one who has this moderate amount of moral and intellectual requisites is capable of an existence which may be called enviable; and unless such a person, through bad laws, or subjection to the will of others, is denied the liberty to use the sources of happiness within his reach, he will not fail to find this enviable existence, if he escape the positive evils of life, the great sources of physical and mental suffering – such as indigence, disease, and the unkindness, worthlessness, or premature loss of objects of affection. The main stress of the problem lies, therefore, in the contest with these calamities, from which it is a rare good fortune entirely to escape; which, as things now are, cannot be obviated, and often cannot be in any material degree mitigated. Yet no one whose opinion deserves a moment's consideration can doubt that most of the great positive evils of the world are in themselves removable, and will, if human affairs continue to improve, be in the end reduced within narrow limits. Poverty, in any sense implying suffering, may be completely extinguished by the wisdom of society, combined with the good sense and providence of individuals. Even that most intractable of enemies, disease, may be indefinitely reduced in dimensions by good physical and moral education, and proper control of noxious influences; while the progress of science holds out a promise for the future of still more direct conquests over this detestable foe. And every advance in that direction relieves us from some, not only of the chances which cut short our own lives, but, what concerns us still more, which deprive us of those in whom our happiness is wrapt up. As for vicissitudes of fortune, and other disappointments connected with worldly circumstances, these are principally the effect either of gross imprudence, of ill-regulated desires, or of bad or imperfect social institutions.

All the grand sources, in short, of human suffering are in a great degree, many of them almost entirely, conquerable by human care and effort; and though their removal is grievously slow – though a long succession of generations will perish in the breach before the conquest is completed, and this world becomes all that, if will and knowledge were not wanting, it might easily be made – yet every mind sufficiently intelligent and generous to bear a part, however small and unconspicuous, in the endeavour, will draw a noble enjoyment from the contest itself, which he would not for any bribe in the form of selfish indulgence consent to be without.

And this leads to the true estimation of what is said by the objectors concerning the possibility, and the obligation, of learning to do without happiness. Unquestionably it is possible to do without happiness; it is done involuntarily by nineteen-twentieths of mankind, even in those parts of our present world which are least deep in barbarism; and it often has to be done voluntarily by the hero or the martyr, for the sake of something which he prizes more than his individual happiness. But this something, what is it, unless the happiness of others or some of the requisites of happiness? It is noble to be capable of resigning entirely one's own portion of happiness, or chances of it: but, after all, this self-sacrifice must be for some end; it is not its own end; and if we are told that its end is not happiness, but virtue, which is better than happiness, I ask, would the sacrifice be made if the hero or martyr did not believe that it would earn for others immunity from similar sacrifices? Would it be made if he thought that his renunciation of happiness for himself would produce no fruit for any of his fellow creatures, but to make their lot like his, and place them also in the condition of persons who have renounced happiness? All honour to those who can abnegate for themselves the personal enjoyment of life, when by such renunciation they contribute worthily to increase the amount of happiness in the world; but he who does it, or professes to do it, for any other purpose, is no more deserving of admiration than the ascetic mounted on his pillar. He may be an inspiriting proof of what men can do, but assuredly not an example of what they should.

Though it is only in a very imperfect state of the world's arrangements that any one can best serve the happiness of others by the absolute sacrifice of his own, yet so long as the world is in that imperfect state, I fully acknowledge that the readiness to make such a sacrifice is the highest virtue which can be found in man. I will add, that in this condition the world, paradoxical as the assertion may be, the conscious ability to do without happiness gives the best prospect of realizing, such happiness as is attainable. For nothing except that consciousness can raise a person above the chances of life, by making him feel that, let fate and fortune do their worst, they have not power to subdue him: which, once felt, frees him from excess of anxiety concerning the evils of life, and enables him, like many a Stoic in the worst times of the Roman Empire, to cultivate in tranquillity the sources of satisfaction accessible to him, without concerning himself about the uncertainty of their duration, any more than about their inevitable end.

Meanwhile, let utilitarians never cease to claim the morality of self-devotion as a possession which belongs by as good a right to them, as either to the Stoic or to the Transcendentalist. The utilitarian morality does recognize in human beings the power of sacrificing their own greatest good for the good of others. It only refuses to admit that the

[j]→ sacrifice is itself a good. A sacrifice which does not increase, or tend to increase, the sum total of happiness, it considers as wasted. The only self-renunciation which it applauds, is devotion to the happiness, or to some of the means of happiness, of others; either of mankind collectively, or of individuals within the limits imposed by the collective interests of mankind.

[k]→ I must again repeat, what the assailants of utilitarianism seldom have the justice to acknowledge, that the happiness which forms the utilitarian standard of what is right in conduct, is not the agent's own happiness, but that of all concerned. As between his own happiness and that of others, utilitarianism requires him to be as strictly impartial as a disinterested and benevolent spectator. In the golden rule of Jesus of Nazareth, we read the complete spirit of the ethics of utility. To do as you would be done by, and to love your neighbour as yourself, constitute the ideal perfection of utilitarian morality. As the means of making

the nearest approach to this ideal, utility would enjoin, first, that laws and social arrangements should place the happiness, or (as speaking practically it may be called) the interest, of every individual, as nearly as possible in harmony with the interest of the whole; and secondly, that education and opinion, which have so vast a power over human character, should so use that power as to establish in the mind of every individual an indissoluble association between his own happiness and the good of the whole; especially between his own happiness and the practice of such modes of conduct, negative and positive, as regard for the universal happiness prescribes; so that not only he may be unable to conceive the possibility of happiness to himself, consistently with conduct opposed to the general good, but also that a direct impulse to promote the general good may be in every individual one of the habitual motives of action, and the sentiments connected therewith may fill a large and prominent place in every human being's sentient existence. If the, impugners of the utilitarian morality represented it to their own minds in this its, true character, I know not what recommendation possessed by any other morality they could possibly affirm to be wanting to it; what more beautiful or more exalted developments of human nature any other ethical system can be supposed to foster, or what springs of action, not accessible to the utilitarian, such systems rely on for giving effect to their mandates.

The objectors to utilitarianism cannot always be charged with representing it in a discreditable light. On the contrary, those among them who entertain anything like a just idea of its disinterested character, sometimes find fault with its standard as being too high for humanity. They say it is exacting too much to require that people shall always act from the inducement of promoting the general interests of society. But this is to mistake the very meaning of a standard of morals, and confound the rule of action with the motive of it. It is the business of ethics to tell us what are our duties, or by what test we may know them; but no system of ethics requires that the sole motive of all we do shall be a feeling of duty; on the contrary, ninety-nine hundredths of all our actions are done from other motives, and rightly so done, if the rule of duty does not condemn them. It is the more unjust to utilitarianism that this particular misapprehension should be made a ground of objection to it, inasmuch as utilitarian moralists have gone beyond almost all others in affirming that the motive has nothing to do with the morality of the action, though much with the worth of the agent. He who saves a fellow creature from drowning does what is morally right, whether his motive be duty, or the hope of being paid for his trouble; he who betrays the friend that trusts him, is guilty of

a crime, even if his object be to serve another friend to whom he is
under greater obligations.

But to speak only of actions done from the motive of duty, and in
direct obedience to principle: it is a misapprehension of the utilitarian mode of thought, to conceive it as implying that people should
fix their minds upon so wide a generality as the world, or society
at large. The great majority of good actions are intended not for the
benefit of the world, but for that of individuals, of which the good of
the world is made up; and the thoughts of the most virtuous man need
not on these occasions travel beyond the particular persons concerned,
except so far as is necessary to assure himself that in benefiting them
he is not violating the rights, that is, the legitimate and authorized
expectations, of any one else. The multiplication of happiness is,
according to the utilitarian ethics, the object of virtue: the occasions
on which any person (except one in a thousand) has it in his power to
do this on an extended scale, in other words to be a public benefactor,
are but exceptional; and on these occasions alone is he called on to
consider public utility; in every other case, private utility, the interest
or happiness of some few persons, is all he has to attend to. Those
alone the influence of whose actions extends to society in general,
need concern themselves habitually about large an object. In the case
of abstinences indeed – of things which people forbear to do from
moral considerations, though the consequences in the particular case
might be beneficial – it would be unworthy of an intelligent agent not
to be consciously aware that the action is of a class which, if practised
generally, would be generally injurious, and that this is the ground of
the obligation to abstain from it. The amount of regard for the public
interest implied in this recognition, is no greater than is demanded by
every system of morals, for they all enjoin to abstain from whatever is
manifestly pernicious to society.

The same considerations dispose of another reproach against the doctrine of utility, founded on a still grosser misconception of the purpose
of a standard of morality, and of the very meaning of the words right
and wrong. It is often affirmed that utilitarianism renders men cold
and unsympathizing; that it chills their moral feelings towards individuals; that it makes them regard only the dry and hard consideration of the consequences of actions, not taking into their moral
estimate the qualities from which those actions emanate. If the assertion means that they do not allow their judgement respecting the
rightness or wrongness of an action to be influenced by their opinion
of the qualities of the person who does it, this is a complaint not

against utilitarianism, but against having any standard of morality at all; for certainly no known ethical standard decides an action to be good or bad because it is done by a good or a bad man, still less because done by an amiable, a brave, or a benevolent man, or the contrary. These considerations are relevant, not to the estimation of actions, but of persons; and there is nothing in the utilitarian theory inconsistent with the fact that there are other things which interest us in persons besides the rightness and wrongness of their actions. The Stoics, indeed, with the paradoxical misuse of language which was part of their system, and by which they strove to raise themselves above all concern about anything but virtue, were fond of saying that he who has that has everything; that he, and only he, is rich, is beautiful, is a king. But no claim of this description is made for the virtuous man by the utilitarian doctrine. Utilitarians are quite aware that there are other desirable possessions and qualities besides virtue, and are perfectly willing to allow to all of them their full worth. They are also aware that a right action does not necessarily indicate a virtuous character, and that actions which are blamable, often proceed from qualities entitled to praise. When this is apparent in any particular case, it modifies their estimation, not certainly of the act, but of the agent. I grant that they are, notwithstanding, of opinion, that in the long run the best proof of a good character is good actions; and resolutely refuse to consider any mental disposition as good, of which the predominant tendency is to produce bad conduct. This makes them unpopular with many people; but it is an unpopularity which they must share with every one who regards the distinction between right and wrong in a serious light; and the reproach is not one which a conscientious utilitarian need be anxious to repel.

If no more be meant by the objection than that many utilitarians look on the morality of actions, as measured by the utilitarian standard, with too exclusive a regard, and do not lay sufficient stress upon the other beauties of character which go towards making a human being lovable or admirable, this may be admitted. Utilitarians who have cultivated their moral feelings, but not their sympathies nor their artistic perceptions, do fall into this mistake; and so do all other moralists under the same conditions. What can be said in excuse for other moralists is equally available for them, namely, that, if there is to be any error, it is better that it should be on that side. As a matter of fact, we may affirm that among utilitarians as among adherents of other systems, there is every imaginable degree of rigidity and of laxity in the application of their standard: some are even puritanically rigorous, while others are as indulgent as can possibly be desired by sinner or by sentimentalist. But on the whole, a doctrine which brings prominently forward the interest that mankind have in the repression and prevention of conduct which violates the moral law, is likely to be inferior to no other in turning the sanctions of opinion again such violations. It is true, the question, What does violate the moral law? is one on which those who recognize different standards of morality are likely now and then to differ. But difference of opinion on moral questions was not first introduced into the world by utilitarianism, while that doctrine does supply, if not always an easy, at all events a tangible and intelligible mode of deciding such differences.

[...]

p⊢→ Again, defenders of utility often find themselves called upon to reply to such objections as this – that there is not time, previous to action, for calculating and weighing the effects of any line of conduct on the general happiness. This is exactly as if any one were to say that it is impossible to guide our conduct by Christianity, because there is not time, on every occasion on which anything has to be done, to read through the Old and New Testaments. The answer to the objection is, that there has been ample time, namely, the whole past duration of the human species. During all that time, mankind have been learning by experience the tendencies of actions; on which experience all the prudence, as well as all the morality of life, are dependent. People talk as if the commencement of this course of experience had hitherto been put off, and as if, at the moment when some man feels tempted to meddle with the property or life of another, he had to begin considering for the first time whether murder and theft are injurious to human happiness. Even then I do not think that he would find the question very puzzling; but, at all events, the matter is now done to his hand.

It is truly a whimsical supposition that, if mankind were agreed in considering utility to be the test of morality, they would remain without any agreement as to what is useful, and would take no measures for having their notions on the subject taught to the young, and enforced by law and opinion. There is no difficulty in proving any ethical standard whatever to work ill, if we suppose universal idiocy q⊢→ to be conjoined with it; but on any hypothesis short of that, mankind must by this time have acquired positive beliefs as to the effects of some actions on their happiness; and the beliefs which have thus come down are the rules of morality for the multitude, and for the philosopher until he has succeeded in finding better. That philosophers might easily do this, even now, on many subjects; that the received code of ethics is by no means of divine right; and that mankind have still much to learn as to the effects of actions on the general happiness,

I admit, or rather, earnestly maintain. The corollaries from the principle of utility, like the precepts of every practical art, admit of indefinite improvement, and, in a progressive state of the human mind, their improvement is perpetually going on.

But to consider the rules of morality as improvable, is one thing; to pass over the intermediate generalizations entirely, and endeavour to test each individual action directly by the first principle, is another. It is a strange notion that the acknowledgement of a first principle is inconsistent with the admission of secondary ones. To inform a traveller respecting the place of his ultimate destination, is not to forbid the use of landmarks and direction-posts on the way. The proposition that happiness is the end and aim of morality, does not mean that no road ought to be laid down to that goal, or that persons going thither should not be advised to take one direction rather than another. Men really ought to leave off talking a kind of nonsense on this subject, which they would neither talk nor listen to on other matters of practical concernment. Nobody argues that the art of navigation is not founded on astronomy, because sailors cannot wait to calculate the Nautical Almanack. Being rational creatures, they go to sea with it ready calculated; and all rational creatures go out upon the sea of life with their minds made up on the common questions of right and wrong, as well as on many of the far more difficult questions of wise and foolish. And this, as long as foresight is a human quality, it is to be presumed they will continue to do. Whatever we adopt as the fundamental principle of morality, we require subordinate principles to apply it by; the impossibility of doing without them, being common to all systems, can afford no argument against any one in particular; but gravely to argue as if no such secondary principles could be had, and as if mankind had remained till now, and always must remain, without drawing any general conclusions from the experience of human life, is as high a pitch, I think, as absurdity has ever reached in philosophical controversy.

[...]

Commentary on Mill

Mill's firm assertion (at [a]⊢→) of at least part of the doctrine of utilitarianism gives a prominent place to the notion of happiness which he goes on to describe as 'pleasure, and the absence of pain'. We will address the full doctrine later on, but first we should look more closely at the notion of happiness.

As we saw, happiness is one translation of Aristotle's notion of *eudaimonia* – a notion intended by him to be the good at which human beings aim in their activities. For this reason, it is not unreasonable to wonder whether Mill's conception of happiness is the same as, or overlaps with, Aristotle's.

On the basis of the paragraph beginning at $\boxed{a}\mapsto$, do you think Mill's conception of happiness does coincide with Aristotle's?

Straight off, there are two features of Mill's notion which would give one pause about answering this question affirmatively. First, the equation of happiness with pleasure (and the absence of pain) certainly seems to mark a difference. For pain and pleasure are most often taken to be feelings – states of mind which one experiences as reactions – and this would seem to place Mill's conception at odds with Aristotle's.

Though one naturally takes 'pleasure' and 'pain' to be feelings, can you think of broader ways in which we use these terms?

Think here of the way some speak of the pleasures of running marathons or climbing mountains, even though these same people would be the first to admit that these involve more than a little physical pain. Or think of the way we speak of losses, whether of loved ones or treasured possessions, as painful.

Second, Mill claims that happiness is central to morality in this way: it figures in the very definition of what it is right (or wrong) to do. This somewhat narrow conception of morality has no obvious counterpart in the *Nicomachean Ethics*. Aristotle certainly considered the idea of agents making choices, but he mainly focuses on the character of such agents – on their virtues (or vices) – and on the kinds of lives that they do, or ought to, lead.

These are clearly differences between Mill's and Aristotle's projects, but they are not quite as stark as the paragraph at $\boxed{a}\mapsto$ might suggest. And even before we investigate these matters further, it is important to bear in mind that Mill certainly thought of his project in the same general terms as Aristotle. That is, Mill intended his notion of happiness as a way of understanding what constituted human good. In the first chapter of *Utilitarianism* he speaks of the search for the *summum bonum* – our greatest good – and he, like Aristotle, thought it reasonable to equate this with human happiness. Moreover, though they have different conceptions of it, both thought that the best way to understand human ethical life was via an understanding of what constitutes human good.

Perhaps sensitive to the very kind of misgiving that Aristotle had about counting pleasure as the highest human good, Mill's defence of utilitarianism opens with a lengthy, and controversial discussion, of this notion.

Read the text from [b]→ to [c]→. Do you find what Mill says an adequate defence of his equation of pleasure and good?

Mill's predecessor, Bentham, had insisted on the equation of pleasure and goodness, and argued that one activity is better than another simply insofar as it gives participants a greater *quantity* of pleasure. A notorious consequence of this is that Bentham had little defence against those who worried that this equation would lead to an overvaluing of bodily pleasures. For in respect of the more elusive pleasures of the intellect – and perhaps engaged as you are in grappling with philosophy, you can well understand this – one finds struggle, and thus a sort of pain.

Just past [c]→, Mill suggests that utilitarians are not limited to distinguishing 'higher pleasures' in terms of their 'greater permanency, safety, uncostliness, etc.'. These features, if they are indeed features of higher pleasures, are not intrinsic to them. That is, they are features that make no special reference to the intrinsic value of the kind of pleasure they are. However, he claims that there is a way of comparing pleasures which can show us that pleasures differ, not only quantitatively, but in quality. The discussion of this begins at [d]→ and finishes at [e]→.

Do you think that Mill makes out a good case for the quantity/quality distinction with respect to pleasure?

Whether or not you think that Mill's way of making this distinction is a good one, the very fact that he makes it raises two further issues. One has important consequences for the consistency of his utilitarianism – and this will be discussed later – and the other is more directly relevant to our attempt to understand what Mill means by happiness.

Mill says that failure to see that higher pleasures – those which depend on our 'higher' faculties – are superior even to a greater quantity of lower pleasures comes from confusing the idea of happiness with that of contentment. And this leads him to conclude (at [e]→): 'it is better to be a human being dissatisfied than a pig satisfied; better to be Socrates dissatisfied than a fool satisfied.' In arguing so vehemently for his conclusion, Mill certainly brings his account of happiness closer to Aristotle's. Though he began by defining happiness in terms of pleasure, he now insists that an obviously psychological notion – contentment – is in fact not what he had in mind when he said that human goodness consisted in happiness. Without insisting that they are saying exactly the same thing, Aristotle's idea of human good as the exercise of our rational faculties, and Mill's idea of it as defined, not by the quantity, but the quality of pleasure, are closer than one might first have thought. Note too that in the paragraph before the conclusion at [e]→, Mill speaks of 'human dignity' as an essential part of happiness. This is scarcely the kind of comment that

someone would make if he took pleasure in the narrow sense to be definitive
of happiness.

Mill's insistence upon the distinction between higher and lower pleasures,
and his championing of the former as necessary ingredients of happiness,
certainly does move him in the direction of the Aristotelian conception. But it
is not yet clear that Mill is entitled to maintain this distinction consistently
with his utilitarianism.

> Why do you think a utilitarian might not be entitled to this distinction
> between higher and lower pleasures?

At the very beginning of the text Mill claims that utilitarianism offers a
criterion of morally right action: such an action is the one which produces the
most happiness. In the passage at $\boxed{f}\mapsto$, and even more clearly at $\boxed{g}\mapsto$, Mill
stresses what is a crucial feature of the criterion: the happiness to be maxi-
mized is not the agent's own happiness, but rather 'the greatest amount of
happiness altogether'. Looking ahead (at $\boxed{k}\mapsto$) he explains this in the clearest
terms: in assessing the amount of happiness that might result from a course of
action, an agent must not favour his own happiness: 'As between his own
happiness and that of others, utilitarianism requires him to be as strictly
impartial as a disinterested and benevolent spectator.'

Utilitarianism thus seems to involve two ingredients: the identification of
human good with happiness, and the idea that in choosing morally we are
required to maximize that good, i.e. to maximize the quantity of happiness.
The problem that many writers have with Mill's quantity/quality distinction
lies in this second ingredient. For how can one maximize the quantity of happiness while insisting that there are constituents of happiness that are qualita-
tively, but not quantitatively, superior? In the paragraph at $\boxed{g}\mapsto$, he does seem
to recognize this difficulty, and states his utilitarian principle in a way that
appears to take account of both quantity and quality. But many have found
difficulties with what he says about the 'rule for measuring' the one against
the other.

> Do you think that what Mill says explains how to accommodate – consis-
> tently and satisfactorily – the quantity/quality distinction within utilitari-
> anism?

At $\boxed{h}\mapsto$, Mill outlines certain other objections to utilitarianism. The basis of
these objections is, as he puts it, that happiness is unsuitable to serve as 'the
rational purpose of human life and action'. And this is because happiness is
either actually unattainable, and/or because it is not something to which we
have any right.

In the paragraphs that follow (up to $\boxed{k}\mapsto$), he confronts these objections, and,
in doing so, takes the opportunity to draw a more rounded, even inspirational,

picture of utilitarianism, one which reveals its deep connections to the social and political reform movement of its time. For example, at $\boxed{i} \vdash\rightarrow$, he claims that human suffering, real as it is, is 'almost entirely conquerable by human care and effort'. And, further on, he finds it entirely reasonable to imagine someone sacrificing their own greatest good for the good of others, noting, at $\boxed{j} \vdash\rightarrow$, that if a sacrifice does not increase the sum total of human happiness, it would be considered 'wasted'.

Before we take up discussion further along, say whether you think Mill deals adequately with the objections that he mentions at $\boxed{h} \vdash\rightarrow$?

In the paragraph marked $\boxed{1} \vdash\rightarrow$, Mill considers an objection that probes a different aspect of his view. As we have seen, Mill's utilitarianism has two main ingredients: an identification of human good with happiness, and the claim that in choosing what it is morally right to do one does, or ought to, choose that action which maximizes the total amount of human happiness. Much of the discussion above is concerned with the nature of happiness and whether it is an appropriate way to capture the notion of human good. However, at $\boxed{1} \vdash\rightarrow$ Mill imagines an objector who sees utilitarianism as setting a standard 'too high for humanity' and as being too 'exacting'.

What exactly is the objection that Mill is here considering?

As we have seen, many find the identification of human good with happiness problematic. But, in trying to understand the present objection, we can put these worries on one side. For the problem Mill identifies at $\boxed{1} \vdash\rightarrow$ concerns the second ingredient of utilitarianism. Supposing, as he does, that rightness does consist in acting so that the consequences of our actions maximize human good in general, Mill imagines someone doubting whether we are capable of being motivated by a disinterested concern for human good.

What is Mill's answer to this objection?

His attempts to deal with this objection are deceptively complicated. Straight off, he argues that the objection confuses the motive of duty towards doing what is right with the understanding of what actually makes an action right. The utilitarian tells us about the second of these, but makes no commitment to the first. Thus, at $\boxed{m} \vdash\rightarrow$, he says: 'He who saves a fellow creature from drowning does what is morally right, whether his motive be duty, or the hope of being paid for his trouble.' However, he obviously doesn't regard this as a complete answer.

At $\boxed{n} \vdash\rightarrow$, he says something which shows a slightly different way of taking the objection, one that has been a persistent worry about utilitarianism. Not so much a confusion about motive and rightness, the issue now is whether, in deciding what is right, one has to consider 'so wide a generality as the world, or society at large'.

Why would this be a problem for the utilitarian?

There are two interconnected reasons for the problem. On the one hand, if deciding what is right requires us to consider the effect of what we do on the whole of society, it will be very difficult to determine what is in fact right in any given case. And, on the other hand, given that everything we do has consequences, even if tiny, for the whole of society, every decision about what to do – and not only those which we intuitively think of as moral – will take on a moral dimension. Together these make the practice of utilitarianism very demanding indeed, and Mill does try to deal with them, albeit briefly (in the remainder of the paragraph after [n]→). What he suggests is that the field of action available to most of us is rather narrower than that of the whole of society, let alone generality of the world. Mill notes that our actions typically have consequences 'for the interest or happiness of some few persons', and therefore that we need only attend to these consequences in deciding what to do.

Is this an adequate reply to the objection that utilitarianism is too demanding?

If what one does actually has consequences, even if slight, that extend beyond a narrow circle of individuals – and most of our actions do have these consequences – then many feel we would need a utilitarian justification for ignoring them. That is, one would have to show that ignoring them can be seen to maximize the good. However, it is unclear how this would work, since one is here tampering with the very notion of maximization that is needed to define what is right.

In the final paragraphs, Mill considers two further objections, one in the paragraphs surrounding the place marked [o]→, and one beginning at [p]→. To the first, Mill says: 'If no more be meant by the objection than that many utilitarians look on the morality of actions, as measured by the utilitarian standard, with too exclusive a regard, and not lay sufficient stress upon the other beauties of character which go towards making a human being lovable or admirable, this may be admitted.' So far, then, from being an objection, Mill claims that the utilitarian criterion of rightness takes precedence over considerations of character and virtue.

The second objection is that, in having to choose a course of action, there is usually no time for the detailed calculations that the utilitarian thinks are necessary for determining the right thing to do. Mill's way of dealing with this objection introduces what many take to be a novelty into the utilitarian doctrine. After defensively pointing out that Christian ethics does not require one to re-read the bible before deciding what it is right to do, he writes (further along, at $\boxed{9}\!\!\rightarrow$): 'mankind must by this time have acquired positive beliefs as to the effects of some actions on their happiness; and the beliefs which have thus come down are the rules of morality for the multitude, and for the philosopher until he has succeeded in finding better'. And, in the next paragraph, he compares these rules of morality to a sailor's use of the 'nautical almanack': 'Being rational creatures they go to sea with it ready calculated; and all rational creatures go out upon the sea of life with their minds made up on the common questions of right and wrong.' In the extensive literature on utilitarianism, what Mill says here is often taken as evidence of his being a 'rule utilitarian'. This is the view that we should use the utilitarian 'greatest happiness' principle primarily to assess our general rules of conduct, rather than applying it, case by case, to specific possible actions.

Is this 'rule-utilitarianism' consistent with the fundamental utilitarian principle that an individual action is right if it maximizes the good, that is, collective happiness?

Aristotle saw good as the central notion in any more detailed account of how our lives should be lived; Mill modified this thought in two important ways. First, he offered a conception of human good which is at once more specific and more controversial than Aristotle's; and, second, he linked this conception more directly to morality. Mill assumes that any moral outlook must be based on a principle which determines, in any specific circumstance, which action is right, and he takes the maximization of happiness to be that criterion. Underlying this idea of maximization is a thought that can seem incontrovertible: given that we have identified what it is that makes various states of affairs good (or bad), then the right action is that which has the best states of affairs as consequences.

Introduction to Foot

Philippa Foot (née Bosanquet, in 1920) is a British philosopher (though she is also the granddaughter of the American President Grover Cleveland) who was educated at Somerville College, Oxford. Most of her academic career has been shared, each year, between a Fellowship at Somerville College and the Griffin Professorship at University of California at Los Angeles (UCLA). She now holds emeritus positions in both institutions. Mrs Foot (as she is most widely known) is a distinguished moral philosopher whose contributions to the subject have always been at once morally serious, philosophically insightful and thoroughly accessible. One way in which her seriousness has shown itself is in the thoughtful development of her career-long search for an objective foundation to morality.

The article from which our text is taken plays an especially important role in this development, and in the topic of this chapter. Having early on decided that the best way to approach moral objectivity is by beginning with our concept of virtue, she found it necessary to say what kind of contribution the virtues make to human good. Given the link that Mill and other utilitarians have forged between the good and happiness, it would have been natural to think that she could find what she needed in utilitarianism. Yet her resistance to utilitarianism has been a cornerstone in her moral philosophy: it is connected to her deepest convictions about the subject, and her anti-utilitarian arguments are more than merely intelligent.

Philippa Foot, 'Utilitarianism and the Virtues' (extracts)

It is remarkable how utilitarianism tends to haunt even those of us who will not believe in it. It is as if we for ever feel that it must be right, although we insist that it is wrong. T. M. Scanlon hits the nail on the head when he observes, in his article 'Contractualism and Utilitarianism', that the theory occupies a central place in the moral philosophy of our time in spite of the fact that, as he puts it, 'the implications of act utilitarianism are wildly at variance with firmly held moral convictions, while rule utilitarianism ... strikes most people as an unstable compromise'.[1] He suggests that what we need to break this spell is to find a better alternative to utilitarian theories, and I am sure that that

$\boxed{\text{a}} \mapsto$ is right. But what I want to do is to approach the business of exorcism more directly. Obviously something drives us towards utilitarianism, and must it not be an assumption or thought which is in some way mistaken? For otherwise why is the theory unacceptable? We must be going wrong somewhere and should find out where it is.

$\boxed{\text{b}} \mapsto$ I want to argue that what is most radically wrong with utilitarianism is its consequentialism, but I also want to suggest that its consequentialist element is one of the main reasons why utilitarianism seems so compelling. I need therefore to say something about the

Philippa Foot, 'Utilitarianism and the Virtues', *Mind* 94 (1985), 196–209. An earlier version appeared in the Proceedings and Addresses of the American Philosophical Association 57 (1983). Copyright: Philippa Foot.
[1]   T. M. Scanlon, 'Contractualism and Utilitarianism', in Amartya Sen and Bernard Williams (eds), *Utilitarianism and Beyond* (Cambridge: Cambridge University Press, 1982), pp. 103–28.

relation between the two theory descriptions 'utilitarian' and 'consequentialist'. Consequentialism in its most general form simply says that it is by 'total outcome', that is, by the whole formed by an action and its consequences, that what is done is judged right or wrong. A consequentialist theory of ethics is one which identifies certain states of affairs as *good* states of affairs and says that the rightness or goodness of actions (or of other subjects of moral judgement) consists in their positive productive relationship to these states of affairs. Utilitarianism as it is usually defined consists of consequentialism together with the identification of the best state of affairs with the state of affairs in which there is most happiness, most pleasure, or the maximum satisfaction of desire. Strictly speaking utilitarianism – taken here as welfare utilitarianism – is left behind when the distribution of welfare is said in itself to affect the goodness of states of affairs; or when anything other than welfare is allowed as part of the good. But it is of course possible also to count a theory as utilitarian if right action is taken to be that which produces 'good states of affairs', whatever these are supposed to be; and then 'utilitarianism' becomes synonymous with 'consequentialism'. By 'utilitarianism' I shall here mean 'welfare utilitarianism', though it is with consequentialism in one form or another that I shall be most concerned.

 Although I believe that what is radically wrong with utilitarianism is its consequentialism, what has often seemed to be most wrong with it has been either welfarism or the sum ranking of welfare. So it has been suggested that 'the good' is not automatically increased by an increase in pleasure, but by non-malicious pleasure, or first-order pleasure, or something of the kind; in order to get over difficulties about the pleasures of watching a public execution or the pleasures and pains of the bigot or the prude.[2] Furthermore distribution principles have been introduced so that actions benefiting the rich more than they harm the poor no longer have to be judged morally worthy. Thus the criteria for the goodness of states of affairs have continually been modified to meet one objection after another; but it seems that the modifications have never been able to catch up with the objections. For the distribution principles and the discounting of certain pleasures and pains did nothing to help with problems about, e.g., the wrongness of inducing cancer in a few experimental subjects to make a substantial advance in finding a cure for the disease. If the theory was to give results at all in line with common moral opinion *rights*

[2] See, e.g., Amartya Sen, 'Utilitarianism and Welfarism', *Journal of Philosophy* 76 (1979): 463–89.

had to be looked after in a way that was so far impossible within even
the modified versions of utilitarianism.

It was therefore suggested, by Amartya Sen, that 'goal rights'
systems should be considered; the idea being that the respecting or
violating of rights should be counted as itself a good or an evil in the
evaluation of states of affairs.[3] This would help to solve some problems because if the respecting of the rights of the subject were weighted
heavily enough the cancer experiment could not turn out to be 'opti-
mific' after all. Yet this seems rather a strange suggestion, because as
Samuel Scheffler has remarked, it is not clear why, in the measure-
ment of the goodness of states of affairs or total outcomes, killings for
instance should count so much more heavily than deaths.[4] But what is
more important is that this 'goal rights' system fails to deal with certain other examples of actions that most of us would want to call
wrong. Suppose, for instance, that some evil person threatens to kill
or torture a number of victims unless we kill or torture one, and suppose that we have every reason to believe that he will do as he says.
Then in terms of their total outcomes (again consisting of the states of
affairs made up of an action and its consequences) we have the choice
between more killings or torturings and less, and a consequentialist
will have to say that we are justified in killing or torturing the one
person, and indeed that we are morally obliged to do it, always supposing that no indirect consequences have tipped the balance of good
and evil. There will in fact be nothing that it will not be right to do to
a perfectly innocent individual if that is the only way of preventing
another agent from doing more things of the same kind.

Now I find this a totally unacceptable conclusion and note that it is
a conclusion not of utilitarianism in particular but rather of consequentialism in any form. So it is the spellbinding force of consequentialism that we have to think about. Welfarism has its own peculiar
attraction, which has to do with the fact that pleasure, happiness, and
the satisfaction of desire are things seen as in some way good. But this
attraction becomes less powerful as distribution principles are added
and pleasures discounted on an *ad hoc* basis to destroy the case for
such things as public executions.

If having left welfarist utilitarianism behind we still find ourselves
unable, in spite of its difficulties, to get away from consequentialism,
there must be a reason for this. What is it, let us now ask, that is so
compelling about consequentialism? It is, I think, the rather simple
thought that it can never be right to prefer a worse state of affairs to

[3] Amartya Sen, 'Rights and Agency', *Philosophy and Public Affairs* 11 (1982): 3–39.
[4] Samuel Scheffler, *The Rejection of Consequentialism*, (Oxford: Clarendon Press, 1982),
pp. 108–12.

a better.[5] It is this thought that haunts us and, incidentally, this thought that makes the move to rule utilitarianism an unsatisfactory answer to the problem of reconciling utilitarianism with common moral opinion. For surely it will be irrational, we feel, to obey even the most useful rule if in a particular instance we clearly see that such obedience will not *have the best results*. Again following Scheffler we ask if it is not paradoxical that it should ever be morally objectionable to act in such a way as to minimize morally objectionable acts of just the same type.[6] If it is a bad state of affairs in which one of these actions is done it will presumably be a worse state of affairs in which several are. And must it not be irrational to prefer the worse to the better state of affairs?

This thought does indeed seem compelling. And yet it leads to an apparently unacceptable conclusion about what it is right to do. So we ought, as I said, to wonder whether we have not gone wrong somewhere. And I think that indeed we have. I believe (and this is the main thesis of the paper) that we go wrong in accepting the idea that there *are* better and worse states of affairs in the sense that consequentialism requires. As Wittgenstein says in a different context, 'The decisive movement in the conjuring trick has been made, and it was the very one that we thought quite innocent'.[7]

Let us therefore look into the idea of a good state of affairs, as this appears in the thought that we can judge certain states of affairs to be better than others and then go on to give moral descriptions to actions related productively to these states of affairs.

We should begin by asking why we are so sure that we even understand expressions such as 'a good state of affairs' or 'a good outcome'; for as Peter Geach pointed out years ago there are phrases with the word 'good' in them, as, e.g., 'a good event', that do *not* at least as they stand have a sense.[8] Following this line one might suggest that philosophers are a bit hasty in using expressions such as 'a better

---

[5] The original version continued 'How could it ever be right, we think, to produce less good rather than more good?'. I have excised this sentence because in the context the use of the expression 'doing more good' suggested an identification which I was at pains to deny. At all times I have allowed *doing good* as an unproblematic notion, because although it does raise many problems, e.g. about different distributions of benefits, it does not raise the particular problems with which I am concerned. I want to insist that however well we might understand what it was to 'do as much good as possible' in the sense of producing maximum benefit, it would not follow that we knew what we meant by expressions such as 'the best outcome' or 'the best state of affairs' as these are used by moral philosophers. Cf. the discussion on page 45 of the present version of this paper.

[6] Scheffler, *The Rejection of Consequentialism*, op. cit, p. 121.

[7] L. Wittgenstein, *Philosophical Investigations* (Macmillan, 1953, and Blackwell, 1958), § 308.

[8] P. Geach, 'Good and Evil', *Analysis* 17 (1956), 33–42.

world'. One may *perhaps* understand this when it is taken to mean a 'deontically better world' defined as one in which fewer duties are left unfulfilled; but obviously this will not help to give a sense to 'better state of affairs' as the consequentialist needs to use this expression, since he is wanting to fix our obligations not to refer to their fulfilment.

Nevertheless it may seem that combinations of words such as 'a good state of affairs' are beyond reproach or question, for such expressions are extremely familiar. Do we not use them every day? We say that it is a good thing that something or other happened; what difficulty can there be in constructing from such elements anything we want in the way of aggregates such as total outcomes which (in principle) take into account all the elements of a possible world and so constitute good states of affairs? Surely no one can seriously suggest that 'good state of affairs' is an expression that we do not understand?'

It would, of course, be ridiculous to query the sense of the ordinary things that we say about its being 'a good thing' that something or other happened, or about a certain state of affairs being good or bad. The doubt is not about whether there is some way of using the words, but rather about the way they appear in the exposition of utilitarian and other consequentialist moral theories. It is important readily to accept the fact that we talk in a natural and familiar way about good states of affairs, and that there is nothing problematic about such usage. But it is also important to see how such expressions actually work in the contexts in which they are at home, and in particular to ask about the status of a good state of affairs. Is it something impersonal to be recognized (we hope) by all reasonable men? It seems, surprisingly, that this is not the case at least in many contexts of utterance of the relevant expressions. Suppose, for instance, that the supporters of different teams have gathered in the stadium and that the members of each group are discussing the game; or that two racegoers have backed different horses in a race. Remarking on the course of events one or the other may say that things are going well or badly, and when a certain situation has developed may say that it is a good or a bad state of affairs. More commonly they will welcome some developments and deplore others, saying 'Oh good!' or 'That's bad!', calling some news good news and some news bad, sometimes describing what has happened as 'a good thing' and sometimes not. We could develop plenty of other examples of this kind, thinking for instance of the conversations about the invention of a new burglar alarm that might take place in the police headquarters and in the robbers' den.

At least two types of utterance are here discernible. For 'good' and its cognates may be used to signal the speaker's attitude to a result judged as an end result, and then he says 'Good!' or 'I'm glad' or 'That's good' where what he is glad about is something welcomed in itself and not for any good it will bring. But a state of affairs may rather be judged by its connection with other things called good. And even what is counted as in itself good may be said to be bad when it brings enough evil in its train.

Now what shall we say about the truth or falsity of these utterances? It certainly seems that they can be straightforwardly true or false. For perhaps what appears to be going to turn out well is really going to turn out badly: what seemed to be a good thing was really a bad thing, and an apparently good state of affairs was the prelude to disaster. 'You are quite wrong' one person may say to another and events may show that he *was* wrong. Nevertheless we can see that this quasi-objectivity, which is not to be questioned when people with similar aims, interests, or desires are speaking together, flies out of the window if we try to set the utterances of those in one group against the utterances of those in another. One will say 'a good thing' where another says 'a bad thing', and it is the same for states of affairs. It would be bizarre to suggest that at the races it really *is* a good thing that one horse or the other is gaining (perhaps because of the pleasure it will bring to the majority, or the good effect on the future of racing) and so that the utterance of one particular punter, intent only on making a packet, will be the one that is true.

This is not to say, however, that what a given person says to be a good thing or a good state of affairs must relate to his own advantage. For anyone may be *interested in* the future of racing, and people commonly are *interested in*, e.g., the success of their friends, saying 'that's a good thing' if one of them looks like winning a prize or getting a job; incidentally without worrying much about whether he is the very best candidate for it.

Now it may be thought that these must be rather special uses of expressions such as 'good state of affairs', because we surely must speak quite differently when we are talking about public matters, as when for instance we react to news of some far-away disaster. We say that the news is bad because a lot of people have lost their lives in an earthquake. Later we may say that things are not as bad as we feared and someone may remark 'that's a good thing'. 'A bad state of affairs', we might remark on hearing the original news about people dead or homeless, and this will usually have nothing to do with harm to us or to our friends.

In this way the case is different from that of the racegoers or the cops and robbers, but this is not of course to imply that what we say on such occasions has a different status from the utterances we have considered so far. For why should its truth not be 'speaker-relative' too, also depending on what the speakers and their group are *interested in* though not now on the good or harm that will come to them themselves? Is it not more plausible to think this than to try to distinguish two kinds of uses of these expressions, one speaker-relative and the other not? For are there really two ways in which the police for instance might speak? And two ways in which the robbers could speak as well? Are we really to say that although when they are both speaking in the speaker-relative way they do not contradict each other, and may both speak truly, when speaking in the 'objective' way one group will speak truly and the other not? What shows that the second way of speaking exists?

What thoughts, one may ask, can we really be supposed to have which must be expressed in the disputed mode? Considering examples such as that of the far-away earthquake we may think that we believe the best state of affairs to be the one in which there is most happiness and least misery, or something of the sort. But considering other examples we may come to wonder whether any such thought can really be attributed to us.

Suppose for instance that when walking in a poor district one of us should lose a fairly considerable sum of money which we had intended to spend on something rather nice. Arriving home we discover the loss and telephone the police on the off chance that our wad of notes has been found and turned in. To our delight we find that it was picked up by a passing honest policeman, and that we shall get it back. 'What a good thing' we say 'that an officer happened to be there.' What seemed to be a bad state of affairs has turned out not to be bad after all: things are much better than we thought they were. And all's well that ends well. But how, it may now be asked, *can* we say that things have turned out better than we thought? Were we not supposed to believe that the best state of affairs was the one in which there was most happiness and least misery? So surely it would have been *better* if the money had not been returned to us but rather found and kept as treasure trove by some poor inhabitant of the region? We simply had not considered that because most of us do not actually *have* the thought that the best state of affairs is the one in which we lose and they gain. Perhaps we should have had this thought if it had been a small amount of money, but this was rather a lot.

No doubt it will seem to many that there must be non-speaker-relative uses of words evaluating states of affairs because moral judgements cannot have speaker-relative status. But if one is inclined, as I am, to doubt whether propositions of this form play any part in the fundamentals of ethical theory there is no objection on this score. It is important however that the preceding discussion has been about propositions of a particular form and nothing has been said to suggest that all judgements about what is good and bad have speaker-relative status. I have not for instance made this suggestion for what Geach called 'attributive' judgements concerning things good or bad of a kind – good knives and houses and essays, or even good actions, motives, or men. If there is some reason for calling these 'speaker-relative' the reason has not been given here. Nor has anything been said about the status of propositions about what is *good for* anyone or anything, or about that in which their good consists.

What has I hope now been shown is that we should not take it for granted that we even know what we are talking about if we enter into a discussion with the consequentialist about whether it can ever be right to produce something other than 'the best state of affairs'.

h⟶ It might be suggested by way of reply that what is in question in these debates is not just the best state of affairs without qualification but rather *the best state of affairs from an impersonal point of view*. But what does this mean? A good state of affairs from an impersonal point of view is presumably opposed to a good state of affairs from *my* point of view or from *your* point of view, and as a good state of affairs from my point of view is a state of affairs which is advantageous to me, and a good state of affairs from your point of view is a state of affairs that is advantageous to you, a good state of affairs from an impersonal point of view presumably means a state of affairs which is generally advantageous, or advantageous to most people, or something like that. About the idea of maximum welfare we are not (or so we are supposing for the sake of the argument) in any difficulty.[9] But an account of the idea of a good state of affairs which simply defines it in terms of maximum welfare is no help to us here. For our problem is that something is supposed to be being said *about* maximum welfare and we cannot figure out what this is.

In a second reply, more to the point, the consequentialist might say that what we should really be dealing with in this discussion is states of affairs which are good or bad, not simply, but *from the moral point of view*. The qualification is, it will be suggested, tacitly understood in moral contexts, where no individual speaker gives his own private interests or allegiances a special place in any debate, the speaker-relativity found in other contexts thus being left behind. This seems to be a pattern familiar from other cases, as, e.g., from discussions in meetings of the governors of public institutions. Why should it not be in a similar way that we talk of a good and a bad thing to happen 'from

---

[9] Cf. footnote 5.

a moral point of view'? And is it not hard to reject the conclusion that right action is action producing *this* 'best state of affairs'?

That special contexts can create special uses of the expressions we are discussing is indeed true. But before we proceed to draw conclusions about moral judgements we should ask why we think that it makes sense to talk about morally good and bad states of affairs, or to say that it is a good thing (or is good that) something happened 'from a moral point of view'. For after all we cannot concoct a meaningful sentence by adding just any qualification of this verbal form to expressions such as these. What would it mean, for instance, to say that a state of affairs was good or bad 'from a legal point of view' or 'from the point of view of etiquette'? Or that, it was a good thing that a certain thing happened from these same 'points of view'? Certain interpretations that suggest themselves are obviously irrelevant, as, for instance, that it is a good state of affairs from a legal point of view when the laws are clearly stated, or a good state of affairs from the point of view of etiquette when everyone follows the rules.

It seems, therefore, that we do not solve the problem of the meaning of 'best state of affairs' when supposed to be used in a non-speaker-relative way simply by tacking on 'from a moral point of view'; since it cannot be assumed that the resulting expression has any sense. Nevertheless it would be wrong to suggest that 'good state of affairs from a moral point of view' is a concatenation of words which in fact has no meaning in *any* of the contexts in which it appears, and to see this we have only to look at utilitarian theories of the type put forward by John C. Harsanyi and R. M. Hare, in which a certain interpretation is implicitly provided for such expressions.[10]

Harsanyi for instance argues that the only *rational* morality is one in which the rightness or wrongness of an action is judged by its relation to a certain outcome, i.e. the maximization of social utility. The details of this theory, which defines social utility in terms of individual preferences, do not concern us here. The relevant point is that within it there appears the idea of an end which is the goal of moral action, and therefore the idea of a best state of affairs from a moral point of view. (It does not of course matter whether Harsanyi uses these words.)

Similarly Hare, by a more elaborate argument from the universalizability and prescriptivity of moral judgements, tries to establish the proposition that one who takes the moral point of view must have as his aim the maximization of utility, reflecting this in one way in his

---

[10] See, e.g., J. C. Harsanyi, 'Morality and the Theory of Rational Behavior', *Social Research* 44 (1977), reprinted in Sen and Williams, *Utilitarianism and Beyond* (Cambridge: Cambridge University Press, 1982), pp. 39–62; and R. M. Hare, *Moral Thinking* (New York: Oxford University Press, 1982).

day-to-day prescriptions and in another in 'critical' moral judgements. So here too a clear sense can be given to the idea of a best state of affairs from a moral point of view: it is the state of affairs which a man aims at when he takes the moral point of view and which in one way or another determines the truth of moral judgements.

Within these theories there is, then, no problem about the meaning of expressions such as 'the best state of affairs from the moral point of view'. It does not follow, however, that those who reject the theories should be ready to discuss the pros and cons of consequentialism in these terms. For unless the arguments given by Hare and Harsanyi are acceptable it will not have been shown that there is any reference for expressions such as 'the aim which each man has in so far as he takes up the moral point of view' or *a fortiori* 'the best state of affairs from the moral point of view'.

If my main thesis is correct this is a point of the first importance. For I am arguing that where non-consequentialists commonly go wrong is in accepting from their opponents questions such as 'Is it ever right to act in such a way as to produce something less than the best state of affairs that is within one's reach?'[11] Summing up the results reached so far we may say that if taken in one way, with no special reference to morality, talk about good states of affairs seems to be speaker-relative. But if the qualification 'from a moral point of view' is added the resulting expression may mean nothing; and it may lack a reference when a special consequentialist theory has given it a sense.

In the light of this discussion we should find it significant that many people who do not find any particular consequentialist theory compelling nevertheless feel themselves driven towards consequentialism by a thought which turns on the idea that there are states of affairs which are better or worse from a moral point of view. What is it that seems to make this an inescapable idea?

Tracing the assumption back in my own mind I find that what seems preposterous is to deny that there are some things that a moral person must want and aim at in so far as he is a moral person and that he will count it 'a good thing' when these things happen and 'a good state of affairs' either when they are happening or when things are disposed in their favour. For surely he must want others to be happy. To deny this would be to deny that benevolence is a virtue – and who wants to deny that?

11 See, e.g., T. Nagel, 'The Limits of Objectivity' in *Tanner Lectures*, vol. I (1980), p. 131, where he says that '... things would be better, what *happened* would be better' if I twisted a child's arm in circumstances where (by Nagel's hypothesis) this was the only way to get medical help for the victims of an accident. He supposes that I might have done something worse if I hurt the child than if I did not do it, but that the total outcome would have been better. It does not, I think, occur to him to question the idea of *things* being better – or *things* being worse.

Let us see where this line of thought will take us, accepting without any reservation that benevolence is a virtue and that a benevolent person must often aim at the good of others and call it 'a good thing' when for instance a far-away disaster turns out to have been less serious than was feared. Here we do indeed have the words 'a good thing' (and just as obviously a 'good state of affairs') necessarily appearing in moral contexts. And the use is explained not by a piece of utilitarian theory but by a simple observation about benevolence.

[k]→   This, then, seems to be the way in which seeing states of affairs in which people are happy as good states of affairs really is an essential part of morality. But it is very important that we have found this end *within* morality, and forming part of it, not standing outside it as the 'good state of affairs' by which moral action in general is to be judged. For benevolence is only one of the virtues, and we shall have to look at the others before we can pronounce on any question about good or bad action in particular circumstances. Off-hand we have no reason to think that whatever is done with the aim of improving the lot of other people will be morally required or even morally permissible. For firstly there are virtues such as friendship which play their part in determining the requirements of benevolence, e.g., by making it consistent with benevolence to give service to friends rather than to strangers or acquaintances. And secondly there is the virtue of justice, taken in the old wide sense in which it had to do with everything *owed*. In our common moral code we find numerous examples of limitations which justice places on the pursuit of welfare. In the first place there are principles of distributive justice which forbid, on grounds of fairness, the kind of 'doing good' which increases the wealth of rich people at the cost of misery to the poor. Secondly, rules such as truth telling are not to be broken wherever and whenever welfare would thereby be increased. Thirdly, considerations about rights, both positive and negative, limit the action which can be taken for the sake of welfare. Justice is primarily concerned with the following of certain rules of fairness and honest dealing and with respecting prohibitions on interference with others rather than with attachment to any end. It is true that the just man must also fight injustice, and here justice like benevolence is a matter of ends, but of course the end is not the same end as the one that benevolence seeks and need not be coincident with it.

I do not mean to go into these matters in detail here, but simply to point out that we find in our ordinary moral code many requirements and prohibitions inconsistent with the idea that benevolence is the whole of morality. From the point of view of the present discussion it would be acceptable to describe the situation in terms of a tension between, for instance, justice and benevolence. But it is not strictly accurate to think of it like this, because that would suggest that someone who does an unjust act for the sake of increasing total happiness has a higher degree of benevolence than one who refuses to do it. Since someone who refuses to sacrifice an innocent life for the sake of increasing happiness is not to be counted as less benevolent than someone who is ready to do it, this cannot be right. We might be tempted to think that the latter would be acting 'out of benevolence' because his aim is the happiness of others, but this seems a bad way of talking. Certainly benevolence does not require unjust action, and we should not call an act which violated rights an act of benevolence. It would not, for instance, be an act of benevolence to induce cancer in one person (or deliberately to let it run its course) even for the sake of alleviating much suffering.

What we should say therefore is that even perfection in benevolence does not imply a readiness to do anything and everything of which it can be said that it is highly probable that it will increase the sum of human happiness. And this, incidentally, throws some light on a certain type of utilitarian theory which identifies the moral assessment of a situation with that of a sympathetic impartial observer whose benevolence extends equally to all mankind.[12] For what, we may ask, are we to suppose about this person's *other* characteristics? Is he to be guided simply and solely by a desire to relieve suffering and increase happiness; or is he also just? If it is said that for him the telling of truth, keeping of promises, and respecting of individual autonomy are to be recommended only in so far as these serve to maximize welfare then we see that the 'impartial sympathetic observer' is by definition one with a utilitarian point of view. So the utilitarians are defining moral assessment in their own terms.

Returning to the main line of our argument we now find ourselves in a better position to see that there indeed is a place *within* morality for the idea of better and worse states of affairs. That there is such a place is true if only because the proper end of benevolence is the good of others, and because in many situations the person who has this virtue will be able to think of good and bad states of affairs, in terms of the general good. It does not, however, follow that he will always be able to do so. For sometimes justice will forbid a certain action, as it forbids the harmful experiment designed to further cancer research; and then it will not be possible to ask whether 'the state of affairs' containing the action and its results will be better or worse than one

---

[12] See Harsanyi, 'Morality and the Theory of Rational Behavior', in Sen and Williams, *Utilitarianism and Beyond*, p. 39.

in which the action is not done. The action is one that *cannot* be done, because justice forbids it, and nothing that has this moral character comes within the scope of the kind of comparison of total outcomes that benevolence may sometimes require. Picking up at this point the example discussed earlier about the morality of killing or torturing to prevent more killings or torturings we see the same principle operating here. If it were a question of riding out to rescue a small number or a large number then benevolence would, we may suppose, urge that the larger number be saved. But if it is a matter of preventing the killing *by* killing (or conniving at a killing) the case will be quite different. One does not have to believe that all rights to non-interference are absolute to believe that *this* is an unjust action, and if it is unjust the moral man says to himself that he cannot do it and does not include it in an assessment he may be making about the good and bad states of affairs that he can bring about.

What has been said in the last few paragraphs is, I suggest, a sketch of what can truly be said about the important place that the idea of maximum welfare has in morality. It is not that in the guise of 'the best outcome' it stands *outside* morality as its foundation and arbiter, but rather that it appears *within* morality as the end of one of the virtues.

When we see it like this, and give expressions such as 'best outcome' and 'good state of affairs' no special meaning in moral contexts other than the one that the virtues give them, we shall no longer think the paradoxical thought that it is sometimes right to act in such a way that the total outcome, consisting of one's action and its results, is less good than some other accessible at the time. In the abstract a benevolent person must wish that loss and harm should be minimized. He does not, however, wish that the whole consisting of a killing to minimize killings should be actualized either by his agency or that of anyone else. So there is no reason on this score to think that he must regard it as 'the better state of affairs'.[13] And therefore there is no reason for the non-consequentialist, whose thought of good and bad states of affairs in moral contexts comes only from the virtues themselves, to describe the refusal as a choice of a worse total outcome. If he does so describe it he will be giving the words the sense they have in his opponents' theories, and it is not surprising that he should find himself in their hands.

We may also remind ourselves at this point that benevolence is not the only virtue which has to do, at least in part, with ends rather than with the observance of rules. As mentioned earlier there belongs to the virtue of justice the readiness to fight for justice as well as to

---

[13]   I have discussed examples of this kind in more detail in 'Morality, Action, and Outcome', in T. Honderich, ed., *Morality and Objectivity: A Tribute to J. L. Mackie* (London: Routledge & Kegan Paul, 1985).

observe its laws; and there belongs to truthfulness not only the avoidance of lying but also that other kind of attachment to truth which has to do with its preservation and pursuit. A man of virtue must be a lover of justice and a lover of truth. Furthermore he will seek the special good of his family and friends. Thus there will be many things which he will want and will welcome, sometimes sharing these aims with others and sometimes opposing them, as when working differentially for his own children or his own friends.[14] Similarly someone who is judging a competition and is a fair judge must try to see to it that the best man wins. The existence of these 'moral aims' will of course give opportunity for the use, in moral contexts, of such expressions as 'a good thing' or 'the best state of affairs'. But nothing of a consequentialist nature follows from such pieces of usage, found here and there within morality.

m⇾   An analogy will perhaps help to make my point. Thinking about good manners we might decide that someone who has good manners tries to avoid embarrassing others in social situations. This must, let us suppose, be one of his aims; and we might even decide that so far as manners is concerned this, or something like it, is the only prescribed *end*. But of course this does not mean that what good manners require of anyone is universally determined by this end. A consequentialist theory of good manners would presumably be mistaken; because good manners, not being solely a matter of purposes, also require that certain things be done or not done: e.g. that hospitality not be abused by frank discussion of the deficiencies of one's host as soon as he leaves the room.[15] So if invited to take part in such discussions a well-mannered person will, if necessary, maintain a silence embarrassing to an interlocutor, because the rule here takes precedence over the aim prescribed. Assuming that this is a correct account of good manners – and it does not of course matter whether it is or not – we can now see the difficulty that arises if we try to say which choice open to the agent results in the best state of affairs from the point of view of manners. In certain contexts the state of affairs containing no embarrassment will be referred to as a good state of affairs, because avoiding embarrassment is by our hypothesis the one *end* prescribed by good manners. But we should not be surprised if the right action from the point of view of good manners is sometimes the one that produces something *other* than this good state of affairs. We have no right to take an end from within the whole that makes up good

---

[14]   See Derek Parfit, 'Prudence, Morality, and the Prisoner's Dilemma', *Proceedings of the British Academy* 65 (1979): 556–64, and Amartya Sen, 'Rights and Agency' op. cit.
[15]   It is customary to wait until later.

manners and turn it, just because it is an *end*, into the single guide to action to be used by the well-mannered man.

[n]→   This analogy serves to illustrate my point about the illegitimacy of moving what is found within morality to a criterial position outside it. But it may also bring to the surface a reason many will be ready to give for being dissatisfied with my thesis. For surely a morality is unlike a code of manners in claiming rational justification for its ordinances? It cannot be enough to say that we *do* have such things as rules of justice in our present system of virtues: the question is whether we should have them, and if so why we should. And the reason this is crucial in the present context is that the justification of a moral code may seem inevitably to involve the very idea that has been called in question in this paper.

This is a very important objection. In its most persuasive form it involves a picture of morality as a rational device developed to serve certain purposes, and therefore answerable to these purposes. Morality, it will be suggested, is a device with a certain object, having to do with the harmonizing of ends or the securing of the greatest possible general good, or perhaps one of these things plus the safeguarding of rights. And the content of morality – what really is right and wrong – will be thought to be determined by what it is rational to require in the way of conduct given that these are our aims. Thus morality is thought of as a kind of tacit legislation by the community, and it is, of course, significant that the early Utilitarians, who were much interested in the rationalizing of actual Parliamentary legislation, were ready to talk in these terms.[16] In moral legislation our aim is, they thought, the general good. With this way of looking at morality there reappears the idea of better and worse states of affairs from the moral point of view. Moreover consequentialism *in some form* is necessarily reinstated. For while there is room on such a model for rational moral codes which enjoin something other than the pursuit of 'the best state of affairs from the moral point of view' this will be only in so far as it is by means of such ordinances that the object of a moral code is best achieved.[17]

[o]→   Thus it may seem that we must after all allow that the idea of a good state of affairs appears at the most basic level in the critical appraisal of any moral code. This would, however, be too hasty a conclusion. Consequentialism in some form follows from the premiss that morality is a device for achieving a certain shared end. But why

[16]   See, e.g., J. Bentham, *An Introduction to the Principles of Legislation* (1789). ch. 3. Section 1.
[17]   For discussions of this possibility, see, e.g., R. Adams, 'Motive Utilitarianism', *The Journal of Philosophy* 73 (1976), and D. Parfit, *Reasons and Persons* (Oxford, Clarendon Press, 1984), pp. 24–8.

should we accept this view of what morality is and how it is to be judged? Why should we not rather see that as itself a consequentialist assumption, which has come to seem neutral and inevitable only in so far as utilitarianism and other forms of consequentialism now dominate moral philosophy?

To counter this bewitchment let us ask awkard questions about who is supposed to *have* the end which morality is supposed to be in aid of. J. S. Mill notoriously found it hard to pass from the premiss that the end of each is the good of each to the proposition that the end of all is the good of all.[18] Perhaps no such *shared end* appears in the foundations of ethics, where we may rather find individual ends and rational compromises between those who have them. Or perhaps at the most basic level lie facts about the way individual human beings can find the greatest goods which they are capable of possessing. The truth is, I think, that we simply do not have a satisfactory theory of morality, and need to look for it. Scanlon was indeed right in saying that the real answer to utilitarianism depends on progress in the development of alternatives. Meanwhile, however, we have no reason to think that we must accept consequentialism in any form. If the thesis of this paper is correct we should be more alert than we usually are to the possibility that we may unwittingly, and unnecessarily, surrender to consequentialism by uncritically accepting its key idea. Let us remind ourselves that the idea of the goodness of total states of affairs played no part in Aristotle's moral philosophy, and that in modern times it plays no part either in Rawls's account of justice or in the theories of more thoroughgoing contractualists such as Scanlon.[19] If we accustom ourselves to the thought that there is simply a blank where consequentialists see 'the best state of affairs' we may be better able to give other theories the hearing they deserve.

Commentary on Foot

At [a]⊢→, Foot describes the central task of the paper as one of 'exorcism'. She believes that we are under the spell of utilitarianism – that something drives us to accept it – and nonetheless she also thinks that there is something fundamentally mistaken in utilitarianism. By exposing this mistake, she believes we can at once understand the utilitarian spell, and free ourselves of it.

---

[18]   J. S. Mill, *Utilitarianism* (1863), Chapter IV.
[19]   J. Rawls, *A Theory of Justice* (Cambridge, Mass: Harvard University Press, 1971); T. M. Scanlon, op. cit.

At $\boxed{b}\rightarrow$ Foot identifies the location of the mistake she finds in utilitarianism. Describe that location.

Utilitarianism is composed of two theses: consequentialism and what Foot calls 'welfarism'. The first of these is that right action is in every case that action whose outcome, or consequence, is the best state of affairs. The second is that one compares the amount of good in different possible states of affairs by finding out how much pleasure, happiness, or satisfaction each one contains. Foot thinks that the fundamental flaw in utilitarianism lies with the first of these – with the thesis of consequentialism. However, at $\boxed{c}\rightarrow$ she notes that it is welfarism that has generally been the target chosen by most critics of utilitarianism.

Give your own summary of Foot's discussion (between $\boxed{c}\rightarrow$ and $\boxed{d}\rightarrow$) of welfarism.

Foot's discussion of welfarism touches only lightly on issues that themselves have led to a huge literature. Without taking much notice of the differences between pleasure, happiness and satisfaction – different notions that utilitarians have used to capture what they regard as the good – she stresses what are arguably two more structural defects. The first is that utilitarians are forced to distinguish between innocent ('non-malicious') pleasures, and those not so innocent, so as to rule out counting as acceptable such things as public executions. And the second is that, though utilitarianism insists that everyone's good counts equally, there are seemingly endless problems in describing acceptable principles for distributing this good. To take a famous example, is it right to take one patient's life so as to produce life-saving organs for five others? Mere adding up of pleasure or happiness suggests that it would be, that five lives gained outweigh the one life lost. But sacrificing someone in this way seems thoroughly unacceptable.

As she points out, the welfarist utilitarian is not without resources for trying to patch up these defects, and she briefly considers the idea of a kind of 'goal-rights' utilitarianism which attempts to deal with the second of them. However, this leads her to what she has already identified as the fundamental source of utilitarian difficulty – its consequentialism – and this sets the agenda for the rest of this commentary. Moreover, this discussion will lead us back to the topic of goodness.

At $\boxed{d}\rightarrow$, Foot asks what makes consequentialism seem so compelling, and she answers: 'It is … the rather simple thought that it can never be right to prefer a worse state of affairs to a better.'

Between $\boxed{d}\rightarrow$ and $\boxed{e}\rightarrow$, and also in footnote 5, Foot says some more about this 'simple thought'. Explain what she says and try either to give an argument for it or to give some examples that test it.

At $\boxed{e}$⊢→, Foot says: 'I believe (and this is the main thesis of the paper) that we go wrong in accepting the idea that there are better and worse states of affairs in the sense that consequentialism requires.' Why precisely do we go wrong? Her detailed answer begins with another question (see the beginning of the paragraph just after $\boxed{e}$⊢→): are we so sure that we even understand what it means to speak of 'a good state of affairs'? For she rightly notes that unless we can make sense of this expression – the right kind of sense – we will not be justified in speaking of better or worse states of affairs, and the simple thought above will have been shown to be empty.

> What reasons does Foot give for thinking that we might not be able to make sense of the idea of a good state of affairs?

As was discussed briefly in the introduction to this chapter, the adjective 'good' often depends for its particular sense on the noun to which it is attached. We can make sense of 'good knife' because, knowing what knives are for, we have some idea of what would count as fulfilling these purposes to some relevantly high standard. However, it is unclear, to say the least, what would count as being a high standard in states of affairs or events. Foot does note that we might think a good state of affairs was one in which people did what was morally required of them, but this doesn't advance matters, because we are looking to the very idea of a good state of affairs to help in defining moral rightness.

> Is this consideration a decisive reason to doubt the intelligibility of the expression 'good state of affairs'?

Foot admits that it isn't decisive, since, as she observes, we do quite commonly speak this way. She notes too that it would be 'ridiculous' to query the sense of such ordinary expressions as 'it would be a good thing', said of something that we might anticipate happening. Yet, despite these concessions, she insists: 'it is important to see how such expressions actually work in the contexts in which they are at home'. And the suspicion is that this further investigation will offer little solace to the utilitarian need to make sense of the expression 'good state of affairs'.

At $\boxed{f}$⊢→, she asks whether a good state of affairs is something impersonal, something to be recognized by all reasonable persons.

> Why is it important at this point to speak of something impersonal that putatively makes a state of affairs good?

The discussion from $\boxed{f}$⊢→ to $\boxed{i}$⊢→ both answers this question, and argues that we cannot plausibly identify 'something impersonal' in the assessments we commonly make of states of affairs. The arguments proceed in what can be identified as two stages. First, Foot offers various examples to make a straight-forward point about one way in which we commonly speak about good out-comes or good states of affairs. For example, when the horse you bet on wins, you might well describe that state of affairs as good, while from my point of view – having backed another horse – it is anything but. What she takes examples like this to suggest is that there seems to be something 'speaker-relative' about our judgements of the goodness of states of affairs. However, if this relativity is really essential to the intelligibility of the phrase 'good state of affairs' – if, that is, there is no reason to think such judgements are imper-sonal – then this spells trouble for the consequentialist. For the appeal to the relative merits of various states of affairs can only ground decisions an agent might make about the rightness or wrongness of some action, if that appeal doesn't depend on the special needs and interests of the agent. I can scarcely convince you that the *morally* right thing to do is to aim for a good state of affairs, if this latter is understood as one that is in *my* interest (or even in *yours*). So, to justify the use in morality of assessments of states of affairs, these must be ones we make from no particular point of view or, perhaps equivalently, from the moral point of view. These possibilities figure in the second stage of Foot's argument, one which starts at $\boxed{h}\!\!\mapsto$.

Summarize these second-stage arguments (from $\boxed{h}\!\!\mapsto$ to $\boxed{i}\!\!\mapsto$), and say whether you think them cogent.

Foot's discussion is summed up at $\boxed{i}\!\!\mapsto$, but before we consider her next move, let's look back at a brief but important comment that she makes at $\boxed{g}\!\!\mapsto$. She notes that her arguments about interest-relativity should not be taken to support the general thesis that all phrases of the form 'good X' are interest-relative. Her concern has been solely with the phrase 'good state of affairs', and her arguments do not therefore entail that, for example, 'good knife', or even 'good action' or 'good person' are interest-relative. Each such case must be examined on its own merits, and so long as one can tell a story which justi-fies the adjective 'good' in each case without adverting to any interests of one or other person or group, that is fine with her. This point is important both for her remaining arguments, and for our work in this chapter. Aristotle cer-tainly aimed to tell us something about human good – enough perhaps to justify our speaking of 'good persons' – and nothing he said there is under-mined by Foot's arguments. With Mill, however, the situation is different. For in spite of his sharing certain general aims with Aristotle, it is important for Mill, and for any consequentialist account of morality, that the notion of a good state of affairs makes sense.

   At $\boxed{i}\!\!\mapsto$, Foot claims that her arguments have shown: either (i) that the expression 'a good state of affairs' is interest-relative, and so useless as a way of defining right action; or (ii) that if qualified by 'from the moral point of view', it needn't be understood as interest-relative, but is either meaningless, or cannot serve as a criterion of right action in the way supposed by consequentialists. Yet, recalling that her aim is to 'exorcise' the spell of utilitarianism, it is crucial not only that she show why the doctrine is wrong, but why it is so widely held. And this is a task she begins at ⌈j⌉↦.

Foot notes first that a moral person would be expected to want others to be happy, and would thus count as good a state of affairs that included that happiness. She says: 'To deny this would be to deny that benevolence is a virtue.' Following through on this line of thought, she claims (in the paragraph beginning at ⌈k⌉↦) that while our commitment to benevolence can give a perfectly good sense to the expression 'good state of affairs' this commitment is *within* morality, and must be placed alongside commitments to virtues other than benevolence.

Foot clarifies and extends this line of thought in the transition from ⌈k⌉↦ to ⌈l⌉↦. Do you find what she says convincing?

In the paragraph before ⌈l⌉↦, Foot condenses her argument into a comment about the ideal observer. Imagining such an observer is a common device that utilitarians, among others, use to dramatize their view: an outcome is said to be right if, in the view of an ideal, impartial and sympathetic observer, it would result in the greatest happiness. Foot acknowledges that such an observer would take into account the happiness of all humankind, and would not be partial, and she agrees that such an observer would therefore be maximally benevolent. But Foot asks: 'what ... are we to suppose about this person's other characteristics?' That is, what other virtues, if any, would such an observer have to recognize? If one says 'none besides an impartial interest in human happiness', this is to build the utilitarian viewpoint into the assessment from the start. But, as she argues in the paragraphs from ⌈l⌉↦ through ⌈m⌉↦, there is not only no compelling reason to do so, there are good reasons against.

Benevolence is certainly a virtue, but there are others. If we imagine that the impartial observer is just, for example, then there may well be states of affairs which, in being unjust, are simply not best, even if they would result in the greatest happiness. To take one case: because we think it unjust to perform a harmful experiment without a subject's consent, then even if this experiment produces a life-saving cure for many other cancer sufferers, we would expect an impartial observer who is just to forbid it. The experiment's consequence might well be a state of affairs in which the most happiness is produced – it could in this way be thought of as benevolent – but, given its injustice, the idea that we might judge it 'best' is a non-starter.

Foot allows that one can talk about good states of affairs, but only from *within* a moral outlook, one which is itself shaped by the range of virtues it recognizes. Among these virtues benevolence is bound to play an important part, since this virtue is central to our relations with each other. Foot thinks that it is this special role for benevolence which gives utilitarianism its perennial appeal. If there is no problem about justice in some specific circumstance, then benevolence is often the single consideration determining the best course of action or social policy. However, we make a mistake when we give to benevolence the even greater role of defining rightness in every case.

At $\boxed{m}$→, Foot offers an analogy intended to support her idea that assessments of states of affairs can only be properly intelligible within some institution. Getting away from morality, she asks us to consider the institution of social manners.

Do you think that this analogy is a good one? Does it help to illuminate Foot's thesis about morality?

Whether or not you answer this question affirmatively, the analogy does serve Foot in another way. As she notes at $\boxed{n}$→, it brings out a question about her view – one which becomes an objection to it – which lurks just beneath the surface.

What is this objection?

Foot imagines her objector saying: 'It cannot be enough to say that we *do* have such things as rules of justice in our present system of virtues; the question is whether we should have them and if so why we should.' What this objector takes to be required is some rational basis for morality, one which doesn't simply assume that what we now regard as virtues are definitive. Such a rational basis could well just bypass Foot's account of the virtues, and, as she says (at $\boxed{o}$→), could well make it 'seem that we must after all allow that the idea of a good state of affairs appears at the most basic level in the critical appraisal of any moral code'.

Do you think that Foot successfully counters this objection?

This objection, and her reply, are the opening moves in a complex and fundamental discussion about the relationship between rationality and morality, a discussion that has been central to Foot throughout her career. For more on her view of how best to link rationality and morality, see her book *Natural Goodness* which is listed in the reference list (also see chapter 5 of this book). However, in the present context, she counts it enough to have shown that we have no reason to accept the idea that we can judge states of affairs better or worse from outside any morality. Moreover, at $\boxed{p}$→, she says something which brings us back to the reading that opened this chapter. She writes: 'Let us remind ourselves that the goodness of total states of affairs played no part in Aristotle's moral philosophy ...'

2

Justice

Introduction

If you are put in charge of distributing food to a hungry population, and you do so by giving a larger share to those whose appearance most pleases you, or to those who promise you favours in return, then you have not done justice, as we would say, to those who happen not to be good-looking, or are not able to offer favours. Justice in this sense is about the distribution of some good: we consider a distribution just when there are reasonable and defensible grounds for deciding who gets what share. While these grounds are not by any means easy to make explicit, and will vary from case to case, neither a person's looks nor ability to do favours would count as good grounds.

Justice also figures centrally in our assessment of legal systems. In a just society, punishments are meted out only on reasonable grounds, and certainly not arbitrarily. Thus, we think that someone deserves punishment only if they are in fact guilty of some crime, and that no system is just if, without good reason, it metes out different punishments to those who have committed the same crime. One could regard justice in punishment as a special case of distributive justice, where what is distributed are harms instead of goods, but there is more to the idea of justice in a legal system than distribution in the narrowest sense. If judges in some society impose long prison sentences on those who overstay their time in parking bays, or if the laws in that society make criminal things like walking slowly or saying 'hello' to passers-by, this would be counted as unjust, even if the distribution of these punishments were completely uniform. One could insist that even the latter kinds of case involve distribution in some sense of the term, since one is after all distributing a prison sentence – unjustly – to someone 'guilty' of no more than walking

slowly. But it would be no less reasonable to think that we have here uncovered
at least a hint of a rather different idea of justice.

The examples of institutions charged with giving out food or meting out
punishments show justice not only in its distributive guise, but also in a social
context. However, we do not speak of justice only in connection with distribution, nor only as a feature of social or legal institutions. We also speak of it
as a virtue of individual agents; we say of them that they are just or unjust,
not because of the way they fulfil some social or institutional role, but instead
because of the way they conduct their lives. Justice in this sense is a character
trait, one which can be put alongside other virtues such as wisdom, honesty,
kindness, courage, and tolerance, whose cultivation we believe to be morally
important. Moreover, it could be argued that justice is not merely one of these
moral virtues, but is central to virtue generally, and hence to morality itself.
That we could think this is partly because 'just' can often serve as a synonym
of 'moral': praising someone for their moral rectitude we can say either that
they are moral or just. But there are more substantial reasons for thinking that
the virtue of justice is perhaps a key to the others.

Consider kindness. We do not regard *any* act of helping others, or being
attentive to their needs, as kindness, since we recognize that such help or consideration could be detrimental to the recipient. What is required for kindness
is what it is natural to describe as a correct moral appreciation of the recipient's circumstances – an appreciation which reveals the help or consideration
to be morally appropriate, and therefore praiseworthy. One perfectly reasonable way to describe someone who possesses the ability to make these sorts of
assessment in acting is to say that they are just. So, someone is thus properly
described as kind when they have not only a disposition or character that
leads them to help others or be attentive, but also a capacity to see what is
just – a capacity to make correct moral judgements about the various situations in which they exercise this disposition. Similar remarks could be made
about the role of justice in relation to other virtues. In sum, justice has a claim
to being the virtue that makes possible the genuine possession of the other
virtues. And the sense of justice that figures here has no immediate connection
with either principles of distribution or features of social and legal systems.

It is somewhat surprising that the notion of justice plays these two roles,
that it can be used both in the evaluation of certain social and political arrangements, and in assessing the moral character of individual agents. Of course, it
could simply be that 'just' merely happens to be used by contemporary speakers in this way; that this English word – and perhaps the equivalent word in
other modern languages – has come to have several different and only dis-
tantly related meanings. However, Plato's *Republic*, written more than two
thousand years ago in a social, political, moral and linguistic context quite
different from our own, shows the concept of justice to have had pretty much
the same breadth for him as it does for us. So, aside from specific questions
about its adequacy, one should approach any specific account of justice with

this question: does the account help us to understand how a single notion can have such breadth of application?

The two texts which figure in this chapter offer what certainly appear to be radically different conceptions of justice. However, the more one looks at each of them, the more one can see resemblances and overlaps, both in the conceptions of justice themselves and in the methods used to arrive at them. In each case, the texts come from much larger works: Plato's *Republic* and Rawls's *A Theory of Justice*. This means that the material in this chapter should only be seen as sketching the conceptions of justice found in those works, though even these sketches contain enough detail to make our explorations rewarding. However, in addition to our more detailed explorations, it will be important to keep two wider issues in focus. On the one hand, there will be the obvious question of how these two conceptions of justice – and the methods used in arriving at them – fit together. And, on the other hand, there is the no less important question of whether what we find in Plato and Rawls can help us understand, and perhaps justify, the breadth of application of the concept of justice. For, given that this concept figures so centrally, an appreciation of its complexities and their interconnections will itself be a contribution to our understanding of morality.

Introduction to Plato (and Socrates)

Though written by Plato, the dialogue from which the first text is taken – the *Republic* – features Socrates as the main character. Since Socrates was a well-known philosopher in his own right, there is thus an obvious need to say something here about both Plato and Socrates. That said, there is little uncontroversial about their lives, and it has been left to generations of scholars to speculate not only about this, but also about how to apportion between them the ideas that figure in the *Republic* and in the other Platonic dialogues that give Socrates the main speaking role.

Plato and Socrates were both Athenian citizens, Socrates being the elder of the two, and he was certainly Plato's teacher, though not in any formal sense. Socrates' dates are generally accepted to be 469–399 BC, and Plato's 427–347 BC. As is often noted, Socrates did not himself produce any written work, and his philosophical reputation comes entirely from what is known about his character, wit and moral seriousness, as detailed in the various Platonic dialogues, but also in the *Memorabilia* of his contemporary, Xenophon, the plays of Aristophanes, and in the works of Aristotle. He is thought to have been the son of a sculptor, though he didn't spend much time in earning a living, perhaps because of an inheritance, though mainly because he lived what by any standards was a radically simple life, one that generated few material needs. (One tradition has it that he was a stonemason.) His life centred wholly around the political and social life of Athens, and he spent his days mainly in discussion of moral and political matters – indeed in debate about these – with those who lived and worked in that city. For underlying reasons which have been argued about down the centuries, he was tried and convicted by those in power in Athens for corrupting the young and undermining religious belief. He was sentenced to death, and, rejecting the very real option of exile, is supposed to have faced his sentence with extraordinary dignity, calmly drinking the hemlock given as the method of execution allowed to Athenian citizens. As to his philosophical positions, very little can be said with any certainty, especially given that he famously insisted that he did not himself know anything. No less famously – even notoriously – he felt that he had to seek knowledge from others by endlessly questioning them about their understanding of, among other notions, virtue, friendship, love, knowledge and piety, and he maintained that a life not examined by such reflective inquiry was not worth living.

Plato came from a wealthy and powerful family in Athens, members of which were deeply implicated in the political turmoil that followed the Athenian defeat at the hands of Sparta in 404 BC. (Socrates' death sentence is often thought to be the indirect result of this turmoil.) As a result, Plato seems to have distanced himself from Athenian politics, though it is known that he travelled to Syracuse in Sicily, and is thought to have given political advice to the ruler of that city. Whatever the truth about Plato's political activities, there is no doubt about his having established a philosophical school in Athens – the Academy – which endured for some centuries. He also wrote a great deal, most of it in dialogue form, and it is from these dialogues that we have gleaned most of what we know, both about his and Socrates' thought.

The *Republic* is one of the longest, and certainly the richest, of Plato's dialogues, and it has a somewhat odd shape. It is generally reckoned to come in the middle period of Plato's writing: the earlier dialogues tend to be short, and have the inconclusiveness one associates with Socrates' method of cross-questioning, whereas the later ones tend to be didactic, and in some cases do not involve Socrates at all. Divided into ten books, the first book of the *Republic* reads like one of the early dialogues in which Socrates cross-questions various characters about their understanding of justice, but in the remaining books one finds Socrates arguing for, typically with very little input from his interlocutors, various philosophical views about justice and other matters.

Given Socrates' emblematic insistence on his lack of philosophical knowledge, commentators have suggested that the first book was originally one of the early dialogues, and that the philosophical doctrines of the later books mark the point at which Plato, in spite of using Socrates as the main character, diverges from his teacher and presents his own views. However, it should be borne in mind that the actual texts we have of the *Republic* and other dialogues date from more than twelve hundred years after Plato wrote, and that most of the conclusions scholars draw about the order of Plato's compositions, and their content, is based mainly on internal evidence from these texts, many of which might have been extensively edited throughout the long period during which they were copied and re-copied. However, putting on one side these vexed issues of authorship, the discussion below will follow tradition in identifying Plato as responsible for the views about justice expressed in the *Republic*.

Our text comes from Books II and IV of the ten books that make up the whole, and it focuses sharply on Plato's account of justice. However, the whole of the *Republic* is concerned, directly or indirectly, with justice, so the selection sketches, rather than details, the Platonic view. (In a parallel way, the second text in this chapter is also a sketch of a contemporary view of justice.)

Though reading the whole of the *Republic* is certainly to be recommended, our selection aims at giving an uncluttered view of the sources and general shape of Plato's views about justice. Moreover, even though it involves severe pruning of Plato's original, enough remains to give one a lively sense of his writing, and his vivid representation of Socrates. Finally, to make it easier to follow the flow of the argument from its inception in Book II to its interim conclusion in Book IV, brief summaries of the excised material will be included at appropriate points (in square brackets), beginning with this comment about the opening book of the *Republic*.

[As mentioned, Book I follows the pattern of other, early, Platonic dialogues. In a realistic dramatic setting, Cephalus, one of the assembled group, comes to speak of justice, thereby inviting Socrates' close cross-examination, first of Cephalus and then of others present who take up the argument. When these further attempts to give a proper account of justice wither under Socratic examination, Thrasymachus rudely breaks into the discussion and offers his own, rather cynical, estimation of justice. The remainder of the book is taken up with Socrates' arguments against Thrasymachus' views. These arguments can seem unconvincing, and Book II opens with Glaucon's plea to Socrates to do better. Finally, note that many or all of the characters in the *Republic* are historical figures: in particular, Thrasymachus – a member of a group of thinkers called 'Sophists' – was known for precisely the kind of views he is shown as espousing in Book I, and Glaucon and Adimantus were Plato's brothers.]

Plato, *Republic* (extracts from Books II–IV)

Book II

a→ When I had said this I supposed that I was done with the subject, but it all turned out to be only a prelude. For Glaucon, who is always an intrepid, enterprising spirit in everything, would not on this

Editors' note: The original footnotes have been renumbered as part of the text has been omitted.

occasion acquiesce in Thrasymachus' abandonment of his case, but said, Socrates, is it your desire to seem to have persuaded us or really to persuade us that it is without exception better to be just than unjust?

Really, I said, if the choice rested with me.

Well, then, you are not doing what you wish. For tell me, do you agree that there is a kind of good which we would choose to possess, not from desire for its after-effects, but welcoming it for its own sake? As, for example, joy and such pleasures as are harmless and nothing results from them afterward save to have and to hold the enjoyment.

I recognize that kind, said I.

And again a kind that we love both for its own sake and for its consequences, such as understanding, sight, and health? For these I presume we welcome for both reasons.

Yes, I said.

And can you discern a third form of good under which fall exercise and being healed when sick and the art of healing and the making of money generally? For of them we would say that they are laborious and painful yet beneficial, and for their own sake we would not accept them, but only for the rewards and other benefits that accrue from them.

Why yes, I said, I must admit this third class also. But what of it?

b→ In which of these classes do you place justice? he said.

In my opinion, I said, it belongs in the fairest class, that which a man who is to be happy must love both for its own sake and for the results.

Yet the multitude, he said, do not think so, but that it belongs to the toilsome class of things that must be practiced for the sake of rewards and repute due to opinion but that in itself is to be shunned as an affliction.

I am aware, said I, that that is the general opinion and Thrasymachus has for some time been disparaging it as such and praising injustice. But I, it seems, am somewhat slow to learn.

Come now, he said, hear what I too have to say and see if you agree with me. For Thrasymachus seems to me to have given up to you too soon, as if he were a serpent that you had charmed, but I am not yet satisfied with the proof that has been offered about justice and injustice. For what I desire is to hear what each of them is and what potency and effect each has in and of itself dwelling in the soul, but to dismiss c→ their rewards and consequences. This, then, is what I propose to do, with your concurrence. I will renew the argument of Thrasymachus and will first state what men say is the nature and origin of justice, secondly, that all who practice it do so reluctantly, regarding it as something necessary and not as a good, and thirdly, that they have plausible grounds for thus acting, since forsooth the life of the unjust man is far better than that of the just man – as they say, though I, Socrates, don't believe it. Yet I am disconcerted when my ears are dinned by the arguments of Thrasymachus and innumerable others. But the case for justice, to prove that it is better than injustice, I have never yet heard stated by any as I desire to hear it. What I desire is to hear an encomium on justice in and by itself. And I think I am most likely to get that from you. For which reason I will lay myself out in praise of the life of injustice, and in so speaking will give you an example of the manner in which I desire to hear from you in turn the dispraise of injustice and the praise of justice. Consider whether my proposal pleases you.

Nothing could please me more, said I, for on what subject would a man of sense rather delight to hold and hear discourse again and again?

That is excellent, he said, and now listen to what I said would be the first topic – the nature and origin of justice.

By nature, they say, to commit injustice is a good and to suffer it is an evil, but that the excess of evil in being wronged is greater than the excess of good in doing wrong, so that when men do wrong and are wronged by one another and taste of both, those who lack the power to avoid the one and take the other determine that it is for their profit to make a compact with one another neither to commit nor to suffer injustice, and that this is the beginning of legislation and of covenants between men, and that they name the commandment of the law the lawful and the just, and that this is the genesis and essential nature of justice – a compromise between the best, which is to do wrong with impunity, and the worst, which is to be wronged and be impotent to get one's revenge. Justice, they tell us, being midway between the two, is accepted and approved, not as a real good, but as a thing honoured in the lack of vigour to do injustice, since anyone who had the power to do it and was in reality 'a man' would never make a compact with anybody neither to wrong nor to be wronged, for he would be mad. The nature, then, of justice is this and such as this, Socrates, and such are the conditions in which it originates, according to the theory.

But as for the second point, that those who practice it do so unwillingly and from want of power to commit injustice, we shall be most likely to apprehend that if we entertain some such supposition as this in thought – if we grant to both the just and the unjust license and power to do whatever they please, and then accompany them in imagination and see whither desire will conduct them. We should then catch the just man in the very act of resorting to the same conduct as the unjust man because of the self-advantage which every creature by its nature pursues as a good, while by the convention of law it is forcibly diverted to paying honor to 'equality.' The license that I mean would be most nearly such as would result from supposing them to have the power which men say once came to the ancestor of Gyges the Lydian. They relate that he was a shepherd in the service of the ruler at that time of Lydia, and that after a great deluge of rain and an earthquake the ground opened and a chasm appeared in the place where he was pasturing, and they say that he saw and wondered and went down into the chasm. And the story goes that he beheld other marvels there and a hollow bronze horse with little doors, and that he peeped in and saw a corpse within, as it seemed, of more than mortal stature, and that there was nothing else but a gold ring on its hand, which he took off, and so went forth. And when the shepherds held their customary assembly to make their monthly report to the king about the flocks, he also attended, wearing the ring. So as he sat there it chanced that he turned the collet of the ring toward himself, toward the inner part of his hand, and when this took place they say that he became invisible to those who sat by him and they spoke of him as absent, and that he was amazed, and again fumbling with the ring turned the collet outward and so became visible. On noting this he experimented with the ring to see if it possessed this virtue, and he found the result to be that when he turned the collet inward he became invisible, and when outward visible, and becoming aware of this, he immediately managed things so that he became one of the messengers who went up to the king, and on coming there he seduced the king's wife and with her aid set upon the king and slew him and possessed his kingdom.

If now there should be two such rings, and the just man should put on one and the unjust the other, no one could be found, it would seem, of such adamantine temper as to persevere in justice and endure to refrain his hands from the possessions of others and not touch them, though he might with impunity take what he wished even from the market place, and enter into houses and lie with whom he pleased, and slay and loose from bonds whomsoever he would, and in all other things conduct himself among mankind as the equal of a god. And in so acting he would do no differently from the other man, but both would pursue the same course. And yet this is a great proof, one might argue, that no one is just of his own will but only from constraint, in the belief that justice is not his personal good, inasmuch as every man, when he supposes himself to have the power to do wrong, does wrong. For that there is far more profit for him personally in injustice than in justice is what every man believes, and believes truly, as the proponent of this theory will maintain. For if anyone who had got such a license within his grasp should refuse to do any wrong or lay his hands on others' possessions, he would be regarded as most pitiable and a great fool by all who took note of it, though they would praise him before one another's faces, deceiving one another because of their fear of suffering injustice. So much for this point.

But to come now to the decision between our two kinds of life, if we separate the most completely just and the most completely unjust man, we shall be able to decide rightly, but if not, not. How, then, is this separation to be made? Thus. We must subtract nothing of his injustice from the unjust man or of his justice from the just, but assume the perfection of each in his own mode of conduct. In the first place, the unjust man must act as clever craftsmen do. A first-rate pilot or physician, for example, feels the difference between impossibilities and possibilities in his art and attempts the one and lets the others go, and then, too, if he does happen to trip, he is equal to correcting his error. Similarly, the unjust man who attempts injustice rightly must be supposed to escape detection if he is to be altogether unjust, and we must regard the man who is caught as a bungler. For the height of injustice is to seem just without being so. To the perfectly unjust man, then, we must assign perfect injustice and withhold nothing of it, but we must allow him, while committing the greatest wrongs, to have secured for himself the greatest reputation for justice, and if he does happen to trip, we must concede to him the power to correct his mistakes by his ability to speak persuasively if any of his misdeeds come to light, and when force is needed, to employ force by reason of his manly spirit and vigor and his provision of friends and money. And when we have set up an unjust man of this character, our theory must set the just man at his side – a simple and noble man, who, in the phrase of Aeschylus, does not wish to seem but to be good. Then we must deprive him of the seeming. For if he is going to be thought just he will have honours and gifts because of that esteem. We cannot be sure in that case whether he is just for justice' sake or for the sake of the gifts and the honours. So we must strip him bare of everything but justice and make his state the opposite of his imagined counterpart. Though doing no wrong he must have the repute of the greatest injustice, so that he may be put to the test as regards justice through not softening because of ill repute and the consequences thereof. But let him hold on his course unchangeable even unto death, seeming all his life to be unjust though being just, so that, both men attaining to the limit, the one of injustice, the other of justice, we may pass judgement which of the two is the happier.

Bless me, my dear Glaucon, said I. How strenuously you polish off each of your two men for the competition for the prize as if it were a statue!

To the best of my ability, he replied, and if such is the nature of the two, it becomes an easy matter, I fancy, to unfold the tale of the sort of life that awaits each. We must tell it, then, and even if my language is somewhat rude and brutal, you must not suppose, Socrates, that it is I who speak thus, but those who commend injustice above justice. What they will say is this, that such being his disposition the just man will have to endure the lash, the rack, chains, the branding iron in his eyes, and finally, after every extremity of suffering, he will be crucified, and so will learn his lesson that not to be but to seem just is what we ought to desire. And the saying of Aeschylus was, it seems, far more correctly applicable to the unjust man. For it is literally true, they will say, that the unjust man, as pursuing what clings closely to reality, to truth, and not regulating his life by opinion, desires not to seem but to be unjust,

> Exploiting the deep furrows of his wit
> From which there grows the fruit of counsels shrewd,[1]

first office and rule in the state because of his reputation for justice, then a wife from any family he chooses, and the giving of his children in marriage to whomsoever he pleases, dealings and partnerships with whom he will, and in all these transactions advantage and profit for himself because he has no squeamishness about committing injustice. And so they say that if he enters into lawsuits, public or private, he wins and gets the better of his opponents, and, getting the better, is rich and benefits his friends and harms his enemies, and he performs sacrifices and dedicates votive offerings to the gods adequately and magnificently, and he serves and pays court to men whom he favours and to the gods far better than the just man, so that he may reasonably expect the favour of heaven also to fall rather to him than to the just. So much better they say, Socrates, is the life that is prepared for the unjust man from gods and men than that which awaits the just.

[...]

[Socrates indicates his willingness to meet Glaucon's challenge, but Glaucon's brother Adimantus insists that the case against justice is not yet complete. However, it is unclear whether the long intervention from Adimantus actually does strengthen the challenge, so we will pick up the thread of argument with Socrates' reply to both of the brothers' speeches. Still, just before doing so, it is worth citing the place in Adimantus' speech where he emphasizes a point that makes Socrates' task that much more difficult. He says:

---

[1] *Septem* 592 sq.

Do not merely show us by argument that justice is superior to injustice, but make clear to us what each in and of itself does to its possessor, whereby the one is evil and the other good. But do away with the repute of both, as Glaucon urged. For unless you take away from either the true repute and attach to each the false, we shall say that it is not justice that you are praising but the semblance, nor injustice you censure but the seeming, and that you really are exhorting us to be unjust but conceal it.]

[...]

g→ Glaucon, then, and the rest besought me by all means to come to the rescue and not to drop the argument but to pursue to the end the investigation as to the nature of each and the truth about their respective advantages. I said then as I thought, The inquiry we are undertaking is no easy one but calls for keen vision, as it seems to me. So, since we are not clever persons, I think we should employ the method of search that we should use if we, with not very keen vision, were bidden to read small letters from a distance, and then someone had observed that these same letters exist elsewhere larger and on a larger surface. We should have accounted it a godsend, I fancy, to be allowed to read those letters first, and then examine the smaller, if they are the same.

Quite so, said Adimantus, but what analogy to this do you detect in the inquiry about justice?

I will tell you, I said. There is a justice of one man, we say, and, I suppose, also of an entire city?

Assuredly, said he.

Is not the city larger than the man?

It is larger, he said.

Then, perhaps, there would be more justice in the larger object, and more easy to apprehend. If it please you, then, let us first look for its quality in states, and then only examine it also in the individual, looking for the likeness of the greater in the form of the less.

I think that is a good suggestion, he said.

If, then, said I, our argument should observe the origin of a state, we should see also the origin of justice and injustice in it?

It may be, said he.

And if this is done, we may expect to find more easily what we are seeking?

Much more.

Shall we try it, then, and go through with it? I fancy it is no slight task. Reflect, then.

We have reflected, said Adimantus. Proceed and don't refuse.

[h]⯈   The origin of the city, then, said I, in my opinion, is to be found in the fact that we do not severally suffice for our own needs, but each of us lacks many things. Do you think any other principle establishes the state?

No other, said he.

As a result of this, then, one man calling in another for one service and another for another, we, being in need of many things, gather many into one place of abode as associates and helpers, and to this dwelling together we give the name city or state, do we not?

By all means.

And between one man and another there is an interchange of giving, if it so happens, and taking, because each supposes this to be better for himself.

Certainly.

Come, then, let us create a city from the beginning, in our theory. Its real creator, as it appears, will be our needs.

Obviously.

Now the first and chief of our needs is the provision of food for existence and life.

Assuredly.

The second is housing and the third is raiment and that sort of thing.

That is so.

Tell me, then, said I, how our city will suffice for the provision of all these things. Will there not be a farmer for one, and a builder, and then again a weaver? And shall we add thereto a cobbler and some other purveyor for the needs of the body?

Certainly.

The indispensable minimum of a city, then, would consist of four or five men.

Apparently.

What of this, then? Shall each of these contribute his work for the common use of all? I mean, shall the farmer, who is one, provide food for four and spend fourfold time and toil on the production of food and share it with the others, or shall he take no thought for them and provide a fourth portion of the food for himself alone in a quarter of the time and employ the other three-quarters, the one in the provision of a house, the other of a garment, the other of shoes, and not have the bother of associating with other people, but, himself for himself, mind his own affairs?

And Adimantus said, But, perhaps, Socrates, the former way is easier.

It would not, by Zeus, be at all strange, said I, for now that you have mentioned it, it occurs to me myself that, to begin with, our several natures are not all alike but different. One man is naturally fitted for one task, and another for another. Don't you think so?

I do.

Again, would one man do better working at many tasks or one at one?

One at one, he said.

And, furthermore, this, I fancy, is obvious – that if one lets slip the right season, the favourable moment in any task, the work is spoiled.

Obvious.

That, I take it, is because the business will not wait upon the leisure of the workman, but the workman must attend to it as his main affair, and not as a bywork.

He must indeed.

The result, then, is that more things are produced, and better and more easily when one man performs one task according to his nature, at the right moment, and at leisure from other occupations.

By all means.

Then, Adimantus, we need more than four citizens for the provision of the things we have mentioned. For the farmer, it appears, will not make his own plow if it is to be a good one, nor his hoe, nor his other agricultural implements, nor will the builder, who also needs many, and similarly the weaver and cobbler.

True.

Carpenters, then, and smiths and many similar craftsmen, associating themselves with our hamlet, will enlarge it considerably.

Certainly.

Yet it still wouldn't be very large even if we should add to them neatherds and shepherds and other herders, so that the farmers might have cattle for plowing, and the builders oxen to use with the farmers for transportation, and the weavers and cobblers hides and fleeces for their use.

It wouldn't be a small city, either, if it had all these.

But further, said I, it is practically impossible to establish the city in a region where it will not need imports.

It is.

There will be a further need, then, of those who will bring in from some other city what it requires.

There will.

And again, if our servitor goes forth empty-handed, not taking with him any of the things needed by those from whom they procure what they themselves require, he will come back with empty hands, will he not?

I think so.

Then their home production must not merely suffice for themselves but in quality and quantity meet the needs of those of whom they have need.

It must.

So our city will require more farmers and other craftsmen.

Yes, more.

And also of other ministrants who are to export and import the merchandise. These are traders, are they not?

Yes.

We shall also need traders, then.

Assuredly.

And if the trading is carried on by sea, we shall need quite a number of others who are expert in maritime business.

Quite a number.

But again, within the city itself how will they share with one another the products of their labor? This was the very purpose of our association and establishment of a state.

Obviously, he said, by buying and selling.

A market place, then, and money as a token for the purpose of exchange will be the result of this.

By all means.

If, then, the farmer or any other craftsman taking his products to the market place does not arrive at the same time with those who desire to exchange with him, is he to sit idle in the market place and lose time from his own work?

By no means, he said, but there are men who see this need and appoint themselves for this service – in well-conducted cities they are generally those who are weakest in body and those who are useless for any other task. They must wait there in the agora and exchange money for goods with those who wish to sell, and goods for money with as many as desire to buy.

This need, then, said I, creates the class of shopkeepers in our city. Or is not 'shopkeepers' the name we give to those who, planted in the agora, serve us in buying and selling, while we call those who roam from city to city merchants?

Certainly.

And there are, furthermore, I believe, other servitors who in the things of the mind are not altogether worthy of our fellowship, but whose strength of body is sufficient for toil; so they, selling the use of this strength and calling the price wages, are designated, I believe, 'wage earners,' are they not?

Certainly.

Wage earners, then, it seems, are the complement that helps to fill up the state.

I think so.

Has our city, then, Adimantus, reached its full growth, and is it complete?

Perhaps.

i→ Where, then, can justice and injustice be found in it? And along with which of the constituents that we have considered do they come into the state?

I cannot conceive, Socrates, he said, unless it be in some need that those very constituents have of one another.

Perhaps that is a good suggestion, said I. We must examine it and not hold back.

First of all, then, let us consider what will be the manner of life of men thus provided. Will they not make bread and wine and garments and shoes? And they will build themselves houses and carry on their work in summer for the most part unclad and unshod and in winter clothed and shod sufficiently. And for their nourishment they will provide meal from their barley and flour from their wheat, and kneading and cooking these they will serve noble cakes and loaves on some arrangement of reeds or clean leaves. And, reclined on rustic beds strewed with bryony and myrtle, they will feast with their children, drinking of their wine thereto, garlanded and singing hymns to the gods in pleasant fellowship, not begetting offspring beyond their means lest they fall into poverty or war.

Here Glaucon broke in, No relishes apparently, he said, for the men you describe as feasting.

True, said I, I forgot that they will also have relishes – salt, of course, and olives and cheese, and onions and greens, the sort of things they boil in the country, they will boil up together. But for dessert we will serve them figs and chick-peas and beans, and they will toast myrtle berries and acorns before the fire, washing them down with moderate potations. And so, living in peace and health, they will probably die in old age and hand on a like life to their offspring.

And he said, If you were founding a city of pigs, Socrates, what other fodder than this would you provide?

Why, what would you have, Glaucon? said I.

What is customary, he replied. They must recline on couches, I presume, if they are not to be uncomfortable, and dine from tables and have dishes and sweetmeats such as are now in use.

j→ Good, said I. I understand. It is not merely the origin of a city, it seems, that we are considering but the origin of a luxurious city. Perhaps that isn't such a bad suggestion, either. For by observation of such a city it may be we could discern the origin of justice and injustice in states. The true state I believe to be the one we have described – the healthy state, as it were. But if it is your pleasure that we contemplate also a fevered state, there is nothing to hinder.

[...]

[The remainder of Book II and the whole of Book III is taken up with a detailed and often puzzling account of the 'fevered' state. What is most important in this account is the state's division into three *functional* units, though how seriously we are meant to take the idea that these are also three classes of real *individuals* is unclear, and has been a source of much debate about the *Republic*.

The first of these units is responsible for the production of goods and services in the state. It consists of all those specializing in farming, manufacturing and trading – the wealth-generating segment of the society – and, while recognized to be important, we are not told much about those engaged in these activities.

The second functional unit is that of the guardians, those whose role is protecting the state from external and internal enemies who would undermine it. Socrates devotes a great deal of space to detailing the education of guardians, much more detail in fact than one would have thought necessary for characterizing justice in the state, and then in the individual. The guardians are described at one point as the 'expert craftsmen of civic liberty', but, given what to us – and perhaps to Plato's contemporaries – is a chilling degree of control in their education, one feels a tension between the life of the guardians and the very idea of civic liberty. The guardians are educated first in music and then gymnastics, but are forbidden from hearing any forms of music or poetry that might undermine their capacity to defend the state. Thus, they are not allowed to hear forms of music or encounter poetry that might make them less fierce, and their physical training is carefully controlled, as is the medical treatment they or anyone else receives. This training is intended to make them determined fighters for the state, but for the guardians there are to be no pleasures of the flesh, nor 'the delights of Attic pastry'.

The third functional unit is introduced only near the end of Book III, and it is in fact a sub-division of the guardian class. After asking about the distinction between rulers and the ruled, Socrates insists that those among the guardians who stand out, presumably for their intellectual capacity and devotion to the cause, should be given the task of ruling. Moreover, the education and way of life of this sub-group of guardians – henceforth 'rulers' – is controlled to an even greater degree than that of ordinary guardians who are in effect the soldiers and police of the state. The text below begins with a description of that way of life given by Socrates at the very end of Book III, and this description is reinforced in the first pages of Book IV.]

[...]

k⟶ Consider then, said I, whether, if that is to be their character, their habitations and ways of life must not be something after this fashion. In the first place, none must possess any private property save the indispensable. Secondly, none must have any habitation or treasure house which is not open for all to enter at will. Their food, in such quantities as are needful for athletes of war sober and brave, they must receive as an agreed stipend from the other citizens as the wages of their guardianship, so measured that there shall be neither superfluity at the end of the year nor any lack. And resorting to a common mess like soldiers on campaign they will live together. Gold and silver, we will tell them, they have of the divine quality from the gods always in their souls, and they have no need of the metal of men nor does holiness suffer them to mingle and contaminate that heavenly possession with the acquisition of mortal gold, since many impious deeds have been done about the coin of the multitude, while that which dwells within them is unsullied. But for these only of all the dwellers in the city it is not lawful to handle gold and silver and to touch them nor yet to come under the same roof with them, nor to hang them as ornaments on their limbs nor to drink from silver and gold. So living they would save themselves and save their city. But whenever they shall acquire for themselves land of their own and houses and coin, they will be householders and farmers instead of guardians, and will be transformed from the helpers of their fellow citizens to their enemies and masters, and so in hating and being hated, plotting and being plotted against, they will pass their days fearing far more and rather the townsmen within than the foemen without – and then even then laying the course of near shipwreck for themselves and the state. For all these reasons, said I, let us declare that such must be the provision for our guardians in lodging and other respects and so legislate. Shall we not?

By all means, said Glaucon.

Book IV

I⟶ And Adimantus broke in and said, What will be your defense, Socrates, if anyone objects that you are not making these men very happy, and that through their own fault? For the city really belongs to them and yet they get no enjoyment out of it as ordinary men do by owning lands and building fine big houses and providing them with suitable furniture and winning the favour of the gods by private sacrifices and

entertaining guests and enjoying too those possessions which you just
now spoke of, gold and silver and all that is customary for those who
are expecting to be happy. But they seem, one might say, to be established in idleness in the city, exactly like hired mercenaries, with nothing to do but keep guard.

Yes, said I, and what is more, they serve for board wages and do not
even receive pay in addition to their food as others do, so that they will
not even be able to take a journey on their own account, if they wish to,
or make presents to their mistresses, or spend money in other directions
according to their desires like the men who are thought to be happy.
These and many similar counts of the indictment you are omitting.

Well, said he, assume these counts too.

What then will be our apology you ask?

Yes.

 By following the same path I think we shall find what to reply. For
we shall say that while it would not surprise us if these men thus
living prove to be the most happy, yet the object on which we fixed
our eyes in the establishment of our state was not the exceptional
happiness of any one class but the greatest possible happiness of the
city as a whole. For we thought that in a state so constituted we
should be most likely to discover justice as we should injustice in the
worst-governed state, and that when we had made these out we could
pass judgement on the issue of our long inquiry. Our first task then,
we take it, is to mould the model of a happy state – we are not isolat-
ing a small class in it and postulating their happiness, but that of the
city as a whole. But the opposite type of state we will consider presently. It is as if we were colouring a statue and someone approached
and censured us, saying that we did not apply the most beautiful pig-
ments to the most beautiful parts of the image, since the eyes, which
are the most beautiful part, have not been painted with purple but
with black. We should think it a reasonable justification to reply,
Don't expect us, quaint friend, to paint the eyes so fine that they will
not be like eyes at all, nor the other parts, but observe whether by
assigning what is proper to each we render the whole beautiful. And
so in the present case you must not require us to attach to the guardians a happiness that will make them anything but guardians. For in
like manner we could clothe the farmers in robes of state and deck
them with gold and bid them cultivate the soil at their pleasure, and
we could make the potters recline on couches from left to right before
the fire drinking toasts and feasting with their wheel alongside to
potter with when they are so disposed, and we can make all the others
happy in the same fashion, so that thus the entire city may be happy.
But urge us not to this, since, if we yield, the farmer will not be a

farmer nor the potter a potter, nor will any other of the types that constitute a state keep its form. However, for the others it matters less. For cobblers who deteriorate and are spoiled and pretend to be the workmen that they are not are no great danger to a state. But guardians of laws and of the city who are not what they pretend to be, but only seem, destroy utterly, I would have you note, the entire state, and on the other hand, they alone are decisive of its good government and happiness. If then we are forming true guardians and keepers of our liberties, men least likely to harm the commonwealth, but the proponent of the other ideal is thinking of farmers and 'happy' feasters as it were in a festival and not in a civic community, he would have something else in mind than a state. Consider, then, whether our aim in establishing the guardians is the greatest possible happiness among them or whether that is something we must look to see develop in the city as a whole, but these helpers and guardians are to be constrained and persuaded to do what will make them the best craftsmen in their own work, and similarly all the rest. And so, as the entire city develops and is ordered well, each class is to be left to the share of happiness that its nature comports.

Well, he said, I think you are right.

And will you then, I said, also think me reasonable in another point akin to this?

What pray?

Consider whether these are the causes that corrupt other craftsmen too so as positively to spoil them.

What causes?

Wealth and poverty, said I.

How so?

Thus! Do you think a potter who grew rich would any longer be willing to give his mind to his craft?

By no means, said he.

But will he become more idle and negligent than he was?

Far more.

Then he becomes a worse potter?

Far worse too.

And yet again, if from poverty he is unable to provide himself with tools and other requirements of his art, the work that he turns out will be worse, and he will also make inferior workmen of his sons or any others whom he teaches.

Of course.

From both causes, then, poverty and wealth, the products of the arts deteriorate, and so do the artisans?

So it appears.

Here, then, is a second group of things, it seems, that our guardians must guard against and do all in their power to keep from slipping into the city without their knowledge.

What are they?

Wealth and poverty, said I, since the one brings luxury, idleness, and innovation, and the other illiberality and the evil of bad workmanship in addition to innovation.

Assuredly, he said. Yet here is a point for your consideration, Socrates – how our city, possessing no wealth, will be able to wage war, especially if compelled to fight a large and wealthy state.

Obviously, said I, it would be rather difficult to fight one such, but easier to fight two.

What did you mean by that? he said.

Tell me first, I said, whether, if they have to fight, they will not be fighting as athletes of war against men of wealth?

Yes, that is true, he said.

Answer me then, Adimantus. Do you not think that one boxer perfectly trained in the art could easily fight two fat rich men who knew nothing of it?

Not at the same time perhaps, said he.

Not even, said I, if he were allowed to retreat and then turn and strike the one who came up first, and if he repeated the procedure many times under a burning and stifling sun? Would not such a fighter down even a number of such opponents?

Doubtless, he said, it wouldn't be surprising if he did.

Well, don't you think that the rich have more of the skill and practice of boxing than of the art of war?

I do, he said.

It will be easy, then, for our athletes in all probability to fight with double and triple their number.

I shall have to concede the point, he said, for I believe you are right.

Well then, if they send an embassy to the other city and say what is in fact true, 'We make no use of gold and silver nor is it lawful for us, but it is for you; do then join us in the war and keep the spoils of the enemy' – do you suppose any who heard such a proposal would choose to fight against hard and wiry hounds rather than with the aid of the hounds against fat and tender sheep?

I think not. Yet consider whether the accumulation of all the wealth of other cities in one does not involve danger for the state that has no wealth.

What happy innocence, said I, to suppose that you can properly use the name city of any other than the one we are constructing.

Why, what should we say? he said.

A greater predication, said I, must be applied to the others. For they are each one of them many cities, not a city, as it goes in the game. There are two at the least at enmity with one another, the city of the rich and the city of the poor, and in each of these there are many. If you deal with them as one you will altogether miss the mark, but if you treat them as a multiplicity by offering to the one faction the property, the power, the very persons of the other, you will continue always to have few enemies and many allies. And so long as your city is governed soberly in the order just laid down, it will be the greatest of cities. I do not mean greatest in repute, but in reality, even though it have only a thousand defenders. For a city of this size that is really one you will not easily discover either among Greeks or barbarians – but of those that seem so you will find many and many times the size of this. Or do you think otherwise?

No, indeed I don't, said he.

Would not this, then, be the best rule and measure for our governors of the proper size of the city and of the territory that they should mark off for a city of that size and seek no more?

What is the measure?

I think, said I, that they should let it grow so long as in its growth it consents to remain a unity, but no further.

Excellent, he said.

Then is not this still another injunction that we should lay upon our guardians, to keep guard in every way that the city shall not be too small, nor great only in seeming, but that it shall be a sufficient city and one?

That behest will perhaps be an easy one for them, he said.

And still easier, haply, I said, is this that we mentioned before when we said that if a degenerate offspring was born to the guardians he must be sent away to the other classes, and likewise if a superior to the others he must be enrolled among the guardians, and the purport of all this was that the other citizens too must be sent to the task for which their natures were fitted, one man to one work, in order that each of them fulfilling his own function may be not many men, but one, and so the entire city may come to be not a multiplicity but a unity.

Why yes, he said, this is even more trifling than that.

These are not, my good Adimantus, as one might suppose, numerous and difficult injunctions that we are imposing upon them, but they are all easy, provided they guard, as the saying is, the one great thing – or instead of great let us call it sufficient.

What is that? he said.

Their education and nurture, I replied. For if a right education makes of them reasonable men they will easily discover everything of this kind – and other principles that we now pass over, as that the possession of wives and marriage, and the procreation of children and all that sort of thing should be made as far as possible the proverbial goods of friends that are common.

Yes, that would be the best way, he said.

And, moreover, said I, the state, if it once starts well, proceeds as it were in a cycle of growth. I mean that a sound nurture and education if kept up create good natures in the state, and sound natures in turn receiving an education of this sort develop into better men than their predecessors both for other purposes and for the production of offspring, as among animals also.

It is probable, he said.

To put it briefly, then, said I, it is to this that the overseers of our state must cleave and be watchful against its insensible corruption. They must throughout be watchful against innovations in music and gymnastics counter to the established order, and to the best of their power guard against them, fearing when anyone says that that song is most regarded among men 'which hovers newest on the singer's lips,'[1] lest haply it be supposed that the poet means not new songs but a new way of song and is commending this. But we must not praise that sort of thing nor conceive it to be the poet's meaning. For a change to a new type of music is something to beware of as a hazard of all our fortunes. For the modes of music are never disturbed without unsettling of the most fundamental political and social conventions, as Damon affirms and as I am convinced.

Set me too down in the number of the convinced, said Adimantus.

It is here, then, I said, in music, as it seems, that our guardians must build their guardhouse and post of watch.

It is certain, he said, that this is the kind of lawlessness that easily insinuates itself unobserved.

Yes, said I, because it is supposed to be only a form of play and to work no harm.

Nor does it work any, he said, except that by gradual infiltration it softly overflows upon the characters and pursuits of men and from these issues forth grown greater to attack their business dealings, and from these relations it proceeds against the laws and the constitution with wanton license, Socrates, till finally it overthrows all things public and private.

[1] *Odyssey* 1.351.

Well, said I, are these things so?

I think so, he said.

Then, as we were saying in the beginning, our youth must join in a more law-abiding play, since, if play grows lawless and the children likewise, it is impossible that they should grow up to be men of serious temper and lawful spirit.

Of course, he said.

And so we may reason that when children in their earliest play are imbued with the spirit of law and order through their music, the opposite of the former supposition happens – this spirit waits upon them in all things and fosters their growth, and restores and sets up again whatever was overthrown in the other type of state.

True indeed, he said.

Then such men rediscover for themselves those seemingly trifling conventions which their predecessors abolished altogether.

Of what sort?

Such things as the becoming silence of the young in the presence of their elders, the giving place to them and rising up before them, and dutiful service of parents, and the cut of the hair and the garments and the fashion of the footgear, and in general the deportment of the body and everything of the kind. Don't you think so?

I do.

Yet to enact them into laws would, I think, be silly. For such laws are not obeyed nor would they last, being enacted only in words and on paper.

How could they?

At any rate, Adimantus, I said, the direction of the education from whence one starts is likely to determine the quality of what follows. Does not like ever summon like?

Surely.

And the final outcome, I presume, we would say is one complete and vigorous product of good or the reverse.

Of course, said he.

For my part, then, I said, for these reasons I would not go on to try to legislate on such matters.

With good reason, said he.

But what, in heaven's name, said I, about business matters, the deals that men make with one another in the agora – and, if you please, contracts with workmen and actions for foul language and assault, the filing of declarations, the impaneling of juries, the payment and exaction of any dues that may be needful in markets or harbours and in general market, police, or harbour regulations and the like – can we bring ourselves to legislate about these?

Nay, 'twould not be fitting, he said, to dictate to good and honourable men. For most of the enactments that are needed about these things they will easily, I presume, discover.

Yes, my friend, provided God grants them the preservation of the principles of law that we have already discussed.

Failing that, said he, they will pass their lives multiplying such petty laws and amending them in the expectation of attaining what is best.

You mean, said I, that the life of such citizens will resemble that of men who are sick, yet from intemperance are unwilling to abandon their unwholesome regimen.

By all means.

And truly, said I, these latter go on in a most charming fashion. For with all their doctoring they accomplish nothing except to complicate and augment their maladies. And they are always hoping that someone will recommend a panacea that will restore their health.

A perfect description, he said, of the state of such invalids.

And isn't this a charming trait in them, that they hate most in all the world him who tells them the truth, that until a man stops drinking and gorging and wenching and idling, neither drugs nor cautery nor the knife, no, nor spells nor periapts nor anything of that kind will be of any avail?

Not altogether charming, he said, for there is no grace or charm in being angry with him who speaks well.

You do not seem to be an admirer of such people, said I.

No, by heaven, I am not.

Neither then, if an entire city, as we were just now saying, acts in this way, will it have your approval, or don't you think that the way of such invalids is precisely that of those cities which being badly governed forewarn their citizens not to meddle with the general constitution of the state, denouncing death to whosoever attempts that – while whoever most agreeably serves them governed as they are and who curries favour with them by fawning upon them and anticipating their desires and by his cleverness in gratifying them, him they will account the good man, the man wise in worthwhile things, the man they will delight to honour?

Yes, he said, I think their conduct is identical, and I don't approve it in the very least.

And what again of those who are willing and eager to serve such states? Don't you admire their valiance and lighthearted irresponsibility?

I do, he said, except those who are actually deluded and suppose themselves to be in truth statesmen because they are praised by the many.

What do you mean? Can't you make allowances for the men? Do you think it possible for a man who does not know how to measure when a multitude of others equally ignorant assure him that he is four cubits tall not to suppose this to be the fact about himself?

Why no, he said, I don't think that.

Then don't be harsh with them. For surely such fellows are the most charming spectacle in the world when they enact and amend such laws as we just now described and are perpetually expecting to find a way of putting an end to frauds in business and in the other matters of which I was speaking because they can't see that they are in very truth trying to cut off a Hydra's head.

Indeed, he said, that is exactly what they are doing.

I, then, said I, should not have supposed that the true lawgiver ought to work out matters of that kind in the laws and the constitution of either an ill-governed or a well-governed state – in the one because they are useless and accomplish nothing, in the other because some of them anybody could discover and others will result spontaneously from the pursuits already described.

What part of legislation, then, he said, is still left for us?

And I replied, For us nothing, but for the Apollo of Delphi, the chief, the fairest, and the first of enactments.

What are they? he said.

The founding of temples, and sacrifices, and other forms of worship of gods, daemons, and heroes, and likewise the burial of the dead and the services we must render to the dwellers in the world beyond to keep them gracious. For of such matters we neither know anything nor in the founding of our city if we are wise shall we entrust them to any other or make use of any other interpreter than the god of our fathers. For this god surely is in such matters for all mankind the interpreter of the religion of their fathers who from his seat in the middle and at the very navel of the earth delivers his interpretation.

Excellently said, he replied, and that is what we must do.

At last, then, son of Ariston, said I, your city may be considered as established. The next thing is to procure a sufficient light somewhere and to look yourself, and call in the aid of your brother and of Polemarchus and the rest, if we may in any wise discover where justice and injustice should be in it, wherein they differ from one another, and which of the two he must have who is to be happy, alike whether his condition is known or not known to all gods and men.

Nonsense, said Glaucon, you promised that you would carry on the search yourself, admitting that it would be impious for you not to come to the aid of justice by every means in your power.

A true reminder, I said, and I must do so, but you also must lend a hand.

Well, he said, we will.

n⟶   I expect then, said I, that we shall find it in this way. I think our city, if it has been rightly founded, is good in the full sense of the word.

Necessarily, he said.

Clearly, then, it will be wise, brave, sober, and just.

Clearly.

Then if we find any of these qualities in it, the remainder will be that which we have not found?

Surely.

Take the case of any four other things. If we were looking for any one of them in anything and recognized the object of our search first, that would have been enough for us, but if we had recognized the other three first, that in itself would have made known to us the thing we were seeking. For plainly there was nothing left for it to be but the remainder.

Right, he said.

And so, since these are four, we must conduct the search in the same way.

Clearly.

And, moreover, the first thing that I think I clearly see therein is the wisdom, and there is something odd about that, it appears.

What? said he.

Wise in very deed I think the city that we have described is, for it is well counselled, is it not?

Yes.

And surely this very thing, good counsel, is a form of wisdom. For it is not by ignorance but by knowledge that men counsel well.

Obviously.

But there are many and manifold knowledges or sciences in the city.

Of course.

Is it then owing to the science of her carpenters that a city is to be called wise and well advised?

By no means for that, but rather mistress of the arts of building.

Then a city is not to be styled wise because of the deliberations of the science of wooden utensils for their best production?

No, I grant you.

Is it, then, because of that of brass implements or any other of that kind?

None whatsoever, he said.

Nor yet because of the science of the production of crops from the soil, but the name it takes from that is agricultural.

I think so.

Then, said I, is there any science in the city just founded by us residing in any of its citizens which does not take counsel about some particular thing in the city but about the city as a whole and the betterment of its relations with itself and other states?

Why, yes, there is.

What is it, said I, and in whom is it found?

It is the science of guardianship or government and it is to be found in those rulers to whom we just now gave the name of guardians in the full sense of the word.

And what term then do you apply to the city because of this knowledge?

Well-advised, he said, and truly wise.

Which class, then, said I, do you suppose will be the more numerous in our city, the smiths or these true guardians?

The smiths, by far, he said.

And would not these rulers be the smallest of all the groups of those who possess special knowledge and receive distinctive appellations?

By far.

Then it is by virtue of its smallest class and minutest part of itself, and the wisdom that resides therein, in the part which takes the lead and rules, that a city established on principles of nature would be wise as a whole. And as it appears these are by nature the fewest, the class to which it pertains to partake of the knowledge which alone of all forms of knowledge deserves the name of wisdom.

Most true, he said.

This one of our four, then, we have, I know not how, discovered, the thing itself and its place in the state.

I certainly think, said he, that it has been discovered sufficiently.

But again there is no difficulty in seeing bravery itself and the part of the city in which it resides for which the city is called brave.

How so?

Who, said I, in calling a city cowardly or brave would fix his eyes on any other part of it than that which defends it and wages war in its behalf?

No one at all, he said.

For the reason, I take it, said I, that the cowardice or the bravery of the other inhabitants does not determine for it the one quality or the other.

It does not.

Bravery too, then, belongs to a city by virtue of a part of itself owing to its possession in that part of a quality that under all conditions will preserve the conviction that things to be feared are precisely those which and such as the lawgiver inculcated in their education. Is not that what you call bravery?

I don't altogether understand what you said, he replied, but say it again.

A kind of conservation, I said, is what I mean by bravery.

What sort of a conservation?

The conservation of the conviction which the law has created by education about fearful things – what and what sort of things are to be feared. And by the phrase 'under all conditions' I mean that the brave man preserves it both in pain and pleasures and in desires and fears and does not expel it from his soul. And I may illustrate it by a similitude if you please.

I do.

You are aware that dyers when they wish to dye wool so as to hold the purple hue begin by selecting from the many colours there be the one nature of the white and then give it a careful preparatory treatment so that it will take the hue in the best way, and after the treatment, then and then only, dip it in the dye. And things that are dyed by this process become fast-coloured and washing either with or without lyes cannot take away the sheen of their hues. But otherwise you know what happens to them, whether anyone dips other colours or even these without the preparatory treatment.

I know, he said, that they present a ridiculous and washed-out appearance.

By this analogy, then, said I, you must conceive what we too to the best of our ability were doing when we selected our soldiers and educated them in music and exercises of the body. The sole aim of our contrivance was that they should be convinced and receive our laws like a dye as it were, so that their belief and faith might be fast-coloured about both the things that are to be feared and all other things because of the fitness of their nature and nurture, and that so their dyes might not be washed out by those lyes that have such dread power to scour our faiths away, pleasure more potent than any detergent or abstergent to accomplish this, and pain and fear, and desire more sure than any lye. This power in the soul, then, this unfailing conservation of right and lawful belief about things to be and not to be feared is what I call and would assume to be courage, unless you have something different to say.

No, nothing, said he, for I presume that you consider mere right opinion about the same matters not produced by education, that which may manifest itself in a beast or a slave, to have little or nothing to do with law and that you would call it by another name than courage.

That is most true, said I.

Well then, he said, I accept this as bravery.

Do so, said I, and you will be right, with the reservation that it is the courage of a citizen. Some other time, if it please you, we will discuss it more fully. At present we were not seeking this but justice, and for the purpose of that inquiry I believe we have done enough.

You are quite right, he said.

Two things still remain, said I, to make out in our city, soberness and the object of the whole inquiry, justice.

Quite so.

If there were only some way to discover justice so that we need not further concern ourselves about soberness.

Well, I, for my part, he said, neither know of any such way nor would I wish justice to be discovered first if that means that we are not to go on to the consideration of soberness. But if you desire to please me, consider this before that.

It would certainly be very wrong of me not to desire it, said I.

Go on with the inquiry then, he said.

I must go on, I replied, and viewed from here it bears more likeness to a kind of concord and harmony than the other virtues did.

How so?

Soberness is a kind of beautiful order and a continence of certain pleasures and appetites, as they say, using the phrase 'master of himself' I know not how, and there are other similar expressions that as it were point us to the same trail. Is that not so?

Most certainly.

Now the phrase 'master of himself' is an absurdity, is it not? For he who is master of himself would also be subject to himself, and he who is subject to himself would be master. For the same person is spoken of in all these expressions.

Of course.

But, said I, the intended meaning of this way of speaking appears to me to be that the soul of a man within him has a better part and a worse part, and the expression self-mastery means the control of the worse by the naturally better part. It is, at any rate, a term of praise. But when, because of bad breeding or some association, the better part, which is the smaller, is dominated by the multitude of the worse, I think that our speech censures this as a reproach, and calls the man in this plight unself-controlled and licentious.

That seems likely, he said.

Turn your eyes now upon our new city, said I, and you will find one of these conditions existent in it. For you will say that it is justly spoken of as master of itself if that in which the superior rules the inferior is to be called sober and self-mastered.

I do turn my eyes upon it, he said, and it is as you say.

And again, the mob of motley appetites and pleasures and pains one would find chiefly in children and women and slaves and in the base rabble of those who are free men in name.

By all means.

But the simple and moderate appetites which with the aid of reason and right opinion are guided by consideration you will find in few and those the best born and best educated.

True, he said.

And do you not find this too in your city and a domination there of the desires in the multitude and the rabble by the desires and the wisdom that dwell in the minority of the better sort?

I do, he said.

If, then, there is any city that deserves to be described as master of its pleasures and desires and self-mastered, this one merits that designation.

Most assuredly, he said.

And is it not also to be called sober in all these respects?

Indeed it is, he said.

And yet again, if there is any city in which the rulers and the ruled are of one mind as to who ought to rule, that condition will be found in this. Don't you think so?

I most emphatically do, he said.

In which class of the citizens, then, will you say that the virtue of soberness has its seat when this is their condition? In the rulers or in the ruled?

In both, I suppose, he said.

Do you see then, said I, that our intuition was not a bad one just now that discerned a likeness between soberness and a kind of harmony?

Why so?

Because its operation is unlike that of courage and wisdom, which residing in separate parts respectively made the city, the one wise and the other brave. That is not the way of soberness, but it extends literally through the entire gamut throughout, bringing about the unison in the same chant of the strongest, the weakest, and the intermediate, whether in wisdom or, if you please, in strength, or for that matter in numbers, wealth, or any similar criterion. So that we should be quite right in affirming this unanimity to be soberness, the concord of the naturally superior and inferior as to which ought to rule in both the state and the individual.

I entirely concur, he said.

Very well, said I, we have made out these three forms in our city to the best of our present judgement. What can be the remaining form that would give the city still another virtue? For it is obvious that the remainder is justice.

Obvious.

Now then, Glaucon, is the time for us like huntsmen to surround the covert and keep close watch that justice may not slip through and get away from us and vanish from our sight. It plainly must be somewhere hereabout. Keep your eyes open then and do your best to descry it. You may see it before I do and point it out to me.

Would that I could, he said, but I think rather that if you find in me one who can follow you and discern what you point out to him you will be making a very fair use of me.

Pray for success then, said I, and follow along with me.

That I will do, only lead on, he said.

And truly, said I, it appears to be an inaccessible place, lying in deep shadows.

It certainly is a dark covert, not easy to beat up.

But all the same, on we must go.

Yes, on.

And I caught view and gave a halloo and said, Glaucon, I think we have found its trail and I don't believe it will get away from us.

I am glad to hear that, said he.

Truly, said I, we were slackers indeed.

How so?

Why, all the time, bless your heart, the thing apparently was tumbling about our feet from the start and yet we couldn't see it, but were most ludicrous, like people who sometimes hunt for what they hold in their hands. So we did not turn our eyes upon it, but looked off into the distance, which was perhaps the reason it escaped us.

What do you mean? he said.

This, I replied, that it seems to me that though we were speaking of it and hearing about it all the time we did not understand ourselves or realize that we were speaking of it in a sense.

That is a tedious prologue, he said, for an eager listener.

Listen then, said I, and learn if there is anything in what I say. For what we laid down in the beginning as a universal requirement when we were founding our city, this I think, or some form of this, is justice. And what we did lay down, and often said, if you recall, was that each one man must perform one social service in the state for which his nature was best adapted.

Yes, we said that.

And again, that to do one's own business and not to be a busybody is justice is a saying that we have heard from many and have very often repeated ourselves.

We have.

This, then, I said, my friend, if taken in a certain sense appears to be justice, this principle of doing one's own business. Do you know whence I infer this?

No, but tell me, he said.

I think that this is the remaining virtue in the state after our consideration of soberness, courage, and intelligence, a quality which made
it possible for them all to grow up in the body politic and which when
they have sprung up preserves them as long as it is present. And
I hardly need to remind you that we said that justice would be the
residue after we had found the other three.

That is an unavoidable conclusion, he said.

But moreover, said I, if we were required to decide what it is whose
indwelling presence will contribute most to making our city good, it
would be a difficult decision whether it was the unanimity of rulers
and ruled or the conservation in the minds of the soldiers of the convictions produced by law as to what things are or are not to be feared,
or the watchful intelligence that resides in the guardians, or whether
this is the chief cause of its goodness, the principle embodied in child,
woman, slave, free, artisan, ruler, and ruled, that each performed his
one task as one man and was not a versatile busybody.

Hard to decide indeed, he said.

A thing, then, that in its contribution to the excellence of a state
vies with and rivals its wisdom, its soberness, its bravery, is this principle of everyone in it doing his own task.

It is indeed, he said.

And is not justice the name you would have to give to the principle
that rivals these as conducting to the virtue of a state?

By all means.

Consider it in this wise too, if so you will be convinced. Will you
not assign the conduct of lawsuits in your state to the rulers?

Of course.

Will not this be the chief aim of their decisions, that no one shall
have what belongs to others or be deprived of his own?

Nothing else but this.

On the assumption that this is just?

Yes.

From this point of view too, then, the having and doing of one's
own and what belongs to oneself would admittedly be justice.

That is so.

Consider now whether you agree with me. A carpenter undertaking
to do the work of a cobbler or a cobbler of a carpenter or their interchange of one another's tools or honors or even the attempt of the
same man to do both – the confounding of all other functions would
not, think you, greatly injure a state, would it?

Not much, he said.

But when, I fancy, one who is by nature an artisan or some kind of
money-maker tempted and incited by wealth or command of votes or

bodily strength or some similar advantage tries to enter into the class of the soldiers or one of the soldiers into the class of counsellors and guardians, for which he is not fitted, and these interchange their tools and their honors or when the same man undertakes all these functions at once, then, I take it, you too believe that this kind of substitution and meddlesomeness is the ruin of a state.

By all means.

The interference with one another's business, then, of three existent classes, and the substitution of the one for the other, is the greatest injury to a state and would most rightly be designated as the thing which chiefly works it harm.

Precisely so.

And the thing that works the greatest harm to one's own state, will you not pronounce to be injustice?

Of course.

This, then, is injustice. Again, let us put it in this way. The proper functioning of the money-makers, the helpers, and the guardians, each doing his own work in the state, being the reverse of that just described, would be justice and would render the city just.

I think the case is thus and no otherwise, said he.

Let us not yet affirm it quite fixedly, I said, but if this form, when applied to the individual man, is accepted there also as a definition of justice, we will then concede the point – for what else will there be to say? But if not, then we will look for something else. But now let us work out the inquiry in which we supposed that, if we found some larger thing that contained justice and viewed it there, we should more easily discover its nature in the individual man. And we agreed that this larger thing is the city, and so we constructed the best city in our power, well knowing that in the good city it would of course be found. What, then, we thought we saw there we must refer back to the individual and, if it is confirmed, all will be well. But if something different manifests itself in the individual, we will return again to the state and test it there and it may be that, by examining them side by side and rubbing them against one another, as it were from the fire sticks we may cause the spark of justice to flash forth, and when it is thus revealed confirm it in our own minds.

Well, he said, that seems a sound method and that is what we must do.

Then, said I, if you call a thing by the same name whether it is big or little, is it unlike in the way in which it is called the same or like?

Like, he said.

Then a just man too will not differ at all from a just city in respect of the very form of justice, but will be like it.

Yes, like.

But now the city was thought to be just because three natural kinds existing in it performed each its own function, and again it was sober, brave, and wise because of certain other affections and habits of these three kinds.

True, he said.

Then, my friend, we shall thus expect the individual also to have these same forms in his soul, and by reason of identical affections of these with those in the city to receive properly the same appellations.

Inevitable, he said.

Goodness gracious, said I, here is another trifling inquiry into which we have plunged, the question whether the soul really contains these three forms in itself or not.

It does not seem to me at all trifling, he said, for perhaps, Socrates, the saying is true that 'fine things are difficult.'

Apparently, said I, and let me tell you, Glaucon, that in my opinion we shall never apprehend this matter accurately from such methods as we are now employing in discussion. For there is another longer and harder way that conducts to this. Yet we may perhaps discuss it on the level of our previous statements and inquiries.

May we not acquiesce in that? he said. I for my part should be quite satisfied with that for the present.

And I surely should be more than satisfied, I replied.

Don't you weary then, he said, but go on with the inquiry.

Is it not, then, said I, impossible for us to avoid admitting this much, that the same forms and qualities are to be found in each one of us that are in the state? They could not get there from any other source. It would be absurd to suppose that the element of high spirit was not derived in states from the private citizens who are reputed to have this quality, as the populations of the Thracian and Scythian lands and generally of northern regions, or the quality of love of knowledge, which would chiefly be attributed to the region where we dwell, or the love of money which we might say is not least likely to be found in Phoenicians and the population of Egypt.

One certainly might, he replied.

This is the fact then, said I, and there is no difficulty in recognizing it.

Certainly not.

But the matter begins to be difficult when you ask whether we do all these things with the same thing or whether there are three things and we do one thing with one and one with another – learn with one part of ourselves, feel anger with another, and with yet a third desire the pleasures of nutrition and generation and their kind, or whether it is with the entire soul that we function in each case when we once begin. That is what is really hard to determine properly.

I think so too, he said.

Let us then attempt to define the boundary and decide whether they are identical with one another in this way.

How?

It is obvious that the same thing will never do or suffer opposites in the same respect in relation to the same thing and at the same time. So that if ever we find these contradictions in the functions of the mind we shall know that it was not the same thing functioning but a plurality.

Very well.

Consider, then, what I am saying.

Say on, he replied.

Is it possible for the same thing at the same time in the same respect to be at rest and in motion?

By no means.

Let us have our understanding still more precise, lest as we proceed we become involved in dispute. If anyone should say of a man standing still but moving his hands and head that the same man is at the same time at rest and in motion we should not, I take it, regard that as the right way of expressing it, but rather that a part of him is at rest and a part in motion. Is not that so?

It is.

Then if the disputant should carry the jest still further with the subtlety that tops at any rate stand still as a whole at the same time that they are in motion when with the peg fixed in one point they revolve, and that the same is true of any other case of circular motion about the same spot – we should reject the statement on the ground that the repose and the movement in such cases were not in relation to the same parts of the objects. But we would say that there was a straight line and a circumference in them and that in respect of the straight line they are standing still since they do not incline to either side, but in respect of the circumference they move in a circle, but that when as they revolve they incline the perpendicular to right or left or forward or back, then they are in no wise at rest.

And that would be right, he said.

No such remarks then will disconcert us or any whit the more make us believe that it is ever possible for the same thing at the same time in the same respect and the same relation to suffer, be, or do opposites.

They will not me, I am sure, said he.

All the same, said I, that we may not be forced to examine at tedious length the entire list of such contentions and convince ourselves that they are false, let us proceed on the hypothesis that this is so, with the understanding that, if it ever appear otherwise, everything that results from the assumption shall be invalidated.

That is what we must do, he said.

Will you not then, said I, set down as opposed to one another assent and dissent, and the endeavour after a thing to the rejection of it, and embracing to repelling – do not these and all things like these belong to the class of opposite actions or passions, it will make no difference which?

None, said he, but they are opposites.

What then, said I, of thirst and hunger and the appetites generally, and again consenting and willing – would you not put them all somewhere in the classes just described? Will you not say, for example, that the soul of one who desires either strives for that which he desires or draws toward its embrace what it wishes to accrue to it, or again, in so far as it wills that anything be presented to it, nods assent to itself thereon as if someone put the question, striving toward its attainment?

I would say so, he said.

But what of not-willing and not-consenting nor yet desiring? Shall we not put these under the soul's rejection and repulsion from itself and generally into the opposite class from all the former?

Of course.

This being so, shall we say that the desires constitute a class and that the most conspicuous members of that class are what we call thirst and hunger?

We shall, said he.

Is not the one desire of drink, the other of food?

Yes.

Then in so far as it is thirst, would it be of anything more than that of which we say it is a desire in the soul? I mean is thirst thirst for hot drink or cold or much or little or in a word for a draught of any particular quality, or is it the fact that if heat is attached to the thirst it would further render the desire – a desire of cold, and if cold of hot? But if owing to the presence of muchness the thirst is much it would render it a thirst for much and if little for little. But mere thirst will never be desire of anything else than that of which it is its nature to be, mere drink, and so hunger of food.

That is so, he said. Each desire in itself is of that thing only of which it is its nature to be. The epithets belong to the quality – such or such.

Let no one then, said I, disconcert us when off our guard with the objection that everybody desires not drink but good drink and not food but good food, because, the argument will run, all men desire good, and so, if thirst is desire, it would be of good drink or of good whatsoever it is, and so similarly of other desires.

Why, he said, there perhaps would seem to be something in that objection.

But I need hardly remind you, said I, that of relative terms those that are somehow qualified are related to a qualified correlate, those that are severally just themselves to a correlate that is just itself.

I don't understand, he said.

Don't you understand, said I, that the greater is such as to be greater than something?

Certainly.

Is it not than the less?

Yes.

But the much greater than the much less. Is that not so?

Yes.

And may we add the onetime greater than the onetime less and that which will be greater than that which will be less?

Surely.

And similarly of the more towards the fewer, and the double towards the half and of all like cases, and again of the heavier towards the lighter, the swifter towards the slower, and yet again of the hot towards the cold and all cases of that kind – does not the same hold?

By all means.

But what of the sciences? Is not the way of it the same? Science, which is just that, is of knowledge which is just that, or is of whatsoever we must assume the correlate of science to be. But a particular science of a particular kind is of some particular thing of a particular kind. I mean something like this. As there was a science of making a house it differed from other sciences so as to be named architecture.

Certainly.

Was not this by reason of its being of a certain kind such as no other of all the rest?

Yes.

And was it not because it was of something of a certain kind that it itself became a certain kind of science? And similarly of the other arts and sciences?

That is so.

This then, said I, if haply you now understand, is what you must say I then meant, by the statement that of all things that are such as to be of something, those that are just themselves only are of things just themselves only, but things of a certain kind are of things of a kind. And I don't at all mean that they are of the same kind as the things of which they are, so that we are to suppose that the science of health and disease is a healthy and diseased science and that of evil and good, evil and good. I only mean that as science became the science not of just the thing of which science is but of some particular kind of thing, namely, of health and disease, the result was that it itself became some kind of science and this caused it to be no longer called simply science but, with the addition of the particular kind, medical science.

I understand, he said, and agree that it is so.

To return to thirst, then, said I, will you not class it with the things that are of something and say that it is what it is in relation to something – and it is, I presume, thirst?

I will, said he, namely of drink.

Then if the drink is of a certain kind, so is the thirst, but thirst that is just thirst is neither of much nor little nor good nor bad, nor in a word of any kind, but just thirst is naturally of just drink only.

By all means.

The soul of the thirsty then, in so far as it thirsts, wishes nothing else than to drink, and yearns for this and its impulse is toward this.

Obviously.

Then if anything draws it back when thirsty it must be something different in it from that which thirsts and drives it like a beast to drink. For it cannot be, we say, that the same thing with the same part of itself at the same time acts in opposite ways about the same thing.

We must admit that it does not.

So I fancy it is not well said of the archer that his hands at the same time thrust away the bow and draw it nigh, but we should rather say that there is one hand that puts it away and another that draws it to.

By all means, he said.

Are we to say, then, that some men sometimes though thirsty refuse to drink?

We are indeed, he said, many and often.

What then, said I, should one affirm about them? Is it not that there is a something in the soul that bids them drink and a something that forbids, a different something that masters that which bids?

I think so.

And is it not the fact that that which inhibits such actions arises when it arises from the calculations of reason, but the impulses which draw and drag come through affections and diseases?

Apparently.

Not unreasonably, said I, shall we claim that they are two and different from one another, naming that in the soul whereby it reckons and reasons the rational, and that with which it loves, hungers, thirsts, and feels the flutter and titillation of other desires, the irrational and appetitive – companion of various repletions and pleasures.

It would not be unreasonable but quite natural, he said, for us to think this.

These two forms, then, let us assume to have been marked off as actually existing in the soul. But now the *thumos*, or principle of high spirit, that with which we feel anger, is it a third, or would it be identical in nature with one of these?

Perhaps, he said, with one of these, the appetitive.

[r] → But, I said, I once heard a story which I believe, that Leontius the son of Aglaion, on his way up from the Piraeus under the outer side of the northern wall, becoming aware of dead bodies that lay at the place of public execution at the same time felt a desire to see them and a repugnance and aversion, and that for a time he resisted and veiled his head, but overpowered in despite of all by his desire, with wide staring eyes he rushed up to the corpses and cried, There, ye wretches, take your fill of the fine spectacle!

I too, he said, have heard the story.

Yet, surely, this anecdote, I said, signifies that the principle of anger sometimes fights against desires as an alien thing against an alien.

Yes, it does, he said.

And do we not, said I, on many other occasions observe when his desires constrain a man contrary to his reason that he reviles himself and is angry with that within which masters him, and that as it were in a faction of two parties the high spirit of such a man becomes the ally of his reason? But its making common cause with the desires against the reason when reason whispers low, Thou must not – that, I think, is a kind of thing you would not affirm ever to have perceived in yourself, nor, I fancy, in anybody else either.

No, by heaven, he said.

Again, when a man thinks himself to be in the wrong, is it not true that the nobler he is the less is he capable of anger though suffering hunger and cold and whatsoever else at the hands of him whom he believes to be acting justly therein, and as I say his spirit refuses to be aroused against such a one?

True, he said.

But what when a man believes himself to be wronged? Does not his spirit in that case seethe and grow fierce – and also because of his suffering hunger, cold, and the like – and make itself the ally of what he judges just? And in noble souls it endures and wins the victory and will not let go until either it achieves its purpose, or death ends all, or, as a dog is called back by a shepherd, it is called back by the reason within and calmed.

Your similitude is perfect, he said, and it confirms our former statements that the helpers are as it were dogs subject to the rulers who are as it were the shepherds of the city.

You apprehend my meaning excellently, said I. But do you also take note of this?

Of what?

That what we now think about the spirited element is just the opposite of our recent surmise. For then we supposed it to be a part of the appetitive, but now, far from that, we say that, in the factions of the soul, it much rather marshals itself on the side of the reason.

By all means, he said.

Is it then distinct from this too, or is it a form of the rational, so that there are not three but two kinds in the soul, the rational and the appetitive? Or just as in the city there were three existing kinds that composed its structure, the money-makers, the helpers, the counsellors, so also in the soul does there exist a third kind, this principle of high spirit, which is the helper of reason by nature unless it is corrupted by evil nurture?

We have to assume it as a third, he said.

Yes, said I, provided it shall have been shown to be something different from the rational, as it has been shown to be other than the appetitive.

That is not hard to be shown, he said, for that much one can see in children, that they are from their very birth chock-full of rage and high spirit, but as for reason, some of them, to my thinking, never participate in it, and the majority quite late.

Yes, by heaven, excellently said, I replied, and further, one could see in animals that what you say is true. And to these instances we may add the testimony of Homer quoted above, 'He smote his breast and chided thus his heart.'[2] For there Homer has clearly represented that in us which has reflected about the better and the worse as rebuking that which feels unreasoning anger as if it were a distinct and different thing.

You are entirely right, he said.

Through these waters, then, said I, we have with difficulty made our way and we are fairly agreed that the same kinds equal in number are to be found in the state and in the soul of each one of us.

That is so.

Then does not the necessity of our former postulate immediately follow, that as and whereby the state was wise, so and thereby is the individual wise?

[2] *Odyssey* 20.17.

Surely.

And so whereby and as the individual is brave, thereby and so is the state brave, and that both should have all the other constituents of virtue in the same way?

Necessarily.

Just too, then, Glaucon, I presume we shall say a man is in the same way in which a city was just.

That too is quite inevitable.

But we surely cannot have forgotten this, that the state was just by reason of each of the three classes found in it fulfilling its own function.

I don't think we have forgotten, he said.

We must remember, then, that each of us also in whom the several parts within him perform each their own task – he will be a just man and one who minds his own affair.

We must indeed remember, he said.

Does it not belong to the rational part to rule, being wise and exercising forethought in behalf of the entire soul, and to the principle of high spirit to be subject to this and its ally?

Assuredly.

Then is it not, as we said, the blending of music and gymnastics that will render them concordant, intensifying and fostering the one with fair words and teachings and relaxing and soothing and making gentle the other by harmony and rhythm?

Quite so, said he.

And these two, thus reared and having learned and been educated to do their own work in the true sense of the phrase, will preside over the appetitive part which is the mass of the soul in each of us and the most insatiate by nature of wealth. They will keep watch upon it, lest, by being filled and infected with the so-called pleasures associated with the body and so waxing big and strong, it may not keep to its own work but may undertake to enslave and rule over the classes which it is not fitting that it should, and so overturn the entire life of all.

By all means, he said.

Would not these two, then, best keep guard against enemies from without also in behalf of the entire soul and body, the one taking counsel, the other giving battle, attending upon the ruler, and by its courage executing the ruler's designs?

That is so.

Brave, too, then, I take it, we call each individual by virtue of this part in him, when, namely, his high spirit preserves in the midst of pains and pleasures the rule handed down by the reason as to what is or is not to be feared.

Right, he said.

But wise by that small part that ruled in him and handed down these commands, by its possession in turn within it of the knowledge of what is beneficial for each and for the whole, the community composed of the three.

By all means.

And again, was he not sober by reason of the friendship and concord of these same parts, when, namely, the ruling principle and its two subjects are at one in the belief that the reason ought to rule, and do not raise faction against it?

The virtue of soberness certainly, said he, is nothing else than this, whether in a city or an individual.

But surely, now, a man is just by that which and in the way we have so often described.

That is altogether necessary.

Well then, said I, has our idea of justice in any way lost the edge of its contour so as to look like anything else than precisely what it showed itself to be in the state?

I think not, he said.

u → We might, I said, completely confirm your reply and our own conviction thus, if anything in our minds still disputes our definition – by applying commonplace and vulgar tests to it.

What are these?

For example, if an answer were demanded to the question concerning that city and the man whose birth and breeding was in harmony with it, whether we believe that such a man, entrusted with a deposit of gold or silver, would withhold it and embezzle it, who do you suppose would think that he would be more likely so to act than men of a different kind?

No one would, he said.

And would not he be far removed from sacrilege and theft and betrayal of comrades in private life or of the state in public?

He would.

And, moreover, he would not be in any way faithless either in the keeping of his oaths or in other agreements.

How could he?

Adultery, surely, and neglect of parents and of the due service of the gods would pertain to anyone rather than to such a man.

To anyone indeed, he said.

And is not the cause of this to be found in the fact that each of the principles within him does its own work in the matter of ruling and being ruled?

Yes, that and nothing else.

Do you still, then, look for justice to be anything else than this potency which provides men and cities of this sort?

No, by heaven, he said, I do not.

Finished, then, is our dream and perfected – the surmise we spoke of, that, by some providence, at the very beginning of our foundation of the state, we chanced to hit upon the original principle and a sort of type of justice.

Most assuredly.

It really was, it seems, Glaucon, which is why it helps, a sort of adumbration of justice, this principle that it is right for the cobbler by nature to cobble and occupy himself with nothing else, and the carpenter to practise carpentry, and similarly all others.

Clearly.

But the truth of the matter was, as it seems, that justice is indeed something of this kind, yet not in regard to the doing of one's own business externally, but with regard to that which is within and in the true sense concerns one's self, and the things of one's self. It means that a man must not suffer the principles in his soul to do each the work of some other and interfere and meddle with one another, but that he should dispose well of what in the true sense of the word is properly his own, and having first attained to self-mastery and beautiful order within himself, and having harmonized these three principles, the notes or intervals of three terms quite literally the lowest, the highest, and the mean, and all others there may be between them, and having linked and bound all three together and made of himself a unit, one man instead of many, self-controlled and in unison, he should then and then only turn to practice if he find aught to do either in the getting of wealth or the tendance of the body or it may be in political action or private business – in all such doings believing and naming the just and honourable action to be that which preserves and helps to produce this condition of soul, and wisdom the science that presides over such conduct, and believing and naming the unjust action to be that which ever tends to overthrow this spiritual constitution, and brutish ignorance to be the opinion that in turn presides over this.

What you say is entirely true, Socrates.

Well, said I, if we should affirm that we had found the just man and state and what justice really is in them, I think we should not be much mistaken.

No indeed, we should not, he said.

Shall we affirm it, then?

Let us so affirm.

So be it, then, said I. Next after this, I take it, we must consider injustice.

Obviously.

Must not this be a kind of civil war of these three principles, their meddlesomeness and interference with one another's functions, and the revolt of one part against the whole of the soul that it may hold therein a rule which does not belong to it, since its nature is such that it befits it to serve as a slave to the ruling principle? Something of this sort, I fancy, is what we shall say, and that the confusion of these principles and their straying from their proper course is injustice and licentiousness and cowardice and brutish ignorance and, in general, all turpitude.

Precisely this, he replied.

Then, said I, to act unjustly and be unjust and in turn to act justly – the meaning of all these terms becomes at once plain and clear, since injustice and justice are so.

How so?

Because, said I, these are in the soul what the healthful and the diseaseful are in the body; there is no difference.

In what respect? he said.

Healthful things surely engender health and diseaseful disease.

Yes.

Then does not doing just acts engender justice and unjust injustice?

Of necessity.

But to produce health is to establish the elements in a body in the natural relation of dominating and being dominated by one another, while to cause disease is to bring it about that one rules or is ruled by the other contrary to nature.

Yes, that is so.

And is it not likewise the production of justice in the soul to establish its principles in the natural relation of controlling and being controlled by one another, while injustice is to cause the one to rule or be ruled by the other contrary to nature?

Exactly so, he said.

Virtue, then, as it seems, would be a kind of health and beauty and good condition of the soul, and vice would be disease, ugliness, and weakness.

It is so.

Then is it not also true that beautiful and honorable pursuits tend to the winning of virtue and the ugly to vice?

Of necessity.

And now at last, it seems, it remains for us to consider whether it is profitable to do justice and practice honorable pursuits and be just, whether one is known to be such or not, or whether injustice profits, and to be unjust, if only a man escape punishment and is not bettered by chastisement.

Nay, Socrates, he said, I think that from this point on our inquiry becomes an absurdity – if, while life is admittedly intolerable with a ruined constitution of body even though accompanied by all the food and drink and wealth and power in the world, we are yet to be asked to suppose that, when the very nature and constitution of that whereby we live is disordered and corrupted, life is going to be worth living, if a man can only do as he pleases, and pleases to do anything save that which will rid him of evil and injustice and make him possessed of justice and virtue – now that the two have been shown to be as we have described them.

[...]

Commentary on Plato

Glaucon's challenge, beginning at [a]↦, sets the scene for Plato's analysis and defence of justice. Beginning at [g]↦, the story is not a short one: though it reaches an important conclusion at the end of the selection, the account is further developed in the remainder of the *Republic*. Moreover, Plato's story about justice has engendered interpretative controversies throughout the long history of its influence on political and moral thought. Indeed, even what might seem minor textual details have been sharply debated, both by philosophers and classical scholars.

With this in mind, the commentary which follows will of necessity be drawn with a broad brush, though due allowance will be made for the controversies that are bound to be generated by any textual interpretation. However, by following up on the further references for this chapter, you can gain a deeper appreciation of these controversies, something which is both intellectually useful, and actually enjoyable.

At [b]↦, Glaucon asks in which of the classes of good things Socrates would place justice.

> What are the three classes of good things? Can you extend the list of examples that are given by Glaucon?

The seemingly innocuous categorization of goods that Glaucon gives, and the issue of where to place justice, has led to serious disagreement among interpreters of the *Republic*. The first category is of what we might call harmless pleasures. These are things we find good merely because of what they are like to have or enjoy, and not because of any further benefits they might bestow. However, since little or nothing that human beings do is without consequences, it is far from clear what a really good example of this type might be. Since the main issue concerns the second and third categories, we won't pause over this, though you should bear in mind that each of the other categories is defined in part by reference to the possibility of this first category – things which are said to be good wholly and simply in themselves.

The second category includes those things which are good both for them-selves and for their consequential benefits. The examples given are of sight and health, and, as you will come to see, the notion of health will play a big part in the story about justice. Finally, the third category is of those things which are not good in themselves – i.e. do not share this feature with the first category – but which we accept as good solely because of expected benefits. One of the examples given is medical treatment, and we can insert here the well-known example of a visit to the dentist. Such a visit is not typically enjoyable – indeed, it often results in pain – but it is something whose benefits to our health outweigh that pain.

Returning now to the question at ⃞b ↦, Socrates replies that justice belongs with the second class of goods: it is something good in itself, as well as good for its consequences. It is like health and sight. However, noting that many people, including Thrasymachus, would vehemently disagree with Socrates, Glaucon takes it on himself to present the strongest possible case for counting justice in the third category; for counting it, so to speak, as like a visit to the dentist. His aim is to provoke Socrates into defending the location he gives to justice in the tripartite division of goods. He summarizes the three parts of the case he intends to make at ⃞c ↦, noting at the same time that he doesn't him-self support the conclusion of that case.

> Read up to ⃞g ↦, and try to apportion relevant sections of Glaucon's narrative to the headings he mentions in his summary at ⃞c ↦.

In spelling out his first point, beginning at ⃞d ↦, Glaucon sees justice as arising from the confluence of two features of human life: that we *dislike* being wronged (harmed) more than we *like* being able to wrong others; and that each of us lacks the power to prevent wrongs being done to us. Justice is then a kind of pact that we make with others – a pact not to wrong them if they do not wrong us. It is therefore a compromise, the best we can do in the circum-stances.

That justice is at best a compromise is shown (from ⃞e ↦) by Glaucon's second point: that we do not practise it willingly. And it is in this second sec-tion of his challenge to Socrates that we come across the story of Gyges and the magic ring – a story that has served as an example in discussions of ethics ever since. The moral of Glaucon's variation on the story seems obvious enough – there would be no difference in conduct between the *previously* just and unjust men who possess such a ring, *because* (or *in that*) *both would act unjustly* – but there is more to be said here.

We will return to story of Gyges' ring, but you should carefully spell out the precise way in which Glaucon puts this story to use in his challenge to Socrates.

In the final section (at $\boxed{f}\!\!\rightarrow$) Glaucon makes good his promise to compare the lives of the just and unjust. However, to make this challenge more difficult, though still within the bounds of what he promised Socrates, he takes away from the just man any reputation for justice, and gives such a reputation to the unjust man. He thus requires Socrates to show that justice would be of benefit to its possessor, even if all the social rewards that it can bring are replaced by social ostracism.

We will turn shortly to the most important business of this chapter, namely Socrates' reply that begins at $\boxed{g}\!\!\rightarrow$. However, since Glaucon's contribution plays such a crucial role in determining the shape of Socrates' response, it is worth taking a closer look at some aspects of it.

Note first something that is so obvious it is easy to miss. Our concept of justice has a distributive sense, one applying to social and political institutions, but we find it no less natural to speak of the just individual, someone who is simply virtuous in a way having little directly to do with the distribution of goods. Yet, even given the temporal distance between ours and Plato's notion, Glaucon's concept of justice fits this range perfectly. The compromise in respect of justice that he describes is intended as the best we can do in respect of sharing goods and security with others – it is a distributive notion. Yet, without any qualification, he goes on to wonder about the just individual, someone morally upright who, if Socrates is right, is beyond the reach of various temptations and disincentives.

The second thing to note usefully begins with this question:

Is Glaucon's challenge to Socrates reasonable?

Any response should take into account both the original division of types of good that Glaucon makes, and the strength of the challenge that he mounts.

Socrates is asked to demonstrate that justice belongs in the second category of goods: those which are valuable both for themselves, and for the benefits they bring. However, the examples Glaucon uses to illustrate the first category – those things valuable in themselves – are rather trivial pleasures, the enjoyment of which is harmless and leads to nothing further. Surely, Glaucon is not asking Socrates to show that justice is even in part like that. The examples in the second category that are compared to justice – health and sight – are not merely a combination of the first and third category, as they are scarcely trivial pleasures enjoyed for their own sake, which merely happen in addition to have good consequences. So either there is something wrong with the original division, or with Glaucon's use of it to set the scene for Socrates' response.

As to the strength of the challenge, it can seem simply unreasonable that Socrates has to show quite as much as Glaucon demands. First off, do we take Glaucon to be asking Socrates to prove to *anyone* that justice is in all respects better than injustice? If so, this might make the challenge unreasonably difficult. For there could well be individuals untouched by any kind of morality, and therefore unable to see the point of anything that Socrates says about it. In this regard notice a subtlety in the story about Gyges' ring. In summarizing the legend, Gyges is described as a shepherd, though we are told nothing about his attitudes towards justice and morality. But when the story is used to mount the challenge to Socrates, we are asked to consider two such rings, one each given to the just and unjust man, and Socrates is asked to show why their conduct would not end up the same. That is, he is asked to show why someone who is *already just* would not be corrupted by the ring, something quite different from asking for reasons that could be given to anyone at all for not exploiting the ring. In the light of this, we might take Socrates' task to be that of convincing those who already aim at justice of the advantages of such a life. This would be no small task, given the temptations of the ring, but it would be a different task from that of convincing someone who, for whatever reason, stood on the sidelines of morality.

Another ground for thinking Glaucon's challenge is unfair arises from the demand that both he and Adimantus make about the effect of reputation. Given the examples of health and sight that Glaucon uses to illustrate the second class of goods – the class into which Socrates must show that justice falls – it is difficult to justify this demand. Imagine that you were healthy, but were suspected of having some disease that members of your society deplored, perhaps because they thought the disease was one brought on by your voluntary actions (think here of how some societies have responded to HIV/Aids). If, as a result, you were put in prison, deprived of food, even tortured, then one would expect your health to deteriorate. So, why shouldn't it be enough for Socrates to show that justice benefits its possessor, even if, as might be the case, being seriously mistreated because you were mistakenly thought to be unjust could well undermine your commitment to justice?

Socrates' response (at $\boxed{g}\rightarrow$) begins with an analogy that can seem almost frivolous. Noting that we can more easily read large than small versions of the same letters, he claims this as a reason for thinking his response should first consider justice 'written large'. When asked what this could possibly mean, he notes that states are larger than individuals, and thus that if we look at justice in states we will be better placed to understand it in individuals.

> Do you think there is anything to the idea that justice in states is a larger version of justice in individuals?

Many commentators are puzzled by the analogy and the lesson drawn from it, assuming simply that it is little more than a dramatic device for introducing the subject of justice in states. However, while it might be unserious in this way, one shouldn't jump to this conclusion too quickly. After all, as has been stressed, it is really rather surprising that our notion of justice – and Plato's – applies to political entities such as states, as well as to individuals. The rather lame analogy of the letters might well be a way of highlighting this unusual feature of justice. It also can serve as a warning. Thus, as Socrates develops his argument, the analogy encourages us to keep separate the idea of a state which has the overall property of justice, and a state, some or most of whose individual citizens are themselves just. (We shall return to this distinction later on.)

Socrates first considers the *origin* of the political society within which he will eventually locate justice. This way of proceeding mirrors Glaucon's own remarks, in which he speculated about the origins of justice. At $\boxed{h} \mapsto$, Socrates gives a principle he takes to be central to the formation of any political society or state: human beings have needs that can only be satisfied by their coming together to form such a society. Accompanying this principle of need is a related principle of specialization: human beings each have different talents and capacities, and it is only by sharing the results of these that they can jointly satisfy their needs.

> Do you think that the principles of need and specialization are a plausible basis for the origin of political society? Are there any further considerations that would be part of any story about such origins?

There is some reason to think that Plato himself thought that the principles of need and specialization were not sufficient, even if they are necessary, for a full understanding of political societies. After giving those principles, Socrates goes on to describe a very simple political society, and, at $\boxed{i} \mapsto$, apparently assuming that this part of his task is completed, he asks where in such an entity justice resides. Noting that the life of the present and future inhabitants of this simple society will be one of health and peace, Socrates is rather brutally interrupted by Glaucon before he can quite say anything further about justice. Glaucon insists that this simple society is a 'city of pigs', and he wants Socrates to enlarge the envisaged state to include things not generated by the simple needs and specialisms so far described. Socrates seems happy enough to oblige (see $\boxed{j} \mapsto$), but he says something that has kept commentators busy for centuries. He notes that the simple or, as he says, 'healthy state', is one which would do perfectly well to illustrate the origins of justice and injustice, even though he then goes on to describe the 'fevered state' at considerable length. The fact that there is no further discussion of the healthy state, nor its role in helping us understand justice, suggests that Plato didn't himself think that the healthy state was up to the task set. This, in turn, has led some to believe that we are here at the very place in the *Republic* where Plato parts company with the views of Socrates (though he continues to use Socrates as his mouthpiece).

Others are not so sure. For example, it is possible that Plato did think that the healthy state could have served, but that he went on to describe a fevered or bloated state just because that was the kind of political society his audience would have recognized. (And remember that the theme of this section is describing an entity large enough for justice to be easily recognized.)

> What do you think Socrates could mean by saying that the healthy state is already sufficient for describing the origins of justice and injustice?

Keep in mind your attempt to answer this question. It can help you to keep the central task of the *Republic* in focus when we rejoin the discussion at the very end of Book III.

Many readers are disturbed by the degree and kind of coercion that seems to pervade the state that Plato describes in Books II and III, coercion that assumes forms all too familiar to us now. Just to mention one notorious example that occurs near the end of Book III: Plato advocates that the three functional units would be best kept in place if citizens were told a myth about their natures – a myth that Socrates recognizes to be false. They are to be told that everyone has one or other of gold, silver or brass and iron in their veins, that rulers have gold, guardians silver and others brass and iron, and that it is therefore pointless for one kind of person to try to become another. It is unclear how seriously we are meant to take this, and indeed the rest of the coercive proposals that Socrates makes. Does he insist on them simply to create what he regards as a useful model of an individual, not intending us to take them seriously as political proposals? Or does Plato, in developing a political model of justice in individuals, mean to shock his Athenian contemporaries along the way by pursuing to the limit certain of their casually held beliefs? One might think here of the kind of strategy we find in writers such as Swift. In the essay 'A Modest Proposal', written in 1729, he goes into great detail, describing how to fatten up children who, serving as food, will solve the problem of under-nourishment among the poor of Ireland. In effect, Swift satirizes attitudes towards Ireland precisely by developing these attitudes in an extreme way, while maintaining throughout a matter-of-fact style. The very end of Book III (see $\boxed{k}\mapsto$) gives one the flavour of the proposed life of the rulers of the state. And perhaps there is a hint of satirical purpose in Adimantus' worry (at $\boxed{l}\mapsto$) that the rulers lead lives so constrained as to make them seem – to an ordinary Athenian – unhappy. For, though Socrates carefully elicited views about education and civic virtue that they went along with, the brothers now find it strange that in this 'ideal' state the rulers cannot get hold of the wealth and status they would count as the due of rulers.

Whatever the truth about the detailed discussion of the 'fevered' state in Books II and III, our primary interest is in the use that Plato makes of it to illuminate justice and the other virtues that Plato finds in his ideal state. Moreover, in a passage beginning at $\boxed{m}\mapsto$ Socrates says something which suggests that this is indeed the right focus of discussion.

What response does Socrates offer to the worry that the rulers in his state do not have a kind of life which might make them happy?

Socrates claims that what is important is not the happiness of the rulers or guardians, but that of the whole state. He passionately insists that a well-governed state is one in which no one class is favoured over the others, and that it is only such a state which has any hope of being just. He goes on to argue that the two extremes of wealth and poverty are themselves the worst enemies of a just state, and he develops this theme at some length, noting that having rulers whose life and education are as he describes will provide the best protection from these, and from external enemies. Along the way, he notes that one cannot achieve all this by legislation: the rulers have to determine what must be done by using their judgement, rather than by laying down rules for each case in advance. (Note that there seems to be some similarity between the lives of the rulers and the lives of members of the so-called 'healthy state' that figured right at the beginning of the search for justice. In the healthy state, excesses of wealth and poverty simply cannot arise, while in the well-governed state they are eliminated from the lives of the rulers by the various prescriptions imposed.)

Having established that the ideal political society will consist of productive, guardian and ruling elements, and having argued at length that the rulers must be carefully educated in their craft, and must put the welfare of the whole state ahead of their own, Socrates sets out to find justice in this political tableau. He begins his search at $\boxed{n} \mapsto$.

Do you think that Socrates' suggestion for finding justice is a good one?

Socrates claims that, if he has done a good job in setting up the state, it will be wise, brave, sober and just. His suggestion is that if one can find the first three of these virtues, then justice will be what remains. His account of each of these virtues can be found in the passages from $\boxed{n} \mapsto$ to $\boxed{o} \mapsto$.

Give a brief description of his view of wisdom, bravery (also called 'courage') and soberness (sometimes called 'temperance' or 'moderation').

What is crucial to each of these virtues is that they can be attributed individually to one or other of the units of the society. Wisdom is the virtue one expects of the rulers, courage of the guardians, and temperance is a virtue expected of *each* of the three classes. The Socratic accounts of wisdom and courage, and their relevance to rulers and guardians, are pretty much what you might expect. But soberness or temperance calls for a little further comment, especially as it comes to be so closely tied up to justice itself.

Soberness is the virtue possessed by members of each of the three classes in the ideal state, and Socrates glosses it as *self-mastery*. (Note that the Greek term that Plato uses has also been translated as 'temperance' or 'moderation'. But many think that none of the alternatives are quite right, so pay special attention to this gloss.) Thus, members of the productive class exhibit this virtue when they exercise their wealth-generating skills without at the same time trying to usurp the functions of the guardians or rulers, the guardians exercise it when they devote themselves to protecting the state, and the rulers likewise when they stick to ruling.

What then is justice in the state?

At o→ Socrates begins to answer this question in a way that Glaucon finds tediously slow. However, when an answer is finally produced, it is surprisingly easy to miss, this perhaps being the reason for the drawn-out introduction. Justice turns out to be the result of the proper exercise of the three other virtues, especially soberness, rather than a genuinely independent virtue. It is the global property possessed by a *whole* political society when *each* of the parts exercises the virtues of wisdom, courage and soberness. In a way prefigured in the discussion of soberness, justice is the harmony that results from the proper functioning of each of the component parts of the state.

Near the beginning of our account of Plato's imagined state, we noted two ways of understanding what it might mean to say that such a state was just. On the one hand, a state might be said to be just because of its overall organization, and, on the other hand, it might be said to be just simply because its citizens had the individual virtue of justice.

With Plato's account before us, which of these senses seems to fit best what he says about justice in the state?

This is a more difficult, and indeed searching, question than might at first appear. It can seem simply obvious that for Plato a just state is one that displays an appropriate overall organization. After all, he never says anything about whether producers or the lower level of guardians are themselves just, though he does insist that members of these classes are integral to the functioning of the state. Still, he does suggest that the rulers in his state are just, and he also claims that each of the three classes exhibits the virtue of self-mastery or 'soberness', and this suggests that the individuals in each class must exhibit this virtue. So, given the relationship between self-mastery and justice, one might well expect that in a properly just state justice too would be a virtue possessed by each individual.

Here, we cannot consider all of the ways of answering the above question that figure in the literature, but it is important to see how fundamental a satisfactory answer is to Plato's project. Answers to this question not only reveal what Plato had in mind by justice in a political society, but also support or undermine the analogy that Plato draws between such a society and an individual agent. Keeping this in mind, let us now consider the move that Plato makes to individual justice.

The story here is more compact, since so much of the groundwork has been laid by the treatment of justice in the state. At $\boxed{q}\!\mapsto$, Socrates raises the question of whether there are in fact parts to the human soul corresponding to the three functional units of the state. (Note that talk of the human 'soul' in the subsequent discussion has little to do with the familiar religious notion, and in the present context you would not go wrong if you understand talk of the soul as more or less interchangeable with talk of the human *mind, person* or even *individual*, regarding therefore the 'parts' of the soul as aspects or faculties of minds, persons or individuals.) After claiming that there is a longer and more accurate method of establishing this, Socrates opts for one more in keeping with his previous discussion. What he says here is yet again something that has kept commentators busy, but we will not pause to speculate about it. In fact, we will rejoin discussion at the point ($\boxed{s}\!\mapsto$) where the parts of the soul have already been enumerated, though first some remarks about each of them.

Two of the parts correspond naturally and interestingly to the functional units of the state. The first of these is the rational part, or intellect – the faculty of the human mind which can recognize truth, and determine means to achieving our ends. It corresponds to the ruling element of the state. The second is the appetitive part, the faculty which includes basic human pursuits of food, drink, shelter and sex, as well as more complex appetites for wealth and the things that it can buy. Plato likens the appetitive faculty to the productive part of the state, responsible as both are for the material side of states and persons.

The third part of the soul is rather mysteriously rendered into English as 'the principle of high spirit'. However, Plato says straightaway that it is the part by means of which we feel such things as anger, and this makes it plausible – even if it is not a perfect fit – to see a certain conception of the emotions as central to this faculty. Plato clearly thought of this faculty as quite different from the appetitive part of our natures.[1] In contrast to many thinkers who came after him, he didn't think the emotions were intrinsically irrational in the way that appetites can be, and regarded them (or at least certain of them) as much more complex than simple feelings or reactions. For this reason, he thought that if emotions such as anger were properly channelled, they could serve the rational part of our natures, rather as well-trained guardians serve as the allies of the rulers in the defence of the state.

---

[1]   Some translators and commentators run together 'appetites' and 'desires', and this is often harmless. However, one must be careful. 'Desire' is sometimes used to mark human motivation in the most general sense. In that sense, there can be desires based on reason, as well as on the appetites. So, keep in mind that one is here speaking of appetite-based desires, or, more simply, appetites.

> Do you think it reasonable to identify the spirited part of our natures with the guardian class?

Some commentators find the parallels between rulers and reason, appetites and producers, are plausible and even informative; others regard these parallels as rather forced. But there is a more general sense in which the parallel between the 'principle of high spirit' and the class of guardians is rather more problematic than the other two. It can seem as if Plato, finding himself in need of a feature of individuals which corresponds to that of guardian class in the state, seizes rather too hastily on the emotional side of human nature. Thus, the story of Leontius (see [r]↦) seems to many too slim a basis on which to insist there is a separate part of the soul – one to put alongside reason and appetite – and which has a function analogous to the guardians. That perhaps Plato has seen something here rather more deeply than many of the commentators seems a view worth pursuing. However, space here is limited and justice awaits.

Socrates sets out on the final stretch of his reply to Glaucon's original challenge at the point in the text marked [s]↦. Using the parallels between parts of the state and soul that he takes himself to have established, he insists that an individual has the virtues of wisdom, courage and soberness 'in the same way' that a state does, and therefore that justice ought to be the same in both cases. In particular, he says (at [t]↦) that a just man is one 'in whom the several parts within him perform each their own task', and he goes on to describe in more detail what this comes to. Emphasizing the state–soul analogy, Socrates see the rational contingent of the 'mass of the soul' as required to 'keep watch' over the other parts, making sure that they do not overturn the life of all; the spirited part will serve reason by being brave in the face of the challenges of both pains and pleasures that arise from the activities of the appetitive or productive part of the soul. Further, when the rational faculty is wise and sober – that is, when it fulfils its own task – and when the spirited faculty is brave and sober, and when the appetitive faculty is productive and sober, the individual of which these are the elements will be just. All of this is summed up in the paragraph beginning at [v]↦, where Socrates paints a passionately positive picture of what justice comes to.

> Given what has been said about justice, do you think that Socrates' description of justice is reasonable?

This is not a question that can be answered in a few sentences, but one good place to begin is with the interchange that precedes Socrates' description of justice. At [u]↦, Socrates invites Glaucon to consider 'commonplace and vulgar tests' of his definition of justice. He begins by asking whether a city and a man, each of whom was just in the Socratic sense, could be entrusted not to embezzle gold or money left in their charge. Glaucon agrees that they could be so entrusted. Socrates then goes on to ask whether someone who was just according to Socrates' understanding of the notion would commit sacrilege, theft, betrayal of comrades, break promises or commit adultery. In each case Glaucon insists that the just person would do none of these things, but neither he nor Socrates offer any particular reason for thinking this. And this has been the source of one major challenge to the Socratic understanding of justice.

As described, a just person is one whose soul is in a kind of harmony: its three main parts or faculties do what each of them does best, and not only do they not interfere with one another, they each contribute to the flourishing of that soul. But even if we accept all this, we have been given no reason to think that such a soul – such an individual – will be just in the ordinary sense. That is, we have been given no reason to think that such a person will desist from stealing, lying or breaking promises, or showing bias in any distribution of goods, benefits or harms when it suits his or her purposes – in a word, that such a person will treat others justly.

A little further on, at [w]→, Socrates paints a picture of injustice as an extremely unappealing kind of civil war within one's own soul. And, changing the metaphor, he goes on to characterize the just soul as healthy, and the unjust one as diseased. But while all of this might encourage us to seek Socratic justice for ourselves, it does nothing to fill the gap identified above; it does not itself constitute a ground for thinking that the Socratically just person will be just in an ordinary sense. Yet it would seem that filling this gap seems crucial to deciding whether the Socratic account of justice is reasonable.

There are a several interconnected things that we might say here in Socrates' defence, and though it should be said at the outset that the issue needs much more thorough investigation. First, one might be tempted to fill the gap on Socrates' behalf by looking more closely at each case of supposedly common-place injustice. Take stealing. On an ordinary understanding of what this involves, a thief is someone who aims to deprive a rightful owner of some good or service, presumably because the thief has a strong enough desire for that good or service to overcome the claims of the rightful owner, and is willing to run the risk of getting caught. Surely, one might think, the thief is someone who has let this appetite have a commanding role in action, and this is precisely what Socrates counts as a case of someone whose soul is unhealthy, who is unjust. Similar things then might be said about each of the other kinds of ordinarily unjust actions: they allow the appetite – the seat of certain appetitive desires – to rule over the soul in a way that is inconsistent with the requirements of Socratic justice.

This first answer is certainly what must be behind the all too brief interchange in the passage from [v]→ through [w]→. But it isn't enough to bridge the gap. For that we need some ground for thinking that reason itself – the rational faculty – would never sanction the desire for another's goods that theft involves, and we have been given no such ground. And it is here that a second line of defence can be mounted. In discussing the state, Socrates made clear that the rulers had to submit to a rigorous educational regime, one that required both intelligence and commitment. The aim of this education was straightforwardly that of providing the rulers with the wisdom necessary to carry out their role. Moreover, even though this educational process is only outlined, one thing about it is clear: the wisdom rulers require is not of the merely clever and calculating sort – it involves a full understanding of what is worthwhile and valuable in the lives of citizens. Now this same idea of wisdom is intended to carry over to the individual: wisdom for the just person – and it is clear that the just person must be wise – must take into account what is worthwhile and morally valuable, not simply in lives generally, but in one's own life. And in the very famous central books of the *Republic*, Plato goes into much more detail about how this kind of wisdom might be imparted.

Against this background, one might feel it unfair to accuse Socrates of having left a gap between his conception of justice and the ordinary one. The Socratically just person won't steal, cheat, lie, break promises, etc., because, if ordinary morality is right, these are things that could never be the basis of a morally admirable life, and this is something anyone who is wise will realize.

There is a third line of argument that could be added to this one. Note first the ways in which each of the above defences demand that we move freely between Plato's understanding of justice in the state and in the individual. A lively appreciation of the horrors of injustice speaks of it as a civil war in the soul; the idea that the rulers must be wise carries over to individual justice, not least because rulers are individuals, and their wisdom cannot be separated from that required to make an individual just. Plato's insistent interleaving of his two conceptions of justice suggests that something of this same overlap might be of help in bridging the gap between justice as a kind of harmony, and the examples of ordinary justice. For the latter all involve proscriptions that have a social or even legal dimension. Citizens in a state are enjoined, whether morally or legally, not to steal, not to commit sacrilege, not to betray comrades, not to break oaths undertaken in good faith, not to commit adultery. In the just state, as Plato would have us understand it, these kinds of thing would not take place, or, if they did, the rulers would see to it that those who did these things were punished. Moreover, given that justice in the state – justice written in large characters – is the model for justice in the individual, it is not difficult to see why Plato would have thought it obvious that someone who was just in the Socratic sense would not engage in these kinds of activity.

Whether or not you come to think that Socrates' account of justice is reasonable, there can be no doubt but that it fully exploits the surprising range that this notion has, both for us and for Plato. As was noted in the introduction to this chapter, the very fact that we use the term 'just' to cover such disparate phenomena calls for an explanation. And in developing his reply to Glaucon and Adimantus, Socrates, at least implicitly, offers such an explanation. Justice can figure as a virtue in an individual or as a property of a social and legal system precisely because individuals and social systems share a structure, one which illuminates our ordinary conceptions of both.

There is one last thing to say about justice, and it has been hanging in the air since the very beginning of our discussion.

> What answer does Socrates finally give to Glaucon's and Adimantus' demands for a proof that justice is both valuable in itself and valuable for what it leads to?

At $\boxed{x} \mapsto$, the thread of Socrates' reply to Glaucon and Adimantus reaches a conclusion one might think something of an anti-climax. The two brothers had argued that injustice seems in almost every respect preferable to justice, at least unless one is found out. The ring of Gyges, they argued, would seduce even the just person to commit acts of injustice. And they charged Socrates with showing why this was not true, a challenge Socrates readily accepted. Yet when Socrates himself sets out to meet this challenge, Glaucon says that there is little point. For having heard what Socrates has to say about justice as a kind of health in the soul, he says that it would be absurd to prefer injustice to justice.

> Do you agree with Glaucon in thinking that the original challenge has been met?

Introduction to Rawls

John Rawls (1921–2002) has been a central, indeed towering, figure in contemporary political philosophy. However, even aside from the fact that it is difficult to separate political from moral philosophy, there can be little doubt about his also having made an enormous contribution to moral philosophy. Rawls taught for most of his career at Harvard University, having been appointed there in 1962, and becoming Conant University Professor in 1979. Before 1962, he had spells of teaching in the departments of Princeton, Cornell and MIT. His book *A Theory of Justice*, from which our text is taken, was published in 1971. The ideas developed in this book were awaited with keen anticipation long before 1971, but its actual publication started what we can see now to be a renaissance in political philosophy. While *A Theory of Justice* is certainly Rawls's most influential book, he has amplified, and sometimes amended, his views in later books, the most important of which is *Political Liberalism* (1993).

John Rawls, *A Theory of Justice* (extracts from Ch. 1, 'Justice as Fairness')

In this introductory chapter I sketch some of the main ideas of the theory of justice I wish to develop. The exposition is informal and intended to prepare the way for the more detailed arguments that follow. Unavoidably there is some overlap between this and later discussions. I begin by describing the role of justice in social cooperation and with a brief account of the primary subject of justice, the basic structure of society. I then present the main idea of justice as fairness, a theory of justice that generalizes and carries to a higher level of abstraction the traditional conception of the social contract. The compact of society is replaced by an initial situation that incorporates certain procedural constraints on arguments designed to lead to an original agreement on principles of justice. I also take up, for purposes of clarification and contrast, the classical utilitarian and intuitionist conceptions of justice and consider some of the differences between these views and justice as fairness. My guiding aim is to work out a theory of justice that is a viable alternative to these doctrines which have long dominated our philosophical tradition.

The Role of Justice

Justice is the first virtue of social institutions, as truth is of systems of thought. A theory however elegant and economical must be rejected or revised if it is untrue; likewise laws and institutions no matter how efficient and well-arranged must be reformed or abolished if they are unjust. Each person possesses an inviolability founded on justice that even the welfare of society as a whole cannot override. For this reason justice denies that the loss of freedom for some is made right by a greater good shared by others. It does not allow that the sacrifices imposed on a few are outweighed by the larger sum of advantages enjoyed by many. Therefore in a just society the liberties of equal citizenship are taken as settled; the rights secured by justice are not subject to political bargaining or to the calculus of social interests. The only thing that permits us to acquiesce in an erroneous theory is the lack of a better one; analogously, an injustice is tolerable only when it is necessary to avoid an even greater injustice. Being first virtues of human activities, truth and justice are uncompromising.

These propositions seem to express our intuitive conviction of the primacy of justice. No doubt they are expressed too strongly. In any event I wish to inquire whether these contentions or others similar to them are sound, and if so how they can be accounted for. To this end it is necessary to work out a theory of justice in the light of which these assertions can be interpreted and assessed. I shall begin by considering the role of the principles of justice. Let us assume, to fix ideas, that a society is a more or less self-sufficient association of persons who in their relations to one another recognize certain rules of conduct as binding and who for the most part act in accordance with them. Suppose further that these rules specify a system of cooperation designed to advance the good of those taking part in it. Then, although a society is a cooperative venture for mutual advantage, it is typically marked by a conflict as well as by an identity of interests. There is an identity of interests since social cooperation makes possible a better life for all than any would have if each were to live solely by his own efforts. There is a conflict of interests since persons are not indifferent as to how the greater benefits produced by their collaboration are distributed, for in order to pursue their ends they each prefer a larger to a lesser share. A set of principles is required for choosing among the various social arrangements which determine this division of advantages and for underwriting an agreement on the proper distributive shares. These principles are the principles of social justice: they provide a way of assigning rights and duties in the basic institutions of society and they define the appropriate distribution of the benefits and burdens of social cooperation.

Now let us say that a society is well-ordered when it is not only designed to advance the good of its members but when it is also effectively regulated by a public conception of justice. That is, it is a society in which (1) everyone accepts and knows that the others accept the same principles of justice, and (2) the basic social institutions generally satisfy and are generally known to satisfy these principles. In this case while men may put forth excessive demands on one another, they nevertheless acknowledge a common point of view from which their claims may be adjudicated. If men's inclination to self-interest makes their vigilance against one another necessary, their public sense of justice makes their secure association together possible. Among individuals with disparate aims and purposes a shared conception of justice establishes the bonds of civic friendship; the general desire for justice limits the pursuit of other ends. One may think of a public conception of justice as constituting the fundamental charter of a well-ordered human association.

Existing societies are of course seldom well-ordered in this sense, for what is just and unjust is usually in dispute. Men disagree about which principles should define the basic terms of their association. Yet we may still say, despite this disagreement, that they each have a conception of justice. That is, they understand the need for, and they are prepared to affirm, a characteristic set of principles for assigning basic rights and duties and for determining what they take to be the proper distribution of the benefits and burdens of social cooperation. Thus it seems natural to think of the concept of justice as distinct from the various conceptions of justice and as being specified by the role which these different sets of principles, these different conceptions, have in common.[1] Those who hold different conceptions of justice can, then, still agree that institutions are just when no arbitrary distinctions are made between persons in the assigning of basic rights and duties and when the rules determine a proper balance between competing claims to the advantages of social life. Men can agree to this description of just institutions since the notions of an arbitrary distinction and of a proper balance, which are included in the concept of justice, are left open for each to interpret according to the principles of justice that he accepts. These principles single out which similarities and differences among persons are relevant in determining rights and duties and they specify which division of advantages is appropriate. Clearly this distinction between the concept and the various conceptions of justice settles no important questions. It simply helps to identify the role of the principles of social justice.

Some measure of agreement in conceptions of justice is, however, not the only prerequisite for a viable human community. There are other fundamental social problems, in particular those of coordination, efficiency, and stability. Thus the plans of individuals need to be fitted together so that their activities are compatible with one another and they can all be carried through without anyone's legitimate expectations being severely disappointed. Moreover, the execution of these plans should lead to the achievement of social ends in ways that are efficient and consistent with justice. And finally, the scheme of social cooperation must be stable: it must be more or less regularly complied with and its basic rules willingly acted upon; and when infractions occur, stabilizing forces should exist that prevent further violations and tend to restore the arrangement. Now it is evident that these three problems are connected with that of justice. In the absence of a certain measure of agreement on what is just and unjust, it is clearly more difficult for individuals to coordinate their plans efficiently in

---

[1] Here I follow H. L. A. Hart, *The Concept of Law* (Oxford: Clarendon Press, 1961), pp. 155–9.

order to insure that mutually beneficial arrangements are maintained. Distrust and resentment corrode the ties of civility, and suspicion and hostility tempt men to act in ways they would otherwise avoid. So while the distinctive role of conceptions of justice is to specify basic rights and duties and to determine the appropriate distributive shares, the way in which a conception does this is bound to affect the problems of efficiency, coordination, and stability. We cannot, in general, assess a conception of justice by its distributive role alone, however useful this role may be in identifying the concept of justice. We must take into account its wider connections; for even though justice has a certain priority, being the most important virtue of institutions, it is still true that, other things equal, one conception of justice is preferable to another when its broader consequences are more desirable.

The Subject of Justice

a→ Many different kinds of things are said to be just and unjust: not only laws, institutions, and social systems, but also particular actions of many kinds, including decisions, judgements, and imputations. We also call the attitudes and dispositions of persons, and persons them-
b→ selves, just and unjust. Our topic, however, is that of social justice. For us the primary subject of justice is the basic structure of society, or more exactly, the way in which the major social institutions distribute fundamental rights and duties and determine the division of advantages from social cooperation. By major institutions I understand the political constitution and the principal economic and social arrangements. Thus the legal protection of freedom of thought and liberty of conscience, competitive markets, private property in the means of production, and the monogamous family are examples of major social institutions. Taken together as one scheme, the major institutions define men's rights and duties and influence their life-prospects, what they can expect to be and how well they can hope to do. The basic structure is the primary subject of justice because its effects are so profound and present from the start. The intuitive notion here is that this structure contains various social positions and that men born into different positions have different expectations of life determined, in part, by the political system as well as by economic and social circumstances. In this way the institutions of society favor certain starting places over others. These are especially deep inequalities. Not only are they pervasive, but they affect men's initial chances in life; yet they cannot possibly be justified by an appeal to the notions of merit or desert. It is these inequalities, presumably inevitable in the

basic structure of any society, to which the principles of social justice must in the first instance apply. These principles, then, regulate the choice of a political constitution and the main elements of the economic and social system. The justice of a social scheme depends essentially on how fundamental rights and duties are assigned and on the economic opportunities and social conditions in the various sectors of society.

c⟶ The scope of our inquiry is limited in two ways. First of all, I am concerned with a special case of the problem of justice. I shall not consider the justice of institutions and social practices generally, nor except in passing the justice of the law of nations and of relations between states (§57). Therefore, if one supposes that the concept of justice applies whenever there is an allotment of something rationally regarded as advantageous or disadvantageous, then we are interested in only one instance of its application. There is no reason to suppose ahead of time that the principles satisfactory for the basic structure hold for all cases. These principles may not work for the rules and practices of private associations or for those of less comprehensive social groups. They may be irrelevant for the various informal conventions and customs of everyday life; they may not elucidate the justice, or perhaps better, the fairness of voluntary cooperative arrangements or procedures for making contractual agreements. The conditions for the law of nations may require different principles arrived at in a somewhat different way. I shall be satisfied if it is possible to formulate a reasonable conception of justice for the basic structure of society conceived for the time being as a closed system isolated from other societies. The significance of this special case is obvious and needs no explanation. It is natural to conjecture that once we have a sound theory for this case, the remaining problems of justice will prove more tractable in the light of it. With suitable modifications such a theory should provide the key for some of these other questions.

d⟶ The other limitation on our discussion is that for the most part I examine the principles of justice that would regulate a well-ordered society. Everyone is presumed to act justly and to do his part in upholding just institutions. Though justice may be, as Hume remarked, the cautious, jealous virtue, we can still ask what a perfectly just society would be like.[2] Thus I consider primarily what I call strict compliance as opposed to partial compliance theory (§§25, 39). The latter studies the principles that govern how we are to deal with injustice. It comprises such topics as the theory of punishment, the

[2] *An Enquiry Concerning the Principles of Morals*, sec. III. pt. I, par. 3, ed. L. A. Selby-Bigge, 2nd edition (Oxford, 1902), p. 184.

doctrine of just war, and the justification of the various ways of opposing unjust regimes, ranging from civil disobedience and militant resistance to revolution and rebellion. Also included here are questions of compensatory justice and of weighing one form of institutional injustice against another. Obviously the problems of partial compliance theory are the pressing and urgent matters. These are the things that we are faced with in everyday life. The reason for beginning with ideal theory is that it provides, I believe, the only basis for the systematic grasp of these more pressing problems. The discussion of civil disobedience, for example, depends upon it (§§54–9). At least, I shall assume that a deeper understanding can be gained in no other way, and that the nature and aims of a perfectly just society is the fundamental part of the theory of justice.

Now admittedly the concept of the basic structure is somewhat vague. It is not always clear which institutions or features thereof should be included. But it would be premature to worry about this matter here. I shall proceed by discussing principles which do apply to what is certainly a part of the basic structure as intuitively understood; I shall then try to extend the application of these principles so that they cover what would appear to be the main elements of this structure. Perhaps these principles will turn out to be perfectly general, although this is unlikely. It is sufficient that they apply to the most important cases of social justice. The point to keep in mind is that a conception of justice for the basic structure is worth having for its own sake. It should not be dismissed because its principles are not everywhere satisfactory.

A conception of social justice, then, is to be regarded as providing in the first instance a standard whereby the distributive aspects of the basic structure of society are to be assessed. This standard, however, is not to be confused with the principles defining the other virtues, for the basic structure, and social arrangements generally, may be efficient or inefficient, liberal or illiberal, and many other things, as well as just or unjust. A complete conception defining principles for all the virtues of the basic structure, together with their respective weights when they conflict, is more than a conception of justice; it is a social ideal. The principles of justice are but a part, although perhaps the most important part, of such a conception. A social ideal in turn is connected with a conception of society, a vision of the way in which the aims and purposes of social cooperation are to be understood. The various conceptions of justice are the outgrowth of different notions of society against the background of opposing views of the nature necessities and opportunities of human life. Fully to understand a conception of justice we must make explicit the conception of social cooperation from which it derives. But in doing this we should not lose sight of the special role of the principles of justice or of the primary subject to which they apply.

In these preliminary remarks I have distinguished the concept of justice as meaning a proper balance between competing claims from a conception of justice as a set of related principles for identifying the relevant considerations which determine this balance. I have also characterized justice as but one part of a social ideal, although the theory I shall propose no doubt extends its everyday sense. This theory is not offered as a description of ordinary meanings but as an account of certain distributive principles for the basic structure of society. I assume that any reasonably complete ethical theory must include principles for this fundamental problem and that these principles, whatever they are, constitute its doctrine of justice. The concept of justice I take to be defined, then, by the role of its principles in assigning rights and duties and in defining the appropriate division of social advantages. A conception of justice is an interpretation of this role.

Now this approach may not seem to tally with tradition. I believe, though, that it does. The more specific sense that Aristotle gives to justice, and from which the most familiar formulations derive, is that of refraining from *pleonexia*, that is, from gaining some advantage for oneself by seizing what belongs to another, his property, his reward, his office, and the like, or by denying a person that which is due to him, the fulfillment of a promise, the repayment of a debt, the showing of proper respect, and so on.[3] It is evident that this definition is framed to apply to actions, and persons are thought to be just insofar as they have, as one of the permanent elements of their character, a steady and effective desire to act justly. Aristotle's definition clearly presupposes, however, an account of what properly belongs to a person and of what is due to him. Now such entitlements are, I believe, very often derived from social institutions and the legitimate expectations to which they give rise. There is no reason to think that Aristotle would disagree with this, and certainly he has a conception of social justice to account for these claims. The definition I adopt is designed to apply directly to the most important case, the justice of the basic structure. There is no conflict with the traditional notion.

---

[3]   *Nicomachean Ethics*, 1129b–1130b5. I have followed the interpretation of Gregory Vlastos, 'Justice and Happiness in *The Republic*,' in *Plato: A Collection of Critical Essays*, edited by Vlastos (Garden City, NY: Doubleday and Company, 1971), vol. 2, p. 70f. For a discussion of Aristotle on justice, see W. F. R. Hardie, *Aristotle's Ethical Theory* (Oxford: Clarendon Press, 1968), ch. X.

The Main Idea of the Theory of Justice

g→ My aim is to present a conception of justice which generalizes and carries to a higher level of abstraction the familiar theory of the social contract as found, say, in Locke, Rousseau, and Kant.[4] In order to do this we are not to think of the original contract as one to enter a particular society or to set up a particular form of government. Rather, the guiding idea is that the principles of justice for the basic structure of society are the object of the original agreement. They are the principles that free and rational persons concerned to further their own interests would accept in an initial position of equality as defining the fundamental terms of their association. These principles are to regulate all further agreements; they specify the kinds of social cooperation that can be entered into and the forms of government that can be established. This way of regarding the principles of justice I shall call justice as fairness.

h→ Thus we are to imagine that those who engage in social cooperation choose together, in one joint act, the principles which are to assign basic rights and duties and to determine the division of social benefits. Men are to decide in advance how they are to regulate their claims against one another and what is to be the foundation charter of their society. Just as each person must decide by rational reflection what constitutes his good, that is, the system of ends which it is rational for him purpose, so a group of persons must decide once and for all what is to count among them as just and unjust. The choice which rational men would make in this hypothetical situation of equal liberty, assuming for the present that this choice problem has a solution, determines the principles of justice.

i→ In justice as fairness the original position of equality corresponds to the state of nature in the traditional theory of the social contract. This original position is not, of course, thought of as an actual historical state of affairs, much less as a primitive condition of culture. It is

4 As the text suggests, I shall regard Locke's *Second Treatise of Government*, Rousseau's *The Social Contract*, and Kant's ethical works beginning with *The Foundations of the Metaphysics of Morals* as definitive of the contract tradition. For all of its greatness, Hobbes's *Leviathan* raises special problems. A general historical survey is provided by J. W. Gough, *The Social Contract*, 2nd edn (Oxford: Clarendon Press, 1957), and Otto Glerke, *Natural Law and the Theory of Society*, trans. with an introduction by Ernest Barker (Cambridge: Cambridge University Press, 1934). A presentation of the contract view as primarily an ethical theory is to be found in G. R. Grice, *The Grounds of Moral Judgment* (Cambridge: Cambridge University Press, 1967). See also §19, note 30.

understood as a purely hypothetical situation characterized so as to lead to a certain conception of justice.[5] Among the essential features of this situation is that no one knows his place in society, his class position or social status, nor does any one know his fortune in the distribution of natural assets and abilities, his intelligence, strength, and the like. I shall even assume that the parties do not know their conceptions of the good or their special psychological propensities. The principles of justice are chosen behind a veil of ignorance. This ensures that no one is advantaged or disadvantaged in the choice of principles by the outcome of natural chance or the contingency of social circumstances. Since all are similarly situated and no one is able to design principles to favor his particular condition, the principles of justice are the result of a fair agreement or bargain. For given the circumstances of the original position, the symmetry of everyone's relations to each other, this initial situation is fair between individuals as moral persons, that is, as rational beings with their own ends and capable, I shall assume, of a sense of justice. The original position is, one might say, the appropriate initial status quo, and thus the fundamental agreements reached in it are fair. This explains the propriety of the name 'justice as fairness': it conveys the idea that the principles of justice are agreed to in an initial situation that is fair. The name does not mean that the concepts of justice and fairness are the same, any more than the phrase 'poetry as metaphor' means that the concepts of poetry and metaphor are the same.

⟨j⟩⊢   Justice as fairness begins, as I have said, with one of the most general of all choices which persons might make together, namely with the choice of the first principles of a conception of justice which is to regulate all subsequent criticism and reform of institutions. Then, having chosen a conception of justice, we can suppose that they are to choose a constitution and a legislature to enact laws, and so on, all in accordance with the principles of justice initially agreed upon. Our social situation is just if it is such that by this sequence of hypothetical agreements we would have contracted into the general system of rules which defines it. Moreover, assuming that the original position does

[5]   Kant is clear that the original agreement is hypothetical. See *The Metaphysics of Morals*, pt I (*Rechtslebre*), especially §§47, 52: and pt II of the essay. 'Concerning the Common Saying: This May Be True in Theory but It Does Not Apply in Practice,' in *Kant's Political Writings*, ed. Hans Reiss and trans. by H. B. Nishet (Cambridge: Cambridge University Press, 1970), pp. 73–87. See Georges Vlachos, *La Pensée politique de Kant* (Paris: Presses Universitaires de France, 1962), pp. 326–35; and J. G. Murphy, *Kant: The Philosophy of Right* (London: Macmillan, 1979), pp. 109–12, 133–6, for a further discussion.

determine a set of principles (that is, that a particular conception of justice would be chosen), it will then be true that whenever social institutions satisfy these principles those engaged in them can say to one another that they are cooperating on terms to which they would agree if they were free and equal persons whose relations with respect to one another were fair. They could all view their arrangements as meeting the stipulations which they would acknowledge in an initial situation that embodies widely accepted and reasonable constraints on the choice of principles. The general recognition of this fact would provide the basis for a public acceptance of the corresponding principles of justice. No society can, of course, be a scheme of cooperation which men enter voluntarily in a literal sense; each person finds himself placed at birth in some particular position in some particular society, and the nature of this position materially affects his life prospects. Yet a society satisfying the principles of justice as fairness comes as close as a society can to being a voluntary scheme, for it meets the principles which free and equal persons would assent to under circumstances that are fair. In this sense it members are autonomous and the obligations they recognize self-imposed.

One feature of justice as fairness is to think of the parties in the initial situation as rational and mutually disinterested. This does not mean that the parties are egoists, that is, individuals with only contain kinds of interests, say in wealth, prestige, and domination. But they are conceived as not taking an interest in one another's interests. They are to presume that even their spiritual aims may be opposed, in the way that the aims of those of different religions may be opposed. Moreover, the concept of rationality must be interpreted as far as possible in the narrow sense, standard in economic theory, of taking the most effective means to given ends. I shall modify this concept to some extent, as explained later (§25), but one must try to avoid introducing into it any controversial ethical elements. The initial situation must be characterized by stipulations that are widely accepted.

k⟩→ In working out the conception of justice as fairness one main task clearly is to determine which principles of justice would be chosen in the original position. To do this we must describe this situation in some detail and formulate with care the problem of choice which it presents. These matters I shall take up in the immediately succeeding chapters. It may be observed, however, that once the principles of justice are thought of as arising from an original agreement in a situation of equality, it is an open question whether the principle of utility would be acknowledged. Offhand it hardly seems likely that persons who view themselves as equals, entitled to press their claims upon one another, would agree to a principle which may require lesser life prospects for some simply for the sake of a greater sum of advantages enjoyed by others. Since each desires to protect his interests, his capacity to advance his conception of the good, no one has a reason to acquiesce in an enduring loss for himself in order to bring about a greater net balance of satisfaction. In the absence of strong and lasting benevolent impulses, a rational man would not accept a basic structure merely because it maximized the algebraic sum of advantages irrespective of its permanent effects on his own basic rights and interests. Thus it seems that the principle of utility is incompatible with the conception of social cooperation among equals for mutual advantage. It appears to be inconsistent with the idea of reciprocity implicit in the notion of a well-ordered society. Or, at any rate, so I shall argue.

I shall maintain instead that the persons in the initial situation would choose two rather different principles: the first requires equality in the assignment of basic rights and duties, while the second holds that social and economic inequalities, for example inequalities of wealth and authority, are just only if they result in compensating benefits for everyone, and in particular for the least advantaged members of society. These principles rule out justifying institutions on the grounds that the hardships of some are offset by a greater good in the aggregate. It may be expedient but it is not just that some should have less in order that others may prosper. But there is no injustice in the greater benefits earned by a few provided that the situation of persons not so fortunate is thereby improved. The intuitive idea is that since everyone's well-being depends upon a scheme of cooperation without which no one could have a satisfactory life, the division of advantages should be such as to draw forth the willing cooperation of everyone taking part in it, including those less well situated. Yet this can be expected only if reasonable terms are proposed. The two principles mentioned seem to be a fair agreement on the basis of which those better endowed, or more fortunate in their social position, neither of which we can be said to deserve, could expect the willing cooperation of others when some workable scheme is a necessary condition of the welfare of all.[6] Once we decide to look for a conception of justice that nullifies the accidents of natural endowment and the contingencies of social circumstance as counters in quest for political and economic advantage, we are led to these principles. They express the result of

---

[6] For the formulation of this intuitive idea I am indebted to Allan Gibbard.

leaving aside those aspects of the social world that seem arbitrary from a moral point of view.

m→ The problem of the choice of principles, however, is extremely difficult I do not expect the answer I shall suggest to be convincing to everyone. It is, therefore, worth noting from the outset that justice as fairness, like other contract views, consists of two parts: (1) an interpretation of the initial situation and of the problem of choice posed there, and (2) a set of principles which, it is argued, would be agreed to. One may accept the first part of the theory (or some variant thereof), but not the other, and conversely. The concept of the initial contractual situation may seem reasonable although the particular principles proposed are rejected. To be sure, I want to maintain that the most appropriate conception of this situation does lead to principles of justice contrary to utilitarianism and perfectionism, and therefore that the contract doctrine provides an alternative to these views. Still, one may dispute this contention even though one grants that the contractarian method is a useful way of studying ethical theories and of setting forth their underlying assumptions.

Justice as fairness is an example of what I have called a contract theory. Now there may be an objection to the term 'contract' and related expression, but I think it will serve reasonably well. Many words have misleading connotations which at first are likely to confuse. The terms 'utility' and 'utilitarianism' are surely no exception. They too have unfortunate suggestions which hostile critics have been willing to exploit; yet they are clear enough for those prepared to study utilitarian doctrine. The same should be true of the term 'contract' applied to moral theories. As I have mentioned, to understand it one has to keep in mind that it implies a certain level of abstraction. In particular, the content of the relevant agreement is not to enter a given society or to adopt a given form of government, but to accept certain moral principles. Moreover, the undertakings referred to are purely hypothetical: a contract view holds that certain principles would be accepted in a well-defined initial situation.

The merit of the contract terminology is that it conveys the idea that principles of justice may be conceived as principles that would be chosen by rational persons, and that in this way conceptions of justice may be explained and justified. The theory of justice is a part, perhaps the most significant part, of the theory of rational choice. Furthermore, principles of justice deal with conflicting claims upon the advantages won by social cooperation; they apply to the relations among several persons or groups. The word 'contract' suggests this plurality as well as the condition that the appropriate division of advantages must be in accordance with principles acceptable to all parties. The condition of publicity for principles of justice is also connoted by the contract phraseology. Thus, if these principles are the outcome of an agreement, citizens have a knowledge of the principles that others follow. It is characteristic of contract theories to stress the public nature of political principles. Finally there is the long tradition of the contract doctrine. Expressing the tie with this line of thought helps to define ideas and accords with natural piety. There are then several advantages in the use of the term 'contract'. With due precautions taken, it should not be misleading.

[n]→   A final remark. Justice as fairness is not a complete contract theory. For it is clear that the contractarian idea can be extended to the choice of more or less an entire ethical system, that is, to a system including principles for all the virtues and not only for justice. Now for the most part I shall consider only principles of justice and others closely related to them; I make no attempt to discuss the virtues in a systematic way. Obviously if justice as fairness succeeds reasonably well, a next step would be to study the more general view suggested by the name 'rightness as fairness'. But even this wider theory fails to embrace all moral relationships, since it would seem to include only our relations with other persons and to leave out of account how we are to conduct ourselves toward animals and the rest of nature. I do not contend that the contract notion offers a way to approach these questions which are certainly of the first importance: and I shall have to put them aside. We must recognize the limited scope of justice as fairness and of the general type of view that it exemplifies. How far its conclusions must be revised once these other matters are understood cannot be decided in advance.

The Original Position and Justification

I have said that the original position is the appropriate initial status quo which insures that the fundamental agreements reached in it are fair. This fact yields the name 'justice as fairness'. It is clear, then, that I want to say that one conception of justice is more reasonable than another, or justifiable with respect to it, if rational persons in the initial situation would choose its principles over those of the other for the role of justice. Conceptions of justice are to be ranked by their acceptability to persons to circumstanced. Understood in this way the question of justification is settled by working out a problem of deliberation: we have to ascertain which principles it would be rational to adopt given the contractual situation. This connects the theory of justice with the theory of rational choice.

If this view of the problem of justification is to succeed, we must, of course, describe in some detail the nature of this choice problem. A problem of rational decision has a definite answer only if we know the beliefs and interests of the parties, their relations with respect to one another, the alternatives between which they are to choose, the procedure whereby they make up their minds, and so on. As the circumstances are presented in different ways, correspondingly different principles are accepted. The concept of the original position, as I shall refer to it, is that of the most philosophically favored interpretation of this initial choice situation for the purposes of a theory of justice.

But how are we to decide what is the most favored interpretation? I assume, for one thing, that there is a broad measure of agreement that principles of justice should be chosen under certain conditions. To justify a particular description of the initial situation one shows that it incorporates these commonly shared presumptions. One argues from widely accepted but weak premises to more specific conclusions. Each of the presumptions should by itself be natural and plausible; some of them may seem innocuous or even trivial. The aim of the contract approach is to establish that taken together they impose significant bounds on acceptable principles of justice. The ideal outcome would be that these conditions determine a unique set of principles; but I shall be satisfied if they suffice to rank the main traditional conceptions of social justice.

One should not be misled, then, by the somewhat unusual conditions which characterize the original position. The idea here is simply to make vivid to ourselves the restrictions that it seems reasonable to impose on arguments for principles of justice, and therefore on these principles themselves. Thus it seems reasonable and generally acceptable that no one should be advantaged or disadvantaged by natural fortune or social circumstances in the choice of principles. It also seems widely agreed that it should be impossible to tailor principles to the circumstances of one's own case. We should insure further that particular inclinations and aspirations, and persons' conceptions of their good do not affect the principles adopted. The aim is to rule out those principles that it would be rational to propose for acceptance, however little the chance of success, only if one knew certain things that are irrelevant from the standpoint of justice. For example, if a man knew that he was wealthy, he might find it rational to advance the principle that various taxes for welfare measures be counted unjust; if he knew that he was poor, he would most likely propose the contrary principle. To represent the desired restrictions one imagines a situation in which everyone is deprived of this sort of information.

One excludes the knowledge of those contingencies which sets men at odds and allows them to be guided by their prejudices. In this manner the veil of ignorance is arrived at in a natural way. This concept should cause no difficulty if we keep in mind the constraints on arguments that it is meant to express. At any time we can enter the original position, so to speak, simply by following a certain procedure, namely, by arguing for principles of justice in accordance with these restrictions.

It seems reasonable to suppose that the parties in the original position are equal. That is, all have the same rights in the procedure for choosing principles; each can make proposals, submit reasons for their acceptance, and so on. Obviously the purpose of these conditions is to represent equality between human beings as moral persons, as creatures having a conception of their good and capable of a sense of justice. The basis of equality is taken to be similarity in these two respects. Systems of ends are not ranked in value; and each man is presumed to have the requisite ability to understand and to act upon whatever principles are adopted. Together with the veil of ignorance, these conditions define the principles of justice as those which rational persons concerned to advance their interests would consent to as equals when none are known to be advantaged or disadvantaged by social and natural contingencies.

There is, however, another side to justifying a particular description of the original position. This is to see if the principles which would be chosen match our considered convictions of justice or extend them in an acceptable way. We can note whether applying these principles would lead us to make the same judgements about the basic structure of society which we now make intuitively and in which we have the greatest confidence; or whether, in cases where our present judgements are in doubt and given with hesitation, these principles offer a resolution which we can affirm on reflection. There are questions which we feel sure must be answered in a certain way. For example, we are confident that religious intolerance and racial discrimination are unjust. We think that we have examined these things with care and have reached what we believe is an impartial judgement not likely to be distorted by an excessive attention to our own interests. These convictions are provisional fixed points which we presume any conception of justice must fit. But we have much less assurance as to what is the correct distribution of wealth and authority. Here we may be looking for a way to remove our doubts. We can check an interpretation of the initial situation, then, by the capacity of its principles to accommodate our firmest convictions and to provide guidance where guidance is needed.

In searching for the most favored description of this situation we work from both ends. We begin by describing it so that it represents generally shared and preferably weak conditions. We then see if these conditions are strong enough to yield a significant set of principles. If not, we look for further premises equally reasonable. But if so, and these principles match our considered convictions of justice, then so far well and good. But presumably there will be discrepancies. In this case we have a choice. We can either modify the account of the initial situation or we can revise our existing judgements, for even the judgements we take provisionally as fixed points are liable to revision. By going back and forth, sometimes altering the conditions of the contractual circumstances, at others withdrawing our judgements and conforming them to principle, I assume that eventually we shall find a description of the initial situation that both expresses reasonable conditions and yields principles which match our considered judgements duly pruned and adjusted. This state of affairs I refer to as reflective equilibrium.[7] It is an equilibrium because at last our principles and judgements coincide; and it is reflective since we know to what principles our judgements conform and the premises of their derivation. At the moment everything is in order. But this equilibrium is not necessarily stable. It is liable to be upset by further examination of the conditions which should be imposed on the contractual situation and by particular cases which may lead us to revise our judgements. Yet for the time being we have done what we can to render coherent and to justify our convictions of social justice. We have reached a conception of the original position.

I shall not, of course, actually work through this process. Still, we may think of the interpretation of the original position that I shall present as the result of such a hypothetical course of reflection. It represents the attempt to accommodate within one scheme both reasonable philosophical conditions on principles as well as our considered judgements of justice. In arriving at the favored interpretation of the initial situation there is no point at which an appeal is made to self-evidence in the traditional sense either of general conceptions or particular convictions. I do not claim for the principles of justice proposed that they are necessary truths or derivable from such truths. A conception of justice cannot be deduced from self-evident premises

---

[7] The process of mutual adjustment of principles and considered judgements is not peculiar to moral philosophy. See Nelson Goodman, *Fact, Fiction, and Forecast* (Cambridge, Mass., Harvard University Press, 1955), pp. 65–8, for parallel remarks concerning the justification of the principles of deductive and inductive inference.

or conditions on principles; instead, its justification is a matter of the mutual support of many considerations, of everything fitting together into one coherent view.

A final comment. We shall want to say that certain principles of justice are justified because they would be agreed to in an initial situation of equality. I have emphasized that this original position is purely hypothetical. It is natural to ask why, if this agreement is never actually entered into, we should take any interest in these principles, moral or otherwise. The answer is that the conditions embodied in the description of the original position are ones that we do in fact accept. Or if we do not, then perhaps we can be persuaded to do so by philosophical reflection. Each aspect of the contractual situation can be given supporting grounds. Thus what we shall do is to collect together into one conception a number of conditions on principles that we are ready upon due consideration to recognize as reasonable. These constraints express what we are prepared to regard as limits on fair terms of social cooperation. One way to look at the idea of the original position, therefore, is to see it as an expository device which sums up the meaning of these conditions and helps us to extract their consequences. On the other hand, this conception is also an intuitive notion that suggests its own elaboration, so that led on by it we are drawn to define more clearly the standpoint from which we can best interpret moral relationships. We need a conception that enables us to envision our objective from afar: the intuitive notion of the original position is to do this for us.

[...]

Commentary on Rawls

In the opening section of *A Theory of Justice* Rawls writes: 'Justice is the first virtue of social institutions, as truth is of systems of thought.'

What do you think he means by this claim?

A Theory of Justice is a book whose continuing influence is partly the result of its generously detailed discussions of many issues in moral and political philosophy. Limited as we are to four sections of its first chapter, we cannot properly take account of this detail, and our focus will be instead on Rawls's sketch of its central idea. In this respect, our treatment of Rawls parallels that given to Plato: the focus in each is on the general outline of their conceptions of justice. Plato's account begins from an interest in the individual virtue of justice: the task given to Socrates in Book II of the *Republic* was that of showing that justice was a virtue that each of us has reason to cultivate. In the claim above, Rawls makes clear that his focus is on justice as a virtue of a political society, and he compares its importance to that of truth in systems of thought. In a system of thought, be it scientific, moral or political, the feature that guides the development of that system is a regard to truth. Similarly, he insists, in the development of a political society, justice should be the aim.

This is no mere rhetorical flourish. Suppose someone claimed that a system of thought should be adopted only if it made its adherents happier. There certainly are those who believe this, but it is most definitely unreasonable. It would be good if the truth also made us happy, but truth comes first in any system of thought. In a precisely parallel way, Rawls claims it to be no less unreasonable to make happiness rather than justice the overriding goal of political society. For both Rawls and Plato, justice does figure in the ultimate happiness of individuals or states, but for neither thinker is happiness fundamental.

While Rawls accepts that the notion of justice has a wide range (see $\boxed{a}\mapsto$), he makes clear (at $\boxed{b}\mapsto$) that his main concern is with the virtue of justice as it shows itself in a social or political context. This contrasts with Plato who at least begins his search with the idea of justice as a virtue in individual moral agents. However, as is also true of Plato, there are significant ways in which Rawls's discussion criss-crosses between the social and the individual notions of justice. We shall return later to discuss this aspect of Rawls's account.

As a preamble to our discussion of Rawls, it is worth getting clear about the context in which justice figures. In a section preceding the selected text, he writes:

> Let us assume, to fix ideas, that a society is a more or less self-sufficient association of persons who in their relations to one another recognise certain rules of conduct as binding and who for the most part act in accordance with them. Suppose further that these rules specify a system of co-operation designed to advance the good of those taking part in it.

How does this description of a society relate to those Plato gives in Book II of the *Republic*?

There are clear resemblances between the two conceptions. Both Plato and Rawls insist that not just any association of persons is what Rawls calls a 'society' and Plato a 'state'. A society is thus not simply a group of persons living side by side. What is required in addition is that the association be one in which members cooperate to achieve their overall good. Aside from its being sensible to think of a society this way, one can see that for Plato the idea of this sort of common aim makes more plausible his comparison between the state and the individual. Rawls does not make direct use of such a comparison, but notice that he requires individuals in any society to have internalized what he calls the 'rules of conduct' which animate the joint enterprise; he speaks of individuals as 'recognizing' these rules. Thus, we can see that even at this early stage, Rawls has in mind a conception of society that shows itself both in its structure – a structure aimed at some overall goal – and in the attitudes of those who live within it.

Just after ⬚b⊢→, Rawls uses the above conception of society to tell us what he regards as the fundamental role of justice.

How does Rawls describe this role?

A good summary answer to this question is given at ⬚e⊢→. For Rawls, a conception of justice as applied to social structures is a standard that we can use to assess the distribution of the very goods these structures make possible. That is, he regards the distribution of rights, duties and the advantages of social cooperation as something built into the basic structure of any society, and justice is properly understood as the concept we must use to evaluate any such distribution.

Rawls stresses the fundamental interdependence of social structures and patterns of distribution. Moreover, even though he is primarily concerned with justice in its social, distributive sense, one should take seriously the fact that it is not merely the distribution of wealth he has in mind. In the passage between ⬚b⊢→ and ⬚c⊢→, Rawls shows that the range of things he imagines distributed by any social structure extends well beyond varieties of wealth. Including as he does rights, duties, and the effects of inequalities in ability and opportunity, he regards distributive justice as of profound importance for the development of individuals in relevant societies. Indeed, Rawls's view implies that individuals are in effect created by the basic social structure within which they live, and therefore that justice, as the notion of assessment of these social structures, is no less crucial to our assessment of moral institutions generally.

Rawls describes his project as that of uncovering the principles which would allow us to say of a society that it was perfectly just (see directly below ⬚d⊢→). This is of course no small task, and he is straightaway careful to spell out two limits to the project. The first is given at ⬚c⊢→, and the second at ⬚d⊢→.

Give a short description of each of these limitations.

The first limits the extent of his project: justice is to be discussed as a feature of the *basic* structure of a society, rather than as a feature of other institutions and practices in that society; it is also supposed that the society is *isolated* from others, so issues such as international justice are put on one side. The second limitation confirms his original description of the project: rather than looking at societies organized in ways that might be considered less than perfectly just, the supposition is that there will be 'strict compliance' with whatever principles of justice come to light. This second limitation means that

Rawls will not concern himself with all the ways there might be for dealing with injustices in a society, e.g. such topics as punishment, civil disobedience, resistance and revolution.

At $\boxed{f}\mapsto$ Rawls wonders whether his project can be said to 'tally with tradition'.

What is the tradition that Rawls has in mind here?

Citing Aristotle, Rawls takes the traditional conception of justice to be that of a pattern of action, one that depends on a character trait – a virtue – of the agent. As Rawls puts it, it is the virtue of refraining from 'gaining some advantage for oneself by seizing what belongs to another, his property, his reward, his office, and the like or by denying a person that which is due to him, the fulfilment of a promise, the repayment of a debt, the showing of proper respect'. Moreover, just as Plato developed a conception of justice different from, but recognizably connected to, this traditional conception, so Rawls intends his own project to 'tally' with this same conception.

Can you say how Rawls thinks his project makes this possible?

The key here is Rawls's claim that what individuals are entitled to – what is due to them – ultimately derives from the basic social structure in which these individuals live, and the conception of justice which governs it.

This is a crucially important claim, both for Rawls's project, and for our understanding of the concept of justice. If true, it offers us a way to understand the connection between the individual and social conceptions of justice. Further, it offers a way to do this which is arguably different from Plato's. Plato used the idea of justice in the state as a *model* for justice in the individual, whereas Rawls suggests a more direct connection. For him the entitlements needed to give substance to an individual's having the virtue of justice are put in place by the requirements of justice in the basic structure of society.

Rawls's project also links to another tradition in the literature on justice. Turning now to the 'main idea' behind the project (at $\boxed{g}\mapsto$), we are told straightaway how much it owes to the social contract approach one finds in Locke, Rousseau and Kant. However, whereas traditional contract theorists imagined individual agents whose subscription to such a contract puts in place a particular political society, Rawls sees his project as more abstract.

In what ways is this so?

There are two ways in which Rawls's project is more abstract. First, the object of the contract is not the establishment of a particular political society; instead it is the selection of the principles of justice which will govern the basic structure of any such society. And, second, the agreement is one made, not simply by individuals as we might find them, but by imagined 'free and rational' individuals who start from an 'initial position of equality'. Both of these crucial defining features of Rawls's project require further elaboration.

In the paragraph beginning at $\boxed{h}\mapsto$, Rawls explains precisely what is involved in the 'contractual' selection of principles of justice. He writes: 'Just as each person must decide by rational reflection what constitutes his good … so a group of persons must decide once and for all what is to count among them as just and unjust.'

> Is Rawls justified in seeing a parallel between these two kinds of choice?

When individuals decide what constitutes their good they must rationally weigh up such things as their resources, talents, abilities and preferences, and, taking these into account alongside their conceptions of what is valuable or worthwhile, they must decide what to do and how to live. What Rawls claims is that something of this same kind of decision process must figure when a group of persons opts for a conception of justice. However, there are two ways in which these two decision processes seem to be different. First, we have seen that Rawls imagines that the group deciding on a conception of justice must begin in an initial position of equality. We will shortly see what he requires to make this possible. But even before we consider what he says, we should be aware that this might well undermine the analogy between an individual's choice of her own good, and group choice of a conception of justice. When an agent comes to decide what is good for her, she might well take other people into account, but her decision is at bottom one that concerns herself. In the case of justice, Rawls wants each individual in the group to ask: what concept of justice do *I* prefer? But, given the pervasive effects of justice on the basic structure of society, this is not a choice that concerns only the individual agent making it.

The second disanalogy is more patent: we would generally expect a rational choice of what is good for an agent to be revisable in the light of that agent's further experience. But Rawls speaks of the choice of justice as 'once and for all'. Moreover, even aside from questions about the relationship between individual choice of good and group choice of justice, someone might wonder whether we should think of justice as something chosen once and for all, rather than something which is modified in the light of further experience.

The paragraphs marked $\boxed{i}\mapsto$ and $\boxed{j}\mapsto$ contain materials relevant to these and other worries. In the paragraph beginning at $\boxed{i}\mapsto$, Rawls first adds some detail to his account of the initial position of equality that he imposes on the choice of principles of justice.

> Rawls speaks of those in the initial position as choosing from 'behind a veil of ignorance'. What does he mean by this?

If each person in the group is fully self-aware – if each knows about his or her abilities, resources and preferences – then it is difficult to see how the choice of a conception of justice could be one made from a position of equality. Those who are more intelligent, or stronger, or more demanding of certain goods than others will shape their conception of justice so as to make sure that they come out best in the social structure determined by that conception. In order to make sure that the choice is in fact made from a position of equality, Rawls radically limits what those in the initial position can know. His thought is that, ignorant as they are of their own natures, ignorant even of their own conceptions of good, they will not be in a position to impose any special conditions on the eventual conception of justice. He writes: 'Since all are similarly situated and no one is able to design principles to favour his particular condition, the principles of justice are the result of a fair agreement or bargain.' From this he derives the idea that his is a conception of 'justice as fairness', though he is careful to note that this is not a way of saying that justice and fairness are the same concept.

The veil of ignorance certainly seems to impose a kind of fairness on the group's choice. Moreover, it goes some way to assuaging the first of the worries discussed above.

> Can you see why this might be so?

Rawls claims that the veil guarantees a 'symmetry' in the relations among those who are given the task of choosing a conception of justice. Though he doesn't put it this way, one could say that the effect of the veil is to make the group effectively homogeneous: they are, in Rawls's words, 'moral persons, . . . rational beings with their own ends', but since they don't know anything about their own natures and good, they are in effect interchangeable. This, in turn, means that there is less difference than was suggested between the case of an individual choosing her own good and a member of this group choosing principles of justice that govern everyone. For the group choice is at bottom one that could have been made by any member of the group. Each is a moral, rational agent who, ignorant of what makes herself different from any other agent, makes a choice of principles of justice that would match the choice of any other member of the group.

That said, the veil of ignorance itself introduces an additional problem for the analogy Rawls sees between an individual's choice of their own good and rational choice made by individuals in the initial position. How can we take seriously the idea of a rational choice made in ignorance of the kinds of thing on which such choice is usually based? After all, if I am told that I have to choose principles governing the distribution of rights, duties and advantages, but, behind the veil of ignorance, I am not allowed to know anything about myself, the usual grounds of choice would seem absent.

We will come to Rawls's response to this later on. But first let us turn briefly to the second worry raised earlier, the one about Rawls's insistence that choice in the initial position is 'once and for all'.

Implicit in the paragraph beginning at $\boxed{j} \mapsto$ is a possible response to this worry.

> Read the whole of that paragraph carefully and see if you can construct a response.

Rawls writes: 'a society satisfying the principles of justice as fairness comes as close as a society can to being a voluntary scheme, for it meets the principles which free and equal persons would assent to under circumstances that are fair'. Chosen under conditions of fairness, Rawls is here suggesting that even if the choice were made over again by a new generation of rational agents, they would choose the same principles. Thus, though he described the original choice as 'once and for all' the same, it would have been more accurate to say that the choice is 'over and again' the same.

Putting on one side for now problems about the circumstances of choice, let us turn to what Rawls says about the choices which equal and rational agents would make in respect of justice. As noted, the detailed exposition and defence of his conception of justice occupy most of *A Theory of Justice*. But we can get a clear enough idea of the shape of that conception from the paragraphs beginning at $\boxed{k} \mapsto$ and $\boxed{l} \mapsto$.

The first of these paragraphs does not give Rawls's own positive view, and its role is rather that of preparing the ground. Still, it is important, for what he does in that paragraph is to suggest that those in the initial position would reject a certain well-known basis for justice.

> What he thinks would be rejected is a conception of justice in which the principle of utility plays an important part. What is that principle, and why does he think it would be rejected?

If the basic structure of society were organized around a principle of utility, then, as Rawls sees it, this would mean that members of the society would be aiming for a distribution of rights, duties and advantages – what together he calls 'goods' – that was maximal. That is, if we could somehow work out the aggregate of all of these goods, then, on a utilitarian distribution, we would find it greater across the society as a whole than it would have been on any other distribution. It is Rawls's further contention that rational agents would never opt for a utilitarian distribution. He writes: 'Since each desires to protect his interests, his capacity to advance his conception of the good, no one has a reason to acquiesce in an enduring loss for himself in order to bring about a greater net balance of satisfaction.' The key here is of course the veil of ignorance. On the utilitarian distribution *some* would get a greater share of the goods, and the sum total of goods would be greater. But there could well be some members of the society who would get considerably less, and one couldn't know whether one was in the one group or the other. So, if rational, one would opt for a more equal distribution, even if this meant a smaller total sum of goods.

This point about utilitarian distribution serves as the introduction to Rawls's favoured conception of justice which he gives in the paragraph beginning at ☐ 1 ⊢→.

What conception of justice does Rawls thinks rational agents would choose?

Rawls claims that they would choose two principles which differ from one another in a crucial respect, but which together provide what he thinks the most defensible conception of justice. The first principle requires equality in the assignment of basic rights and duties, and the second requires that any divergence from equality in the distribution of social or economic goods and status can only be tolerated if this inequality works in favour of the least advantaged members of society.

The first principle is one of unqualified equality, indeed it is one of unqualifiable equality. That is, while there can be some kind of compromise within the basically egalitarian second principle, the first is not negotiable. When it comes to basic rights and duties, there can be no trade-offs, even if, after the veil of ignorance is lifted, one or another group in the society shows themselves willing to exchange some right, for example one concerning some aspect of their freedom, for economic gain. Rawls makes much of this in *A Theory of Justice*, but the non-negotiability of equality in the first principle seems to him obviously right from the start.

The second principle concerns *only* social and economic goods – not rights and duties – and is a sharp restriction on a utilitarian distribution of those goods. The latter would certainly allow quite unequal distributions, so long as the net balance in the society of these social and economic goods were greater. Rawls insists on strict equality except in the special case in which those who would end up least advantaged in fact get a larger share than they would otherwise have done.

What justification does Rawls give for these principles of justice?

Rawls asks us to imagine ourselves having to decide on principles of justice that will once and for all determine the basic structure of society. Moreover, we are to imagine that whatever is decided will substantially determine the kinds of moral agent there are in the society with that basic structure. While it is the distributive kind of justice that is of immediate concern, the individual moral virtue of justice – our individual sense of justice – is both affected by the basic distribution and figures crucially in the background to the decision. (More on this last point below.) With so much at stake, Rawls insists that the imagined decision cannot be left in the hands of those who might well aim to further their own interests. The initial position imposes a veil of ignorance on the participants, so that there is a kind of fairness in any decision they reach about justice. Rawls argues that his principles are the only ones that any rational agent would choose because only those principles are 'the result of leaving aside those aspects of the social world that seem arbitrary from a moral point of view' (see the last sentence of the paragraph beginning [l]→). Any individual making the momentous choice of principles of justice would want a notion of justice that would not severely and permanently disadvantage her if she happened not to be endowed with what we would justifiably think of as undeserved advantages such as social position, wealth or intelligence.

Independently of whether you think the two basic principles of justice that Rawls sketches are correct, there is more to be said about his way of arriving at them. This is precisely something he himself urges at [m]→, where he separates the question of our starting point – the problem of choice in the initial position – from that of the principles we would arrive at from that starting point. So, in the last part of this commentary, we will look more closely at what he says about 'the initial position and its justification'. Moreover, aside from helping us better understand Rawls's conception of justice, this investigation will suggest certain links between his and Plato's projects.

In the paragraph beginning at [o]→ Rawls reviews his earlier description of the initial position, and suggests it is the best way of setting out the conditions on rational choice that lead to a conception of justice.

> Is Rawls right to think that we can in fact best arrive at a conception of justice by seeing it as the result of rational choice in the circumstances he describes?

This question is in a way more fundamental than the question of whether the initial position and its veil of ignorance lead to Rawls's actual principles of justice. For it requires us to decide whether a group of people trying to make a rational choice of principles – a choice constrained by the veil of ignorance – is a justifiable way to ensure that the principles chosen are those of justice. Rawls insists that it is, because the principles one ends up with are those that affect the lives of every member of the group and also because, in imagining such a group in the first place, one is treating them as equal moral agents. He says (see [P]→) 'the purpose of these conditions is to represent equality between human beings as moral persons, as creatures having a conception of their good and capable of a sense of justice'. And he imposes the veil of ignorance to ensure that these conditions of equality and therefore fairness are not disturbed by the rational deliberations of the group.

Many commentators have wondered whether the veil of ignorance isn't too strong a constraint. After all, when we make a choice that will affect the course of our lives in a fundamental way, we usually have to have some idea of what we ourselves are like – what we want and need – in order to make such choice a reasonable one. Yet it would seem that the veil prevents anyone from having this knowledge. Rawls's discussion of this issue comes later in the book, but his basic response is simple enough: while veiling knowledge of the *particular* features of individuals who do the choosing, he allows them to have a clear idea of *general* features of human need, interest and desire.

> Do you think that such general knowledge is enough to make the choice of principles of justice reasonable?

This is too large a question to be answered here, but it is important to have raised it. Dealing with it forces us to consider the nature of the knowledge one must have in order to think properly about justice, and this is certainly something we must understand before we can feel comfortable with the contractual idea that Rawls advocates.

That said, the idea that justice is best seen as resulting from the rational deliberations of a collection of individuals, each equal and each having a sense of justice, can be given a rather different justification, one that Rawls considers in the paragraphs following $\boxed{q} \mapsto$. (We are here returning, as promised, to a point made earlier.) He suggests that we can test the principles rationally chosen by those in an initial position of fairness by comparing them with the intuitive conception of justice we each have. And he goes on, at $\boxed{r} \mapsto$, to describe this as working 'from both ends'.

> What does Rawls mean here by 'working from both ends'?

The paragraph beginning at $\boxed{r} \mapsto$ introduces a notion that has been taken up in philosophical discussions, not merely in ethics but more widely. Rawls dubs this notion *reflective equilibrium*, but it wouldn't be wrong to think this a merely fancier way of saying that one is exploring some concept from both 'ends' or perspectives. Whatever it is called, what is most important is that one be clear about these two perspectives, reflection on which leads to some kind of equilibrium. As Rawls explains, one is the project of imagining a group of people charged with making a rational choice about the principles of justice which will then govern the basic structure of their society. Working from this end, one puts conditions on the choice and sees what kinds of principles emerge. The other end begins with our everyday intuitions about what is just or unjust. As the introduction to this chapter suggested, neither a distribution of goods on the basis of people's looks, nor a meting out of severe punishment for walking slowly, strike us as just. Of course, there will be all sorts of cases in which our intuitions will be less clear-cut, cases in which there will be genuine conflict. Still, starting off with intuitions we can all accept, we can see whether they fit with the principles of justice got from the other end – from the imaginative project of group choice. What Rawls suggests is that, in those cases where there is no such fit, we can either change the conditions that govern the project to arrive at new principles, or we can consider jettisoning the everyday intuitions that led to conflict. It is this trade-off that, in the best case, Rawls thinks can lead to an equilibrium between principle and intuition, a reflective equilibrium.

Though not discussed in our Plato commentary, at one point Plato describes a procedure close to Rawls's notion of reflective equilibrium. A few lines below the point marked $\boxed{\text{p}}\!\!\rightarrow$ in the text of the *Republic*, Socrates notes that if we find discrepancies between our conceptions of justice in the state and in the individual, we will have to revise the one or the other. His says of this procedure that it involves rubbing sticks together so as to 'cause the sparks of justice to flash forth'. This image could well serve to describe the relationship between Rawls's project and our intuitions about justice. Rawls asks us to rub together the conception of justice got by rational choice in an initial position and the conception that comes piecemeal in the various intuitions we all have about what is, or is not, just. This is not exactly the same juxtaposition that Socrates described, but it is close. Moreover, this shared insight into a kind of reflective equilibrium is a cue for thinking more generally about the relationship between Plato's and Rawls's conceptions of justice, and we will end this commentary on justice with some reflections on this relationship.

Rawls's project aims at discovering and justifying a conception of justice that will govern the basic structure of society. Except for noting that this project is not in conflict with what he calls traditional conceptions of justice, he says little directly about justice as an individual moral virtue. Plato's project begins with the task of describing and justifying that individual virtue, though he does so by first considering that same virtue in political society. These two projects can look very different, but if one steps back a bit they are more closely related than they might at first seem. In each case, there are close and intriguing connections between these two aspects of the concept of justice.

Can you think of at least two respects in which the projects of Plato and Rawls overlap?

Plato models his conception of justice as an individual virtue on justice in the state, but there are many different ways of understanding the idea of a *model*. At its most superficial, a model merely suggests features of the notion thereby modelled. However, the interplay between the two notions of justice in the *Republic* suggests something more substantive. For example, when later in the *Republic* Plato considers various forms of injustice in states, he claims that each corresponds to a kind of unjust individual, and he seems thereby to be claiming, at a minimum, a formative influence in both directions between political society and individual characters. Rawls quite explicitly makes what is a similar point: the principles of justice that would be chosen by those in the initial position are so fundamental to the basic structure of a society that they would undoubtedly shape the characters of those living in that society.

However, it is one thing to think that the basic structure of a society shapes the characters of its members, and another to think that one and the same notion of justice applies both to societies and to those characters. Plato certainly seems to have used justice in this dual way, and, as noted in the introduction to the chapter, it is not difficult to find that use in ordinary speech. What then of Rawls's use of the notion?

On the one hand, we have seen that, though he never takes it in a narrowly distributive sense, he intends to restrict his discussion of justice to its social and political context. But, on the other hand, if you look back to the paragraph marked [n]→, Rawls claims that his conception of justice 'can be extended to the choice of an entire ethical system, that is, to a system including principles for all the virtues and not only for justice'. Though, for reasons of space, it is not something Rawls pursues, this claim suggests an interesting way in which the social and individual uses of 'justice' might be linked. As we have seen, we do sometimes speak of individuals who are morally admirable as 'just'; the word is sometimes used more or less synonymously with 'moral'. One reason for this is the pivotal role justice plays in relation to other virtues: an act of benevolence is one in which an agent contributes to another's good, but it only counts genuinely as benevolence if the contribution is compatible with justice. But Rawls's claim at [n]→ offers another reason: the contractarian idea that lies behind his theory of justice is one that also lies behind our conception of 'more or less an entire ethical system'.

In this way our notion of justice, and our notions of the other virtues that constitute morality, are linked no less closely for Rawls than for Plato. Moreover, even the ground for the linkage is, in a way, shared. Plato thought that the social and political structure of the state was a substantial model of the individual, and that this explained the connection between the social and individual notions of justice, as well as the pivotal role of the latter. Rawls never claims that the state or society is a model of the individual, but, in insisting that the device of rational social choice lies behind both justice and the ethical life generally, his account of justice can be understood, perhaps surprisingly, as broadly Platonic.

Write a few paragraphs considering ways in which Plato's and Rawls's accounts of justice resemble or differ from one another.

3

Reasons for Action

Introduction

We commonly speak about ourselves, persons we know or members of other cultures as having moral outlooks. Indeed, having something that we would recognize as a moral outlook, even if it were one highly contested, seems part of what it is to be a grown-up and non-pathological human being. But what is a moral outlook? As you would expect, this is too big a question to be answered in any substantial way in a few pages. But sketching the outlines of an answer is one useful way of bringing the issue of this chapter into sharp focus.

At the very minimum, a moral outlook is a set of opinions or views. Not opinions about just anything, but rather about a specific, if broad, subject matter. Thus, it is natural to speak about someone's moral outlook as made up of views about what makes this or that action *right*, which kinds of character traits count as *virtues*, and – not least – which of the possible ways of leading a life are *admirable* or *worthwhile*. Opinions about these topics are often expressed, and this can lead to lively discussion. But one can have a moral outlook without articulating part, or even most, of it. As can happen with other sorts of belief, those about rightness, virtue and worthwhileness often remain unarticulated, even to those whose moral outlook it is. Indeed, it might even be true – though I am not insisting on it here – that there are many elements of our moral outlooks that cannot be articulated. (There will be more about this in our discussion of the second reading in this chapter.)

While there is little doubt that a moral outlook consists in opinions, views or beliefs about a particular subject matter, this can only be part of the story. Even when we recognize that the subject matter is a special one, concerned as it is with the notions of right, virtue and worth, there is still something missing. What needs to be said in addition is that moral outlooks figure importantly in the actions and lives of those who hold them. A moral outlook is not simply a set of opinions about some subject matter, one merely suited to study and contemplation; it is related to how we act, and the choices we make.

While something of this sort needs to be said, claiming that moral out-looks 'figure importantly' in how we act and live, is unhelpfully weak. Yet, if we try to make the claim stronger by saying, for example, that the opin-ions that make up our moral outlooks determine our actions and choices, we run the risk of making ourselves seem better than we are. For, though morality is connected with acting and choosing, many of us can be found professing moral opinions without actually acting on them. Nor is this gap between thought and action rare or exceptional. What is needed, then, is some way of describing the relationship between moral outlooks and actions which is precise enough to be genuinely informative, and is at the same time not implausibly strong. It is here that the notion of a reason for action can help.

Leaving morality on one side for the moment, let's focus on the notion of a reason. A simple example will serve. Jones is sitting comfortably reading a book, when he notices that the sky is darkening, and threatens rain. He thinks about the washing that he put out on the line that morning, and realizes that if it does rain, the nearly dry washing will be soaked. It is plausible then to say that the threatening sky gives Jones a reason to go out and take the washing in. Does this mean that Jones will in fact retrieve the washing? The answer to this is by no means clear. In saying that Jones has a reason to do something, call it 'X', we are not committed to thinking that Jones will in fact do X. It is by no means uncommon for us to have reasons to do things which we do not act on. For example, Jones might recognize the threatening sky as a reason to take in the washing, but he might feel that he has a stronger reason for con-tinuing to read his book. Perhaps he is on the last chapter, and stopping now will ruin the denouement. Then again, Jones might just be, as we say, lazy: he has reason to take in the washing, but he just doesn't feel like getting out of his chair. However, whatever else we say, if our reason-giving statement is true, it stops us from thinking of Jones as a mere bystander for whom the fact about the weather is irrelevant.

Let's look a bit deeper at what makes some circumstance reason-giving. Suppose that Jones was so engrossed in his book that he didn't even notice the threatening sky. Suppose too that Jones's friend Green does notice it, and is fully aware of the threat it poses to Jones's washing. Would Green be justi-fied in saying that Jones, engaged as he is in reading, nonetheless has a reason to take in the washing? That is, does Jones himself have to be aware of how things are in respect of the weather in order for it to be true that he has a reason to take in the washing? In this case, one might think this is not so. After all, we might well think that Jones does have a reason because he put out the washing and were he to notice the weather, he would be inclined to take it in. But, as you will see, in more complex cases, the question of how knowledge (or belief) leads to an agent's reasons can be difficult to decide.

Somewhat separate from the question whether Jones's needs to be aware of a circumstance in order for it to give him a reason is the question of whether knowledge or belief – what are generally called *cognitive* states – are themselves all that are needed for reasons. Thus, some might argue that Jones's having a reason for taking in the washing does not result simply from his believing that it is about to rain, but also requires his desiring his washing dry. Obviously, most people who put out washing do want it to dry. But suppose that Jones realizes that if his laundry were soaked, he couldn't go out that evening, and further suppose that he would rather stay in. In this case, what he most wants is for it to rain on his washing, and it can seem odd to say, given this desire, that he has a reason to take the washing in. Admittedly, the circumstances are unusual, but they are not implausible. And what they seem to show is that the threat of rain only constitutes a reason for Jones to take in the washing if he *wants* his washing to be dry.

Wanting (or desiring) is a quite different kind of mental state from knowing (or believing). As noted, the latter are *cognitive* states – they are states of mind recording how things are or how they are thought to be. When such cognitive states accurately reflect how the world is we say they are true. In contrast, desires, wants, needs and the like are often called *conative* states. They do not reflect how things are, they rather indicate how some agent would like them to be. Encouraged by the story about Jones not wanting to go out that evening, one might think that a reason simply has to be a *mixture* of knowing (or believing) and desiring. That is, one might think that a reason only counts as such if it is an amalgam of the appropriate cognitive and conative mental states of an agent. But, as you will see, this is by no means a settled question. However, even our inconclusive discussion has important consequences for the earlier problem about moral outlooks.

The problem was generated by our needing to say something about how moral outlooks are related to the actions and choices of those who hold them. Recognizing it as implausible that human beings are invariably motivated by their moral outlooks to act and choose in certain ways, we need to say something less strong. But we still want what we say to be strong enough to be informative about that connection. The notion of a reason for action seems just right for this purpose.

As in our simple example, Jones could have a reason to take in the washing, even though he might well not actually be motivated to do it. Similarly, we could say that someone might have opinions about morality which constitute a moral outlook, and which give that person reasons to act and choose, even though on occasion – or even more generally – these reasons fall short of motivating action. Perhaps they are overridden by other reasons that an agent takes herself to have; or perhaps there is a kind of laziness that prevents a particular opinion that is part of her moral outlook from motivating the choice or action that it is a reason for.

This slack gives us a realistic picture of the relationship between moral outlooks and action. On the one hand, we do not have to insist that agents who hold particular moral outlooks invariably act in accordance with them. But, on the other hand, these agents are no mere bystanders – they find themselves with reasons to act that are dictated by their moral outlooks. For given that a moral outlook is a set of opinions furnishing agents with reasons, we can see them as indicators, not simply of cognitive achievement, but of character – indicators of what a person will find reason to do when faced with various moral choices.

In providing an agent with reasons for action and choice, moral outlooks are distinguished from other kinds of outlook. Those who have studied chemistry or history certainly have what we could think of as outlooks on chemical or historical matters. Indeed, if we needed to know about chemistry or history, these are precisely the sort of persons we would ask. But one can know someone to be an expert in chemistry or history without really knowing the first thing about their moral character – about the kinds of thing they will find reason to do when they are faced with moral choices. In contrast, someone who adopts a particular moral outlook seems to be taking a cognitive stance towards matters of right, virtue and worth, while at the same time being susceptible to reasons that issue from that stance.

Most would agree that the notion of a reason for action plays a crucial part in the proper characterization of a moral outlook. But as was hinted earlier, when one looks more closely at what a reason involves, agreement is more difficult to find. The contrast in the previous paragraph between history or chemistry and morality suggests that a moral outlook is essentially a set of beliefs about right, virtue and worth which by itself imposes reasons on the holder of that outlook. Yet, as we saw in the example of Jones, it is by no means clear that agents come under the sway of reasons simply because of what they know or believe, that is, simply because of their cognitive capacities. Indeed, there has been a forceful advocacy of a picture in which cognition plays at best a secondary role, and where something only comes to be a reason in the first place, if an agent has some desire, need or interest – some conative or 'pro-attitude' – directed towards the relevant action. It is precisely this sort of controversy that will be played out between Hume and McDowell in the passages below.

As a last word before getting down to work on these texts, it is worth emphasizing what is at stake. As has been suggested, the notion of a reason plays a pivotal role in moral outlooks. Just because of this, a proper conception of reasons can exert real leverage on our understanding of moral outlooks and, hence, on our understanding of morality itself. So, what might at times be a finely drawn and highly detailed discussion of the issues that separate Hume from McDowell can have substantial consequences for our understanding of moral value, character and action.

Introduction to Hume

David Hume (1711–76) was born and died in Edinburgh, but travelled extensively in the middle part of his life. He is regarded by most as the greatest philosopher who wrote in English, and by many as one of the three or four most important philosophers of all time. Both through his writings and his personality he influenced many French philosophers of the Enlightenment, and philosophers such as Immanuel Kant in Germany. Books I (Of the Understanding) and II (Of the Passions) of his *A Treatise of Human Nature* were published in 1739 (when he was twenty-eight) and Book III (Of Morals) was published a year later. Both readings come from the *Treatise* (as it is usually referred to): the first comes from Book II and the second from Book III. In addition to the *Treatise*, Hume's philosophical writings include *An Enquiry Concerning Human Understanding* (1748) and *An Enquiry Concerning the Principles of Morals* (1751), as well as many other philosophical and literary essays. Especially important, and too controversial to be published in his lifetime, is *The Dialogues Concerning Natural Religion* (1779). In addition to his enormous philosophical output, during the 1750s Hume published a six-volume *History of England*, a work that had considerable popularity, contributing to Hume's income and thereby to his independence.

David Hume, *A Treatise of Human Nature* (extracts from II.III.iii, 'Of the Influencing Motives of the Will', and III.I.i, 'Moral Distinctions Not Derived from Reason')

[…]

a →
Nothing is more usual in philosophy, and even in common life, than to talk of the combat of passion and reason, to give the preference to reason, and to assert that men are only so far virtuous as they conform themselves to its dictates. Every rational creature, 'tis said, is oblig'd to regulate his actions by reason; and if any other motive or principle challenge the direction of his conduct, he ought to oppose it, 'till it be entirely subdu'd, or at least brought to a conformity with that superior principle. On this method of thinking the greatest part of moral philosophy, ancient and modern, seems to be founded; nor is there an ampler field, as well for metaphysical arguments, as popular

declamations, than this suppos'd pre-eminence of reason above passion. The eternity, invariableness, and divine origin of the former have been display'd to the best advantage: The blindness, unconstancy and deceitfulness of the latter have been as strongly insisted on. In order to shew the fallacy of all this philosophy, I shall endeavour to prove *first*, that reason alone can never be a motive to any action of the will; and *secondly*, that it can never oppose passion in the direction of the will.

 The understanding exerts itself after two different ways, as it judges from demonstration or probability; as it regards the abstract relations of our ideas, or those relations of objects, of which experience only gives us information. I believe it scarce will be asserted, that the first species of reasoning alone is ever the cause of any action. As it's proper province is the world of ideas, and as the will always places us in that of realities, demonstration and volition seem, upon that account, to be totally remov'd, from each other. Mathematics, indeed, are useful in all mechanical operations, and arithmetic in almost every art and profession: But 'tis not of themselves they have any influence. Mechanics are the art of regulating the motions of bodies *to some design'd end or purpose*; and the reason why we employ arithmetic in fixing the proportions of numbers, is only that we may discover the proportions of their influence and operation. A merchant is desirous of knowing the sum total of his accounts with any person: Why? but that he may learn what sum will have the same *effects* in paying his debt, and going to market, as all the particular articles taken together. Abstract or demonstrative reasoning, therefore, never influences any of our actions, but only as it directs our judgement concerning causes and effects; which leads us to the second operation of the understanding.

'Tis obvious, that when we have the prospect of pain or pleasure from any object, we feel a consequent emotion of aversion or propensity, and are carry'd to avoid or embrace what will give us this uneasiness or satisfaction. 'Tis also obvious, that this emotion rests not here, but making us cast our view on every side, comprehends whatever objects are connected with its original one by the relation of cause and effect. Here then reasoning takes place to discover this relation; and according as our reasoning varies, our actions receive a subsequent variation. But 'tis evident in this case, that the impulse arises not from reason, but is only directed by it. 'Tis from the prospect of pain or pleasure that the aversion or propensity arises towards any object: And these emotions extend themselves to the causes and effects of that object, as they are pointed out to us by reason and experience. It can never in the least concern us to know, that such objects are causes, and such others effects, if both the causes and effects be indifferent to us. Where the objects themselves do not affect us, their connexion can never give them any influence; and 'tis plain, that as reason is nothing but the discovery of this connexion, it cannot be by its means that the objects are able to affect us.

[h]→ Since reason alone can never produce any action, or give rise to volition, I infer, that the same faculty is as incapable of preventing volition, or of disputing the preference with any passion or emotion. This consequence is necessary. 'Tis impossible reason cou'd have the latter effect of preventing volition, but by giving an impulse in a contrary direction to our passion; and that impulse, had it operated alone, wou'd have been able to produce volition. Nothing can oppose or retard the impulse of passion, but a contrary impulse; and if this contrary impulse ever arises from reason, that latter faculty must have an original influence on the will, and must be able to cause, as well as hinder any act of volition. But if reason has no original influence, 'tis impossible it can withstand any principle, which has such an efficacy, or ever keep the mind in suspence a moment. Thus it appears, that the principle, which opposes our passion, cannot be the same with reason, and is only call'd so in an improper sense. We speak not strictly and philosophically when we talk of the combat of passion and of reason.

[i]→ Reason is, and ought only to be the slave of the passions, and can never pretend to any other office than to serve and obey them. As this opinion may appear somewhat extraordinary, it may not be improper to confirm it by some other considerations.

[j]→ A passion is an original existence, or, if you will, modification of existence, and contains not any representative quality, which renders it a copy of any other existence or modification. When I am angry, I am actually possest with the passion, and in that emotion have no more a reference to any other object, than when I am thirsty, or sick, or more than five foot high. 'Tis impossible, therefore, that this passion can be oppos'd by, or be contradictory to truth and reason; since this contradiction consists in the disagreement of ideas, consider'd as copies, with those objects, which they represent.

What may at first occur on this head, is, that as nothing can be contrary to truth or reason, except what has a reference to it, and as the judgements of our understanding only have this reference, it must follow, that passions can be contrary to reason only so far as they are *accompany'd* with some judgement or opinion. According to this principle, which is so obvious and natural, 'tis only in two senses, that

[k]→ any affection can be call'd unreasonable. First, When a passion, such as hope or fear, grief or joy, despair or security, is founded on the supposition of the existence of objects, which really do not exist. Secondly, When in exerting any passion in action, we chuse means insufficient for the design'd end, and deceive ourselves in our judgement of causes

and effects. Where a passion is neither founded on false suppositions, nor chuses means insufficient for the end, the understanding can neither justify nor condemn it. 'Tis not contrary to reason to prefer the destruction of the whole world to the scratching of my finger. 'Tis not contrary to reason for me to chuse my total ruin, to prevent the least uneasiness of an *Indian* or person wholly unknown to me. 'Tis as little contrary to reason to prefer even my own acknowledg'd lesser good to my greater, and have a more ardent affection for the former than the latter. A trivial good may, from certain circumstances, produce a desire superior to what arises from the greatest and most valuable enjoyment; nor is there any thing more extraordinary in this, than in mechanics to see one pound weight raise up a hundred by the advantage of its situation. In short, a passion must be accompany'd with some false judgement, in order to its being unreasonable; and even then 'tis not the passion, properly speaking, which is unreasonable, but the judgement.

The consequences are evident. Since a passion can never, in any sense, be call'd unreasonable, but when founded on a false supposition, or when it chuses means insufficient for the design'd end, 'tis impossible, that reason and passion can ever oppose each other, or dispute for the government of the will and actions. The moment we perceive the falshood of any supposition, or the insufficiency of any means our passions yield to our reason without any opposition. I may desire any fruit as of an excellent relish; but whenever you convince me of my mistake, my longing ceases. I may will the performance of certain actions as means of obtaining any desir'd good; but as my willing of these actions is only secondary, and founded on the supposition, that they are causes of the propos'd effect; as soon as I discover the falshood of that supposition, they must become indifferent to me.

'Tis natural for one, that does not examine objects with a strict philosophic eye, to imagine, that those actions of the mind are entirely the same, which produce not a different sensation, and are not immediately distinguishable to the feeling and perception. Reason, for instance, exerts itself without producing any sensible emotion; and except in the more sublime disquisitions of philosophy, or in the frivolous subtilties of the schools, scarce ever conveys any pleasure or uneasiness. Hence it proceeds, that every action of the mind, which operates with the same calmness and tranquillity, is confounded with reason by all those, who judge of things from the first view and appearance. Now 'tis certain, there are certain calm desires and tendencies, which, tho' they be real passions, produce little emotion in the mind, and are more known by their effects than by the immediate feeling or sensation. These desires are of two kinds; either certain instincts originally implanted in our natures, such as benevolence and resentment, the love of life, and kindness to children; or the general appetite to good, and aversion to evil, consider'd merely as such. When any of these passions are calm, and cause no disorder in the soul, they are very readily taken for the determinations of reason, and are suppos'd to proceed from the same faculty, with that, which judges of truth and falshood. Their nature and principles have been suppos'd the same, because their sensations are not evidently different.

[...]

It has been observ'd, that nothing is ever present to the mind but its perceptions; and that all the actions of seeing, hearing, judging, loving, hating, and thinking, fall under this denomination. The mind can never exert itself in any action, which we may not comprehend under the term of *perception*; and consequently that term is no less applicable to those judgements, by which we distinguish moral good and evil, than to every other operation of the mind. To approve of one character, to condemn another, are only so many different perceptions.

Now as perceptions resolve themselves into two kinds, viz. *impressions* and *ideas*, this distinction gives rise to a question, with which we shall open up our present enquiry concerning morals, *Whether 'tis by means of our* ideas *or* impressions *we distinguish betwixt vice and virtue, and pronounce an action blameable or praise-worthy?* This will immediately cut off all loose discourses and declamations, and reduce us to something precise and exact on the present subject.

Those who affirm that virtue is nothing but a conformity to reason; that there are eternal fitnesses and unfitnesses of things, which are the same to every rational being that considers them; that the immutable measures of right and wrong impose an obligation, not only on human creatures, but also on the Deity himself: All these systems concur in the opinion, that morality, like truth, is discern'd merely by ideas, and by their juxta-position and comparison. In order, therefore, to judge of these systems, we need only consider, whether it be possible, from reason alone, to distinguish betwixt moral good and evil, or whether there must concur some other principles to enable us to make that distinction.

If morality had naturally no influence on human passions and actions, 'twere in vain to take such pains to inculcate it; and nothing wou'd be more fruitless than that multitude of rules and precepts, with which all moralists abound. Philosophy is commonly divided

into *speculative* and *practical*; and as morality is always compre-
hended under the latter division, 'tis supposed to influence our passions and actions, and to go beyond the calm and indolent judgements
of the understanding. And this is confirm'd by common experience,
which informs us, that men are often govern'd by their duties, and are
deter'd from some actions by the opinion of injustice, and impell'd to
others by that of obligation.

[q]→ Since morals, therefore, have an influence on the actions and affections, it follows, that they cannot be deriv'd from reason; and that
because reason alone, as we have already prov'd, can never have any
such influence. Morals excite passions, and produce or prevent
actions. Reason of itself is utterly impotent in this particular. The
rules of morality, therefore, are not conclusions of our reason.

No one, I believe, will deny the justness of this inference; nor is
there any other means of evading it, than by denying that principle,
on which it is founded. As long as it is allow'd, that reason has no
influence on our passions and actions, 'tis in vain to pretend, that
morality is discover'd only by a deduction of reason. An active prin-
[r]→ ciple can never be founded on an inactive; and if reason be inactive in
itself, it must remain so in all its shapes and appearances, whether it
exerts itself in natural or moral subjects, whether it considers the
powers of external bodies, or the actions of rational beings.

It would be tedious to repeat all the arguments, by which I have
prov'd,[1] that reason is perfectly inert, and can never either prevent or
produce any action or affection. 'Twill be easy to recollect what has
been said upon that subject. I shall only recall on this occasion one of
these arguments, which I shall endeavour to render still more conclusive,
and more applicable to the present subject.

Reason is the discovery of truth or falshood. Truth or falshood
consists in an agreement or disagreement either to the *real* relations of
ideas, or to *real* existence and matter of fact. Whatever, therefore, is
not susceptible of this agreement or disagreement, is incapable of
being true or false, and can never be an object of our reason. Now 'tis
evident our passions, volitions, and actions, are not susceptible of any
such agreement or disagreement; being original facts and realities,
compleat in themselves, and implying no reference to other passions,
volitions, and actions. 'Tis impossible, therefore, they can be pronounced
either true or false, and be either contrary or conformable to reason.

[s]→ This argument is of double advantage to our present purpose. For it
proves *directly*, that actions do not derive their merit from a conformity

---

[1] Book II. Part III. sect. iii. See above pp. 148–52.

to reason, nor their blame from a contrariety to it; and it proves the same truth more *indirectly*, by shewing us, that as reason can never immediately prevent or produce any action by contradicting or approving of it, it cannot be the source of moral good and evil, which are found to have that influence. Actions may be laudable or blameable; but they cannot be reasonable or unreasonable: Laudable or blameable, therefore, are not the same with reasonable or unreasonable. The merit and demerit of actions frequently contradict, and sometimes controul our natural propensities. But reason has no such influence. Moral distinctions, therefore, are not the offspring of reason. Reason is wholly inactive, and can never be the source of so active a principle as conscience, or a sense of morals.

But perhaps it may be said, that tho' no will or action can be immediately contradictory to reason, yet we may find such a contradiction in some of the attendants of the action, that is, in its causes or effects. The action may cause a judgement, or may be *obliquely* caus'd by one, when the judgement concurs with a passion; and by an abusive way of speaking, which philosophy will scarce allow of, the same contrariety may, upon that account, be ascrib'd to the action. How far this truth or falshood may be the source of morals, 'twill now be proper to consider.

[...]

Commentary on Hume

As noted, the first extract comes from Book II of the *Treatise*, and it is not directly concerned with morality. Still, as was true of our discussion of Jones and his washing, we can gain insight into the notion of a reason from contexts not directly concerned with morality; insight which comes eventually to determine what we say about specifically moral reasons. You can think of the two Hume extracts in the same way: in the first he offers us a general conception of reasons, and in the second he applies it to the special case of morality.

In the paragraph beginning at [a]↦ Hume sets out what he takes to be the standard or traditional view of the relationship between reason and passion.

> Say in your own words what that view is.

Hume insists that the standard view which sees reason as often locked in combat with passion is mistaken. We will come to this. But before we do, it is important to understand what Hume means by each of *reason* and *passion*. Let's begin with the latter.

In the opening section of Book II (Of the Passions), Hume writes:

> As all the perceptions of the mind may be divided into impressions and
> ideas, so the impressions admit of another division into original and
> secondary. ... Original impressions or impressions of sensation are such
> as without any antecedent perception arise in the soul, from the consti-
> tution of the body, from the animal spirits, or from the application of
> objects to the external organs. Secondary, or reflective impressions are
> such as proceed from some of these original ones, either immediately or
> by the interposition of its idea. Of the first kind are all the impressions
> of the senses, and all bodily pains and pleasures: Of the second are the
> passions, and other emotions resembling them.[1]

Unless you have some familiarity with Book I of the *Treatise*, the terminology
that Hume uses here is bound to be opaque. However, without getting too
deeply involved, we can gloss what he says as follows. The contents of any
human mind (Hume calls these contents 'perceptions') can be classified in
several ways. One way which Hume discussed at length in Book I is the division
of perceptions into *impressions* and *ideas*. An impression is some lively mental
episode such as the sensations we experience of light, colour, pressure, smell –
what we think of as effects of the world on our senses – as well as sensations
of our own bodies, including those of pain and pleasure. It also includes, as
will be discussed below, certain of the passions or emotions. In contrast, an
idea for Hume is a less vivid, less lively, copy of an impression; it is that
mental item held in the mind after the impression has passed, and is made
available to us by memory and imagination. Ideas are important in helping us
understand Hume's notion of reason, but for now let's continue with our
attempt to understand what he means by passions.

In the passage from the opening of Book II cited above, Hume divides
impressions into those which are *original* and those *secondary*. Original
impressions are those which result, as Hume writes, 'from the constitution of
the body, from the animal spirits, or from the application of objects to the
external organs'. These include the sensory sensations and bodily awareness
of pleasures and pains listed above. A secondary impression is one which is
triggered either directly by some original one or by some intervening idea.
That is, these have the liveliness required of impressions, but they are triggered by the experience of some other impression, or by our entertaining
some idea. Hume counts the emotions and passions as secondary impressions.
Some examples might help make this clearer.

Imagine that you experience a bodily pain – you have a pain impression –
when you touch a hot object. Hume suggests that this pain impression might

---

[1] *Treatise*, II, I, i.

trigger an impression of disagreeableness, an impression which leads you to pull your hand away. This secondary impression counts for Hume as the direct passion or emotion he calls aversion. Other examples of these second-ary, but direct, impressions include desire, grief, joy, hope and fear.

Imagine next that you call to mind an idea, say, the idea of some project you have successfully completed. This idea might give rise to a certain impression, say, an impression of pleasure or contentment, and Hume counts this impression as indirect (because it follows an idea, not another impression) and thinks of this further impression as the passion or emotion of pride. Other such indirect passions include vanity, love, hatred, envy, pity and malice. Unlike the direct passions, these depend on the idea that gives rise to them. An impression of pleasure only counts as pride if it is brought about by the idea of something for which you are in some sense responsible. Pleasure brought about by the idea of a sunset cannot count as pride.

Leaving aside the details, what is important for understanding Hume's arguments about the relation between reason and passion is his view of passion or emotion as mental features which are essentially vivid – emotions are impressions – and which have the capacity to move us. Thus, Hume counts desires for various things, as well as aversion to them, as basic or direct emotions, and finds these implicated in a whole range of further, secondary emotions such as pride.

Look now at the passage marked $\boxed{b}\rightarrow$. Hume here outlines the shape of the argument against the traditional idea that reason is in more or less constant battle with passion.

What are the key notions that figure in this outline?

The link between the two points that Hume makes is that of the will. He first insists that reason cannot by itself influence the will, and next that reason cannot oppose the influence on the will exerted by passion. Implicit in all this is the idea that one or another of the passions, as described above, do in fact influence the will. More specifically, Hume assumes that desire, or aversion – or some elaboration of these indirect emotions such as love, hatred or pride – have the capacity to initiate action, and that reason lacks this capacity. We will examine Hume's insistence on this relation between passion and will shortly, but first a few comments about Hume's notion of reason.

The sentence marked $\boxed{c}\rightarrow$ encapsulates what we need to know about Hume's conception of reason. In that sentence, Hume speaks of the 'under-standing', but throughout the *Treatise*, he uses 'reason', 'reasoning' and 'understanding' more or less interchangeably. The basic idea is that reason or, equivalently, the understanding, aspires to knowledge, and in Book I (Of the Understanding) Hume offers an account of the origins and nature of such knowledge. What he says at ⌐c⌐→ is a summary of that account. Such knowledge as we have has one of two sources: it arises directly from an investigation of ideas – this is what he calls demonstration; or it arises from our recognition of the connections among ideas that figure in experience – this is what he means by probability. A good example of the first is geometric knowledge. If we look into the very idea of a triangle, we discover that the three internal angles of any triangle have 180°. This is something proved by Euclid, and Hume regards this, and other mathematical knowledge, as a perfect example of knowledge by demonstration. A good example of the second is our knowledge that fire burns wood. Unlike the geometrical case, we cannot determine that fire burns wood just by examining the idea of fire. However, through experience, we have come to connect the idea of fire with the idea of violent combustion of wood that is our idea of burning. Because this connection depends on experience, it lacks the certainty of demonstrative reasoning; it is therefore characterized as probabilistic.

For our purposes, it is not important to go further into the details of these two sources of knowledge. All one needs to keep in mind is that for Hume the proper role of reason, or, equivalently, the understanding, is the acquisition of knowledge, and that demonstration and probabilistic reasoning are the two ways to get it.

Let's now return to Hume's arguments against the traditional view of the opposition between reason and passion. These arguments determine the shape of Hume's account of motivation, and, once we have got hold of this, we will be in a position to grasp the consequences of that account for morality.

At ⌐d⌐→, Hume claims that the result of any piece of *demonstrative* reasoning cannot by itself motivate us to act, and he offers as his reason for this the sentence beginning at ⌐e⌐→.

Do you find his reason compelling?

Many people do find it compelling. Thus, someone who comes to know, for example, that $12 \times 72 = 864$ has used reason to acquire this piece of knowledge. But there doesn't seem to be anything intrinsically motivating about what is thereby known. If we are told that someone has acquired knowledge of this arithmetical fact, we would not thereby think he would act or have reason to act one way rather than another. That is, we wouldn't expect such action unless we had some independent grasp of his desires, aversions, likes, dislikes, needs, etc. – things that Hume has classified as passions or emotions. Hume's example (at ⌐f⌐→) of the merchant who works out his account with some client is intended as a concrete illustration of the fact that demonstrative reasoning – by itself – does not initiate action. But he allows that this same example might reveal a role for the second aspect of reason – probabilistic reasoning – in influencing the will. But does it?

According to Hume, probabilistic reasoning is responsible for our recognizing cause–effect relationships, a recognition fundamental to the conduct of any human life. The earlier example of fire and burning is one simple instance, but a moment's reflection would reveal that we couldn't so much as function in the world if we couldn't depend, as we do, on a kind of regularity in the events which take place within it. Confidently putting one foot in front of the other as you walk down the street depends upon your expectations of the continued support of the ground. Yet, in spite of the importance of cause–effect reasoning, Hume insists (at $\boxed{g}\!\rightarrow$) that it does not by itself influence the will, that it is not itself a motive force behind actions.

> Crucial to Hume's claim at $\boxed{g}\!\rightarrow$ is what he says just before this. Is what he says convincing?

As with his earlier claim about the secondary role of demonstrative reasoning, Hume doesn't so much argue for his view as assert it. In the text just above $\boxed{g}\!\rightarrow$ he says that 'the impulse [to an action] arises not from reason, but is only directed by it', and he goes on to insist that the prospect of pleasure and pain, and the passion that this prospect gives rise to, is what is ultimately responsible for the relevant 'impulse'. If you find what he says plausible – and, as noted above, many do – then you might well be convinced. But, strictly speaking, Hume has offered no independent argument for his insistence that reason alone cannot direct action. That is, he has as yet offered no argument which might convince someone who didn't already agree with him.

We will consider below how he tries to bolster the position, but first have a look at the paragraph beginning at $\boxed{h}\!\rightarrow$. In this paragraph, Hume argues that we are not justified in speaking 'strictly and philosophically' of the combat between reason and passion. And near the end of this paragraph he makes a claim (at $\boxed{i}\!\rightarrow$) that has echoed for more than two hundred years in discussions of morality.

> Explain what he means by the claim that reason is the 'slave of the passions'. Does his claim here go beyond those discussed earlier?

The consequences for morality of Hume's claims about reason and passion figure in the second Hume text (from *Treatise*, Book III). But we are not yet done with Hume's discussion of reasons and motivation, and must now consider the way in which Hume attempts to strengthen his argument for the motivational impotency of reason. He recognizes that this needs doing – see the sentence after the one marked $\boxed{i}\!\rightarrow$; and at $\boxed{j}\!\rightarrow$ he sets about doing it.

> What do you think Hume means by claiming that a passion is an original existence? (This is not an easy question to answer without some background, though you should get some inkling of how to go about it just from reading the paragraph beginning at $\boxed{j}\!\rightarrow$.)

When we describe someone as having a thought or belief, our description specifies what that thought or belief is about – its content – and this content is not optional. Saying merely that George has a belief is not enough: in describing George's state of mind, it is necessary to say more – to say, for example, that he has the belief *that today will be sunny*. The idea that thoughts and beliefs have such content is what Hume is alluding to when he speaks about their 'representative quality'. George's belief represents that today will be sunny – his belief represents in a specific way how things are or might be – and this representative aspect is what accounts for beliefs being judged true or false. Moreover, it is this representative aspect that Hume denies to the passions when he describes them as 'original existences'. Thus, he says that when someone is angry, what is felt has 'no reference to any other object'. This of course doesn't mean that the anger isn't directed at something, or indeed caused by something. It simply means that the state of anger, unlike the state of believing, cannot be judged to be true or false, accurate or inaccurate. For an experience or state to be an original existence is, for Hume, for it to lack any pretension to represent how things are. That is why he says that being thirsty, sick or more than five foot high are also original existences.

The distinction between original existences and those that represent allows Hume to mount what he thinks is his most telling argument against the idea of a combat between reason and passion. In outline, the argument runs as follows: (i) the states of mind that reason generates are representational, and they can be judged to be true or false; (ii) any state of mind which supports reason does so by supporting the truth of its judgements, and conflicts with reason by contradicting that supposed truth; (iii) passions, not being representational, cannot directly either support or conflict with reason, and can only be contrary to reason if they are accompanied by judgements of reason. Only these latter have the representational feature necessary for such conflict. So, passions cannot really support or conflict with reason.

> At $\boxed{k} \rightarrow$, Hume considers two circumstances in which a passion can be called unreasonable, and neither of these undermines the above argument. Explain what these two circumstances are, and say whether you think what Hume says about them is true.

In a very famous passage beginning at $\boxed{l} \rightarrow$ Hume states the conclusion of his argument with a grand rhetorical flourish.

> Do think that what Hume says about our preferences in these examples is right?

Whatever one's intuitions about Hume's examples, he presses his point home with several further observations about the passion of desire or preference.

What is Hume's explanation for the fact that an apparently weak desire can sometimes gain the upper hand in influencing the will?

In the paragraph beginning at $\boxed{m}$→, Hume re-states his argument. He then devotes the remaining three paragraphs of Section iii to explaining why it is so natural to confuse the products of reason and passion, and to thus conclude – he thinks mistakenly – that they can be in conflict with each other.

What role does his notion of a 'calm passion' play in this explanation?

Hume both insists and argues that passions – desires, loves, hates, among others – are what move us to act, and that, while reason might well guide our actions, it cannot by itself ever initiate them. This view, interesting in itself, figures centrally in Hume's account of morality, and for this we turn now to the second extract from the *Treatise*.

The first two paragraphs of the second Hume extract re-state his general account of what is 'present to the mind'. Hume calls these contents of the mind *perceptions*, using this term to cover thinking and judging, desiring, hating and loving, as well as what we would most naturally think of as per-ceptions, such as hearing and seeing. This re-statement leads him to pose a question about morality (at $\boxed{n}$→), and Hume stresses the importance of this question by putting it in italics.

Can you spell out Hume's question in your own words?

As Hume makes clear in the paragraph beginning at $\boxed{o}$→, he imagines that many will answer this question affirmatively: they will insist that reason – the juxtaposition and comparison of ideas – is the origin of the obligations that morality imposes on us. But Hume thinks he can demonstrate that this is not so. In the next few paragraphs he uses the arguments about reason and pas-sion from Book II in answering the question at $\boxed{n}$→ negatively. Because we have already examined these arguments, it will be easy to see how Hume uses them in the present context.

The key to the transfer of these arguments is in the paragraph beginning at $\boxed{p}$→, and you should try to summarize the point made in that paragraph.

At $\boxed{q}$→ Hume both summarizes the point of the previous paragraph and employs it in answering his question at $\boxed{n}$→. In the previous paragraph, he claimed it to be a matter of 'common experience' that morals do influence action, that we are often governed by what we take to be our duties, and are deterred or impelled to act in various ways on the basis of our assessment of certain actions as just or unjust. As he puts it in the paragraph beginning at $\boxed{q}$⊢→, 'morals excite passions, and produce or prevent actions'. However, Hume takes himself to have established in Book II that reason alone cannot excite passions – cannot produce or prevent actions. The processes of thinking through our ideas and juxtaposing them – what Hume calls reasoning – can lead us to knowledge, or at least belief, about the world, but these mental items do not *by themselves* initiate any action. Hume then draws the conclusion that morals, by which he means the recognition of our duties, views about justice and injustice as well as right and wrong, cannot themselves be the products of reason. As he says at $\boxed{r}$⊢→: 'An active principle [here he means our appreciation of morals] can never be founded on an inactive [by which he means reason].'

Two paragraphs later, after summarizing his arguments concerning the supposed combat of reason and passion, he notes (at $\boxed{s}$⊢→) that there is a 'double advantage' to be got from applying these arguments to the case of morals.

What do you think are the two advantages he speaks of?

Hume insists that there are two argumentative strands supporting his contention that reason is not the source of morality. The first one – he describes it as the direct one – is that reason cannot deliver verdicts about the justness or rightness of any action. This strand relies on Hume's view that actions and the passions which motivate them are not representations: unlike a belief, an action or a passion does not represent things as being a certain way. Thus, an action or a passion cannot derive whatever merit it has from 'conformity to reason', i.e. from such an action or passion being a correct representation.

The second strand is the one Hume characterizes as 'indirect'. Leaving on one side the issue of the representational nature of actions or passions, Hume takes himself to have shown that reason cannot by itself initiate actions. Only passions – desires, emotions and the like – can do that. However, given that morality is bound up with actions and the motivations we have for them, the sole basis for morality cannot be reason.

Together, Hume's arguments have had an enormous influence on how philosophers have come to think about morality. Moreover, they are quite novel: though philosophers have struggled from the beginning with the undoubted link between morality and action, Hume is perhaps the first to exploit that link to put limits on the role of reason in morality.

One can appreciate why many feel a reluctance to credit the whole of what makes up a moral outlook to human cognitive capacities, that is, the capacities to acquire belief and knowledge about the world. Surely, as was discussed in the introduction to this chapter, morality is not merely a matter of knowing or believing certain things; it is as much and crucially a matter of living and acting in accordance with what one knows. Or if, as was noted, that is misleadingly strong, it is a matter of finding, in such knowledge and belief, reasons or demands for living and acting in certain ways, whether or not we live up to those demands. What we have seen in Hume's *Treatise* is an attempt to go beyond mere reluctance here. His arguments are intended to make us give up the very idea that a moral outlook could be something purely cognitive, that such an outlook could be solely the product of those cognitive capacities that Hume calls 'reason' or 'understanding'. For him, a moral outlook is at bottom an expression of our passions – an expression of the desires and emotions we bring to our reasoned contemplation of the world. As he says in the section of the *Treatise* following the second of our two extracts, 'morality is more properly felt than judged of'.

Introduction to McDowell

John McDowell, born in 1942, is currently Professor of Philosophy in the University of Pittsburgh, having started his career at University College, Oxford. In the past three decades, McDowell has made major contributions to philosophy of language, philosophy of mind, metaphysics, epistemology, and, more pertinently to the present chapter, to moral philosophy. In 1994 he published a version of the John Locke lectures that he gave in Oxford in 1991 under the title *Mind and World* and this book has become a source, inspiration and target for philosophical discussions across the academic world. He has also published two important collections of his papers: *Mind, Language and Reality* (1999) and *Mind, Value and Reality* (1998), and the selection comes from the latter volume.

The text below focuses on the issue of the linkages between moral judgement and reasons for action raised by Hume, but the article from which it is excerpted has broader aims. In the commentary which follows, something will be said about this, but it should be possible to understand the central points made with only minimal grasp of their fuller context.

John McDowell, 'Are Moral Requirements Hypothetical Imperatives?' (extracts)

[…]

a ↦   I suppose the general doubt is on these lines. A view of how things
b ↦   are is a state or disposition of one's cognitive equipment. But the psychological states we are considering are to suffice, on their own, to show how certain actions appeared in a favourable light. That requires that their possession entails a disposition of the possessor's will. And will and

---

Editor's note: The original footnotes have been renumbered as some sources have been added.

belief – the appetitive and the cognitive – are distinct existences; so a state that presents itself as cognitive but entails an appetitive state must be, after all, only impurely cognitive, and contain the appetitive state as a part. If such a state strikes its possessor as cognitive, that is because he is projecting his states of will on to the world (a case of the mind's propensity to spread itself upon objects). The appetitive state should be capable in principle of being analysed out, leaving a neutrally cognitive residue. Thus where it appears that a conception of how things are exhausts an agent's reason for acting in a certain way, an analysed and less misleading formulation of the reason will be bipartite: it will specify, first, a neutral conception of the facts, available equally to someone who sees no reason to act in the way in question, and second, a desire, which combines with that conception of the facts to make the action attractive to its possessor.

[c] → This paper is primarily addressed to those who are vulnerable to the *ad hominem* argument. In their view, since the line of thought I have just sketched falsifies the workings of prudential explanations of behaviour, it simply cannot be generally right. In the rest of this section I shall make some remarks, not *ad hominem*, about the general issue; but a proper discussion is impossible here.

There is room for scepticism about whether it is acceptable to discount the appearances in the way the objection urges. Explanation of behaviour by reasons purports to show the favourable light in which an [d] → agent saw his action. If it strikes an agent that his reason for acting as he does consists entirely in his conception of the circumstances in which he acts, then an explanation that insists on analysing that seemingly cognitive state into a less problematically cognitive state combined with a separate desire, while it will show the action as attractive from the standpoint of the psychological states it cites, is not obviously guaranteed to get the favourable light right. If one accepts an explanation of the analysing sort, one will not be baffled by inability to find any point one can take the agent to have seen in behaving as he did; but what leaves one unpuzzled is not thereby shown to be a *correct* explanation.

[e] → The analysis will nevertheless seem compulsory, if the objection seems irresistible. If the world is, in itself, motivationally inert, and is also the proper province of cognitive equipment, it is inescapable that a strictly cognitive state – a conception of how things are, properly so called – cannot constitute the whole of a reason for acting. But the idea of the world as motivationally inert is not an independent hard datum. It is simply the metaphysical counterpart of the thesis that states of will and cognitive states are distinct existences, which is exactly what is in question.

If a conception of a set of circumstances can suffice on its own to explain an action, then the world view it exemplifies is certainly not the kind of thing that could be established by the methods of the natural sciences. But the notion of the world, or how things are, that is appropriate in this context is a metaphysical notion, not a scientific one: world views richer than that of science are not scientific, but not on that account unscientific (a term of opprobrium for answers other than those of science to science's questions). To query their status as world views on the ground of their not being scientific is to be motivated not by science but by scientism.

f⟶ **6.** It is not to be denied that behaviour that is in fact virtuous can in some cases be found unsurprising through being what one would expect anyway, given an acceptably ascribed desire that is independently intelligible. That is why sheer bafflement at virtuous behaviour in general is very difficult to imagine. At some points even the rankest outsider would be able to attain a measure of comprehension of virtuous actions in terms of desires that people just naturally have: for instance the desire that people related to them in various ways should not suffer. Such coincidences constitute possible points of entry for an outsider trying to work his way into appreciation of a moral outlook. Similarly, they perhaps partly explain how it is possible to acquire a moral outlook of one's own (not the same topic, since one can understand a moral outlook without sharing it).

g⟶ What is questionable is whether there need *always* be an independently intelligible desire to whose fulfilment a virtuous action, if rational at all, can be seen as conducive.

h⟶ Charitable behaviour aims at an end, namely the good of others, (See Foot 'Morality as a System of Hypothetical Imperatives', p. 165.[1]) It does not follow that a full specification of the agent's reason for a charitable act would need to add a desire to his conception of the circumstances in which he acted. For prudent behaviour equally aims at an end, namely one's own future happiness. The desire for the good of others is related to charity as the desire for one's own future happiness is related to prudence; not, then, as a needed extra ingredient in formulations of reasons for acting. Rather, the desire is ascribed, as in the prudential case, simply in recognition of the fact that a charitable person's special way of conceiving situations by itself casts a favourable light on charitable actions. Of course a desire ascribed in this purely consequential way is not independently intelligible.

i⟶ It does not seem plausible that any purely natural fellow-feeling or benevolence, unmediated by the special ways of seeing situations that are characteristic of charity as it is thought of above, would issue in

---

[1]   P. Foot, *Virtues and Vices* (Oxford: Blackwell, 1978).

j→ behaviour that exactly matched that of a charitable person; the objects of a purely natural benevolence could not be guaranteed to coincide in all cases with the good of others as a possessor of the virtue would conceive it. It seems still less plausible that virtuous behaviour in general could be duplicated by means of the outcomes of independently intelligible desires.

Mrs Foot sometimes seems to suggest that if someone acts in a way he takes to be morally required, and his behaviour cannot be shown to be rational as a case of conformity to a hypothetical imperative, then he must be blindly obeying an inculcated code. (See 'Reasons for Action and Desires', p. 155: 'Perhaps we have been bewitched by the idea that we *just do* have reason to obey this part of our moral code'.[2] She does not endorse this thought, which is about honesty; but she seems to put it forward as the sole alternative to the thought that we should explain honest behaviour in terms of desires.) But if we deny that virtuous behaviour can always be explained as the outcome of independently intelligible desires, we do not thereby commit ourselves

k→ to its being mere obedience to a code. There need be no possibility of reducing virtuous behaviour to rules. In moral upbringing what one learns is not to behave in conformity with rules of conduct, but to see situations in a special light, as constituting reasons for acting; this perceptual capacity, once acquired, can be exercised in complex novel circumstances, not necessarily capable of being foreseen and legislated for by a codifier of the conduct required by virtue, however wise and thoughtful he might be.

On this view, independently intelligible desires will take an outsider only some of the distance towards full understanding of virtuous behaviour. In the first place, there will be some actions that simply cannot be explained as the outcomes of such desires. Second, if one sticks with explanations in terms of independently intelligible desires at the points of entry, where such explanations do make actions unpuzzling, one will not have the full picture even of those actions: if they manifest a virtuous person's distinctive way of seeing things, they must be explicable also in terms of exercises of that perceptual capacity, which need no supplementing with desires to yield full specifications of reasons. (This need not imply that the initial explanations, at the points of entry, were wrong. Someone can have two separate reasons for what he does; perhaps he can do it for both of them. If so, we need not suppose – as Kant perhaps did – that an action's being the outcome of a natural desire disqualifies it as a manifestation of virtue.)

---

[2] Ibid.

[l]→ §4 suggests that if someone could not see the force of prudential considerations, one might appropriately protest: 'You don't know what it means for a fact to concern your future.' Rather similarly, in urging behaviour one takes to be morally required, one finds oneself saying things like this: 'You don't know what it means that someone is shy and sensitive.' Conveying what a circumstance means, in this loaded sense, is getting someone to see it in the special way in which a virtuous person would see it. In the attempt to do so, one exploits contrivances similar to those one exploits in other areas where the task is to back up the injunction 'See it like this': helpful juxtapositions of cases, descriptions with carefully chosen terms and carefully placed emphasis, and the like. (Compare, for instance, what one might do and say to someone who says 'Jazz sounds to me like a mess, a mere welter of uncoordinated noise.') No such contrivances can be guaranteed success, in the sense that failure would show irrationality on the part of the audience. That, together with the importance of rhetorical skills to their successful deployment, sets them apart

[m]→ from the sorts of thing we typically regard as paradigms of argument. But these seem insufficient grounds for concluding that they are appeals to passion as opposed to reason: for concluding that 'See it like this' is really a covert invitation to feel, quite over and above one's view of the facts, a desire that will combine with one's belief to recommend acting in the appropriate way.

  Failure to see what a circumstance means, in the loaded sense, is of course compatible with competence, by all ordinary tests, with the language used to describe the circumstance; that brings out how loaded the notion of meaning involved in the protest is. Notice that, as the example of 'shy and sensitive' illustrates, the language used to express a special reason-constituting conception of a situation need not be explicitly evaluative.

[n]→ The question 'Why should I conform to the dictates of morality?' is most naturally understood as asking for an extra-moral motivation that will be gratified by virtuous behaviour. So understood, the question has no answer. What may happen is that someone is brought to see things as a virtuous person does, and so stops feeling the need to ask it. Situation by situation, he knows why he should behave in the relevant ways; but what he now has is a set of answers to a different interpretation of the question.[3]

---

[3] See pp. 152–3 of D. Z. Phillips, 'In Search of the Moral "Must": Mrs Foot's Fugitive Thought' [*Philosophical Quarterly* 27 (1977): 140–57] – an article from which I profited in writing this paper.

7. We have, then, an apparent contrast between two ways in which an agent's view of how things are can function in explaining his actions. In one, exemplified by the case of taking one's umbrella (§3), the agent's belief about how things are combines with an independently intelligible desire to represent the action as a good thing from the agent's point of view. In the other, a conception of how things are suffices on its own to show us the favourable light in which the action appeared. Beliefs about one's future well-being standardly operate in the second way, according to the concession of §3; so, according to the suggestion I am making in this paper, do moral reasons.

With reasons that function in the second way, it is not false that they weigh with people only if they have a certain desire. But that is just because the ascription of the desire in question follows from the fact that the reasons weigh as they do. It would be wrong to infer that the conceptions of situations that constitute the reasons are available equally to people who are not swayed by them, and weigh with those who are swayed only contingently on their possession of an independent desire. That would be to assimilate the second kind of reason to the first. To preserve the distinction, we should say that the relevant conceptions are not so much as possessed except by those whose wills are influenced appropriately. Their status as reasons is hypothetical only in this truistic sense: they sway only those who *have* them.

When we envisaged a person immune to the force of prudential considerations, we supposed that he might have an idiosyncratic understanding of what it was for a fact to concern his own future (§4). Particular facts about his own future, by themselves, would leave him cold. Now we might imagine equipping him with a separate desire, for the welfare of the future person he takes to be involved in the relevant facts. Then his conception of those facts might move him to action, with their influence conditional on his possession of that extra desire. But the resulting behaviour, only hypothetically called for by his conception of the facts, would match ordinary prudent behaviour only externally. It would be wrong to conclude that ordinary prudent behaviour is likewise only hypothetically commanded.

Similarly, someone who lacks a virtuous person's distinctive view of a situation might perhaps be artificially induced into a simulacrum of a virtuous action by equipping him with an independent desire. His conception of the situation would then be influencing his will hypothetically. But it would be wrong to conclude that a virtuous person's actions are likewise only hypothetically commanded by his conceptions of such situations. (§6 suggests, anyway, a special difficulty about the idea that virtuous behaviour might be thus artifically duplicated across the board.)

According to this position, then, a failure to see reason to act virtuously stems, not from the lack of a desire on which the rational influence of moral requirements is conditional, but from the lack of a distinctive way of seeing situations. If that perceptual capacity is possessed and exercised, it yields non-hypothetical reasons for acting. Now the lack of a perceptual capacity, or failure to exercise it, need show no irrationality. (It might be argued that not to have the relevant conception of one's own future, in the prudential case, would be irrational; but a parallel argument in the moral case would lack plausibility.) Thus we can grant Mrs Foot's premise – that it is possible without irrationality to fail to see reason to act as morality requires – without granting her conclusion – that moral requirements exert a rational influence on the will only hypothetically. The gap opens because we have undermined the assumption that a consideration can exert a rational influence on a will otherwise than hypothetically only if it is recognizable as a requirement by all rational people.

[...]

Commentary on McDowell

At [c]⇥ McDowell notes that the overall argument of his paper is addressed to those philosophers whose position is vulnerable to what he calls an *ad hominem* argument. As we will come to see, he is concerned with those philosophers who adopt a certain view of prudential reasons, reasons affecting an agent's own welfare, but who fail to apply this same view to moral reasons – reasons that concern the welfare of those other than the agent herself. It is *ad hominem* because only those philosophers who hold a certain conception of prudential reasons are vulnerable. However, in the paragraphs immediately following the one marked [c]⇥, he makes some remarks about more general issues regarding reasons for action, remarks that touch on the conception of reasons we found above in Hume. These form a useful backdrop to the more obviously *ad hominem* considerations which we will return to in due course.

At [d]⇥ McDowell mentions an objection to his own position – a position that is intended to capture how we ordinarily think about moral reasons for action – and registers his doubt about whether the objection is genuinely damaging. Before we can appreciate McDowell's doubts, we have to go back a bit to make sure that the objection itself (given at [a]⇥) is clear. Moreover, this is a particularly important thing to do independently of understanding McDowell's strategy. For, though the wording is not exactly Hume's, the objection is recognizably Humean. We shall do this in two stages.

First, look at the sentence that begins in the line marked by $\boxed{\text{b}}\mapsto$. This is a brief description of the picture of reasons and action that McDowell would like to defend.

What is this picture?

The picture here is perhaps best explained with an example. Suppose that Jones has a close friend who has suffered a recent bereavement and is very much in need of help and support. Jones thinks to himself: given the way things are with my friend, I must arrange to visit him this evening. On the picture suggested above, this can be described in more general terms by saying that a particular cognitive state of Jones's – his *knowledge* of how things stand in respect of his friend – suffices for Jones to have a reason to see the friend that very evening. Having such a reason is, in McDowell's way of putting it, seeing the relevant action in a favourable light, and McDowell stresses that seeing it in this way is just what we would expect of a virtuous agent. In effect, a virtuous agent is someone who possesses a certain kind of knowledge – possesses, that is, a specific cognitive state – which alone determines what that agent will find reason to do.

What follows $\boxed{\text{b}}\mapsto$ and fills out the rest of this paragraph is the objection that McDowell imagines being made to this picture.

Spell out this objection. Can you see the connection between this objection and Hume's view of reason and action?

It is not difficult to see the legacy of Hume in the objection. One can even imagine the objector to McDowell's position being Hume himself. Where McDowell finds Jones's cognitive state alone determining his will, Hume insists this is not possible. Instead, he will say, given that Jones's mental state does determine his will, there must be a passion or desire – McDowell speaks here of 'appetitive' states – somehow included in what might seem a cognitive state. The idea here is that what seems a cognitive state would be better *analysed* as a neutral, cognitive appreciation of how things are, and an added passion or desire. Thus, one might take Jones's mental state to consist of two ingredients: a purely cognitive recording of the fact that a certain person is suffering, and at the same time a desire to alleviate that suffering. Moreover, Hume has several interconnected ways of explaining why a state which is in reality a combination of reason and passion can seem to us (as it did to McDowell) a purely cognitive one. McDowell mentions the Humean idea that our minds have 'a propensity to spread upon objects'. In the present example, this would mean Jones's projecting his desire to alleviate his friend's suffering on to the world, perhaps by his thinking that the visit would be a kindness. But, as Hume would insist, strictly speaking such kindness is not a feature of the situation, but is only an element of Jones's emotional reaction to the situation – one which is projected when he (or we) describe the situation as one demanding kindness. Or, as Hume also thinks, when we experience a 'calm passion', as we might in this case, we can easily mistake it for something that has its sole origin in reason.

Returning now to McDowell's expression of scepticism about the Humean objection, look first at $\boxed{d}\mapsto$. McDowell's point from there to the remainder of this paragraph is that, while one might well think it possible to 'analyse' Jones's state into a neutral cognitive component and a motivating desire, this is not mandatory. And, more importantly, it is not guaranteed to capture accurately the particular way in which Jones sees the situation as favouring the action he intends. McDowell sums up this first point by noting that the two-component picture might leave one unpuzzled by Jones's acting as he does – that is, by his visiting his friend – but that this is not enough to show that the two-component story is itself the correct explanation of Jones's action.

> How does McDowell support the suggestion that the two-component analysis might not capture the favourable light in which someone like Jones might see a certain proposed course of action?

If you have read the text carefully, you will see that he has offered no support for this suggestion. This is a matter we will return to later. However, his strategy doesn't yet require it. The next paragraph, the one beginning at $\boxed{e}\mapsto$, shows why. McDowell maintains that the Humean two-component picture is one that seems compulsory only if one adheres to a rather suspect view of what it is to have knowledge. It is this suspect view that is the target of the remarks he promised at the end of the paragraph beginning at $\boxed{c}\mapsto$.

> What does McDowell think is wrong with the Humean picture?

If the world is, as McDowell puts it 'motivationally inert', and cognition simply aims to record how the world is, then it simply couldn't be the case that cognitive states could themselves provide agents with reasons for acting. As we saw, this picture is precisely the one advocated by Hume. But McDowell does not believe that we are compelled to adopt this picture. He says that it is not an independently supported 'hard datum'; it is, he insists, not something we have to accept. Moreover, in the paragraph which concludes the section he hints at a reason why the Humean picture has so many adherents in contemporary philosophy. The methods of science are certainly an important way we find out things about the world, and it is plausible to think that the judgements got by these methods are in fact motivationally inert. But, McDowell insists, there is no reason to think that the only kinds of cognitive judgements we arrive at are those got by the methods of science. As he says, to think that science is the only way to find out what is true is a metaphysical claim, not one that comes from science itself.

Of course, these high-level remarks about science and metaphysics do not themselves constitute a convincing argument against the Humean picture, nor were they intended to. Instead, they serve as a reminder that what Hume offers is itself an unsupported, and hence not compulsory, claim about the nature of cognition. They serve also to remind us that many writers find Hume's picture attractive because there is a tendency to think that science is the only source of our knowledge, a view McDowell derides as 'scientism'.

Let us turn now to the more specific arguments that McDowell offers against certain advocates of the Humean picture. These are the arguments that he identified as *ad hominem*, and our discussion will make clearer what kind of advocacy is in question.

At ⟨f⟩-> McDowell makes a point that could be considered a concession to those, like Hume, who insist that a virtuous agent's reason for action must include some desire that could be ascribed to the agent. But he introduces a qualification to the ascription that has important consequences.

Can you characterize this qualification?

McDowell says that we might be able to ascribe to a virtuous agent desires that are 'independently intelligible'. What he means here by 'independent' needs to be spelled out a little.

Begin with the plausible thought that many people just do, for example, desire that those near to them do not suffer. Desires of this kind are not specifically related to any particular situation that agents might face. It is this that makes them independently intelligible. Like the desire for food, for sustenance or for shelter from the cold, they just do figure in an agent's psychological make-up, and can be understood independently of any particular moral choice.

McDowell sees such desires as important to the possibility of understanding what it is to have a moral outlook. Thus, appealing to such desires might help an outsider understand our sort of moral outlook, one in which kindness is a virtue. This outsider could ascribe to us the desire that our friends do not suffer, and this, together with his appreciation of the circumstances in which such suffering might take place, would show him why we act to avoid those circumstances. Equally, one could imagine a child being taught about these sorts of desires, thereby taking the first steps towards sharing our moral outlook. However, in conceding that desires can play these sorts of role in respect of reasons, McDowell is not conceding that the Humean picture is right. For, as he forcefully says at ⟨g⟩->, these sorts of independently intelligible desires are not always going to help us understand a virtuous person's reasons for acting.

In the paragraph beginning at ⬛h⬛↦, and going on to the end of the selection, McDowell both explains why, and fills in many details of his anti-Humean conception of reasons.

> Just as an initial exercise in following McDowell's line of argument, outline the moves that McDowell makes in the paragraph beginning at ⬛h⬛↦

Using charity as an example, McDowell first observes something no one is likely to deny: charitable behaviour aims at the good of others. More specifically, in undertaking a particular charitable act, an agent has in view the good of some other person; that person's good provides her with a reason for aiming to act in the way she does. (McDowell cites an article by Philippa Foot here – it is listed in Further Reading at the end of the book – and, as you will see, it is her particular conception of reasons that is his target.) He then applies the point made at ⬛g⬛↦ to this observation. In understanding the charitable person's reason for acting, we do not bring in an *independently intelligible* desire for the good of the person. Remember that such a desire is one that could be ascribed to an agent independently of the particular situation faced. McDowell's point, then, is that any desire we might attribute to the relevant agent is one which depends on the actual circumstance in which the good of some other person figures. Its intelligibility is thus *dependent* on the particular circumstances that would fulfil that good.

The distinction between dependent and independent desires is not one that Hume himself envisaged, but it has important consequences for his view, and for our notion of a reason for action. Hume argued that cognitive states do not give us reasons for acting, though moral opinions do. From this he concluded that morality could not be based solely on cognition. In contrast, on the McDowell picture, the recognition that some friend is in need can produce in an agent the desire to meet that particular need. This desire is one that is *not* intelligible independently of one's coming to know of the friend's need, so it is itself the result of cognition. But this means that while we might still say, *with Hume*, that desires are necessary for us to have reasons to act, we can also say, *against Hume*, that cognition alone can sometimes produce those desires in us.

Could a Humean deny this by insisting that the charitable agent just does come equipped with a desire that is independent of coming to know of another's need? Couldn't the model here be that of an agent who has, for example, desires for food, and shelter, which can be specified independently of the circumstances that might turn them into reasons for determinate action? There are two things that McDowell says about this. The first is at ⬛i⬛↦. Here he has in mind Foot's paper in which she concedes that prudential reasons – reasons directed to our own future welfare – depend only on our knowing what is in fact required by our welfare. Our desires for our own welfare are then seen as dependent, and hence produced by our knowing what is in our future interest.

McDowell's point is that because of this concession, she is not in a position to resist his making the same point about charity that she did about prudence. This is the *ad hominem* strategy that was remarked on earlier. It applies to Foot because of her view of prudence, but someone could resist it by insisting that prudence too involves independently intelligible desires.

Leaving this point on one side because we do not have the Foot paper in front of us, turn now to the paragraph marked [i]→.

> What is McDowell's objection here to the idea that a charitable agent is one who just does have independently intelligible desires to do in each case what is required by charity?

McDowell claims that it is not plausible that a charitable person's behaviour would be matched by an agent possessed *both* of a kind of natural benevolence towards others generally *and* a motivationally neutral knowledge of another person's situation. He explains why, only briefly, at [j]→.

> Whether or not you agree with him, try to put into your own words McDowell's claim at [j]→.

Here is one way to expand McDowell's claim. An agent possessed of the virtue of charity knows, case by case, what that virtue requires her to do, and, knowing this, she comes to see doing those things in a favourable light. In other words, what she knows about a given situation gives her a reason to do some quite specific thing. Compare such an agent with someone who is naturally benevolent, someone who, as we might say, has a generalized desire to help others. Is there any reason to think that this generalized (and independently intelligible) desire will result in actions that are reliably charitable? McDowell says that there is no guarantee that this will be so, but one could go further than this. The figure of an agent who is naturally benevolent, but who sometimes brings about more harm than good, is a familiar one. What would it take to turn such a naturally benevolent agent into a genuinely virtuous one? In outline, the answer to this is easy: such an agent would have to learn how to channel his natural benevolence into genuinely constructive actions; he would in effect have to train his generalized desire so that he came to desire the appropriate outcome on a case-by-case basis. However, in giving this answer, McDowell's point is conceded. For, if natural benevolence requires someone to know case by case which action is to be viewed favourably, then the appeal to natural benevolence is idle. What matters is not that someone has the *independent* desires that constitute general benevolence, but instead the *dependent* desires that follow from judgements about the merits of each case.

Changing direction a little – but not changing the subject – McDowell considers whether an appeal to moral codes or sets of rules can be used to undermine his claim that reasons can result solely from what an agent knows about some situation. As you will see, this is not a change of subject, because someone might naturally think that if moral reasons do not include desires, then this must be because agents are following some kind of code or set of rules, *rather than* because they have the knowledge that McDowell attributes to the virtuous agent. He cites Foot as hinting at this, but it is not necessary to appeal to her paper to see why someone might think this.

Many find convincing Hume's claim that cognition alone doesn't account for our having reason to act, and we saw that McDowell, while not accepting it, can see how a certain view of science might be thought to lend it support. McDowell's own defence of the role of cognition might shake that conviction, but, given the strength of support for a broadly Humean view, there is a natural tendency to look around for some other way to explain the phenomena that McDowell describes. It is here that the notion of rules or a code comes in. One can find a perfect model of this kind of agent in the bureaucrat who says: 'I am only doing what the rules prescribe.'

We recognize that the bureaucrat does not necessarily desire the outcome that he finds reason to enact, but we recognize too that the bureaucrat's reasons do not have a purely cognitive basis. This is because we allow that strict adherence to a set of rules or code can serve for some as a source of reasons. Extending this model, it might be tempting to explain McDowell's charitable agent along the same lines. Agreeing with him that an independent benevolent desire doesn't capture what we are after, we might think of the charitable agent as one who is following a code that spells out what is required by charity, case by case. This extension is further encouraged by the stance towards morality that many people naturally adopt, namely, that it is indeed concerned with rules for acting one way or another.

If virtue consists in the adherence to a code, it would seem that we could understand why moral considerations give us reasons for acting, without our having to see them as purely cognitive, and yet without our having to find appropriate desires in each case. As with the bureaucrat, an agent following a moral code might well not have an independently intelligible desire to act as the code requires; adhering to a relevant rule does the work instead. (That said, the determined Humean might insist that desires play some role in adopting the code in the first place.)

At [k]⊢→ and just after, McDowell responds to this possibility. Do you find his response convincing?

McDowell claims that virtue cannot be understood in terms of a code because any agent aiming to act as virtue requires is bound to encounter circumstances which could not have been anticipated in any codification, however carefully it was originally drawn up. As he notes, only by having a moral upbringing that allows one 'to see situations in a special light, as constituting reasons for acting' can we ensure the flexibility not catered for by explicit rules.

Note that McDowell uses a perceptual analogy here – he speaks about seeing situations – and this underlines his commitment to the anti-Humean position about reasons. After all, what one gets by perception is knowledge of, or at least belief about, how things are. Insofar as the virtuous agent's reasons result from a kind of perception of a situation, these reasons are grounded on cognition rather than passion and desire.

Indirect support for McDowell's attitude towards any codification of morality comes from his discussion in the paragraph beginning at ⌐l¬→. If there were a code whose explicit rules showed the virtuous agent what he had reason to do in some specific circumstance, then it should be possible to say what those rules were. But as McDowell notes, both in the case of prudence and morality, no such explicitness seems achievable. In the case of prudence, if someone simply couldn't see why doing something was in his best interest – even when it was – there is little anyone could say to convince him. As McDowell notes, one would end up thinking that the agent didn't know what it meant for that fact to concern his future, and this would clearly be a cognitive failure. Similarly, there is no reason to think that an agent who finds reason to act virtuously could articulate that reason in anything like the way we would expect of someone following an explicit rule. For example, finding reason to treat another person with particular consideration, the virtuous agent might say: 'He is shy and sensitive, and it would be wrong to be too demanding in his case.' If this explanation is challenged by someone who cannot see why being shy and sensitive is a reason, it would be difficult to imagine the virtuous agent having much more to say than, as McDowell puts it: 'You simply don't know what it means that someone is shy and sensitive.' As in the case of prudence, and as in many others having no connection with morality – McDowell cites the appreciation of jazz – one is required to see things in certain ways, but there is no guarantee that one can say anything which forces another person to see it the same way. But this is scarcely evidence that there is some code, even an implicit one, that the virtuous agent is following, and that could be cited in an effort to convince someone who saw no reason to act as the virtuous agent intends. Nor is it, McDowell claims at ⌐m¬→, evidence that what is involved is an appeal to feeling rather than cognition.

The paragraph beginning at ⌐n¬→ raises an issue that can seem slightly off to the side of the discussion so far.

> Can you see the connection between the point of this paragraph and the position that McDowell has developed?

Familiarity with Foot's article would make McDowell's point at ⌐n¬→ easier to understand, but, even without it, a careful reading of the material from ⌐o¬→ to the end of the selection can serve. (In any case, this material offers a very useful and clear summary of both the Humean position and McDowell's alternative – a summary that we will return to below.) After doing this reading, go back to the passage beginning at $\boxed{p}$⊢→. McDowell claims that someone lacking a particular perceptual capacity would not thereby be branded as irrational.

Is this true?

If we take the notion of a perceptual capacity in its most literal sense, the claim is unlikely to be challenged. We certainly wouldn't count someone irrational who was, for example, unable to distinguish red from green because of colour blindness. Of course, as is clear from McDowell's text, he is using the idea of a perceptual capacity in an extended, though still natural, sense. For we speak of perceiving what is the case – for example, perceiving (seeing) that it takes hard work to succeed – even though perception in the narrower sense of vision, hearing, etc., is not in question. It is by means of this latter sense that McDowell characterizes the virtuous agent – the agent who perceives a situation as favouring a reason to act in one way rather than another. What McDowell claims at $\boxed{p}$⊢→ is that an agent who is unable to see relevant situations as the virtuous agent does is not thereby irrational. (Though, of course, an egregious failure here might lead us to think such an agent immoral. In the parenthetical remark, McDowell notes that we may have a contrast here between prudence and morality: the agent who lacks a proper conception of his own future welfare might well be thought irrational, as well of course as imprudent.)

Here is how the point made at $\boxed{p}$⊢→ connects up with the paragraph at $\boxed{n}$⊢→. In the latter, McDowell admitted that it was hopeless to think that one could provide an 'extra-moral motivation' to an agent who simply didn't see why he should 'conform to the dictates of morality'.

What do you think McDowell might mean by 'extra-moral motivation'?

An extra-moral motivation is one which would move someone who was not already moved by moral considerations, someone usually described as 'amoral'. McDowell's point is that if it were irrational to fail to see things as the virtuous agent would, then we could perhaps hope to have some leverage on such an agent. We could say: 'in not conforming to the dictates of morality, you are being irrational'. But, at $\boxed{p}$⊢→, this possibility is ruled out.

In the view of Foot, and others, the relevant extra-moral motivation is bound to be something like 'having appropriate desires or feelings'. So, she would take failure of an agent to act as a virtuous one as a sign that the relevant desires or feelings were missing. Moreover, she would take this as also explaining why we cannot use extra-moral arguments to change such an agent's attitudes. As Foot and Hume would be likely to claim: 'you cannot use argument to convince someone to desire or feel something'. McDowell counters this with his own picture, one in which it is not desire or feeling that is crucial, but rather an ability to perceive situations as the virtuous agent does. Hume and Foot explain the impossibility of giving extra-moral grounds for being moral by citing the non-cognitive nature of feelings. Again, in contrast, McDowell explains this impossibility by noting that an agent could suffer from a kind of cognitive blindness in respect of morality which is not itself irrational, and is therefore not something we can change by arguments appealing to non-moral considerations.

Having reached the end of our discussion of McDowell, let us finish this chapter with a brief review, not of details, but of what is at stake in the debate between Hume and McDowell. It would be useful in this connection to re-read McDowell from ⊙→ to the end of the selection.

Hume claimed, and in various ways argued, that any reason one might have for doing something, or making some choice, must involve passions, feelings or desires driving such action or choice. When this view of reasons is applied to morality, it radically constrains our understanding of individual agents' moral outlooks. In the Humean picture, moral outlooks cannot be essentially cognitive: a moral outlook will consist of an agent's affective (conative) states, supplemented, guided, but certainly not determined by, that agent's recognition of how things are. McDowell challenges this picture of reasons and tries thereby to make room for the idea that a moral outlook be constituted by its holder's cognitive states – constituted, that is, by what agents know, case by case, about the situations they face. As he takes pains to point out, passions, feelings and desires can still play a role, but, in being dependent on an agent's appreciation of how things are, they are more products of a moral outlook than its determinants.

Why is it important to decide whether moral outlooks are, or are not, essentially cognitive? Aside from relevance of this question to the metaphysics and epistemology of moral value – concerns that might be thought narrowly philosophical – answers to this question have direct consequences for moral practice. For one thing, ways of handling disagreements depend on whether a moral outlook is cognitive. Argument, while not guaranteed to work, is at least appropriate to disagreements about what is the case, whereas some form of enticement or reward better suits differences in feeling. Similarly, approaches to moral development and education are bound to vary depending on whether we expect children to come to know or feel what is right, virtuous or worthwhile, though one must be cautious about hasty conclusions here. For, even in McDowell's picture, independently intelligible desires can play a role in the earliest stages of development. Appeal to a child's natural inclinations might well be the best way to get the child started on the path to acquiring a moral outlook, even though a mature outlook will only be fully intelligible as a form of knowledge.

4

Subjectivism and Objectivism

Introduction to the Problem

Moral philosophy encompasses two spheres of inquiry. There is 'normative ethics', which is an extension of our everyday ethical reflection in that it inquires into *first order* questions about the rights and wrongs of this or that practice. (When is euthanasia permissible? Is smacking children always wrong?) Normative ethics argues for this or that ethical conclusion about a given ethical problem, and for this reason it is sometimes referred to as 'applied ethics'. The second sphere of moral philosophical inquiry is 'meta-ethics'. This kind of ethics is *second order*. The notion of 'second order' ethics can seem rather alien, so let's take a moment to anchor it in two more straightforward examples. A first order desire is a desire for something (a cream cake perhaps), and a second order desire is a desire about a desire (for instance, the desire to stop having the desire for cream cakes). Similarly, a first order belief is a belief about something (about the weather, perhaps), and a second order belief is a belief about a belief (for instance, the belief that my belief that it's sunny is true). Just as second order desires are desires about desires, and second order beliefs are beliefs about beliefs, so we might think of second order ethics as ethics about ethics – meta-ethics is *about* first order ethics. Centrally, meta-ethics asks questions about the status of our moral judgements and beliefs. It asks, for instance, how far our moral conclusions are truth-apt (able to be true or false), or how far they can constitute knowledge. Underpinning such questions is the cardinal issue in meta-ethics, namely, whether, or how far, moral values are objective; that is, whether or how far they are independent of our subjective responses and judgements.

Much of the meta-ethical literature bears witness to a tension between two contrary pressures in our ethical thinking. There is a pressure in the direction of *objectivism* about moral value: our ordinary moral thought and talk seems to display a robust commitment to the objectivity of moral values. Imagine you are facing a difficult moral decision – perhaps you work for a large corporation which you have discovered is embroiled in corruption. Do you have an obligation to blow the whistle, even at some professional and probably personal cost? It seems we typically confront these sorts of moral questions as if they have an objectively correct answer – an answer we must discover elsewhere than in our own subjective responses, and which will bind us regardless of how we happen to feel about it. In trying to work out what is the morally right thing to do, it seems we generally take ourselves to be attempting to discern some objective moral fact of the matter.

Conversely, however, our everyday moral consciousness also witnesses a pressure in the direction of *subjectivism*. Moral judgements are intrinsically action-guiding (or so it is widely, if not unanimously, assumed) which means that the moral values at work in these judgements have power to produce or constrain action. If I say to someone 'It was cruel to ridicule him like that in public', then I am expressing a judgement which is such as to impact on my interlocutor's actions: my moral comment puts a pressure on her to refrain from that sort of thing in the future, and perhaps try to make amends. Moral statements, needless to say, are not guaranteed to make a practical impact, for the people they are addressed to may have more powerful countervailing motivations; so let us simply say that they are apt to influence action. This is what philosophers mean when they say that moral values have 'motivational force', or 'action-guiding power', or that they are essentially 'practical'. The action-guiding power of moral values creates a pressure in the direction of subjectivism insofar as action, in general, requires a subjective impulse on the part of the agent – on the simplest construal, action requires something like a desire to do the thing in question.

Given these contradictory pressures, it is not surprising that philosophical views about the nature of value are diverse, and range from objectivists who take their philosophical cues from the objectivizing tendencies in our pre-theoretical moral thought and talk, to subjectivists who insist that we can make best philosophical sense of these objectivizing tendencies by explaining them away. The extracts that follow, from J. L. Mackie and Thomas Nagel, provide classic illustrations of the case for subjectivism on the one hand, and the case for objectivism on the other hand. Published in 1977 and 1986 respectively, they together present some of the key ideas that continue to structure the debate about the status of moral value as it is conducted today.

Introduction to Mackie

J. L. Mackie was born in Sydney, Australia, in 1917. He taught at the University of Sydney, and at Otago University, Dunedin, New Zealand, then moved to

England where he taught first at the University of York, and then, from 1967 until his death in 1981, at the University of Oxford. Mackie made major contributions to moral philosophy, philosophy of religion, and metaphysics, as well as to the interpretation of Locke and Hume. Mackie's particular brand of moral subjectivism (whose essence is captured in this extract from the first chapter of his book *Ethics: Inventing Right and Wrong*) is profoundly influenced by Hume's moral philosophy, but is also distinctively Mackie's own position. The driving idea in Mackie's view is that a mistaken commitment to the objectivity of moral value is incorrigibly built into our everyday moral thought and talk. And he advanced an 'error theory' about that commitment, which permits us to continue with our everyday moralizing-as-usual, while maintaining, when we have our philosophical hats on, a sceptical meta-ethical attitude. These ideas remain an intriguing and powerful influence in philosophical debates about the metaphysical status of moral value, and, more generally, the relation of sceptical philosophy to the non-sceptical commitment inherent in first order moral thinking.

J. L. Mackie, *Ethics: Inventing Right and Wrong* (extracts from Ch. 1, 'The Subjectivity of Values')

Moral Scepticism

There are no objective values. This is a bald statement of the thesis of this chapter, but before arguing for it I shall try to clarify and restrict it in ways that may meet some objections and prevent some misunderstanding.

The statement of this thesis is liable to provoke one of three very different reactions. Some will think it not merely false but pernicious; they will see it as a threat to morality and to everything else that is worthwhile, and they will find the presenting of such a thesis in what purports to be a book on ethics paradoxical or even outrageous. Others will regard it as a trivial truth, almost too obvious to be worth mentioning, and certainly too plain to be worth much argument. Others again will say that it is meaningless or empty, that no real issue is raised by the question whether values are or are not part of the fabric of the world. But, precisely because there can be these three different reactions, much more needs to be said.

The claim that values are not objective, are not part of the fabric of the world, is meant to include not only moral goodness, which might be most naturally equated with moral value, but also other things that could be more loosely called moral values or disvalues – rightness and wrongness, duty, obligation, an action's being rotten and contemptible, and so on. It also includes non-moral values, notably aesthetic ones, beauty and various kinds of artistic merit. I shall not discuss these explicitly, but clearly much the same considerations apply to aesthetic and to moral values, and there would be at least some initial implausibility in a view that gave the one a different status from the other.

Since it is with moral values that I am primarily concerned, the view I am adopting may be called moral scepticism. But this name is likely to be misunderstood: 'moral scepticism' might also be used as a name for either of two first order views, or perhaps for an incoherent mixture of the two. A moral sceptic might be the sort of person who says 'All this talk of morality is tripe,' who rejects morality and will take no notice of it. Such a person may be literally rejecting all moral judgements; he is more likely to be making moral judgements of his own, expressing a positive moral condemnation of all that conventionally passes for morality; or he may be confusing these two logically incompatible views, and saying that he rejects all morality, while he is in fact rejecting only a particular morality that is current in the society in which he has grown up. But I am not at present concerned with the merits or faults of such a position. These are first order moral views, positive or negative: the person who adopts either of them is taking a certain practical, normative, stand. By contrast, what I am discussing is a second order view, a view about the status of moral values and the nature of moral valuing, about where and how they fit into the world. These first and second order views are not merely distinct but completely independent: one could be a second order moral sceptic without being a first order one, or again the other way round. A man could hold strong moral views, and indeed ones whose content was thoroughly conventional, while believing that they were simply attitudes and policies with regard to conduct that he and other people held. Conversely, a man could reject all established morality while believing it to be an objective truth that it was evil or corrupt.

[...]

Standards of Evaluation

One way of stating the thesis that there are no objective values is to say that value statements cannot be either true or false. But this formulation, too, lends itself to misinterpretation. For there are certain kinds of value statements which undoubtedly can be true or false, even if, in the sense I intend, there are no objective values. Evaluations of many sorts are commonly made in relation to agreed and assumed standards. The classing of wool, the grading of apples, the awarding of prizes at sheepdog trials, flower shows, skating and diving championships, and even the marking of examination papers are carried out in relation to standards of quality or merit which are peculiar to each particular subject-matter or type of contest, which may be explicitly laid down but which, even if they are nowhere explicitly stated, are fairly well understood and agreed by those who are recognized as judges or experts in each particular field. Given any sufficiently determinate standards, it will be an objective issue, a matter of truth and falsehood, how well any particular specimen measures up to those standards. Comparative judgements in particular will be capable of truth and falsehood: it will be a factual question whether this sheepdog has performed better than that one.

The subjectivist about values, then, is not denying that there can be objective evaluations relative to standards, and these are as possible in the aesthetic and moral fields as in any of those just mentioned. More than this, there is an objective distinction which applies in many such fields, and yet would itself be regarded as a peculiarly moral one: the distinction between justice and injustice. In one important sense of the word it is a paradigm case of injustice if a court declares someone to be guilty of an offence of which it knows him to be innocent. More generally, a finding is unjust if it is at variance with what the relevant law and the facts together require, and particularly if it is known by the court to be so. More generally still, any award of marks, prizes, or the like is unjust if it is at variance with the agreed standards for the contest in question: if one diver's performance in fact measures up better to the accepted standards for diving than another's, it will be unjust if the latter is awarded higher marks or the prize. In this way the justice or injustice of decisions relative to standards can be a thoroughly objective matter, though there may still be a subjective element in the interpretation or application of standards. But the statement that a certain decision is thus just or unjust will not be objectively prescriptive: in so far as it can be simply true it leaves open the question whether there is any objective requirement to do what is just and to refrain from what is unjust, and equally leaves open the practical decision to act in either way.

Recognizing the objectivity of justice in relation to standards, and of evaluative judgements relative to standards, then, merely shifts the question of the objectivity of values back to the standards themselves. The subjectivist may try to make his point by insisting that there is no objective validity about the choice of standards. Yet he would clearly be wrong if he said that the choice of even the most basic standards in any field was completely arbitrary. The standards used in sheepdog trials clearly bear some relation to the work that sheepdogs are kept to do, the standards for grading apples bear some relation to what people generally want in or like about apples, and so on. On the other hand, standards are not as a rule strictly validated by such purposes. The appropriateness of standards is neither fully determinate nor totally indeterminate in relation to independently specifiable aims or desires. But however determinate it is, the objective appropriateness of standards in relation to aims or desires is no more of a threat to the denial of objective values than is the objectivity of evaluation relative to standards. In fact it is logically no different from the objectivity of goodness relative to desires. Something may be called good simply in so far as it satisfies or is such as to satisfy a certain desire; but the objectivity of such relations of satisfaction does not constitute in our sense an objective value.

[...]

The Claim to Objectivity

[...]

Objectivism about values is not only a feature of the philosophical tradition. It has also a firm basis in ordinary thought, and even in the meanings of moral terms. No doubt it was an extravagance for
[f]→ Moore to say that 'good' is the name of a non-natural quality, but it would not be so far wrong to say that in moral contexts it is used as if it were the name of a supposed non-natural quality, where the description 'non-natural' leaves room for the peculiar evaluative, prescriptive, intrinsically action-guiding aspects of this supposed quality. This point can be illustrated by reflection on the conflicts and swings of opinion in recent years between non-cognitivist and naturalist views about the central, basic, meanings of ethical terms. If we reject the view that it is the function of such terms to introduce objective values into discourse about conduct and choices of action,
[g]→ there seem to be two main alternative types of account. One (which has importantly different subdivisions) is that they conventionally express either attitudes which the speaker purports to adopt towards whatever it is that he characterizes morally, or prescriptions or recommendations, subject perhaps to the logical constraint of universalizability. Different views of this type share the central thesis that ethical terms have, at least partly and primarily, some sort of noncognitive, non-descriptive, meaning. Views of the other type hold

that they are descriptive in meaning, but descriptive of natural features, partly of such features as everyone, even the non-cognitivist, would recognize as distinguishing kind actions from cruel ones, courage from cowardice, politeness from rudeness, and so on, and partly (though these two overlap) of relations between the actions and some human wants, satisfactions, and the like. I believe that views of both these types capture part of the truth. Each approach can account for the fact that moral judgements are action-guiding or practical. Yet each gains much of its plausibility from the felt inadequacy of the other. It is a very natural reaction to any non-cognitive analysis of ethical terms to protest that there is more to ethics than this, something more external to the maker of moral judgements, more authoritative over both him and those of or to whom he speaks, and this reaction is likely to persist even when full allowance has been made for the logical, formal, constraints of full-blooded prescriptivity and universalizability. Ethics, we are inclined to believe, is more a matter of knowledge and less a matter of decision than any non-cognitive analysis allows. And of course naturalism satisfies this demand. It will not be a matter of choice or decision whether an action is cruel or unjust or imprudent or whether it is likely to produce more distress than pleasure. But in satisfying this demand, it introduces a converse deficiency. On a naturalist analysis, moral judgements can be practical, but their practicality is wholly relative to desires or possible satisfactions of the person or persons whose actions are to be guided; but moral judgements seem to say more than this. This view leaves out the categorical quality of moral requirements. In fact both naturalist and non-cognitive analyses leave out the apparent authority of ethics, the one by excluding the categorically imperative aspect, the other the claim to objective validity or truth. The ordinary user of moral language means to say something about whatever it is that he characterizes morally, for example a possible action, as it is in itself, or would be if it were realized, and not about, or even simply expressive of, his, or anyone else's, attitude or relation to it. But the something he wants to say is not purely descriptive, certainly not inert, but something that involves a call for action or for the refraining from action, and one that is absolute, not contingent upon any desire or preference or policy or choice, his own or anyone else's. Someone in a state of moral perplexity, wondering whether it would be wrong for him to engage, say, in research related to bacteriological warfare, wants to arrive at some judgement about this concrete case, his doing this work at this time in these actual circumstances; his relevant characteristics will be part of the subject of the judgement, but no relation between him and the proposed action will be part of the predicate. The question is not, for example, whether he really wants to do this work, whether it will satisfy or dissatisfy him, whether he will in the long run have a pro-attitude towards it, or even whether this is an action of a sort that he can happily and sincerely recommend in all relevantly similar cases. Nor is he even wondering just whether to recommend such action in all relevantly similar cases. He wants to know whether this course of action would be wrong in itself. Something like this is the everyday objectivist concept of which talk about non-natural qualities is a philosopher's reconstruction.

[...]

k|→ I conclude, then, that ordinary moral judgements include a claim to objectivity, an assumption that there are objective values in just the sense in which I am concerned to deny this. And I do not think it is going too far to say that this assumption has been incorporated in the basic, conventional, meanings of moral terms. Any analysis of the meanings of moral terms which omits this claim to objective, intrinsic, prescriptivity is to that extent incomplete; and this is true of any non-cognitive analysis, any naturalist one, and any combination of the two.

If second order ethics were confined, then, to linguistic and conceptual analysis, it ought to conclude that moral values at least are objective: that they are so is part of what our ordinary moral statements mean: the traditional moral concepts of the ordinary man as well as of the main line of western philosophers are concepts of objective value. But it is precisely for this reason that linguistic and conceptual analysis is not enough. The claim to objectivity, however ingrained in our language and thought, is not self-validating. It can and should be questioned. But the denial of objective values will have to be put forward not as the result of an analytic approach, but as an 'error theory', a theory that although most people in making moral judgements implicitly claim, among other things, to be pointing to something objectively prescriptive, these claims are all false. It is this that makes the name 'moral scepticism' appropriate.

But since this is an error theory, since it goes against assumptions ingrained in our thought and built into some of the ways in which language is used, since it conflicts with what is sometimes called common sense, it needs very solid support. It is not something we can accept lightly or casually and then quietly pass on. If we are to adopt this view, we must argue explicitly for it. Traditionally it has been supported by arguments of two main kinds, which I shall call the argument from relativity and the argument from queerness, but these can, as I shall show, be supplemented in several ways.

The Argument from Relativity

The argument from relativity has as its premiss the well-known variation in moral codes from one society to another and from one period
to another, and also the differences in moral beliefs between different
groups and classes within a complex community. Such variation is in
itself merely a truth of descriptive morality, a fact of anthropology
which entails neither first order nor second order ethical views. Yet it
may indirectly support second order subjectivism: radical differences
between first order moral judgements make it difficult to treat those
judgements as apprehensions of objective truths. But it is not the mere
occurrence of disagreements that tells against the objectivity of values.
Disagreement on questions in history or biology or cosmology does
not show that there are no objective issues in these fields for investiga-
tors to disagree about. But such scientific disagreement results from
speculative inferences or explanatory hypotheses based on inadequate
evidence, and it is hardly plausible to interpret moral disagreement in
the same way. Disagreement about moral codes seems to reflect people's adherence to and participation in different ways of life. The
causal connection seems to be mainly that way round: it is that people
approve of monogamy because they participate in a monogamous
way of life rather than that they participate in a monogamous way of
life because they approve of monogamy. Of course, the standards may
be an idealization of the way of life from which they arise: the monogamy in which people participate may be less complete, less rigid,
than that of which it leads them to approve. This is not to say that
moral judgements are purely conventional. Of course there have been
and are moral heretics and moral reformers, people who have turned
against the established rules and practices of their own communities
for moral reasons, and often for moral reasons that we would endorse.
But this can usually be understood as the extension, in ways which,
though new and unconventional, seemed to them to be required for
consistency, of rules to which they already adhered as arising out of
an existing way of life. In short, the argument from relativity has
some force simply because the actual variations in the moral codes are
more readily explained by the hypothesis that they reflect ways of life
than by the hypothesis that they express perceptions, most of them
seriously inadequate and badly distorted, of objective values.

But there is a well-known counter to this argument from relativity,
namely to say that the items for which objective validity is in the first
place to be claimed are not specific moral rules or codes but very general basic principles which are recognized at least implicitly to some

extent in all society – such principles as provide the foundations of what Sidgwick has called different methods of ethics: the principle of universalizability, perhaps, or the rule that one ought to conform to the specific rules of any way of life in which one takes part, from which one profits, and on which one relies, or some utilitarian principle of doing what tends, or seems likely, to promote the general happiness. It is easy to show that such general principles, married with differing concrete circumstances, different existing social patterns or different preferences, will beget different specific moral rules; and there is some plausibility in the claim that the specific rules thus generated will vary from community to community or from group to group in close agreement with the actual variations in accepted codes.

The argument from relativity can be only partly countered in this way. To take this line the moral objectivist has to say that it is only in these principles that the objective moral character attaches immediately to its descriptively specified ground or subject: other moral judgements are objectively valid or true, but only derivatively and contingently – if things had been otherwise, quite different sorts of actions would have been right. [...]

The Argument from Queerness

Even more important, however, and certainly more generally applicable, is the argument from queerness. This has two parts, one metaphysical, the other epistemological. If there were objective values, then they would be entities or qualities or relations of a very strange sort, utterly different from anything else in the universe. Correspondingly, if we were aware of them, it would have to be by some special faculty of moral perception or intuition, utterly different from our ordinary ways of knowing everything else. These points were recognized by Moore when he spoke of non-natural qualities, and by the intuitionists in their talk about a 'faculty of moral intuition'. Intuitionism has long been out of favour, and it is indeed easy to point out its implausibilities. What is not so often stressed, but is more important, is that the central thesis of intuitionism is one to which any objectivist view of values is in the end committed: intuitionism merely makes unpalatably plain what other forms of objectivism wrap up. Of course the suggestion that moral judgements are made or moral problems solved by just sitting down and having an ethical intuition is a travesty of actual moral thinking. But, however complex the real process, it will require (if it is to yield authoritatively prescriptive conclusions) some input of this distinctive sort, either premises or forms of argument or both. When we ask the awkward question, how we can be aware of this authoritative prescriptivity, of the truth of these distinctively ethical premises or of the cogency of this distinctively ethical pattern of reasoning, none of our ordinary accounts of sensory perception or introspection or the framing and confirming of explanatory hypotheses or inference or logical construction or conceptual analysis, or any combination of these, will provide a satisfactory answer; 'a special sort of intuition' is a lame answer, but it is the one to which the clear-headed objectivist is compelled to resort.

o⟶ Indeed, the best move for the moral objectivist is not to evade this issue, but to look for companions in guilt. For example, Richard Price argues that it is not moral knowledge alone that such an empiricism as those of Locke and Hume is unable to account for, but also our knowledge and even our ideas of essence, number, identity, diversity, solidity, inertia, substance, the necessary existence and infinite extension of time and space, necessity and possibility in general, power, and causation. If the understanding, which Price defines as the faculty within us that discerns truth, is also a source of new simple ideas of so many other sorts, may it not also be a power of immediately perceiving right and wrong, which yet are real characters of actions?

This is an important counter to the argument from queerness. The only adequate reply to it would be to show how, on empiricist foundations, we can construct an account of the ideas and beliefs and knowledge that we have of all these matters. I cannot even begin to do that here, though I have undertaken some parts of the task elsewhere. I can only state my belief that satisfactory accounts of most of these can be given in empirical terms. If some supposed metaphysical necessities or essences resist such treatment, then they too should be included, along with objective values, among the targets of the argument from queerness.

[…]

p⟶ Plato's Forms give a dramatic picture of what objective values would have to be. The Form of the Good is such that knowledge of it provides the knower with both a direction and an overriding motive; something's being good both tells the person who knows this to pursue it and makes him pursue it. An objective good would be sought by anyone who was acquainted with it, not because of any contingent fact that this person, or every person, is so constituted that he desires this end, but just because the end has to-be-pursuedness somehow built into it. Similarly, if there were objective principles of right and wrong, any wrong (possible) course of action would have not-to-be-doneness somehow built into it.

[…]

Another way of bringing out this queerness is to ask, about anything that is supposed to have some objective moral quality, how this is linked with its natural features. What is the connection between the natural fact that an action is a piece of deliberate cruelty – say, causing pain just for fun – and the moral fact that it is wrong? It cannot be an entailment, a logical or semantic necessity. Yet it is not merely that the two features occur together. The wrongness must somehow be 'consequential' or 'supervenient'; it is wrong because it is a piece of deliberate cruelty. But just what *in the world* is signified by this 'because'? And how do we know the relation that it signifies, if this is something more than such actions being socially condemned, and condemned by us too, perhaps through our having absorbed attitudes from our social environment? It is not even sufficient to postulate a faculty which 'sees' the wrongness: something must be postulated which can see at once the natural features that constitute the cruelty, and the wrongness, and the mysterious consequential link between the two. Alternatively, the intuition required might be the perception that wrongness is a higher order property belonging to certain natural properties; but what is this belonging of properties to other properties, and how can we discern it? How much simpler and more comprehensible the situation would be if we could replace the moral quality with some sort of subjective response which could be causally related to the detection of the natural features on which the supposed quality is said to be consequential.

[...]

Patterns of Objectification

Considerations of these kinds suggest that it is in the end less paradoxical to reject than to retain the common-sense belief in the objectivity of moral values, provided that we can explain how this belief, if it is false, has become established and is so resistant to criticisms. This proviso is not difficult to satisfy.

On a subjectivist view, the supposedly objective values will be based in fact upon attitudes which the person has who takes himself to be recognizing and responding to those values. If we admit what Hume calls the mind's 'propensity to spread itself on external objects', we can understand the supposed objectivity of moral qualities as arising from what we can call the projection or objectification of moral attitudes. This would be analogous to what is called the 'pathetic fallacy', the tendency to read our feelings into their objects. If a fungus, say, fills us with disgust, we may be inclined to ascribe to the fungus itself a non-natural quality of foulness. But in moral contexts there is more than this propensity at work. Moral attitudes themselves are at least partly social in origin: socially established – and socially necessary – patterns of behaviour put pressure on individuals, and each individual tends to internalize these pressures and to join in requiring these patterns of behaviour of himself and of others. The attitudes that are objectified into moral values have indeed an external source, though not the one assigned to them by the belief in their absolute authority. Moreover, there are motives that would support objectification. We need morality to regulate interpersonal relations, to control some of the ways in which people behave towards one another, often in opposition to contrary inclinations. We therefore want our moral judgements to be authoritative for other agents as well as for ourselves: objective validity would give them the authority required. Aesthetic values are logically in the same position as moral ones; much the same metaphysical and epistemological considerations apply to them. But aesthetic values are less strongly objectified than moral ones; their subjective status, and an 'error theory' with regard to such claims to objectivity as are incorporated in aesthetic judgements, will be more readily accepted, just because the motives for their objectification are less compelling.

But it would be misleading to think of the objectification of moral values as primarily the projection of feelings, as in the pathetic fallacy. More important are wants and demands. As Hobbes says, 'whatsoever is the object of any man's Appetite or Desire, that is it, which he for his part calleth *Good*'; and certainly both the adjective 'good' and the noun 'goods' are used in non-moral contexts of things because they are such as to satisfy desires. We get the notion of something's being objectively good, or having intrinsic value, by reversing the direction of dependence here, by making the desire depend upon the goodness, instead of the goodness on the desire. And this is aided by the fact that the desired thing will indeed have features that make it desired, that enable it to arouse a desire or that make it such as to satisfy some desire that is already there. It is fairly easy to confuse the way in which a thing's desirability is indeed objective with its having in our sense objective value. The fact that the word 'good' serves as one of our main moral terms is a trace of this pattern of objectification.

[...]

Another way of explaining the objectification of moral values is to say that ethics is a system of law from which the legislator has been removed. This might have been derived either from the positive law of a state or from a supposed system of divine law. There can be no doubt that some features of modern European moral concepts are traceable to the theological ethics of Christianity. The stress on quasi-imperative notions, on what ought to be done or on what is wrong in a sense that is close to that of 'forbidden', are surely relics of divine commands. Admittedly, the central ethical concepts for Plato and Aristotle also are in a broad sense prescriptive or intrinsically action-guiding, but in concentrating rather on 'good' than on 'ought' they show that their moral thought is an objectification of the desired and the satisfying rather than of the commanded. Elizabeth Anscombe has argued that modern, non-Aristotelian, concepts of *moral* obligation, *moral* duty, of what is *morally* right and wrong, and of the *moral* sense of 'ought' are survivals outside the framework of thought that made them really intelligible, namely the belief in divine law. She infers that 'ought' has 'become a word of mere mesmeric force', with only a 'delusive appearance of content', and that we would do better to discard such terms and concepts altogether, and go back to Aristotelian ones.

There is much to be said for this view. But while we can explain some distinctive features of modern moral philosophy in this way, it would be a mistake to see the whole problem of the claim to objective prescriptivity as merely local and unnecessary, as a post-operative complication of a society from which a dominant system of theistic belief has recently been rather hastily excised. [...]

The apparent objectivity of moral value is a widespread phenomenon which has more than one source: the persistence of a belief in something like divine law when the belief in the divine legislator has faded out is only one factor among others. There are several different patterns of objectification, all of which have left characteristic traces in our actual moral concepts and moral language.

[...]

Commentary on Mackie

Mackie's first concern is to characterize the form of subjectivism or 'moral scepticism' for which he will argue. He opens with the bald definitive claim that 'There are no objective values', but at |a|→ he is concerned to distinguish his particular moral scepticism from two other sceptical views with which it might easily be confused.

> What are the two views with which Mackie says his own 'moral scepticism' risks being conflated? What is a 'first order' moral view and how does it contrast with the view Mackie will argue for?

Mackie imagines a kind of moral sceptic who rejects morality per se and takes no part in moral thinking. Such a person would be a complete amoralist.

He also imagines someone who rejects all that passes for morality, but who remains committed to some alternative moral code. Such a person would not be an amoralist, but might engage in some of the dismissive rhetoric of the amoralist. Both of these characters express first order moral views – that is, they express a view about the content of a given moral code or codes (about, for instance, the rights and wrongs of eating meat, or smacking children, or abortion, or euthanasia). By contrast, Mackie's moral scepticism is not a view about any piece of morality in particular, but rather it is a view about the nature of moral value per se. At $\boxed{b} \mapsto$ he distinguishes it as a second order view, a view about the very nature of moral values, whatever those values might be. In particular, he will be concerned with the metaphysical status of moral values – the question of whether or not they have an objective existence, or whether or not they are, to use his evocative phrase, 'part of the fabric of the world'.

Mackie goes on to acknowledge at $\boxed{c} \mapsto$ that there is a kind of objectivity of judgement that is available in the moral, just as it is available in other realms of evaluative judgement, such as the judgement of a sheepdog trial or the grading of apples.

> State in your own words what sort of objectivity of judgement is common to these spheres.

The reason morality permits a certain objectivity of judgement is that it permits judgement relative to agreed standards, just as there are agreed standards in the judging of sheepdog trials or the grading of apples.

Further, he notes at $\boxed{d} \mapsto$ that there is an objective distinction between just and unjust judgements available here.

> Explain in your own words what this distinction between just and unjust judgements consists in. Think up one or two examples of your own.

His point is that severe deviations from the agreed standards of judgement will produce an objectively unjust decision – if a sheepdog who scatters the sheep willy-nilly to the four corners of the field wins the prize, the judges have made an objectively unjust decision. However, in order to render this point compatible with his scepticism about the objectivity of values, he claims at $\boxed{e} \mapsto$ that the fact that certain judgements or decisions may be objectively unjust still leaves it an open question whether there is an objective requirement to judge justly and/or refrain from judging unjustly.

> Do you agree with this latter point? Doesn't Mackie's acknowledgement that evaluative judgements made relative to agreed standards are objectively just or unjust put real pressure on his subjectivism about value? (How could one hold both that someone's evaluative judgement was objectively unjust **and** that they had no objective obligation to judge differently?)

Mackie's argument, however, is that the recognition that evaluative judgements can be objectively just or unjust makes no difference to the subjectivist's case. His scepticism simply shifts its aim away from judgements themselves and towards the standards that govern those judgements.

Next Mackie suggests that a tendency for objectivist assumptions is in evidence both in the philosophical tradition and in our ordinary ethical thought and talk. At ⟨f⟩↦ he specifically mentions the philosopher G. E. Moore who argued (in a work entitled *Principia Ethica*, published in 1903) for the idea that moral properties, and in particular the central moral property 'good', were *non-natural* properties. That is to say, he argued that goodness was a real and objective feature of the world but not a natural feature such as the features that any natural science might investigate.

Perhaps some general background comment is called for here. Objectivism about moral values can be argued for on a naturalist picture, so that moral values or properties are presented as natural properties of a human world. On such views the conception of nature is implicitly or explicitly generous, including in its remit the historical and cultural dimension of human life. But those who tend towards a more narrowly construed conception of nature (perhaps because they regard the 'fabric of the world' as excluding anything that could not be investigated by the physical sciences) tend to think that if moral properties were objective, they would have to be strictly non-natural properties. Moore is an objectivist: he affirms the existence of such properties. (He is also a cognitivist: he holds that moral statements are truth-apt.) By contrast, a subjectivist such as Mackie denies the existence of such properties. (Mackie too can be categorized as a cognitivist, because even while he holds that there are no objective values for our moral talk to describe, he nonetheless takes it that our moral talk *purports* to describe such values. This leads him, as we shall see, to the conclusion that our normal moral talk is systematically false.)

> What are the two sorts of account of the meaning of ethical terms which Mackie describes at ⟨g⟩↦?

He describes two types of view. One kind of view says that ethical terms are prescriptive. They prescribe action either obliquely by expressing positive or negative attitudes towards whatever it is that is being morally characterized, or more squarely by expressing explicit prescriptions for or against it. Non-cognitivist views of this type share the key idea that the meaning of ethical terms has an essential non-descriptive element. That is what renders them manifestly able to explain the action-guiding power of ethical statements. The other type of view, by contrast, presents ethical terms as descriptive. Such views are described as 'naturalist' because (in Mackie's conception of naturalism) moral terms are descriptive of natural features of the world that underpin ethical distinctions between, say, courageous and cowardly behaviour – standing firm or running away in the face of the enemy, for instance. But, crucially,

they are also descriptive of relations between actions and human wants, satisfactions, and so on. This is the element that renders such views manifestly
able to account for the action-guiding power of moral statements. Mackie
says that both sorts of view have the merit of explaining the action-guiding-
ness of moral talk, but that they only capture part of the truth.

At $\boxed{h} \mapsto$ Mackie describes a 'natural reaction to any non-cognitive analysis
of ethical terms', i.e. a natural reaction to any view presenting moral claims as
not truth-apt.

> Describe in your own words the 'natural reaction' that Mackie has in mind.
> Can you think of an example to back it up?

The reaction in question is to object that ethical matters are surely something
we *can* have knowledge of – one might think one can know, for instance, that
severely beating children is cruel and wrong – whereas any non-cognitive
account deems it that such things are ultimately a matter of human decision
or invention.

Mackie acknowledges that naturalist ethical views can honour our intuition
that ethics is not a matter of decision. But he goes on to argue at $\boxed{i} \mapsto$ that by
the same token naturalist views run into a problem.

> What is the problem or 'deficiency' that Mackie attributes to naturalist
> views at $\boxed{i} \mapsto$?

The problem is that naturalist views relativize the action-guiding quality of
ethical statements to the desires or wants of the agent. This means they cannot
honour the further objectivist intuition we tend to have about morality: that
its authority over us is 'categorical' – that is, it binds us regardless of our
desires, wants and so on. So neither naturalism nor non-cognitivism can really
incorporate our objectivist intuitions about morality. Non-cognitivism leaves
out the claim to moral knowledge or truth; naturalism leaves out the sense of
morality's absolute authority. At $\boxed{j} \mapsto$ Mackie goes on to argue that our ordinary moral thinking contains a commitment to both of these objectivist
aspects.

> Do you agree that our ordinary moral thinking contains both these
> objectivist commitments? Can you think of examples that would support
> and/or undermine Mackie's claim?

At $\boxed{k} \mapsto$ Mackie states his general conclusion that ordinary moral judgements
include a claim to objectivity. And he infers from this that meta-ethics must
not limit itself to linguistic and conceptual analysis.

> Why does Mackie say that conceptual and linguistic analysis are not enough?

The argument here is that if our moral terms and concepts contain an implicit claim to objectivity, then any philosophical analysis of these things is bound to be objectivist. For Mackie observes that the claim to objectivity, however intrinsic to our moral thought and talk, is not self-validating, and philosophy should be able to question it. He goes on to claim that the subjectivist's or sceptic's denial of objective values should be put forward in the form of an 'error theory'.

What does Mackie mean by an 'error theory'? What is the error in question?

The idea is that all our moral judgements implicitly make a false claim: that they point to something objectively prescriptive. This false claim is the error in question, and the 'error theory' is simply the theory that our ethical thought and talk has the error built into it. He goes on to support his error theory with two kinds of argument.

What is the first kind of argument Mackie uses to defend his error theory? Specify the key points and see if you can think of objections.

The first argument Mackie presents is the 'argument from relativity'. It starts from the premise that there is moral variation between different societies and through different historical eras. The observation is then made that such moral disagreement reflects commitments to different ways of life; and the conclusion is drawn that people endorse a given moral code because they participate in that way of life, and not the other way round. This argument thus lends some support to subjectivism (see $\boxed{1}\mapsto$) – morality arises out of a shared way of life rather than out of diverse and therefore largely failed attempts to perceive objective morality. Subjectivism looks like a better explanation of the diversity of moral codes than the alternative objectivist hypothesis, that all these moral codes are more or less badly distorted versions of objective moral values.

At $\boxed{m}\mapsto$ Mackie considers an objection to the argument from relativity.

What is the objection Mackie considers, and how does he respond to it?

Somebody might claim that the objectivist case does not rest on the idea that *all* moral principles and judgements relate to objective values, but only those most basic and general principles that underpin them; and these are more or less common to all moral cultures.

But Mackie responds by arguing that this point does not constitute a powerful objection to the argument from relativity, since the sort of objectivism available on this view would not be very objectivist: while some basic moral principles would be objectively valid, still most of our moral judgements would only have objective status in a derivative and contingent sense – if society had been different, then different sorts of expressions of these basic principles would have been in force, and different actions would have been right.

At n⊢→ Mackie presents the second argument against the idea that moral values are objective.

> What is the second argument against the objectivity of moral values? Reading from n⊢→, see if you can specify its two key components.

The second and, as he sees it, more important argument that Mackie employs to defend the proposed error theory of moral value is his 'argument from queerness'. The first of its two components is a metaphysical point: if there were objective values figuring as part of the 'fabric of the world', then they would be metaphysically very odd things (whether conceived as entities, qualities or relations). He substantiates his claim at P⊢→ with the thought that such objective values would have to be akin to Plato's Form of the Good – something such that knowledge of it automatically furnishes the subject with a motivation to act accordingly.[1] As Mackie puts it, the theory of objective moral values would have to have 'to-be-pursuedness' somehow built into it, and this, he claims, is a very odd idea.

> How does Mackie go on further to bring out and support his argument from queerness?

He raises the question of how any supposed objective moral quality of an action would be related to the relevant non-evaluative (what he calls natural) properties of the action. In the case of a cruel action, for instance, how would the moral quality of wrongness be related to the action's natural features such as that the person was inflicting pain just for fun? He finds that the relation between the evaluative moral property and the non-evaluative natural property is suspiciously mysterious. The evaluative property would have to be somehow consequential or dependent upon the non-evaluative property, and yet it is very hard to see what this relation could amount to. He finishes the point by exclaiming how much simpler the subjectivist picture makes things, according to which there is no objective moral quality but instead a subjective human response which bears a causal relation to the perception of the natural features of the act. Our awareness that the pain is being inflicted just for fun causes us to respond with one or another sort of revulsion and disapproval.

> Looking back to o⊢→, what does Mackie claim is the objectivist's best reply to the argument from queerness?

---

[1] If you are interested in looking up Plato's idea of the Forms, see *Republic*, Book 6, 506b–509b.

The point, which he attributes to the eighteenth-century philosopher Richard Price, who was an advocate of 'intuitionism' (the objectivist view that we can perceive moral reality by way of a distinctive faculty of moral intuition), is that there are many things we do not and should not characterize as mere figments of an objectivist imagination yet which can seem metaphysically strange, at least from an empiricist point of view. Examples include number, identity, substance, and causation. (Empiricism is the school of philosophical thought that originates classically in the work of the eighteenth-century philosophers, John Locke and David Hume, the latter being a particular influence on Mackie's ethical philosophy. Perhaps the definitive idea of empiricism is that the elements of mind – our beliefs, our concepts – are all ultimately derived from sensory experience.)

> What is Mackie's response to this objection? How strong a response is it?

He says that the only adequate reply to the objection would be to present a full empiricist account of all these other things – number, identity, causation, etc. – which explained how they were not metaphysically queer after all, and how our knowledge of them is not epistemologically puzzling either. And he says that if any of number, identity or causation, etc., should prove resistant to such an account, then they should be regarded, along with objective values, as vulnerable to the argument from queerness.

Mackie's subjectivism attributes a global error to our moral thought and talk, and so part of his argumentative burden must be to explain how and why this error is so deeply ingrained in us.

> Reading from 9 → state in your own words the different 'patterns of objectification' that Mackie presents. Where appropriate, see if you can think of your own examples.

First he invokes what Hume called the mind's 'propensity to spread itself on external objects'. The suggestion is that we have a deep-seated tendency to project our own subjective responses on to the objects we are responding to. His example is that our disgust at a fungus may lead us to attribute a non-natural property of foulness to the fungus itself.

Second, he points out that moral attitudes are at least partly socially established, so it is true that morality has a source external to the individual's subjective responses. But it is not outside the realm of subjective response per se, since the social establishment of morality will be a matter of collectively established patterns of subjective moral response.

Third, Mackie observes that the social need to regulate behaviour creates a strong motivation to characterize moral values as objective: if they appear as objective then they are more likely to hold sway over people even in the face of contrary inclinations. This explains how we have less investment in the objectivity of aesthetic values, so that people are less resistant to subjectivism in the aesthetic sphere.

Fourth, he invokes the claim made by Thomas Hobbes (a seventeenth-century philosopher) that 'whatsoever is the object of any man's Appetite or Desire, that is it, which he for his part calleth *Good*', and the idea here is that we have a deeply entrenched habit of reversing the direction of dependence between our valuing something and the thing's having value. We tend to think we value something because it is objectively valuable, when really the thing has value simply because we value it.

Fifth, he cites Elizabeth Anscombe's view that our commitment to the objectivity of moral values is a historical residue from a time when there was a collective belief in a divine authority behind morality.

> What is Mackie's overall conclusion as to the explanation of our apparently incorrigible objectivist leanings?

He concludes that there are a number of different 'patterns of objectification' that we go in for and that these patterns have left their mark on our moral concepts and language.

> Do you find that the patterns of objectification which Mackie describes add up to a good explanation of the objectivism he has claimed is built into our moral thought and talk? Why couldn't we correct our objectivist error by changing, perhaps gradually, our moral concepts and language? Or perhaps, simply, by changing our allegedly objectivist assumptions? Is it really plausible to say that our natural moral consciousness is as heavily theory-laden as Mackie claims? Give a response to these questions in your own words.

Mackie presents and rejects one model of the objectivity of moral values: the metaphysical objectivity of moral values as real entities, properties or relations in the fabric of the world. His concern to refute moral objectivism takes the form of a concern to refute moral realism conceived as akin to realism about empirical matters. Our next reading, however, explores and defends a different conception of moral objectivity, which is aligned with a different idea of moral realism.

Introduction to Nagel

Thomas Nagel is Professor of Philosophy and Law at New York University. Born in Belgrade, Yugoslavia (now Serbia), in 1937, he first taught philosophy at the University of California, Berkeley (1963–6), then moved to Princeton University, where he stayed until his move to NYU in 1980. He is one of our most eminent living philosophers, and he has made significant contributions not only to ethics but also, notably, to political philosophy and philosophy of mind. His ideas in these different areas are unified by the organizing idea that human beings are capable of both subjective and objective views of their activities, and that these different perspectives cannot always be rendered compatible.

Thomas Nagel, *The View from Nowhere* (extracts from Ch. VIII, 'Value')

Realism and Objectivity

Objectivity is the central problem of ethics. Not just in theory, but in life. The problem is to decide in what way, if at all, the idea of objectivity can be applied to practical questions, questions of what to do or want. To what extent can they be dealt with from a detached point of view towards ourselves and the world? [...] The possibility of ethics and many of its problems can be best understood in terms of the impact of objectivity on the will. If we can make judgements about how we should live even after stepping outside of ourselves, they will provide the material for moral theory.

a⟶   In theoretical reasoning objectivity is advanced when we form a new conception of reality that includes ourselves as components. This involves an alteration or at least an extension of our beliefs. In the sphere of values or practical reasoning, the problem is different. As in the theoretical case, we must take up a new, comprehensive viewpoint after stepping back and including our former perspective in what is to be understood. But here the new viewpoint will be not a new set of beliefs, but a new or extended set of values. We try to arrive at normative judgements, with motivational content, from an impersonal standpoint. We cannot use a non-normative criterion of objectivity, for if values are objective, they must be so in their own right and not through reducibility to some other kind of objective fact. They have to be objective *values*, not objective anything else.

Here as elsewhere there is a connection between objectivity and realism, though realism about values is different from realism about b⟶   empirical facts. Normative realism is the view that propositions about what gives us reasons for action can be true or false independently of

Editors' note: The original footnotes have been renumbered as parts of the text have been omitted.

how things appear to us, and that we can hope to discover the truth by transcending the appearances and subjecting them to critical assessment. What we aim to discover by this method is not a new aspect of the external world, called value, but rather just the truth about what we and others should do and want.

It is important not to associate this form of realism with an inappropriate metaphysical picture: it is not a form of Platonism. The claim is that there are reasons for action, that we have to discover them instead of deriving them from our preexisting motives – and that in this way we can acquire new motives superior to the old. We simply aim to reorder our motives in a direction that will make them more acceptable from an external standpoint. Instead of bringing our thoughts into accord with an external reality, we try to bring an external view into the determination of our conduct.

c⊢→ The connection between objectivity and truth is therefore closer in ethics than it is in science. I do not believe that the truth about how we should live could extend radically beyond any capacity we might have to discover it (apart from its dependence on nonevaluative facts we might be unable to discover). The subject matter of ethics *is* how to engage in practical reasoning and the justification of action once we expand our consciousness by occupying the objective standpoint – not something else about action which the objective standpoint enables us to understand better. Ethical thought is the process of bringing objectivity to bear on the will, and the only thing I can think of to say about ethical truth in general is that it must be a possible result of this process, correctly carried out. I recognize that this is empty. If we wish to be more specific, all we can do is to refer to the arguments that persuade us of the objective validity of a reason or the correctness of a normative principle (and a given principle may be established in more than one way – got at from different starting points and by different argumentative routes).

Perhaps a richer metaphysic of morals could be devised, but I don't know what it would be. The picture I associate with normative realism is not that of an extra set of properties of things and events in the world, but of a series of possible steps in the development of human motivation which would improve the way we lead our lives, whether or not we will actually take them. We begin with a partial and inaccurate view, but by stepping outside of ourselves and constructing and comparing alternatives we can reach a new motivational condition at a higher level of objectivity. Though the aim is normative rather than descriptive, the method of investigation is analogous in certain respects to that of seeking an objective conception of what there is. We first form a conception of the world as centreless – as containing ourselves and other beings with particular points of view. But the question we then try to answer is not 'What can we see that the world contains, considered from this impersonal standpoint?' but 'What is there reason to do or want, considered from this impersonal standpoint?'

The answer will be complex. As in metaphysics, so in the realm of practical reason the truth is sometimes best understood from a detached standpoint; but sometimes it will be fully comprehensible only from a particular perspective within the world. If there are such subjective values, then an objective conception of what people have reasons to do must leave room for them. [...] But once the objective step is taken, the possibility is also open for the recognition of values and reasons that are independent of one's personal perspective and have force for anyone who can view the world impersonally, as a place that contains him. If objectivity means anything here, it will mean that when we detach from our individual perspective and the values and reasons that seem acceptable from within it, we can sometimes arrive at a new conception which may endorse some of the original reasons but will reject some as false subjective appearances and add others.

So without prejudging the outcome – that is, how much of the domain of practical reasons can be objectively understood – we can see what the objectifying impulse depends on. The most basic idea of practical objectivity is arrived at by a practical analogue of the rejection of solipsism in the theoretical domain. Realism about the facts leads us to seek a detached point of view from which reality can be discerned and appearance corrected, and realism about values leads us to seek a detached point of view from which it will be possible to correct inclination and to discern what we really should do. Practical objectivity means that practical reason can be understood and even engaged in by the objective self.

This assumption, though powerful, is not yet an ethical position. It merely marks the place which an ethical position will occupy if we can make sense of the subject. It says that the world of reasons, including my reasons, does not exist only from my own point of view. I am in a world whose character is to a certain extent independent of what I think, and if I have reasons to act it is because the person who I am has those reasons, in virtue of his condition and circumstances. The basic question of practical reason from which ethics begins is not 'What shall I do?' but 'What should this person do?'

This sets a problem and indicates a method of attacking it. The problem is to discover the form which reasons for action take, and whether it can be described from no particular point of view. The method is to begin with the reasons that appear to obtain from my own point of view and those of other individuals, and ask what the best perspectiveless account of those reasons is. As in other domains, we begin from our position inside the world and try to transcend it by regarding what we find here as a sample of the whole.

That is the hope. But the claim that there are objective values is permanently controversial, because of the ease with which values and reasons seem to disappear when we transcend the subjective stand-point of our own desires. It can seem, when one looks at life from outside, that there is no room for values in the world at all. So to say: 'There are just people with various motives and inclinations, some of which they may express in evaluative language; but when we regard all this from outside, all we see are psychological facts. The ascent to an objective view, far from revealing new values that modify the sub-jective appearances, reveals that appearances are all there is: it enables us to observe and describe our subjective motives but does not pro-duce any new ones. Objectivity has no place in this domain except what is inherited from the objectivity of theoretical and factual ele-ments that play a role in practical reasoning. Beyond that it applies here with a nihilistic result: nothing is objectively right or wrong because objectively nothing matters; if there are such things as right and wrong, they must rest on a subjective foundation.'

I believe this conclusion is the result of a mistake comparable to the one that leads to physicalism, with its attendant reductionist elabora-tions. An epistemological criterion of reality is being assumed which pretends to be comprehensive but which in fact excludes large domains in advance without argument.

The assumption is surreptitious, but natural. Values can seem really to disappear when we step outside of our skins, so that it strikes us as a philosophical *perception* that they are illusory. This is a characteris-tic Humean step: we observe the phenomenon of people acting for what they take to be reasons, and *all we see* [...] are certain natural facts; that people are influenced by certain motives, or would be if they knew certain things.

We are continually tempted to reoccupy Hume's position by the difficulties we encounter when we try to leave it. Skepticism, Platonism, reductionism, and other familiar philosophical excesses all make their appearance in ethical theory. Particularly attractive is the reaction to skepticism which reinterprets the whole field, ethics included, in completely subjective terms. [...] This conceals the retreat from realism by substituting a set of judgements that in some way resemble the originals.

The only way to resist Humean subjectivism about desires and reasons for action is to seek a form of objectivity appropriate to the subject. This will not be the objectivity of naturalistic psychology. It must be argued that an objective view limited to such observations is not correct. Or rather, not necessarily correct, for the point is that an objective view of ourselves should leave room for the apprehension of reasons – should not exclude them in advance.

They seem to be excluded in advance if the objective standpoint is assumed to be one of pure observation and description.[1] When we direct this sort of attention to what appears subjectively as a case of acting for reasons and responding to good and evil, we get a naturalistic account that seems to give the complete objective description of what is going on. Instead of normative reasons, we see only a psychological explanation.

But I believe it is a mistake to give these phenomena a purely psychological reading when we look at them from outside. What we see, unless we are artificially blind, is not just people being moved to act by their desires, but people acting and forming intentions and desires for reasons, good or bad. That is, we recognize their reasons *as reasons* – or perhaps we think they are bad reasons – but in any case we do not drop out of the evaluative mode as soon as we leave the subjective standpoint. The recognition of reasons as reasons is to be contrasted with their use purely as a form of psychological explanation [...]. The latter merely connects action with the agent's desires and beliefs, without touching the normative question whether he *had* an adequate reason for acting – whether he should have acted as he did. If this is all that can be said once we leave the point of view of the agent behind, then I think it would follow that we don't really act for reasons at all. Rather, we are caused to act by desires and beliefs, and the terminology of reasons can be used only in a diminished, nonnormative sense to express this kind of explanation.

The substitution of an account in which values or normative reasons play no part is not something that simply falls out of the objective view. It depends on a particular objective claim that can be accepted only if it is more plausible than its denial: the claim that our sense that the world presents us with reasons for action is a subjective illusion, produced by the projection of our preexisting motives onto the world, and that there aren't objectively any reasons for us to do anything – though of course there are motives, some of which mimic normative reasons in form.

But this would have to be established: it does not follow from the idea of objectivity alone. When we take the objective step, we don't

---

[1] Cf. G. E. M. Anscombe, 'Causality and Determination', Inaugural lecture, Cambridge University, 1971, in *Metaphysics and the Philosophy of Mind: Collected Philosophical Papers vol. III* (University of Minnesota Press, 1981), p. 137: 'This often happens in philosophy; it is argued that 'all we "find" is such-and-such, and it turns out that the arguer has excluded from his idea of "finding" the sort of thing he says we don't "find".'

leave the evaluative capacity behind automatically, since that capacity does not depend on antecedently present desires. We may find that it continues to operate from an external standpoint, and we may conclude that this is not just a case of subjective desires popping up again in objective disguise. I acknowledge the dangers of false objectification, which elevates personal tastes and prejudices into cosmic values. But it isn't the only possibility.

Antirealism

Where does the burden of proof lie with respect to the possibility of objective values? Does their possibility have to be demonstrated before we can begin to think more specifically about which values are revealed or obliterated by the objective standpoint? Or is such an inquiry legitimate so long as objective values haven't been shown to be *im*possible?

I think the burden of proof has been often misplaced in this debate, and that a defeasible presumption that values need not be illusory is entirely reasonable until it is shown not to be. Like the presumption that things exist in an external world, the presumption that there are real values and reasons can be defeated in individual cases, if a purely subjective account of the appearances is more plausible. And like the presumption of an external world, its complete falsity is not self-contradictory. The reality of values, impersonal or otherwise, is not entailed by the totality of appearances any more than the reality of a physical universe is. But if either of them is recognized as a possibility, then its reality in detail can be confirmed by appearances, at least to the extent of being rendered more plausible than the alternatives. So a lot depends on whether the possibility of realism is admitted in the first place.

It is very difficult to argue for such a possibility, except by refuting arguments against it. [...] What is the result when such an argument is refuted? Is the contrary possibility in a stronger position? I believe so: in general, there is no way to prove the possibility of realism; one can only refute impossibility arguments, and the more often one does this the more confidence one may have in the realist alternative. So to consider the merits of an admission of realism about value, we have to consider the reasons against it – against its possibility or against its truth. I shall discuss three. They have been picked for their apparent capacity to convince.

The first type of argument depends on the unwarranted assumption that if values are real, they must be real objects of some other kind. John Mackie, in his book *Ethics*, denies the objectivity of values by saying that they are 'not part of the fabric of the world', and that if they were, they would have to be 'entities or qualities or relations of a very strange sort, utterly different from anything else in the universe' (Mackie, p. 38).[2] He clearly has a definite picture of what the universe is like, and assumes that realism about value would require crowding it with extra entities, qualities, or relations, things like Platonic Forms or Moore's non-natural qualities. But this assumption is not correct. The objective badness of pain, for example, is not some mysterious further property that all pains have, but just the fact that there is reason for anyone capable of viewing the world objectively to want it to stop. The view that values are real is not the view that they are real occult entities or properties, but that they are real values: that our claims about value and about what people have reason to do may be true or false independently of our beliefs and inclinations. No other kinds of truths are involved. Indeed, no other kinds of truths *could* imply the reality of values. This applies not only to moral values but also to prudential ones, and even to the simple reasons people have to do what will achieve their present aims.

In discussion, Mackie objected that his disbelief in the reality of values and reasons did not depend on the assumption that to be real they must be strange entities or properties. As he says in his book, the point applies directly to reasons themselves. For whatever they are they are not needed to explain anything that happens, and there is consequently no reason to believe in their existence.

But this raises the same issue. Mackie meant that reasons play no role in causal explanations. But it begs the question to assume that this sort of explanatory necessity is the test of reality for values. The claim that certain reasons exist is a normative claim, not a claim about the best causal explanation of anything. To assume that only what has to be included in the best causal theory of the world is real is to assume that there are no irreducibly normative truths.

However, there is another difficulty here which I'm not sure how to deal with. If there are normative truths, they enter into normative rather than causal explanations of the existence of particular reasons or the rightness or wrongness of particular actions. But our apprehension of these truths also explains our acquisition of new motives, and ultimately it can influence our conduct. Even if we set aside the issues about free will and the intentional explanation of action, [...] there is a problem here about the relation between normative and causal explanation. It is not clear whether normative realism is compatible with the hypothesis that all our normative beliefs can be accounted for by some kind of naturalistic psychology.

[2]   J. L. Mackie, *Ethics* (Harmondsworth: Penguin, 1977).

Gilbert Harman formulates the problem thus:

> Observation plays a role in science that it does not seem to play in ethics. The difference is that you need to make assumptions about certain physical facts to explain the occurrence of the observations that support a scientific theory, but you do not seem to need to make assumptions about any moral facts to explain the occurrence of ... so-called moral observations ... In the moral case, it would seem that you need only make assumptions about the psychology or moral sensibility of the person making the moral observation.[3]

Any defender of realism about values must claim that the purely psychological account is incomplete, either because normative explanations are an additional element or because they are somehow present in certain types of psychological explanations – perhaps in a way like that in which explanations of belief by logical reasoning can be simultaneously causal and justificatory (if in fact they can be). So when, for example, we become convinced by argument that a distinction is morally relevant, the explanation of our conviction can be given by the content and validity of the argument.

While we cannot prove the purely psychological, antirealist account to be false – so that it remains literally true that you don't *need* to explain normative judgements in terms of normative truths – I believe the most plausible account will refer to such truths, even at the most elementary level. To dispense with them is too radical a denial of the appearances. If I have a severe headache, the headache seems to me to be not merely unpleasant, but a bad thing. Not only do I dislike it, but I think I have a reason to try to get rid of it. It is barely conceivable that this might be an illusion, but if the idea of a bad thing makes sense at all, it need not be an illusion, and the true explanation of my impression may be the simplest one, namely that headaches are bad, and not just unwelcome to the people who have them.

Everything depends on whether the idea makes sense. If the possibility of real values is admitted, specific values become susceptible to a kind of observational testing, but it operates through the kind of explanation appropriate to the subject: normative explanation. In physics, one infers from factual appearances to their most plausible explanation in a theory of how the world is. In ethics, one infers from appearances of value to their most plausible explanation in a theory

[3] G. Harman, [*The Nature of Morality* (Oxford University Press, 1977)] p. 6; this is his formulation of the problem, not his proposed solution.

of what there is reason to do or want. All the inferences will rely on general ideas of reality that do not derive from appearance – the most important being the general idea of objective reality itself. And in both science and ethics some of the appearances will turn out to be mistaken and to have psychological explanations of a kind that do not confirm their truth.

My belief that the distinction between appearance and reality applies here is based not on a metaphysical picture, but on the capacity of a realistic approach to make sense of our thoughts. If we start by regarding appearances of value as appearances of something, and then step back to form hypotheses about the broader system of motivational possibilities of which we have had a glimpse, the result is a gradual opening out of a complex domain which we apparently discover. The method of discovery is to seek the best normative explanation of the normative appearances. I believe that the actual results of this method tend to confirm the realistic assumption behind it – though I recognize that a sceptic may object that the results are contaminated by the assumption itself and cannot therefore supply independent confirmation.

Let me now turn to the second argument against realism. Unlike the first, it is not based on a misinterpretation of moral objectivity. Instead, it tries to represent the unreality of values as an objective discovery. The argument is that if claims of value have to be objectively correct, and if they are not reducible to any other kind of objective claim, then we can just see that all positive value claims must be false. Nothing has any objective value, because objectively nothing matters at all. If we push the claims of objective detachment to their logical conclusion, and survey the world from a standpoint completely detached from all interests, we discover that there is *nothing* – no values left of any kind: things can be said to matter at all only to individuals within the world. The result is objective nihilism.

I don't deny that the objective standpoint tempts one in this direction. [...] But I believe this can seem like the required conclusion only if one makes the mistake of assuming that objective judgements of value must emerge from the detached standpoint alone. It is true that with nothing to go on but a conception of the world from nowhere, one would have no way of telling whether anything had value. But an objective view has more to go on, for its data include the appearance of value to individuals with particular perspectives, including oneself. In this respect practical reason is no different from anything else. Starting from a pure idea of a possible reality and a very impure set of appearances, we try to fill in the idea of reality so as to make some partial sense of the appearances, using objectivity as a method. To find out what the world is like from outside we have to approach it from within: it is no wonder that the same is true for ethics.

And indeed, when we take up the objective standpoint, the problem is not that values seem to disappear but that there seem to be too many of them, coming from every life and drowning out those that arise from our own. It is just as easy to form desires from an objective standpoint as it is to form beliefs. Probably easier. Like beliefs, these desires and evaluations must be criticized and justified partly in terms of the appearances. But they are not just further appearances, any more than the beliefs about the world which arise from an impersonal standpoint are just further appearances.

The third type of argument against the objective reality of values is an empirical argument. It is also perhaps the most common. It is intended not to rule out the possibility of real values from the start, but rather to demonstrate that even if their possibility is admitted, we have no reason to believe that there are any. The claim is that if we consider the wide cultural variation in normative beliefs, the importance of social pressure and other psychological influences to their formation, and the difficulty of settling moral disagreements, it becomes highly implausible that they are anything but pure appearances.

Anyone offering this argument must admit that not every psychological factor in the explanation of an appearance shows that the appearance corresponds to nothing real. Visual capacities and elaborate training play a part in explaining the physicist's perception of a cloud-chamber track, or a student's coming to believe a proposition of geometry, but the nature of the particle and the truth of the proposition also play an essential part in these explanations. No one has produced a general account of the kinds of psychological explanation that discredit an appearance. But some sceptics about ethics feel that because of the way we acquire moral beliefs and other impressions of value, there are grounds for confidence that here, nothing real is being talked about.

I find the popularity of this argument surprising. The fact that morality is socially inculcated and that there is radical disagreement about it across cultures, over time, and even within cultures at a time is a poor reason to conclude that values have no objective reality. Even where there is truth, it is not always easy to discover. Other areas of knowledge are taught by social pressure, many truths as well as falsehoods are believed without rational grounds, and there is wide disagreement about scientific and social facts, especially where strong interests are involved which will be affected by different answers to a disputed question. This last factor is present throughout ethics to a uniquely high degree: it is an area in which one would expect extreme variation of belief and radical disagreement however objectively real the subject actually was. For comparably motivated disagreements about matters of fact, one has to go to the heliocentric theory, the theory of evolution, the Dreyfus case, the Hiss case, and the genetic contribution to racial differences in IQ.

Although the methods of ethical reasoning are rather primitive, the degree to which agreement can be achieved and social prejudices transcended in the face of strong pressures suggests that something real is being investigated, and that part of the explanation of the appearances, both at simple and at complex levels, is that we perceive, often inaccurately, that there are certain reasons for action, and go on to infer, often erroneously, the general form of the principles that best account for those reasons.

Again let me stress that this is not to be understood on the model of perception of features of the external world. The subject matter of our investigations is how to live, and the process of ethical thought is one of motivational discovery. The fact that people can to some extent reach agreement on answers which they regard as objective suggests that when they step outside of their particular individual perspectives, they call into operation a common evaluative faculty whose correct functioning provides the answers, even though it can also malfunction and be distorted by other influences. It is not a question of bringing the mind into correspondence with an external reality which acts causally on it, but of reordering the mind itself in accordance with the demands of its own external view of itself.

I have not discussed all the possible arguments against realism about values, but I have tried to give general reasons for skepticism about such arguments. It seems to me that they tend to be supported by a narrow preconception of what sorts of truths there are, and that this is essentially question-begging. Nothing said here will force a reductionist to give up his denial of normative realism, but perhaps it has been shown to be a reasonable position. I should add that the search for objective principles makes sense even if we do not assume that all of ethics or human value is equally objective. Objectivity need not be all or nothing. So long as realism is true in some of these areas, we can reasonably pursue the method of objective reflection as far as it will take us.

[...]

Types of Generality

The search for generality is one of the main impulses in the construction of an objective view – in normative as in theoretical matters. One takes the particular case as an example, and forms hypotheses about what general truth it is an example of. There is more than one type of generality, and no reason to assume that a single form will apply to every type of value. Since the choice among types of generality defines some of the central issues of moral theory, let me describe the options.

[m]→   One respect in which reasons may vary is in their breadth. A principle may be general in the sense that it applies to everyone but be quite narrow in content; and it is an open question to what extent narrower principles of practical reason (don't lie; develop your talents) can be subsumed under broader ones (don't hurt others; consider your long-term interests), or even at the limit under a single widest principle from which all the rest derive. Reasons may be universal, in other words, without forming a unified system that always provides a method for arriving at determinate conclusions about what one should do.

A second respect in which reasons vary is in their *relativity to the agent*, the person for whom they are reasons. The distinction between reasons that are relative to the agent and reasons that are not is an extremely important one.[4] If a reason can be given a general form which does not include an essential reference to the person who has it, it is an *agent-neutral* reason. For example, if it is a reason for anyone to do or want something that it would reduce the amount of wretchedness in the world, then that is a neutral reason. If on the other hand the general form of a reason does include an essential reference to the person who has it, it is an *agent-relative* reason. For example, if it is a reason for anyone to do or want something that it would be in *his* interest, then that is a relative reason. In such a case, if something were in Jones's interest but contrary to Smith's, Jones would have reason to want it to happen and Smith would have the same reason to want it not to happen. (Both agent-relative and agent-neutral reasons are objective, if they can be understood and affirmed from outside the viewpoint of the individual who has them.)

A third way in which reasons may vary is in their degree of externality, or independence of the concerns of sentient beings. Most of the apparent reasons that initially present themselves to us are intimately connected with interests and desires, our own or those of others, and

---

[4] In Nagel [*The Possibility of Altruism* (Oxford University Press, 1970; repr. Princeton University Press, 1978)] I marked it by speaking of 'subjective' and 'objective' reasons, but since those terms are being put to different use here, I shall adopt Parfit's terms, 'agent-relative' and 'agent-neutral' (Parfit [*Reasons and Persons* (Oxford University Press, 1984)], p. 143). Often I shall shorten these to 'relative' and 'neutral'; and sometimes I shall refer to the corresponding values as 'personal' and 'impersonal'.

often with experiential satisfaction. But it seems that some of these interests give evidence that their objects have an intrinsic value which is not merely a function of the satisfaction that people may derive from them or of the fact that anyone wants them – a value which is not reducible to their value *for* anyone. I don't know how to establish whether there are any such values, but the objectifying tendency produces a strong impulse to believe that there are – especially in aesthetics, where the object of interest is external and the interest seems perpetually capable of criticism in light of further attention to the object. The problem is to account for external values in a way which avoids the implausible consequence that they retain their practical importance even if no one will *ever* be able to respond to them. (So that if all sentient life is destroyed, it will still be a good thing if the Frick Collection survives.)

There may be other significant dimensions of variation. I want to concentrate on these because they locate the main controversies about what ethics is. Reasons and values that can be described in these terms provide the material for objective judgements. If one looks at human action and its conditions from outside and considers whether some normative principles are plausible, these are the forms they will take.

The actual acceptance of a general normative judgement will have motivational implications, for it will commit you under some circumstances to the acceptance of reasons to want and do things yourself.

This is most clear when the objective judgement is that something has agent-neutral or impersonal value. That means anyone has reason to want it to happen – and that includes someone considering the world in detachment from the perspective of any particular person within it. Such a judgement has motivational content even before it is brought back down to the particular perspective of the individual who has accepted it objectively.

Relative reasons are different. An objective judgement that some kind of thing has agent-relative value commits us only to believing that someone has reason to want and pursue it if it is related to him in the right way (being in his interest, for example). Someone who accepts this judgement is not even committed to wanting it to be the case that people in general are influenced by such reasons. The judgement commits him to wanting something only when its implications are drawn for the individual person he happens to be. With regard to others, the content of the objective judgement concerns only what *they* should do or want.

Judgements of both these kinds, as well as others, are evoked from us when we take up an objective standpoint, and the pressure to combine intelligibly the two standpoints toward action can lead to the refinement and extension of such judgements.

The choice among normative hypotheses is difficult and there is no general method of making it, any more than there is a general method of selecting the most plausible objective account of the facts on the basis of the appearances. The only 'method' here or elsewhere, is to try to generate hypotheses and then to consider which of them seems most reasonable, in light of everything else one is fairly confident of. Since we may assume that not every alternative has been thought of, the best we can hope for is a comparison among those available, not a firm solution.

This is not quite empty, for it means at least that logic alone can settle nothing. We do not have to be shown that the denial of some kind of objective value is self-contradictory in order to be reasonably led to accept its existence. There is no constraint to pick the weakest or narrowest or most economical principle consistent with the initial data that arise from individual perspectives. Our admission of reasons beyond these is determined not by logical entailment, but by the relative plausibility of those normative hypotheses – including the null hypothesis – that are consistent with the evidence.

In this respect ethics is no different from anything else: theoretical knowledge does not arise by deductive inference from the appearances either. The main difference is that our objective thinking about practical reasons is very primitive and has difficulty taking even the first step. Philosophical scepticism and idealism about values are much more popular than their metaphysical counterparts. Nevertheless, I believe they are no more correct. Although no single objective principle of practical reason like egoism or utilitarianism covers everything, the acceptance of some objective values is unavoidable – not because the alternative is inconsistent but because it is not *credible*. Someone who, as in Hume's example (*Treatise*, bk. 2, pt. 3, sec. 3), prefers the destruction of the whole world to the scratching of his finger may not be involved in a contradiction or in any false expectations, but there is something the matter with him nonetheless, and anyone else not in the grip of an overnarrow conception of what reasoning is would regard his preference as objectively wrong.

But even if it is unreasonable to deny that anyone ever objectively has a reason to do anything, it is not easy to find positive objective principles that *are* reasonable. In particular it is not easy to follow the objectifying impulse without distorting individual life and personal relations. We want to be able to understand and accept the way we live from outside, but it may not always follow that we should control our lives from inside by the terms of that external understanding. Often the objective viewpoint will not be suitable as a replacement for the subjective, but will coexist with it, setting a standard with which the subjective is constrained not to clash. In deciding what to do, for example, we should not reach a result different from what we could decide objectively that that *person* should do – but we need not arrive at the result in the same way from the two standpoints.

Sometimes, also, the objective standpoint will allow us to judge how people should be or should live, without permitting us to translate this into a judgement about what they have reasons to do. For in some respects it is better to live and act not for reasons, but because it does not occur to us to do anything else. This is especially true of close personal relations. Here the objective standpoint cannot be brought into the perspective of action without diminishing precisely what it affirms the value of. Nevertheless, the possibility of objective affirmation is important. We should be *able* to view our lives from outside without extreme dissociation or distaste, and the extent to which we should live without considering the objective point of view or even any reasons at all is itself determined largely from that point of view.

[...]

Commentary on Nagel

Realism and objectivity

Nagel begins at ⟨a⟩→ by presenting a conception of objectivity in general. Whereas in the extract from Mackie the notion of objectivity was used to pick out a metaphysical idea – the idea of something's existing independently from human minds – in this extract from Nagel the notion of objectivity is used to pick out an epistemic idea, the idea that questions of practical reason (what should I do?) have an objectively correct answer, so that there can be objectively correct moral judgements.

> What is Nagel's general model of objectivity? See if you can think of your own example to illustrate an increase in objectivity of the kind he describes.

Nagel takes objectivity primarily as an epistemic idea, as a feature of our beliefs or views of the world. On this conception, objectivity comes in degrees. It is increased when we stand back from one point of view on the world and take up a more inclusive purview which includes the former viewpoint. Supposing, for example, that you are responding to the fact that your child has been accused of bullying at school. Your first reaction might well be to say this is impossible, that your son would never do such a thing, and so on. Imagine that, for whatever reason, it turns out that in fact he has been bullying one of his classmates. In order for you to achieve a more objective view of the matter, you need to take a step back, so that you include in your new purview the fact that your first reaction to the accusation was one of an adoring parent and that adoring parents do not see everything there is to see about their children. To take up a more objective view is to take up a more detached or impersonal view.

> What, on Nagel's view, is the difference between objectivity in theoretical reasoning and objectivity in evaluative or practical reasoning?

In the sphere of theoretical reasoning (this includes the empirical theoretical reasoning of science) the upshot of stepping back and including our former perspective in what is to be understood will be a new set of beliefs. By contrast, in the sphere of evaluative reasoning the upshot is a new or extended set of values. In the moral sphere, increases in the objectivity of our views lead to increases in the objectivity of our values. This is how we bring objectivity to bear in our motivations, in our will.

At $\boxed{\text{b}} \mapsto$ he observes the close connection between (this kind of) objectivity of values and realism about values.

> What, according to Nagel, is normative realism (i.e. realism about values)? And what does he say is the difference between realism about values and realism about empirical facts?

Nagel is clear that realism about values should not be conflated with realism about empirical facts. He characterizes normative realism as the idea that the truth of evaluative propositions transcends (is independent of) how things seem subjectively to be. He adds that we can hope to discover this truth by taking up the objective standpoint and engaging in critical assessment of our moral responses. But this idea that we generally have the critical wherewithal to discover moral reality is not an article of faith. Rather it is a corollary of his conception of normative realism, for, as he argues at $\boxed{\text{c}} \mapsto$, in ethics the connection between objectivity and truth is very close. The very idea of ethical truth just falls out of our capacity to occupy the objective standpoint: he says he cannot give the concept of ethical truth any more content than that it is what we arrive at if we fully succeed in bringing objectivity to bear in our ethical thinking.

Nagel's normative realism, then, does not posit evaluative entities of any kind as part of the external world. And he argues that to think so would be to associate realism about values with an inappropriate metaphysical picture – one appropriate to realism about empirical facts but not realism about values.

(Compare Mackie on what sort of realism the objectivity of moral values would amount to.) Whereas empirical realism allows for the possibility that the nature of empirical reality may ultimately outstrip our capacity to find out about it and understand it (it is possible that the ultimate mysteries of the physical universe remain permanently beyond our ken), in the sphere of ethical thinking realism does not permit this kind of gap between ethical truth and our powers of critical ethical reflection.

So far Nagel has talked only positively about increasing objectivity in our ethical views or judgements. But at ⌐d⌐→ he explains that the need for objectivity is in some degree countered by a need to retain some element of subjectivity.

> What is it, on Nagel's view, that limits the desirability of objectivity in ethical thinking?

The point is that sometimes in ethics the truth will be fully intelligible only from a particular perspective on the world. We could be too detached, too impersonal to grasp some ethical truths, and so our efforts at objectivity need to be appropriately adjusted to this limitation. More broadly, he seems to suggest that perhaps the relevant degree of objectivity that is desirable in the ethical involves the transcendence of one's personal standpoint as an individual, in order to arrive at an altered set of values, perhaps a set that will have force for anyone capable of taking up such an impersonal standpoint.

Nagel is not assuming this is possible; rather he is setting up the idea of normative realism in order that it may be investigated. He says that his method will be to begin with the reasons that appear to obtain from individuals' points of view, and to ask what the best perspectiveless account of those reasons is.

> How does Nagel explain at ⌐e⌐→ the fact that the claim to objective values is permanently controversial?

It is all too easy, he says, when we stand outside the subjective standpoint of our own desires and inclinations to have the impression that there is nothing left over in the way of values. It can seem – as it does on Mackie's picture – that all we are confronted with are people doing things not for moral reasons but rather because of some set of subjective impulses, impulses which perhaps create an illusion of objective moral reasons.

Nagel argues that our impression that values disappear when we step outside our own skins is the result of a surreptitious mistaken assumption. He says at ⌐f⌐→ that the assumption comes to us as if it were a philosophical *perception*. And he regards this assumption as doing falsely reductive work elsewhere in philosophy too, in the philosophy of mind, by encouraging physicalism: the view that the proper account of our mental lives (our consciousness, our experiences, our beliefs) is to be given in purely physical terms of states and processes of the brain.

Try and explain in your own words the nature of the assumption that Nagel criticizes.

The assumption Nagel regards as mistaken is traced to a methodological step that is characteristic of Hume: to take up the position of an outside observer on some human practice, and find that all one really *sees* there is some set of natural facts – for instance, that when such and such happens, people tend to behave in this or that manner. The perfectly natural idea that what one might be in a position to *see* is that people are acting for reasons comes, in this sort of methodological move, to seem outlandish. Nagel describes the assumption embedded in Hume's methodological step as 'an epistemological assumption', because the assumption is that if you do not have the impression of *seeing* the phenomenon on the surface of human behaviour, then it is not real; it must be an illusion of some sort, classically the result of projection.

How, at g ⟩→, does Nagel suggest we might resist Humean subjectivism about reasons?

Simply, by first identifying the form of objectivity that is appropriate to values (as opposed to empirical facts). That has been the aim of this first section.

Anti-realism

Nagel opens this section with the question of where the burden of proof lies in the debate between realists and anti-realist about values. He states his view that the onus of proof lies with the anti-realist in that it is reasonable to assume our values are not 'illusory' unless proven otherwise. He says the only available strategy for the realist is to refute anti-realist arguments and hope that realism gradually comes to seem more and more convincing as a result.

What argument does Nagel give against Mackie's anti-realist view of values?

Having quoted from Mackie's argument from queerness, Nagel argues that the assumption that moral realism requires us to countenance new and bizarre entities, qualities or relations in our metaphysics is false. On the contrary, Nagel argues, all it requires is that our claims about value and what people have reason to do in this or that situation be true or false, independently of what we may happen to believe or want. That our moral questions should have objective answers does not require any new metaphysical commitment of the kind Mackie supposes.

What response on Mackie's part does Nagel recount at i ⟩→; and how does Nagel counter it?

Nagel reports that Mackie objected to the idea that his scepticism about value depended on the argument from queerness, and he directs attention to another argument offered elsewhere in his book, which relies on the idea that values and reasons were, strictly speaking, explanatorily redundant: we can give a full (physical) causal explanation of why everything in the world happens without having to mention values or reasons at all. Nagel argues that this argument is question-begging in the same way that the argument from queerness was: why assume that this sort of explanatory necessity is the test for the reality of values?

> What is the difficulty at [j]⟶ which Nagel says he is unsure how to deal with?

The difficulty is that the advocate of normative realism must insist that there could not be a complete causal explanation of events that made no mention of values or reasons for actions. And yet there is a plausible case (made, for instance, by Gilbert Harman) for the idea that one does not need to make mention of any moral facts or objective values in order to explain our moral 'observations'; all the explanatory work can be done by pointing to the psychology (moral sensibility) of the subject.

Still, Nagel continues on the basis that his case for normative realism does not rest on proving that reasons are an irreplaceable part of any complete causal explanation. Rather, he mounts his case on the grounds that the presumption that values and reasons are real makes best sense of our normative thinking and, in particular, of our capacity to step back and increase the objectivity of our point of view. This process presents itself as one of normative discovery – discovery of what our reasons for action in fact are.

> What is the second argument against normative realism, which Nagel considers at [k]⟶? And how does he counter it?

The argument is for 'objective nihilism'; that is, for the view that objectively there are no values of any kind. Such a view is arrived at by taking the stepping-back process to its logical extreme, so that we take up a maximally objective view of the world from a standpoint that is devoid of all interests, devoid of all perspective (recall the title of Nagel's book: *The View From Nowhere*).

Nagel responds with the point that the move to objective nihilism depends on a false assumption: that if values were objective they would be visible on the maximally objective view of the world. Rather, they are in view on (what Nagel simply calls) the objective view, which presents us with human individuals and the appearances of value to those individuals. With this data in view, normative realism naturally takes hold as we try to make best sense of those appearances. That is, the idea that values and reasons are real flows from our attempts to make sense of these appearances, as we subject them to critical scrutiny: some turn out to be true and others do not.

> Describe in your own words the third argument against normative realism, which Nagel discusses at ⌊l⌋→. How does Nagel respond?

This anti-realist argument is addressed not to the very possibility that there are real values, but instead presses the case that certain appearances of radical contingency in ethical life – the moral diversity between cultures, the difficulty of resolving moral disagreements, the role of socialization in establishing any given morality – render moral realism implausible. (Recall Mackie's argument from relativity, which exemplifies precisely the argumentative strategy in question.)

Nagel argues that the considerations mentioned are entirely inconclusive. The achievement of scientific knowledge too requires a certain social training, and there is often radical disagreement between scientific communities, especially where people have strong interests in one or another view, as they tend to in the ethical case. Truth, Nagel emphasizes, is not always easy to discover, and his point is that disagreement over moral matters is no conclusive argument against normative realism. (Recall that such inconclusiveness was acknowledged by Mackie when he advanced his own argument from relativity.)

At ⌊m⌋→ Nagel distinguishes three kinds of generality as applied to values. The first is what he calls breadth, which relates to the content of a value or principle. Among reasons that are universal (they apply to everyone), there are variations of breadth. Moral principles whose content means that the principles are not very broad – his examples are: don't lie; develop your talents – can be seen as instances of other principles whose content is broader: don't hurt others; consider your long-term interests. Lying to someone is an instance of the broader phenomenon of hurting others, and developing your talents an instance of the broader phenomenon of considering your long-term interests.

> Think up your own example of a relatively narrow principle which might be subsumed under a broader one.

The second kind of generality is relativity to the agent. The terminology used contrasts reasons that are agent-relative with those that are agent-neutral, and the distinction turns on whether the expression of the reason makes essential reference to the particular agent or not. For instance, you have a reason to be well prepared for a certain job interview; but another candidate for the same job has no reason to want you to be well prepared. Your reason to be well prepared is an agent-relative reason; its rational force is relative to you in particular.

The third kind of generality is degree of independence from the concerns of sentient beings. This is quite an abstract idea but it is well captured in the example given about its being a good thing (not *for* anyone, just a good-thing-full-stop) if the wonderful private art collection at the Frick Museum in New York should survive, even if there's no one around to enjoy it. This is a particular idea of absolute value, and it could be seen as positioned at the extreme of a single continuum with agent-relative and agent-neutral reasons. On one end of the continuum there are agent-relative reasons (reasons whose force depends upon features of the particular individual agent); then moving along the continuum we find agent-neutral reasons (reasons whose force is dependent on no contingent features of the individual agent, so that they apply to everyone); and then, at the very extreme, there are reasons whose force is independent of features (contingent or otherwise) of *all* sentient life.

Some people might be sceptical that there are any absolutely valuable things in this last, very strong sense. But others will share the intuition that there's something to it: consider, for instance, the idea that it would be bad-full-stop if a certain unknown micro-organism in an undiscovered depth of the Antarctic were to die out, even if no sentient beings knew about the species, or could ever be remotely affected by its extinction. These sorts of examples tend to enlist our more consequentialist intuitions – intuitions about the value inherent in states of affairs, including those states of affairs that do not involve sentient beings. (See chapter 1 for discussion of utilitarianism, the form of consequentialism that takes general happiness to be the good.) We might express such intuitions in terms of the world being a better place with the micro-organism in it. We feel there's some sort of a total net loss when such things happen. Here our moral intuitions seem close to being aesthetic ones.

At $\boxed{n}$ → Nagel explains the different ways in which agent-relative and agent-neutral reasons can generate motivations for action. Agent-relative reasons generate motivations for the individual they are relative to. To invoke my previous example, the individual who wants the job has an agent-relative reason to be well prepared for the interview, and other things being equal that reason gives rise to a motivation to be well prepared. Agent-neutral reasons generate motivations regardless of who the agent is – they are, precisely, neutral or impersonal in this respect. But note the general point that the generation of motivations for action does not guarantee that the motivation in question is the overriding one in the agent's psychology. For the agent may have countervailing motivations – most obviously she might be a morally bad or lazy person; or, alternatively, a good person who has a stronger moral reason to do something else instead. Most poignantly, we may find we have conflicting moral reasons of different sorts – one agent-relative and the other agent-neutral. This can make for moral dilemmas such as when, as the lifeguard, someone has a reason to save the weakest swimmers first, yet as a husband he has a reason to save his wife first. But the possibility of such clashes is not confined to dilemma situations. Part of Nagel's general message is that moral life consists essentially in the standing obligation to combine the personal and the impersonal points of view, and the effort to do this can lead to the refinement of our judgement, even while it may also, on rare occasion, lead to painful no-win dilemmas.

Why does Nagel say at ⊡→ that it is inevitable that we accept some objective values?

He has explained that there is no method special to normative reasoning except the general policy of considering all the options and going for the one that seems more reasonable, all things considered. But this natural style of rational reflection itself commits us to holding some values as objective. He recalls Hume's example of the character who prefers the destruction of the whole world to the scratching of his finger, and notes that only a philosopher in the grip of a narrowly rationalistic conception of what constitutes reasoning would think that such a character was not making some kind of objective error of reason. (Hume's point was precisely that while this character has clearly immoral sentiments, he cannot be charged with any error of reason.[1]) If we start off thinking that reasoning can only be either formal deduction or empirical induction, then no wonder we find the idea of practical reasoning difficult to substantiate philosophically. But if we start off with open minds about the possibility of normative reasoning, and we observe how human beings actually go about it, perhaps we won't find it such a misfit idea that there can be objectively correct practical reasoning.

However, Nagel goes on to acknowledge at ⊡→ that it is very difficult to come up with a positive proposal for objective normative principles. And one of the difficulties here is that as we aim for objectivity, and in particular agent-neutrality, we tend to find we distort the values that are really at work in personal life. It may be that the sorts of moral motives that are appropriate in public life – motives deriving from principles couched in impersonal terms, such as giving to each according to need, for instance – might not be appropriate as motivations in personal life, where special relationships create distinctly partial reasons, and partial motivations, such as the motivation to help one's own child first, no matter if there are other children in greater need of help.

Now, champions of the impersonal view might try to subsume such partial, agent-relative reasons under the remit of impersonal, agent-neutral principles by saying that the motive to help one's own child first is an instance of a general moral principle that parents have special responsibility for their own children – a principle from which we might derive reasons of an impersonal form for mothers to help their own children first. Certainly we aim to be able, at the end of the day, to stand back and check that our agent-relative reasons are morally permissible – that is what Nagel means when he talks about the objective viewpoint setting a standard with which the subjective must be able to coexist. But philosophers who regard the role of partial and personal reasons in ethical life as irreducible to impartial reasons will insist that the impersonal

---

[1] For the Hume, see Ch. 3 this volume pp. 148–62.

version cannot replace the personal one. If a mother helps her own child first, her ethical motive may quite properly be irreducibly personal: she helps him simply because he's her son. Indeed, we might think there was something profoundly wrong with her, including morally wrong with her, if her primary motive took any other form. This is what Nagel is getting at when he says that the objective viewpoint will often not be suitable as a replacement for the subjective one, and that sometimes it is better to act not for reasons at all but simply 'because it does not occur to us to do anything else'. An irreducible kernel of ethical life may consist of actions done entirely spontaneously out of love, compassion, friendship and so on, as opposed to being done on principle or for any specified reason relating to these values. If love, compassion and friendship are among the things we most value, then forcing the relevant motives into the impersonal mould would do violence to the very things we most value. Further, it would be to mistake the nature of the demand that objectivity makes on moral consciousness.

These issues of the place of the personal and the impersonal viewpoints in moral life run through moral philosophy as a whole, and we shall soon encounter them again, when we come to Kant and Williams in the next pair of readings. Kant's moral philosophy seems to require that the agent take up the impersonal point of view as a prerequisite for doing actions of moral worth; Williams mounts a critique of the conception of morality in which this model of objectivity culminates.

5

Morality and Obligation

Introduction to the Problem

Moral philosophy is always answerable to our pre-theoretical moral intuitions, and a responsible strategy on the part of any moral philosopher is to begin by characterizing our pre-theoretical moral thinking and then proceed to theorize it. This does not mean that philosophy must simply aim to imitate all aspects of everyday moral thinking. On the contrary, as our theoretical efforts bring increased coherence and systematicity to our moral thinking, it may be that aspects of our pre-theoretical attitudes get revised. We have already seen this mechanism at work in Mackie's meta-ethics: he characterizes our pre-theoretical moral attitudes as inherently objectivist, but then on general philosophical grounds proceeds to characterize that objectivism as an error. But the method applies at the first order level of normative ethical attitudes too. If we were to start out with an intuition that, for example, smacking children is a morally acceptable form of discipline, still it is quite possible that philosophical reflection should bring us to see it as a form of domestic violence, which as such is not morally acceptable. Nevertheless, for some of our most entrenched moral intuitions, there may be no theoretical argument strong enough to overturn the intuition. For instance, we may have a deep-seated intuition that, although lying is in general wrong, there are many circumstances in which it is entirely permissible (even obligatory) to tell a lie in order to save a life. And if a given moral theory says otherwise, then most of us would stand by the intuition and change the theory.

Now our pre-theoretical moral thinking is not just a cluster of first order intuitions about what's right and what's wrong, what is morally permissible and what is not. Our pre-theoretical moral thinking also contains some commitments of a meta-ethical sort. Commitments, for instance, about how far our moral judgements are absolute or, by contrast, contingent upon the moral attitudes of the individual agent or, more generally, the culture. We saw, in the extract from Mackie, how one philosopher characterizes our pre-theoretical meta-ethical commitments – Mackie depicts moral subjects as having a natural and unchangeable commitment to the metaphysical objectivity of moral values. But philosophers' characterizations of pre-theoretical moral thinking may vary, and if our pre-theoretical thinking is in fact something of a mixed bag of commitments and attitudes that might even be in some tension with one another, this will make for magnified differences writ large in the theories of different philosophers.

One aspect of our pre-theoretical moral thought is that morality can be absolutely binding on us, so that if, for instance, duty requires us to keep a solemnly made death-bed promise, we *must* fulfil that promise, even if we frankly do not want to. One philosopher – as we shall see in the extract from Immanuel Kant – might pick this out as essential to our conception of moral worth, so that moral worth comes to be precisely delineated as residing in actions done from the motive of duty, construed as acting purely because morality requires it. Another philosopher, however – and we shall see this in the extract from Bernard Williams – might problematize this conception of moral worth by focusing on different aspects of our pre-theoretical moral thinking. He may emphasize that we do not always see moral injunctions as absolute obligations. For instance, there are occasions on which it would be morally good to do something, even though it remains morally permissible not to do it – doing a stranger a good turn, for instance. If acting out of kindness, love, friendship or loyalty to another person can seem paradigmatic of morally good action, then acting purely for duty's sake can come to seem something of a special case. Indeed someone who takes ethically good sentiments to be morally fundamental might find the precisely delineated duty-conception of moral worth to be not only misguided, but even morally distasteful. Thus magnified philosophical disagreements can arise from differing characterizations of pre-theoretical moral consciousness.

The two readings for this chapter, then, illustrate how different views of pre-theoretical moral thinking can lead to such magnified theoretical differences. The first presents key elements of one of the most influential and systematic moral philosophies ever produced, namely, that advanced by Kant. The extract is taken from Section II of his *Groundwork of the Metaphysics of Morals*, in which he sets out the formal case for his moral philosophy. The second reading is a classic statement of the opposition. It is from the final chapter of Williams's *Ethics and the Limits of Philosophy*, in which he criticizes the Kantian conception of duty, or moral obligation, and offers a diagnostic analysis: it is motivated by the misplaced fear that if morality is not founded on something a priori (something absolute, and non-contingent) then it fails to have any authority over us at all. This pair of readings draws the lines of the ongoing debate about the nature of moral authority that continues to fascinate in moral philosophy.

Introduction to Kant

Immanuel Kant was born in 1724 in Königsberg, East Prussia. He lectured at the University of Königsberg and in 1770 gained the Chair of Logic and Metaphysics. He lived and worked there all his life, until 1804 when he died at the remarkable age of eighty. Kant wrote many great works of philosophy, including the 'three critiques', *Critique of Pure Reason* (1781), *Critique of Practical Reason* (1788), and *Critique of Judgement* (1790), and his different philosophical works fit together to comprise a whole systematic philosophy. He wrote *Groundwork of the Metaphysics of Morals* in 1785, in which he constructs the formal foundation for his deontological (duty-based) moral philosophy. In the extract reproduced here he makes mention of the future work he was already planning to write (and which is implied in the title of the *Groundwork*), namely, *The Metaphysics of Morals*, which he went on to publish in 1797, and which offers a detailed account of different duties relating to a range of substantive moral issues. Together with the *Critique of Practical Reason*, these comprise his major works of moral philosophy, though his other moral philosophical writings include, for instance, one of his most well-known and indeed controversial essays, 'On a Supposed Right to Lie from Philanthropy' (1797), which argues that it is absolutely never permissible to lie. In systematic philosophy, and indeed philosophy quite generally, Kant is a giant whose influence permeates the whole discipline. In moral philosophy, the theory whose structure he sets out in the *Groundwork* is the explicit source of an entire tradition of deontological thinking.

Immanuel Kant, *Groundwork of the Metaphysics of Morals* (extracts from Section II, 'Transition from Popular Moral Philosophy to Metaphysics of Morals')

Everything in nature works in accordance with laws. Only a rational being has the capacity to act *in accordance with the representation* of laws, that is, in accordance with principles, or has a *will*. Since *reason*

[a] ⇒ is required for the derivation of actions from laws, the will is nothing

Editors' note: The original footnotes have been renumbered as parts of the text have been omitted; Kant's own notes are marked with an asterisk.

other than practical reason. If reason infallibly determines the will, the actions of such a being that are cognized as objectively necessary are also subjectively necessary, that is, the will is a capacity to choose *only that* which reason independently of inclination cognizes as practically necessary, that is, as good. However, if reason solely by itself does not adequately determine the will; if the will is exposed[1] also to subjective conditions (certain incentives) that are not always in accord with the objective ones; in a word, if the will is not *in itself* completely in conformity with reason (as is actually the case with human beings), then actions that are cognized as objectively necessary are subjectively contingent, and the determination of such a will in conformity with objective laws is *necessitation*: that is to say, the relation of objective laws to a will that is not thoroughly good is represented as the determination of the will of a rational being through grounds of reason, indeed, but grounds to which this will is not by its nature necessarily obedient.

|b|→   The representation of an objective principle, insofar as it is necessitating for a will, is called a command (of reason), and the formula of the command is called an **imperative**.

All imperatives are expressed by an *ought* and indicate by this the relation of an objective law of reason to a will that by its subjective constitution is not necessarily determined by it (a necessitation). They say that to do or to omit something would be good, but they say it to a will that does not always do something just because it is represented to it that it would be good to do that thing. Practical good, however,

|c|→   is that which determines the will by means of representations of reason, hence not by subjective causes but objectively, that is, from grounds that are valid for every rational being as such. It is distinguished from the *agreeable*, as that which influences the will only by means of feeling[2] from merely subjective causes, which hold only for the senses of this or that one, and not as a principle of reason, which holds for everyone.

|d|→   A perfectly good will would, therefore, equally stand under objective laws (of the good), but it could not on this account be represented as *necessitated* to actions in conformity with law since of itself, by its subjective constitution, it can be determined only through the representation of the good. Hence no imperatives hold for the *divine* will and in general for a *holy* will: the 'ought' is out of place here, because volition[3] is of itself necessarily in accord with the law. Therefore

---

[1]   *unterworfen*
[2]   *Empfindung*
[3]   *das Sollen ... das Wollen*

imperatives are only formulae expressing the relation of objective laws of volition in general to the subjective imperfection of the will of this or that rational being, for example, of the human will.

Now, all imperatives command either *hypothetically* or *categorically*. The former represent the practical necessity of a possible action as a means to achieving something else that one wills (or that it is at least possible for one to will). The categorical imperative would be that which represented an action as objectively necessary of itself, without reference to another end.

Since every practical law represents a possible action as good and thus as necessary for a subject practically determinable by reason, all imperatives are formulae for the determination of action that is necessary in accordance with the principle of a will which is good in some way. Now, if the action would be good merely as a means *to something else* the imperative is *hypothetical*; if the action is represented as *in itself* good, hence as necessary in a will in itself conforming to reason, as its principle, *then it is categorical*.

[...]

The question of how the imperative of *morality* is possible is undoubtedly the only one needing a solution, since it is in no way hypothetical and the objectively represented necessity can therefore not be based on any presupposition, as in the case of hypothetical imperatives. Only we must never leave out of account, here, that it cannot be made out *by means of any example*, and so empirically, whether there is any such imperative at all, but it is rather to be feared that all imperatives which seem to be categorical may yet in some hidden way be hypothetical. For example, when it is said 'you ought not to promise anything deceitfully,' and one assumes that the necessity of this omission is not giving counsel for avoiding some other ill – in which case what is said would be 'you ought not to make a lying promise lest if it comes to light you destroy your credit' – but that an action of this kind must be regarded as in itself evil and that the imperative of prohibition is therefore categorical: one still cannot show with certainty in any example that the will is here determined merely through the law, without another incentive, although it seems to be so; for it is always possible that covert fear of disgrace, perhaps also obscure apprehension of other dangers, may have had an influence on the will. Who can prove by experience the nonexistence of a cause when all that experience teaches is that we do not perceive it? In such a case, however, the so-called moral imperative, which as such appears to be categorical and unconditional, would in fact be only a pragmatic precept that makes us attentive to our advantage and merely teaches us to take this into consideration.

[g]→   We shall thus have to investigate entirely a priori the possibility
of a *categorical* imperative, since we do not here have the advantage of its reality being given in experience, so that the possibility
would be necessary not to establish it but merely to explain it.[4] In
the meantime, however, we can see this much: that the categorical
imperative alone has the tenor of[5] a practical law; all the others can
indeed be called *principles* of the will but not laws, since what it is
necessary to do merely for achieving a discretionary purpose can be
regarded as in itself contingent and we can always be released from
the precept if we give up the purpose; on the contrary, the unconditional command leaves the will no discretion[6] with respect to the
opposite, so that it alone brings with it that necessity which we
require of a law.

Second, in the case of this categorical imperative or law of morality
the ground of the difficulty (of insight into its possibility) is also very
[h]→   great. It is an a priori synthetic practical proposition;[7] and since it is
so difficult to see the possibility of this kind of proposition in theoretical cognition, it can be readily gathered that the difficulty will be
no less in practical cognition.

          [...]

[i]→   When I think of a *hypothetical* imperative in general I do not know
beforehand what it will contain; I do not know this until I am given
the condition. But when I think of a *categorical* imperative I know at
once what it contains. For, since the imperative contains, beyond the
[j]→   law, only the necessity that the maxim[8] be in conformity with this law,
while the law contains no condition to which it would be limited,
nothing is left with which the maxim of action is to conform but the
universality of a law as such; and this conformity alone is what the
imperative properly represents as necessary.

---

[4]   *und also die Möglichkeit nicht zur Festsetzung, sondern bloss zur Erklärung nötig wäre*
[5]   *als ... laute*
[6]   *dem Willen kein Belieben ... frei läßt*
*[7]   I connect the deed with the will, without a presupposed condition from any inclination, a
priori and hence necessarily (though only objectively, i.e., under the idea of a reason having
complete control over all subjective motives). This is, therefore, a practical proposition that
does not derive the volition of an action analytically from another volition already presupposed
(for we have no such perfect will), but connects it immediately with the concept of the will of
a rational being as something that is not contained in it.
*[8]   A *maxim* is the subjective principle of acting, and must be distinguished from the *objective*
principle, namely the practical law. The former contains the practical rule determined by reason
conformably with the conditions of the subject (often his ignorance or also his inclinations),
and is therefore the principle in accordance with which the subject *acts;* but the law is the objective principle valid for every rational being, and the principle in accordance with which he
ought to act, i.e., an imperative.

k⊢→   There is, therefore, only a single categorical imperative and it is this: *act only in accordance with that maxim through which you can at the same time will that it become a universal law.*

Now, if all imperatives of duty can be derived from this single imperative as from their principle, then, even though we leave it undecided whether what is called duty is not as such an empty concept, we shall at least be able to show what we think by it and what the concept wants to say.

Since the universality of law in accordance with which effects take place constitutes what is properly called *nature* in the most general sense (as regards its form) – that is, the existence of things insofar as it is determined in accordance with universal laws – the

l⊢→   universal imperative of duty can also go as follows: *act as if the maxim of your action were to become by your will a* **universal law of nature.**

m⊢→   We shall now enumerate a few duties in accordance with the usual division of them into duties to ourselves and to other human beings

n⊢→   and into perfect and imperfect duties.[9]

1. Someone feels sick of life because of a series of troubles that has grown to the point of despair, but is still so far in possession of his reason that he can ask himself whether it would not be contrary to his duty to himself to take his own life. Now he inquires whether the maxim of his action could indeed become a universal law of nature. His maxim, however, is: from self-love I make it my principle to shorten my life when its longer duration threatens more troubles than it promises agreeableness. The only further question is whether this principle of self-love could become a universal law of nature. It is then seen at once that a nature whose law it would be to destroy life itself by means of the same feeling whose destination[10] is to impel toward the furtherance of life would contradict itself and would therefore not subsist[11] as nature; thus that maxim could not possibly be a law of nature and, accordingly, altogether opposes the supreme principle of all duty.

---

*9   It must be noted here that I reserve the division of duties entirely for a future *Metaphysics of Morals*, so that the division here stands only as one adopted at my discretion (for the sake of arranging my examples). For the rest, I understand here by a perfect duty one that admits no exception in favor of inclination, and then I have not merely external but also internal *perfect duties;* although this is contrary to the use of the word adopted in the schools, I do not intend to justify it here, since for my purpose it makes no difference whether or not it is granted me.

10   *Bestimmung*

11   *bestehen*

2. Another finds himself urged by need to borrow money. He well knows that he will not be able to repay it but sees also that nothing will be lent him unless he promises firmly to repay it within a determinate time. He would like to make such a promise, but he still has enough conscience to ask himself: is it not forbidden and contrary to duty to help oneself out of need in such a way? Supposing that he still decided to do so, his maxim of action would go as follows: when I believe myself to be in need of money I shall borrow money and promise to repay it, even though I know that this will never happen. Now this principle of self-love or personal advantage is perhaps quite consistent with my whole future welfare, but the question now is whether it is right. I therefore turn the demand of self-love into a universal law and put the question as follows: how would it be if my maxim became a universal law? I then see at once that it could never hold as a universal law of nature and be consistent with itself, but must necessarily contradict itself. For, the universality of a law that everyone, when he believes himself to be in need, could promise whatever he pleases with the intention of not keeping it would make the promise and the end one might have in it itself impossible, since no one would believe what was promised him but would laugh at all such expressions as vain pretenses.

3. A third finds in himself a talent that by means of some cultivation could make him a human being useful for all sorts of purposes. However, he finds himself in comfortable circumstances and prefers to give himself up to pleasure than to trouble himself with enlarging and improving his fortunate natural predispositions.[12] But he still asks himself whether his maxim of neglecting his natural gifts, besides being consistent with his propensity to amusement, is also consistent with what one calls duty. He now sees that a nature could indeed always subsist with such a universal law, although (as with the South Sea Islanders) the human being should let his talents rust and be concerned with devoting his life merely to idleness, amusement, procreation – in a word, to enjoyment; only he cannot possibly **will** that this become a universal law or be put in us as such by means of natural instinct. For, as a rational being he necessarily wills that all the capacities in him be developed, since they serve him and are given to him for all sorts of possible purposes.

Yet a *fourth*, for whom things are going well while he sees that others (whom he could very well help) have to contend with great hardships, thinks: what is it to me? let each be as happy as heaven

---

[12] *Naturanlagen*

wills or as he can make himself; I shall take nothing from him nor even envy him; only I do not care to contribute anything to his welfare or to his assistance in need! Now, if such a way of thinking were to become a universal law the human race could admittedly very well subsist, no doubt even better than when everyone prates about sympathy and benevolence and even exerts himself to practice them occasionally, but on the other hand also cheats where he can, sells the right of human beings or otherwise infringes upon it. But although it is possible that a universal law of nature could very well subsist in accordance with such a maxim, it is still impossible to **will** that such a principle hold everywhere as a law of nature. For, a will that decided this would conflict with itself, since many cases could occur in which one would need the love and sympathy[13] of others and in which, by such a law of nature arisen from his own will, he would rob himself of all hope of the assistance he wishes for himself.

These are a few of the many actual duties, or at least of what we take to be such, whose derivation[14] from the one principle cited above is clear. We must *be able to will* that a maxim of our action become a universal law: this is the canon of moral appraisal of action in general. Some actions are so constituted that their maxim cannot even be *thought* without contradiction as a universal law of nature, far less could one *will* that it *should* become such. In the case of others that inner impossibility is indeed not to be found, but it is still impossible to *will* that their maxim be raised to the universality of a law of nature because such a will would contradict itself. It is easy to see that the first is opposed to strict or narrower (unremitting)[15] duty, the second only to wide (meritorious) duty; and so all duties, as far as the kind of obligation (not the object of their action) is concerned, have by these examples been set out completely in their dependence upon the one principle.

If we now attend to ourselves in any transgression of a duty, we find that we do not really will that our maxim should become a universal law, since that is impossible for us, but that the opposite of our maxim should instead remain a universal law, only we take the liberty of making an *exception* to it for ourselves (or just for this once) to the advantage of our inclination. Consequently, if we weighed all cases from one and the same point of view, namely that of reason, we would find a contradiction in our own will, namely that a certain principle be objectively necessary as a universal law and yet subjectively not

---

[13] *Teilnehmung*
[14] reading *Ableitung* instead of *Abteilung*, "classification".
[15] *unnachlaßlich*

hold universally but allow exceptions. Since, however, we at one time regard our action from the point of view of a will wholly conformed with reason but then regard the very same action from the point of view of a will affected by inclination, there is really no contradiction here but instead a resistance[16] of inclination to the precept of reason (*antagonismus*), through which the universality of the principle (*universalitas*) is changed into mere generality (*generalitas*) and the practical rational principle is to meet the maxim half way. Now, even though this cannot be justified in our own impartially rendered judgement, it still shows that we really acknowledge the validity of the categorical imperative and permit ourselves (with all respect for it) only a few exceptions that, as it seems to us, are inconsiderable and wrung from us.

[q]→ We have therefore shown at least this much: that if duty is a concept that is to contain significance and real lawgiving for our actions it can be expressed only in categorical imperatives and by no means in hypothetical ones; we have also – and this is already a great deal – set forth distinctly and as determined for every use the content of the categorical imperative, which must contain the principle of all duty (if there is such a thing at all). But we have not yet advanced so far as to prove a priori that there really is such an imperative, that there is a practical law, which commands absolutely of itself and without any incentives, and that the observance of this law is duty.

For the purpose of achieving this it is of the utmost importance to take warning that we must not let ourselves think of wanting to derive the reality of this principle from the *special property of human nature*. For, duty is to be practical unconditional necessity of action and it must therefore hold for all rational beings (to which alone an imperative can apply at all) and *only because of this* be also a law for all human wills. On the other hand, what is derived from the special natural constitution of humanity – what is derived from certain feelings and propensities and even, if possible, from a special tendency that would be peculiar to human reason and would not have to hold necessarily for the will of every rational being – that can indeed yield a maxim for us but not a law; it can yield a subjective principle on which we might act if we have the propensity and inclination,[17] but not an objective principle on which we would be *directed* to act even though every propensity, inclination, and natural tendency of ours were against it – so much so that the sublimity and inner dignity of the command in a duty is all the more manifest the fewer are the

---

[16] *Widerstand*
[17] *nach welchem wir handeln zu dürfen Hang und Neigung haben*

subjective causes in favor of it and the more there are against it, without thereby weakening in the least the necessitation by the law or taking anything away from its validity.

Here, then, we see philosophy put in fact in a precarious position, which is to be firm even though there is nothing in heaven or on earth from which it depends or on which it is based. Here philosophy is to manifest its purity as sustainer of its own laws, not as herald of laws that an implanted sense or who knows what tutelary nature whispers to it, all of which – though they may always be better than nothing at all – can still never yield basic principles that reason dictates and that must have their source entirely and completely a priori and, at the same time, must have their commanding authority from this: that they expect nothing from the inclination of human beings but everything from the supremacy of the law and the respect owed it or, failing this, condemn the human being to contempt for himself and inner abhorrence.

Hence everything empirical, as an addition[18] to the principle of morality, is not only quite inept for this; it is also highly prejudicial to the purity of morals, where the proper worth of an absolutely good will – a worth raised above all price – consists just in the principle of action being free from all influences of contingent grounds, which only experience can furnish. One cannot give too many or too frequent warnings against this laxity, or even mean cast of mind, which seeks its principle among empirical motives and laws; for, human reason in its weariness gladly rests on this pillow and in a dream of sweet illusions (which allow it to embrace a cloud instead of Juno) it substitutes for morality a bastard patched up from limbs of quite diverse ancestry, which looks like whatever one wants to see in it but not like virtue for him who has once seen virtue in her true form.[19]

[...]

Commentary on Kant

The first thing that happens in this extract is that Kant tells us something about how he is using the notion of the *will*.

---

[r] →*18   To behold virtue in her proper form is nothing other than to present morality stripped of any admixture of the sensible and of any spurious adornments of reward or self-love. By means of the least effort of his reason everyone can easily become aware of how much virtue then eclipses everything else that appears charming to the inclinations, provided his reason is not altogether spoiled for abstraction.

19   *Zutat*, literally "an ornament".

What does Kant mean by 'will'?

He argues that only rational beings have the capacity to act on principle – as opposed to acting on instinct, desire or other forms of mere inclination. (Humans are the only natural species of rational beings we know of, but we can conceive of other sorts of rational being – a god-like being, for instance.) Kant conceives acting on principle as acting 'in accordance with the representation of laws'. Since reason is required for a law to issue in an action, he infers that the will is none other than practical reason. (Note that, for Kant, the will is not a matter of wishes, wants or desires, so his use of the term is quite different from our popular use of it.) Kant goes on to characterize the distinctively human experience of acting on principle.

Explain in your own words Kant's conception of what it is for a human being to act on principle, on reason.

Kant draws a contrast between two sorts of being or agent: one whose will is automatically or 'infallibly' in tune with reason, and one whose will is susceptible to incentives that may conflict with reason. Human beings exemplify this latter category, so that when we act on principle we experience this as bending our wills to the dictates of reason; we experience it as a form of 'necessitation'. We might say that when humans act on reason, we *require* ourselves to do so, for acting according to reason does not simply come naturally, but is always open to possible challenge from some countervailing inclination (it is not, after all, always convenient or congenial to do the morally right thing). That is the form that acting on reason takes for human beings, because our will is not, as Kant puts it '*in itself* completely in conformity with reason'. In this sense, human wills are not 'thoroughly good' – not guaranteed to be in tune with reason.

What is the meaning of Kant's contrast between an action's being 'cognized as objectively necessary' and an action's being cognized as 'subjectively necessary'?

Recall the distinction between beings with a thoroughly rational will and beings with a less-than-thoroughly rational will. For the former, all actions cognized as objectively necessary (required by law) are guaranteed also to be cognized as subjectively necessary. For such beings there can be no conflict between the dictates of reason and the dictates of mere inclination. But, for human beings, there is no guarantee that actions perceived by the agent as objectively necessary will also be subjectively necessary; that is, someone may perceive that reason requires her to keep a promise she made to water a neighbour's plants, and yet some countervailing inclination – sheer laziness, perhaps – may prevail in her will so that she does not in fact keep the promise.

In the psychology of human beings, there can be a disunity between what is objectively necessary and what is subjectively necessary; a gap between what one ought to do and what one is in fact motivated to do.

How, at b↦, does Kant introduce the notion of an 'imperative', and why?

Requirements of practical reason are 'objective principles' of action – they hold for all rational beings – and for a human will their authority is 'necessitating'. That is why such a principle is a *command* of reason, and it is what renders statements that express them 'imperatives'. Imperatives are 'ought' statements that relate an objective law of reason to a less-than-thoroughly rational will. It is by way of imperatives that reason can command the human will.

At c↦, what does Kant say distinguishes 'practical good' from 'the agreeable'? Can you think of your own example to illustrate his distinction?

The distinction here is between two kinds of determination of the will. Sometimes a practical end or purpose determines the will as a matter of reason, such as when the practical good of helping someone is a purpose that imposes a practical requirement on us all, whether we like it or not. By contrast, sometimes an end or purpose determines the will only by means of feeling, such as when we help someone just because we care about them.

Kant's special concern here, as elsewhere, is that what is special about reason's authority over us is that its authority is absolute – no amount of disinterest or distaste on our part (nothing subjective in us) can relieve us of these sorts of obligations. (His first moves in the *Groundwork* – in the Preface and in Section I – explicitly embrace a conception of morality as essentially composed of absolutely authoritative imperatives.) That is why he is in this Section so concerned to establish the difference between the imperatives of reason, of 'practical good', as opposed to the imperatives of that which is only contingently 'agreeable'. The former, unlike the latter, depend on no subjective contingency in us. Only pure reason can be absolutely or unconditionally authoritative, and because he takes it that the imperatives of morality, if there are such, are absolutely authoritative, he holds that they must be requirements of pure reason.

What does Kant mean at d↦ by a 'perfectly good will'? He mentions two examples of such a will; what are they?

The idea of a 'perfectly good will' is just the idea already advanced of a will that is '*in itself* completely in conformity with reason' or 'thoroughly good'. He goes on to mention both 'the divine will' and 'a holy will', apparently as two examples of a perfectly good will – the will of God, and (more mysteriously – it remains unclear exactly what Kant has in mind) the will of an extraordinarily good (perhaps Christ-like?) being.

> What is Kant's distinction, given at $\boxed{e}\mapsto$, between a hypothetical imperative and a categorical imperative? Explain this distinction in your own words, and think of an example of each.

Central to Kant's moral philosophy is this distinction between hypothetical and categorical imperatives. We use the former all the time in means–end, or instrumental, practical reasoning: if you want your toothache to stop, go to the dentist; if you want to please your friend, cook her dinner (and wash it up). But Kant's idea is that if we ever engage in distinctively moral reasoning, then our imperatives are not conditional on any interest or desire, but are precisely unconditional: keep your promises; do not be cruel; play fair. The unconditionality of categorical imperatives is what furnishes their absolute authority.

> Why does Kant say at $\boxed{f}\mapsto$ that we cannot demonstrate by way of example the functioning of categorical imperatives in action? Elaborate your own example of a categorical imperative so that it exemplifies an action apparently done from duty but in fact done from some other motive.

Kant is aware that any example of an action apparently done in obedience to a categorical imperative might yet have been done from some hypothetical motive after all. One cannot conclusively interpret a person's motives by observing their actions. This is why he concludes at $\boxed{g}\mapsto$ that his argument for the possibility of categorical imperatives will have to be entirely a priori – it will have to be entirely non-empirical, because no empirical evidence for the possibility could be conclusive.

At $\boxed{h}\mapsto$ Kant states a very real difficulty in countenancing the possibility of a categorical imperative, namely, that such imperatives would be propositions of a frankly extraordinary sort: a priori synthetic practical propositions.

> Explain what is meant by the idea that categorical imperatives are (i) a priori and (ii) synthetic.

Historically, analytic propositions have generally been understood as propositions which, if true, are true in virtue of the meanings of their terms – the canonical example is 'all bachelors are unmarried men'. By contrast, synthetic propositions, if true, are true in virtue of how things are in the world – for example, 'many bachelors enjoy the bachelor lifestyle'. (Subsequently, this orthodoxy has been challenged, particularly the idea that the distinction between analytic and synthetic marks more than a merely cosmetic difference.) Traditionally it has been assumed that synthetic propositions can only

be known a posteriori (known from experience). A canonical example of a
synthetic proposition might be a proposition of empirical science, and certainly it seems we can only have a posteriori knowledge of such propositions,
since science is precisely a matter of investigating the natural world by empirical methods. Correspondingly, it has also been traditionally assumed that the
only sort of proposition that can be known a priori ('from first principles' –
precisely not from any experience or empirical investigation) are analytic
propositions. It is primarily this that Kant is detracting from here in his conception of moral propositions as synthetic and a priori. It is not controversial
to class moral propositions as synthetic, for there was and is no orthodoxy
claiming they were analytic. What is controversial, and difficult to grasp, is
the idea that we can know such propositions a priori. (Kant was also a detrac-
tor from the orthodoxy that mathematical propositions were analytic. He
held that the propositions of mathematics were synthetic, and thus that mathematical knowledge too was synthetic a priori. Hence his mention at $\boxed{\text{h}}\!\!\rightarrow$ of
the difficulty of seeing 'the possibility of this kind of proposition in theoretical
cognition'.)

> Why does Kant claim at $\boxed{\text{i}}\!\!\rightarrow$ that when he thinks of a categorical impera-
> tive in general he knows at once what it contains, whereas this is not so
> when he thinks of a hypothetical imperative in general?

A hypothetical imperative is, as we have already seen, just a practical imperative that depends (is 'conditional') upon some contingent aim or interest on
the part of the agent – '*If you want to pass your exam*, do some revision'.
We might express such imperatives to each other without bothering to make
the (italicized) antecedent explicit – one might simply tell someone to do some
revision – but the authority of the practical reason is no less conditional, and
the form of the imperative is no less hypothetical. In such an imperative, the
authority is dependent on the antecedent of the condition being satisfied, so
that if you don't care whether or not you pass the exam, the reason to revise
that is expressed in the imperative does not apply to you. This means that if
one thinks of a hypothetical imperative *in general* (as opposed to thinking of
a particular example of one) something crucial is missing, namely, the particular antecedent on which any such imperative depends. By contrast, the authority of categorical imperatives depends on nothing that is omitted in the idea of
a categorical imperative in general. Categorical imperatives are peculiarly
empty – they are purely formal – for their authority is, according to Kant,
dependent only on the agent's general obligation as a rational being to refrain
from contradiction in his practical reasoning, as in his theoretical reasoning.
(The claim that failing to adhere to duty involves a contradiction in practical
reason will become clear later on, at $\boxed{\text{p}}\!\!\rightarrow$.)

Note Kant's footnoted use of the term 'maxim' at $\boxed{\text{k}}\!\!\rightarrow$. This is an important
concept in his theory, so read the footnote carefully.

Kant defines 'maxim' as 'the subjective principle of acting', and this means one's (most basic) reason for doing a given action. When we do an action we might have various reasons for doing it, and we might have various motivations in mind when we do it, but not all of these will constitute the maxim of one's action. A maxim is the explanatorily basic *principle* governing one's action, and so it must be suitably general in form.

This point is worth expanding a little by way of illustration. If I am in a queue to buy my train ticket for the 8.06 to Brighton, and I'm anxiously aware that it is already gone 8 o'clock, then I might jump the queue to get my ticket in time to catch my train. If I do jump the queue, then while I might have the thought 'It's already gone 8 o'clock' present in my mind as a powerful motivating factor, this thought is not the maxim of my action. Rather, the maxim of my action is something more explanatorily basic and more general. It is (something like): 'Whenever queuing for a ticket would make me miss my train, I jump the queue.'

Kant explains in his footnote that a maxim is a *subjective* principle of acting. That means it's a practical principle that applies specifically to the individual agent, the individual subject of the action. By contrast, an *objective* principle of acting is a practical principle that applies to *all* agents, and Kant captures this universality in the idea of a 'law', an imperative that any agent ought to adhere to.

Once again, the idea here is that all categorical imperatives are expressions of a single formal idea: the idea of rational agents acting in conformity with reason as such; bending their will to a law purely because it is a law. (Do not be misled, however, by the claim that there is only a single categorical imperative. We should hear that claim as a claim about the singularity of the categorical imperative in general. For it is crucial to Kant's theory that the categorical imperative in general – the parent categorical imperative, as we might think of it – issues in many offspring categorical imperatives, namely, all the particular duties we derive from it.)

'Act only in accordance with that maxim through which you can at the same time will that it become a universal law.' This formulation of the categorical imperative is known as the Formula of Universal Law (sometimes abbreviated to FUL). It expresses an absolute requirement that we restrict our actions to those done for a special class of reasons, namely, those that we can 'will' as a reason acted on by all. Remember that what Kant means by 'will' refers to our practical reason, so the idea of 'willing' a reason as a universal law is the idea that we can make sense of it as a reason acted on by all. Hence the FUL expresses the imperative that we act only on reasons that are universalizable.

> What is the next formulation of the categorical imperative that Kant gives us? How does it differ from FUL?

At ☐1⟩ Kant offers a slightly different expression of the categorical imperative: 'Act as if the maxim of your action were to become by your will a universal law of nature.' This is often referred to as the Formula of Nature, which can be abbreviated to FN. He introduces it by way of the idea that everything that happens according to universal laws (for instance, the law expressed by the categorical imperative) can be called 'nature'; it is possible to re-express the categorical imperative in terms of a law of nature. (As with all four different expressions of the categorical imperative that Kant gives in Section II, FUL and FN are meant to be entirely equivalent in meaning.)

At ☐m⟩ Kant enumerates four examples of duties. He tells us that these illustrations exemplify two duties to ourselves and two duties to others; and that they also exemplify two 'perfect' duties and two 'imperfect' duties. At ☐n⟩ he flags a footnote that gives us a handle on the distinction. (In the footnote he also describes duties as 'internal' and 'external', which corresponds to 'to ourselves' and 'to others'.)

> Read his footnote carefully and see if you can express in your own words the distinction he is employing between perfect and imperfect duties. Now read through all four illustrations and ask yourself, firstly, which two exemplify duties to ourselves, and which two exemplify duties to others; and, secondly, which two exemplify perfect duties and which two imperfect duties.

He says that perfect duties admit 'no exception in favor of inclination', and this implies that imperfect duties do admit some exception in favour of inclination. But what exactly can this mean? Surely no duties as such allow exceptions to be made on grounds of mere inclination? As we read the four illustrations we shall see that the perfect duties are highly specified in what they demand of the agent, so that there is no latitude of choice in how the agent fulfils her duty. These duties express direct injunctions against suicide, and against making false promises, so the agent must simply refrain from either of those sorts of action. By contrast, the imperfect duties must be construed as allowing some latitude for inclination, since any other reading could make them impossible to fulfil. These duties express injunctions against failing to develop one's natural talents, and failing to help others. So the agent must find a way of refraining from doing either of these things, and we can immediately see that she may have some choice in how to do that. If, for instance, you have a range of natural talents, it may be you choose to develop them all to some extent, or to focus instead on achieving excellence in one or two. All duties command fulfilment, but there are different ways of fulfilling imperfect duties, and it is up to the agent how she does it.

Each illustration shows the moral reasoning Kant is presenting as requisite for doing actions of moral worth; that is, doing actions from the motive of duty. The first illustration concerns the duty not to commit suicide. Our despairing man, we are told, still has enough grip on his reason to ask himself whether or not taking his own life would be morally forbidden, that is, whether or not it would be contrary to duty. Accordingly, he runs the test of the categorical imperative. First, he formulates his maxim: 'from self-love I make it my principle to shorten my life when its longer duration threatens more trouble than it promises agreeableness.' This is an expression of the most basic reason on which he would be acting if he were to end his life – if going on living is a worse prospect than ending it all, he'll end it all. Second, he asks himself whether he can will the maxim as a universal law; that is, he asks whether there could be a coherent practice in which everyone acted on such a maxim. Kant takes it that the answer to this question is swiftly arrived at: one cannot will the maxim in question as a universal law. He concludes this on the grounds that there is a contradiction in the idea of a law of nature that used a principle, namely self-love, for the two contradictory purposes of furthering life and destroying life. One cannot will the maxim as a universal law of nature because there is something incoherent about employing the principle of self-love in the way our suicidal man is considering. Thus the would-be suicide discovers that the action he is considering is not morally permissible, and that he has a duty to refrain.

The second illustration concerns the duty not to make false promises. A man is desperate for money and considers securing a personal loan on the pretence that he will be able to repay it. He formulates his maxim: 'when I believe myself to be in need of money I shall borrow money and promise to repay it, even though I know that this will never happen'. He then asks himself if he can will this as a universal law, and again Kant claims that he would at once see that he cannot, for such a law would not be consistent with itself. He concludes this on the ground that such a principle would be self-defeating, since if people were free to make such false promises whenever they were in need of money (or whatever) then they would not in fact be able to secure the loans (or other help) that they want, because the promisee would not believe a word they said. There can be no effective institution of promising about X in circumstances C where the practical context is governed by a universal law of false promising about X in C, for it would be known in advance by all concerned that this would-be 'promise' will not be honoured, and so the attempt to make any such promise miscarries from the start. Thus the maxim would be self-defeating when universalized – it could not achieve its purpose ('it would make the promise and *the end one might have in it* itself impossible').

Before moving on to the third and fourth illustrations, note that the first two have turned on the agent's maxim containing a contradiction when universalized at the moment when the agent tries to imagine or conceive such a universal practice – the moment of *conception*. In both these examples, the agent is unable even to imagine a practice in which the maxim in question is a universal law. But we should note in advance that this is only one moment at which the agent may encounter contradiction. At $\boxed{\text{o}}{\mapsto}$, immediately after Kant finishes presenting his four illustrations, he will distinguish two moments at which the agent who is running the categorical imperative test may discover contradiction: the first, already familiar to us, is the moment he attempts to *conceive* or imagine the universal practice; the second is the moment he tries to *will* that imagined universal practice. Thus, as the agent runs the test in respect of any maxim destined to fail it, he may discover either what in the secondary literature is often called a 'contradiction in conception', or, alternatively (for a maxim whose universalization *can* be imagined), a 'contradiction in the will'. These first two illustrations, then, have involved the agent discovering that the universalized version of his maxim is incoherent because there is a contradiction in conception – the agent cannot even get so far as a coherent conception of a practice in which the maxim functions as a universal law.

The third illustration relates to the duty to develop one's natural talents or capacities. A man is inclined not to bother with any such self-cultivation, because he is doing fine as it is and prefers the life of easy amusements and pleasures. But when he asks himself whether his maxim is morally permissible, he finds that while the universalized version of his maxim can be imagined, and indeed it would be consistent with human 'subsistence', he nonetheless cannot will the maxim in universalized form. He cannot will it, because (according to Kant) any rational being wills the development of his own capacities, as even if he doesn't happen to need them now, he *might* need them 'for all sorts of possible purposes'.

The fourth illustration presents us with a man whose life is going well, but who sees that others around him are suffering hardship that he could help relieve if he chose to. His first reaction is to embrace a policy of selfish individualism: he won't help others, and nor will he ask others for help. But then he applies the test of the categorical imperative, asking himself whether he can will this prospective maxim as a universal law. He cannot, claims Kant, for (once again) although the human race could subsist while operating such a law, and there is no difficulty in imagining a universal practice of this maxim, still one cannot will such a law. One cannot will it, because such a law would be in conflict with something that any rational being wills, namely, that one does not close off potential channels of help and assistance that one might turn out to need.

Kant's case for these duties of self-cultivation and helping others might seem to be argued for on strangely prudential terms. That is, he might seem to be suggesting that we have a duty to help others and to cultivate our natural talents because it's in our interests to do so. This had better not be his argument, and indeed it isn't. His case rests only on an idea of what any rational being would will, and he claims respectively that any rational being would will the availability of his own developed capacities and the availability of help from others, for he may need them. This reveals Kant's conception of the rational being at this point as a potentially needy being, a being vulnerable to certain sorts of contingency. That fits for human practical rationality; but it might be objected that Kant's case here only holds firm specifically for *human* rational beings, rather than rational beings per se. There could, after all, be other, more robust rational beings whose survival and well-being was not remotely needy or vulnerable, so that it would be entirely implausible to suggest that such beings necessarily will that their natural talents be cultivated, or that they leave open channels of help from others. If Kant's argument here does depend on features of the specifically human condition, this would seem to undermine his cardinal claim that matters of duty are all derived from pure reason – rationality per se – and so undermine his ambition to show that the imperatives of morality are derived entirely a priori. Rather, on this reading, some duties would be based on reasoning specific to rational beings who are susceptible to various sorts of need.

> Bearing in mind the distinction between maxims that one cannot even *conceive* as universal laws, and maxims that one can imagine but cannot *will* as universal laws, review the four illustrations and remind yourself which illustrations fall into which category – 'contradiction in conception' or 'contradiction in the will'.

At $\boxed{\text{o}}\!\mid\!\rightarrow$ Kant makes his distinction between the two moments at which contradiction may be discovered in a universalized maxim – the moment of conception, and the moment of willing. He also now introduces the terminology of 'strict or narrower (unremitting)' duties as opposed to 'wide (meritorious)' duties, a distinction previously alluded to in terms of 'perfect' as opposed to 'imperfect' duties. Strict duties require a specific action or omission (don't make the false promise), whereas wide duties are less specified and so leave some flexibility in how one fulfils them (developing your talent as a philosopher may be enough to fulfil the duty to develop your natural talents, even while you may leave other talents undeveloped). Kant says that strict duties derive from contradictions in conception, and that only wide duties derive from contradictions in the will. Kant clearly intends that his first two illustrations exemplify contradiction in conception – recall that the would-be suicide and the would-be false promiser are unable even to conceive their maxims as universal laws.[1] And he says that the second two illustrations exemplify contradiction in the will – recall that the would-be bearer of uncultivated capacities and the would-be selfish individualist can imagine universal practices of their maxims, but they cannot will them.

All four illustrations describe an agent considering an action, checking whether or not it is morally permissible by running the test of the categorical imperative. But what happens next? Clearly, on discovering he has a duty to refrain from the action he was considering, the agent may indeed choose to refrain (thereby performing an act of moral worth); or, alternatively, he may choose to go ahead anyway and do something he knows to be morally wrong, perhaps saying to himself 'just this once'.

At $\boxed{p}\mapsto$ Kant gives a description of what is going on when we decide to do something we have discovered is morally impermissible. He describes us, when we do such acts, as making an exception to a universal law that we continue to will even while flouting it (this universal law is the universalized version of the 'opposite of our maxim'). To take up the example of false promising, let us imagine that the agent has already discovered that to make a false promise would be morally forbidden, for he has found he cannot will false promising as a universal law. His not being able to will false promising as a universal law equally establishes that he does will the principle of refraining from false promising as a universal law. Now, if he goes ahead and makes a false promise anyway, he wills his maxim subjectively – that is, as a practical principle applied just to him, as the exception to the rule. This generates a contradiction in his own will, for he already wills the *opposite of his maxim* and now he wills his *maxim* too, the first being willed as an objective or universal practical principle, and the second as a subjective practical principle applied to him 'just this once' as the exception to the rule. Whenever we flout a duty, our will is the locus of a collision between a universal practical principle and its one-off practical negation. Thus, when we do immoral actions we are embroiled in a 'contradiction in our own will'.

> Now that we have depicted the agent testing the moral permissibility of his maxim, and then flouting duty by going ahead with an action he has found to be forbidden, we have encountered a total of three possible kinds of contradiction in practical rationality. Can you review them?

---

[1] The precise interpretation of exactly what sort of contradiction is involved in the contradiction in conception test is much debated. For a discussion of the different interpretations, see Christine Korsgaard, *Creating the Kingdom of Ends*, ch. 3, 'Kant's Formula of Universal Law', listed below in Further Reading.

We have already seen that in running the test of the categorical imperative, if the agent encounters contradiction, it could be *either* a contradiction in conception *or* a contradiction in the will. Now, given Kant's account of what is going on when an agent flouts a recognized duty, we find that if an agent does a forbidden action, he incurs a contradiction in his own will. This last possible moment of contradiction in practical reasoning is crucial to Kant's moral system, because it is the lynchpin of his general conception of immoral action as *irrational* action. But if we are rational animals, how come we can find it so easy to flout duty? Kant goes on to explain a sort of moral double-think that we go in for when we flout the moral law, a double-think that reflects the fact that the human will – human practical rationality – is permanently vulnerable to countervailing motivations of inclination. He describes how the 'contradiction in our own will' that we incur when we act against duty is a matter of inclination *resisting* reason, so that in our minds we transform the universal prohibition on our desired action into a mere generality (something which does permit exceptions), in order that it resembles nearly enough a permission to act on our maxim just this once. The suggestion here is that the fact that we go in for this sort of double-think when we do morally prohibited things reveals our more funda-mental commitment to reason, since otherwise we would not need to go to such psychological lengths.

Finally, in this extract from the middle section of the *Groundwork*, Kant summarizes what he takes himself to have shown so far. At $\boxed{q}$→ he says he takes his arguments to have shown that if there is a morality, a moral law, it must be expressed in categorical imperatives and not hypothetical impera-tives. He has also given the content of such a law by way of the Formula of Universal Law and Formula of Nature, which entail that morality requires us to act only on maxims we can universalize. But he has not yet established that there is such a thing as moral law, as duty; that is, he has explored our pre-theoretical conception of morality but he has not yet tried to establish that human and any other rational animals really have wills that are capable of being commanded by the moral law (this task he reserves for Section III of the *Groundwork*).

He goes on to remind us how important it is to his conception of morality that it be derived from law and not from any natural or otherwise implanted inclination, however reliable. For Kant, the 'inner dignity' of acting from duty depends entirely on the action's stemming purely from duty itself. So much so that he remarks how this dignity is 'all the more manifest' the less supported it is by inclination. That is, the fact that an action is brought about purely by an agent's sense of duty is most evident when the agent lacks any other motive to do it, and perhaps even has some motive not to do it. Sometimes Kant is unfairly read as if he most admires those actions done by people who have nothing but mean and selfish inclinations but whose sense of duty overcomes those mean inclinations to produce an action of moral worth. One does catch a whiff of this from the text, but it is not at all what Kant says. His point is simply that the moral worth of an action is most easily identified, most prominent, when it stands alone in the agent's psychology. Nevertheless, we may still question the plausibility of identifying all moral worth in an impartial style of motivation, conceived as psychologically self-standing and detached from the other motives (love, compassion, kindness) that we commonly regard as at the core of what is good.

The theme of 'purity' is particularly to the fore in these last three paragraphs of the excerpt, and the purity of moral motivation is a matter of the motive of duty being free from contamination by mere inclination, however benevolent. It is not that Kant regards it as in any way bad if people have good inclinations that make it easier for them to act from duty. The point is rather that when we are investigating the nature of the authority that moral imperatives have over us, we must focus on the possibility of acting from duty alone, and in Kant's theory that is a matter of acting on pure reason – reason that is unconditional upon any empirical motives (any motives arising from feelings or interests), for such motives are contingent and so cannot necessitate action in, as Kant sees it, the distinctive manner of morality. Such empirical motives can produce hypothetical imperatives, but not categorical ones. If we want to see 'virtue in her true form' we must, as he says in the footnote at ⃞r ↦, view virtue in separation from the various rewards of morally good action that tend to inspire positive inclinations to conduct oneself in conformity with duty. Doing the right thing purely because it's right is the only thing that furnishes an action with moral worth. For Kant, an action that may conform outwardly with duty but which in fact flows not from the motive of duty but perhaps from some motley admixture of inclinations or interests is a Frankenstein's monster of a motive. By contrast, the pure motive of duty, untouched by any empirical motive, is what characterizes virtue in its true form.

Introduction to Williams

Bernard Williams was born in Essex, England, in 1929. He taught first in London at University College, then as Professor at Bedford College, moving to Cambridge in 1967 to take up the Knightbridge Chair of Philosophy. In 1979 he was elected Provost of King's College, Cambridge, where he stayed until 1987 when he left for Berkeley, California. He came back to Britain in 1990, returning to Oxford as White's Professor of Moral Philosophy, from which he retired in 1996, and returned to All Souls until 2003, the year of his death. Williams served on a number of government committees, most notably chairing in 1979 the Committee on Obscenity and Censorship. He received a knighthood in 1999.

One of the most eminent and influential philosophers of his generation, Williams's thinking exerts a major influence, most especially in ethics and political philosophy. He wrote one of the most widely read studies in the field on the philosophy of Descartes, and contributed much to the recent revival of interest in Nietzsche, but he is perhaps most well-known for his work in the philosophy of value, and in particular his critiques of Utilitarianism and Kantianism. His critical stance can be characterized in the broad by a resistance to the systematization of ethical thinking that is typical of moral *theory* as such, which he argued to be inherently falsifying of moral life and moral sensibility. One prominent aspect of the falsification of our ethical thinking by this style of theory is that it represents morality as fundamentally impersonal, when the opposite is true: much of Williams's philosophy can be read as working out the implications of the idea that ethical life flows from a radically first-personal source – what, as an individual, one cares about, what moves one, and what makes one's life worth living.

Bernard Williams, *Ethics and the Limits of Philosophy* (extracts from Ch. 10, 'Morality, the Peculiar Institution')

Earlier I referred to morality as a special system, a particular variety of ethical thought. I must now explain what I take it to be, and why we would be better off without it.

The important thing about morality is its spirit, its underlying aims, and the general picture of ethical life it implies. In order to see them, we shall need to look carefully at a particular concept, *moral obligation*. The mere fact that it uses a notion of obligation is not what makes morality special. There is an everyday notion of obligation, as one consideration among others, and it is ethically useful. Morality is distinguished by the special notion of obligation it uses, and by the significance it gives to it. It is this special notion that I shall call 'moral obligation'. Morality is not one determinate set of ethical thoughts.

Editors' note: The original footnotes have been renumbered as parts of the text have been omitted.

It embraces a range of ethical outlooks; and morality is so much with us that moral philosophy spends much of its time discussing the differences between those outlooks, rather than the difference between all of them and everything else. They are not all equally typical or instructive examples of the morality system, though they do have in common the idea of moral obligation. The philosopher who has given the purest, deepest, and most thorough representation of morality is Kant. But morality is not an invention of philosophers. It is the outlook, or, incoherently, part of the outlook, of almost all of us.

In the morality system, moral obligation is expressed in one especially important kind of deliberative conclusion – a conclusion that is directed toward what to do, governed by moral reasons, and concerned with a particular situation. (There are also general obligations, and we shall come back to them later.) Not every conclusion of a particular moral deliberation, even within the morality system, expresses an obligation. To go no further, some moral conclusions merely announce that you *may* do something. Those do not express an obligation, but they are in a sense still governed by the idea of obligation: you ask whether you are under an obligation, and decide that you are not.

This description is in terms of the output or conclusion of moral deliberation. The moral considerations that go into a deliberation may themselves take the form of obligations, but one would naturally say that they did not need to do so. I might, for instance, conclude that I was under an obligation to act in a certain way, because it was for the best that a certain outcome should come about and I could bring it about in that way. However, there is a pressure within the morality system to represent every consideration that goes into a deliberation and yields a particular obligation as being itself a general obligation; so if I am now under an obligation to do something that would be for the best, this will be because I have some general obligation, perhaps among others, to do what is for the best. We shall see later how this happens.

The fact that moral obligation is a kind of practical conclusion explains several of its features. An obligation applies to someone with respect to an action – it is an obligation to do something – and the action must be in the agent's power. '*Ought* implies *can*' is a formula famous in this connection. As a general statement about *ought* it is untrue, but it must be correct if it is taken as a condition on what can be a particular obligation, where that is practically concluded. If my deliberation issues in something I cannot do, then I must deliberate again. The question of what counts as in the agent's power is notoriously problematical, not only because of large and unnerving theories claiming that everything (or everything psychological) is determined, but also because it is simply unclear what it means to say that someone can act, or could have acted, in a certain way. To say anything useful about these problems needs a wide-ranging discussion that I shall not attempt in this book.[1] What I shall have to say here, however, will suggest that morality, in this as in other respects, encounters the common problems in a peculiarly acute form.

Another feature of moral obligations in this sense is that they cannot conflict, ultimately, really, or at the end of the line. This will follow directly from the last point, that what I am obliged to do must be in my power, if one grants a further principle (it has been called the 'agglomeration principle'), that if I am obliged to do X and obliged to do Y, then I am obliged to do X and Y. This requirement, too, reflects the practical shape of this notion of obligation. In an ordinary sense of 'obligation' not controlled by these special requirements, obligations obviously can conflict. One of the most common occasions of mentioning them at all is when they do.[2]

[...]

[d]→ Moral obligation is inescapable. I may acquire an obligation voluntarily, as when I make a promise: in that case, indeed, it is usually said that it has to be voluntarily made to be a promise at all, though there is a gray area here, as with promises made under constraint. In other cases, I may be under an obligation through no choice of mine. But, either way, once I am under the obligation, there is no escaping it, and the fact that a given agent would prefer not to be in this system or bound by its rules will not excuse him; nor will blaming him be based on a misunderstanding. Blame is the characteristic reaction of the morality system. [...] Remorse or self-reproach or guilt [...] is the characteristic first-personal reaction within the system, and if an agent never felt such sentiments, he would not belong to the morality system or be a full moral agent in its terms. The system also involves blame between persons, and unless there were such a thing, these first-personal reactions would doubtless not be found, since they are formed by internalization. But it is possible for particular agents who belong to the system never to blame anyone, in the sense

---

[1] I touch briefly on some points later in this chapter. Most discussions of free will do not pay enough attention to the point that causal explanation may have a different impact on different parts of our thought about action and responsibility. It is worth consideration that deliberation requires only *can*, while blame requires *could have*.

[2] I have discussed the question of conflict in several essays, in *Problems of the Self* (1976) and *Moral Luck* (1982) (both Cambridge: Cambridge University Press). It is important that, if it were logically impossible for two actual obligations to conflict, I could not get into a situation of their conflicting even through my own fault. What is it supposed that I get into?

of expressing blame and perhaps even of feeling the relevant sentiments. They might, for instance, be scrupulously sceptical about
what was in other people's power. The point that self-blame or
remorse requires one's action to have been voluntary is only a special
application of a general rule, that blame of anyone is directed to the
voluntary. The moral law is more exigent than the law of an actual
liberal republic, because it allows no emigration, but it is unequivocally just in its ideas of responsibility.

[...]

The sense that moral obligation is inescapable, that what I am
obliged to do is what I *must* do, is the first-personal end of the conception already mentioned, that moral obligation applies to people
even if they do not want it to. The third-personal aspect is that moral
judgement and blame can apply to people even if, at the limit, they
want to live outside that system altogether. From the perspective of
morality, there is nowhere outside the system, or at least nowhere for
a responsible agent. Taking Kant's term, we may join these two aspects
in saying that moral obligation is *categorical*.

I shall come back later to people outside the system. There is more
that needs to be said first about what a moral obligation is for someone within the system. It is hard to agree that the course of action
which, on a given occasion, there is most moral reason to take must
e⊦→ necessarily count as a moral obligation. There are actions (also policies, attitudes, and so on) that are either more or less than obligations.
They may be heroic or very fine actions, which go beyond what is
obligatory or demanded. Or they may be actions that from an ethical
point of view it would be agreeable or worthwhile or a good idea to
do, without one's being required to do them. The point is obvious in
terms of people's reactions. People may be greatly admired, or merely
well thought of, for actions they would not be blamed for omitting.
How does the morality system deal with the considerations that
seemingly do not yield obligations?

One way in which the central, deontological, version of morality
deals with them is to try to make as many as possible into obligations.
(It has a particular motive for the reductivist enterprise of trying to
make all ethical considerations into one type.) [...]

It is a mistake of morality to try to make everything into obligations. But the reasons for the mistake go deep. Here we should recall
f⊦→ that what is *ordinarily* called an obligation does not necessarily have
to win in a conflict of moral considerations. Suppose you are under
an everyday obligation – to visit a friend, let us say (a textbook
example), because you have promised to. You are then presented
with a unique opportunity, at a conflicting time and place, to further

significantly some important cause. (To make the example realistic, one should put in more detail; and, as often in moral philosophy, if one puts in the detail the example may begin to dissolve. There is the question of your friend's attitude toward the cause and also toward your support of the cause. If he or she favours both, or merely the second, and would release you from the promise if you could get in touch, only the stickiest moralist would find a difficulty. If the friend would not release you, you may wonder what sort of friend you have ... But it should not be hard for each person reading this to find some example that will make the point.) You may reasonably conclude that you should take the opportunity to further the cause.[3] But obligations have a moral stringency, which means that breaking them attracts blame. The only thing that can be counted on to cancel this, within the economy of morality, is that the rival action should represent another and more stringent obligation. Morality encourages the idea, *only an obligation can beat an obligation.*[4]

[...]

In order to see around the intimidating structure that morality has made out of the idea of obligation, we need an account of what obligations are when they are rightly seen as merely one kind of ethical consideration among others. This account will help to lead us away from morality's special notion of moral obligation, and eventually out of the morality system altogether.

g⊢→ We need, first, the notion of *importance*. Obviously enough, various things are important to various people (which does not necessarily

[3] The example is of a conflict between an obligation and a consideration that is not at first sight an obligation. It may very readily represent another conflict as well, between private and public. For various considerations on this, and particularly on the role of utilitarian considerations in public life, see the essays in Stuart Hampshire, ed., *Public and Private Morality* (New York: Cambridge University Press, 1978).

[4] Morality encourages the idea, certainly in cases of this kind, but it does not always insist on it, at least in the form that an obligation of mine can be overridden only by another obligation of mine. If some vital interest of mine would have to be sacrificed in order to carry out a promise, particularly if the promise were relatively unimportant, even the severest moralist may agree that I would have the right to break the promise, without requiring that I would be under an obligation to do so (I owe this point to Gilbert Harman). This is correct but, unless the promise is very trivial, the severe moralist will agree, I suspect, only if the interests involved are indeed vital. This suggests an interpretation under which my obligation would indeed be beaten by an obligation, but not one of mine. In insisting that only vital interests count, it is likely that the moralist, when he says that I have the right to safeguard my interest, does not mean simply that I may do that, but that I have what has been called a claim-right to do so: that is to say, others are under an obligation not to impede me in doing so. Then my original obligation will be canceled by an obligation *of the promissee*, to waive his or her right to performance.

mean that those things are important for those people's interests). This involves a relative notion of importance, which we might also express by saying that someone *finds* a given thing important. Beyond this merely relative idea, we have another notion, of something's being, simply, important (important *überhaupt*, as others might put it, or important *period*). It is not at all clear what it is for something to be, simply, important. It does not mean that it is important to the universe: in that sense, nothing is important. Nor does it mean that it is as a matter of fact something that most human beings find important; nor that it is something people ought to find important. I doubt that there can be an incontestable account of this idea; the explanations people give of it are necessarily affected by what they find important.

It does not matter for the present discussion that this notion is poorly understood. I need only three things of it. One is that there is such a notion. Another is that if something is important in the relative sense to somebody, this does not necessarily imply that he or she thinks it is, simply, important. It may be of the greatest importance to Henry that his stamp collection be completed with a certain stamp, but even Henry may see that it is not, simply, important. A significant ideal lies in this: people should find important a number of things that are, simply, important, as well as many things that are not, and they should be able to tell the difference between them.

[h]→ The third point is that the question of importance, and above all the question of what is, simply, important, needs to be distinguished from questions of *deliberative priority*. A consideration has high deliberative priority for us if we give it heavy weighting against other considerations in our deliberations. [...]

Importance has some connections with deliberative priority, but they are not straightforward. There are many important things that no one can do much about, and very many that a given person can do nothing about. Again, it may not be that person's business to do anything: there is a deliberative division of labor. Your deliberations are not connected in a simple way even with what is important to you. If you find something important, then that will affect your life in one way or another, and so affect your deliberations, but those effects do not have to be found directly in the content of your deliberations.

[...]

[i]→ There is one kind of ethical consideration that directly connects importance and deliberative priority, and this is obligation. It is grounded in the basic issue of what people should be able to rely on. People must rely as far as possible on not being killed or used as a resource, and on having some space and objects and relations with

other people they can count as their own. It also serves their interests if, to some extent at least, they can count on not being lied to. One way in which these ends can be served, and perhaps the only way, is by some kind of ethical life; and, certainly, if there is to be ethical life, these ends have to be served by it and within it. *One* way in which ethical life serves them is by encouraging certain motivations, and *one* form of this is to instil a disposition to give the relevant considerations a high deliberative priority – in the most serious of these matters, a virtually absolute priority, so that certain courses of action must come first, while others are ruled out from the beginning. An effective way for actions to be ruled out is that they never come into thought at all, and this is often the best way. One does not feel easy with the man who in the course of a discussion of how to deal with political or business rivals says, 'Of course, we could have them killed, but we should lay that aside right from the beginning.' It should never have come into his hands to be laid aside. It is characteristic of morality that it tends to overlook the possibility that some concerns are best embodied in this way, in deliberative silence.

[...]

[j]→ When a deliberative conclusion embodies a consideration that has the highest deliberative priority and is also of the greatest importance (at least to the agent), it may take a special form and become the conclusion not merely that one should do a certain thing, but that one *must*, and that one cannot do anything else. We may call this a conclusion of practical necessity. Sometimes, of course, 'must' in a practical conclusion is merely relative and means only that some course of action is needed for an end that is not at all a matter of 'must'. 'I must go now' may well be completed '... if I am to get to the movies' where there is no suggestion that I have to go to the movies: I merely am going to the movies. We are not concerned with this, but with a 'must' that is unconditional and *goes all the way down*.

It is an interesting question, how a conclusion in terms of what we must do, or equally of what we cannot do, differs from a conclusion expressed merely in terms of what we have most reason to do; in particular, how it can be stronger, as it seems to be. (How, in deliberation, can anything stronger be concluded in favour of a course of action than that we have most reason to take it?) I shall not try to
[k]→ discuss this question here.[5] What is immediately relevant is that practical necessity is in no way peculiar to ethics. Someone may conclude that he or she unconditionally must do a certain thing, for reasons

---

[5] I have made a suggestion about it in 'Practical Necessity', *Moral Luck*, pp. 124–32.

of prudence, self-protection, aesthetic or artistic concern, or sheer self-assertion. In some of these cases (basic self-defence, for instance), an ethical outlook may itself license the conclusion. In others, it will disapprove of it. The fundamental point is that a conclusion of practical necessity is the same sort of conclusion whether it is grounded in ethical reasons or not.

Practical necessity, and the experience of reaching a conclusion with that force, is one element that has gone into the idea of moral obligation (this may help to explain the sense, which so many people have, that moral obligation is at once quite special and very familiar). Yet practical necessity, even when it is grounded in ethical reasons, does not necessarily signal an obligation. The course of action the agent 'must' take may not be associated with others' expectations, or with blame for failure. The ethically outstanding or possibly heroic actions I mentioned before, in being more than obligations, are not obligatory, and we cannot usually be asked to do them or be blamed for not doing them. But the agent who does such a thing may feel that he must do it, that there is no alternative for him, while at the same time recognizing that it would not be a demand on others. The thought may come in the form that it is a demand on him, but not on others, because he is different from others; but the difference will then typically turn out to consist in the fact that he is someone who has this very conviction. His feelings, indeed, and his expectations of feelings he will have if he does not act, may well be like those associated with obligations (more like them than morality admits[6]).

I have already mentioned Kant's description of morality as categorical. When he claimed that the fundamental principle of morality was a Categorical Imperative, Kant was not interested in any purely logical distinction between forms of what are literally imperatives. He was concerned with the recognition of an *I must* that is unconditional and goes all the way down, but he construed this unconditional practical necessity as being peculiar to morality. He thought it was unconditional in the sense that it did not depend on desire at all: a course of action presented to us with this kind of necessity was one we had

[6]   How alike? This touches on an important question that I cannot pursue here, the distinction between guilt and shame. For a detailed discussion, see now *Shame and Necessity* (California University Press, 1993), especially chapter 4 and endnote 1. There is such a distinction, and it is relevant to ethics, but it is much more complex than is usually thought. Above all, it is a mistake to suppose that guilt can be distinguished as a mature and autonomous reaction that has a place in ethical experience, whereas shame is a more primitive reaction that does not. Morality tends to deceive itself about its relations to shame. For some suggestive remarks on the distinction, see Herbert Morris, 'Guilt and Shame', in *On Guilt and Innocence* (Berkeley: University of California Press, 1976).

reason to take *whatever we might happen to want,* and it was only moral reasons that could transcend desire in that way. As I have introduced it, however, practical necessity need not be independent of desire in so strong a sense. I distinguished a 'must' that is unconditional from one that is conditional on a desire *that the agent merely happens to have;* but a conclusion of practical necessity could itself be the expression of a desire, if the desire were not one that the agent merely happened to have, but was essential to the agent and had to be satisfied. The difference between this conception of practical necessity and Kant's is not of course merely a matter of definition or of logical analysis. Kant's idea of practical necessity is basically this more familiar one, but it is given a particularly radical interpretation, under which the only necessary practical conclusions are those absolutely unconditioned by any desire. For Kant there could be a practical conclusion that was radically unconditioned in this way, because of his picture of the rational self as free from causality, and because there were reasons for action which depended merely on rational agency and not on anything (such as a desire) that the agent might not have had.[7]

[…]

In truth, almost all worthwhile human life lies between the extremes that morality puts before us. It starkly emphasizes a series of contrasts: between force and reason, persuasion and rational conviction, shame and guilt, dislike and disapproval, mere rejection and blame. The attitude that leads it to emphasize all these contrasts can be labelled its *purity.* The purity of morality, its insistence on abstracting the moral consciousness from other kinds of emotional reaction or social influence, conceals not only the means by which it deals with deviant members of its community, but also the virtues of those means. It is not surprising that it should conceal them, since the virtues can be seen as such only from outside the system, from a point of view that can assign value to it, whereas the morality system is closed in on itself and must consider it an indecent misunderstanding to apply to the system any values other than those of morality itself.

---

[7]   This is connected with the differing conceptions of the self entertained by Kant and by his Hegelian critics: see chapter 1, note 6, *Ethics and the Limits of Philosophy.* It is important here to distinguish two different ideas. Other people, and indeed I myself, can have an 'external' idea of different ideals and projects that I might have had, for instance if I had been brought up differently: there are few reasons for, and many reasons against, saying that if I had been brought up differently, it would not have been me. This is the area of metaphysical necessity. But there is a different area, of practical necessity, concerned with what are possible lines of action and possible projects for me, granted that I have the ideals and character I indeed have. This is the level at which we must resist the Kantian idea that the truly ethical subject is one for whom nothing is necessary except agency itself. This is also closely related to the matter of real interests, discussed in chapter 3 of *Ethics and the Limits of Philosophy.*

The purity of morality itself represents a value. It expresses an ideal, presented by Kant, once again, in a form that is the most unqualified and also one of the most moving: the ideal that human existence can be ultimately just. Most advantages and admired characteristics are distributed in ways that, if not unjust, are at any rate not just, and some people are simply luckier than others. The ideal of morality is a value, moral value, that transcends luck. It must therefore lie beyond any empirical determination. It must lie not only in trying rather than succeeding, since success depends partly on luck, but in a kind of trying that lies beyond the level at which the capacity to try can itself be a matter of luck. The value must, further, be supreme. It will be no good if moral value is merely a consolation prize you get if you are not in worldly terms happy or talented or good-humoured or loved. It has to be what ultimately matters.

This is in some ways like a religious conception. But it is also unlike any real religion, and in particular unlike orthodox Christianity. The doctrine of grace in Christianity meant that there was no calculable road from moral effort to salvation; salvation lay beyond merit, and men's efforts, even their moral efforts, were not the measure of God's love.[8] Moreover, when it was said by Christianity that what ultimately mattered was salvation, this was thought to involve a difference that anyone would recognize as a difference, as *the* difference. But the standpoint from which pure moral value has its value is, once more, only that of morality itself. It can hope to transcend luck only by turning in on itself.

The ideals of morality have without doubt, and contrary to a vulgar Marxism that would see them only as an ideology of unworldiness, played a part in producing some actual justice in the world and in mobilizing power and social opportunity to compensate for bad luck in concrete terms. But the idea of a value that lies beyond all luck is an illusion, and political aims cannot continue to draw any conviction from it. Once again, the other conceptions of morality cannot help us. They can only encourage the idea, which always has its greedy friends, that when these illusions have gone there can be no coherent ideas of social justice, but only efficiency, or power, or uncorrected luck.

Many philosophical mistakes are woven into morality. It misunderstands obligations, not seeing how they form just one type of ethical consideration. It misunderstands practical necessity, thinking it peculiar to the ethical. It misunderstands ethical practical necessity, thinking it peculiar to obligations. Beyond all this, morality makes people think that, without its very special obligation, there is only

---

[8] This is why I [have] said [...] that Kant's conception was like that of the Pelagian heresy, which did adjust salvation to merit.

inclination; without its utter voluntariness, there is only force; without its ultimately pure justice, there is no justice. Its philosophical errors are only the most abstract expressions of a deeply rooted and still powerful misconception of life.

Commentary on Williams

This extract is from the final chapter of Williams's defining work, *Ethics and the Limits of Philosophy*, and already the chapter title, 'Morality, the Peculiar Institution', subtly invites comment. If one happens to know that 'the peculiar institution' was the euphemism for slavery used by the American Confederacy,[1] and if one bears in mind Nietzsche's famous castigation of Christian morality as a morality for 'slaves', then one will twig the deliciously embedded Nietzschean joke. As we shall see, part of Williams's critique of the morality system pertains to its pretensions to a species of obligation that is absolutely authoritative. The idea of an absolutely authoritative 'Thou shalt not' is of course fundamental to Christian morality, at least in the style of the Old Testament, though for Williams's purposes the most relevant historical antecedent to the morality system is not so much Christianity, but more specifically the moral philosophy of Kant. Williams regards the target of his criticism as a powerful philosophical construct that is ultimately as misleading as it is moving. But he also emphasizes, at $\boxed{a}\mapsto$, that the morality system is not merely a philosophical invention: 'It is the outlook, or, incoherently, part of the outlook, of almost all of us.'

Williams characterizes 'morality' (the morality system) by reference to the special notion of obligation it makes central to ethical thinking, and he calls it 'moral obligation'. (Recall the kind of obligation to which Kant's conception of duty gives rise. The conscientious would-be false promiser discovers he has a duty to refrain; that is, he discovers an absolutely authoritative obligation to refrain from actions of that sort.) By contrast, there is an everyday notion of obligation – as applies, roughly speaking, whenever there is a consideration that bears on what one should do – which is ethically useful. In drawing his distinction between the everyday and the distinctively 'moral' uses of obligation, Williams introduces a contrast between two vocabularies: the 'moral' and the 'ethical'. Since he is engaged in a critique of something (the morality system) that he is willing simply to call 'morality', he needs some other vocabulary he can use ingenuously and uncritically to talk about moral life in the more relaxed sense that remains independent of the morality system's idea of morality. For that purpose he employs the vocabulary of the ethical, and as his view emerges we might see its most general claim as the complaint

---

[1] Tim Chappell, 'Bernard Williams', *Stanford Encyclopedia of Philosophy* (entry first published Feb 2006), note 11: <http://plato.stanford.edu/entries/williams-bernard>.

that the ethical is distorted when it is viewed through the lens of the morality system. For these argumentative purposes, he rejects the vocabulary of the 'moral' and recommends the vocabulary of the 'ethical'; but he is not disputing about a word. Rather, restricting the vocabulary of the 'moral' for the morality system he aims to criticize, and reserving the vocabulary of the 'ethical' for the conception of morality he wishes to endorse, is a useful device, and an appropriate one, inasmuch as our ordinary usage would tend to present morality as something rather specific and special, and ethics as something broader. This fits with Williams's rejection of the idea that morality is a sharply delineated practical sphere (that there is a well-defined and distinctive category of practical reasons that are 'moral' reasons), and his endorsement of a more relaxed philosophical conception of how ethical thinking fits into the broad category of practical reason.

In contrast with the everyday, non-specific notion of an obligation, Williams now begins (in the paragraph immediately following $\boxed{a}{\rightarrow}$) to identify the specific conception of obligation that characterizes the morality system.

As you read on through the piece, focus your mind on the five key features of the morality system's notion of obligation that are picked out for discussion, and ask yourself whether you agree with Williams's view of them as features of an undesirably restrictive conception of morality.

The fundamental starting point is that in the morality system moral obligation is a practical *conclusion*: it governs what an agent should do *all things considered* in a particular situation. Williams's point is not that in the morality system every moral conclusion expresses an obligation to do some particular action, for sometimes the conclusion might merely be a permission to do it. Rather, the point is that obligation is the primary or controlling moral idea, so that even when the moral conclusion is a permission, still that permission is granted by concluding that one is not under an obligation to refrain. (Recall that in Kant's theory a practical permission is granted only with the discovery that the prospective action passes the test of the categorical imperative.) In the morality system, the liberty to do the action that one is considering derives entirely from the discovery of the absence of an obligation to refrain: 'you ask whether you are under an obligation, and decide that you are not.'

At $\boxed{b}{\rightarrow}$ Williams anticipates his claim that there is a pressure within the morality system to represent every consideration, every reason, contributing to a moral deliberation as itself an obligation. Exactly what this pressure is will become clearer at $\boxed{f}{\rightarrow}$.

With the basic idea in place of moral obligation as a kind of practical conclusion – an all-things-considered obligation to do something – Williams goes on (in the paragraph immediately after $\boxed{b}{\rightarrow}$) to specify a number of related features of this conception of obligation. First, given that an obligation is an obligation for someone to do something, the action must be in the agent's power. Williams mentions a well-known philosophical slogan here, which expresses the point, albeit, in his view, in over-generalized form: *ought* implies *can*. While it may be quite true that no one could have a conclusive moral obligation to do something in circumstances where they lack the power to do it, the slogan in fact expresses the stronger idea that it cannot be the case that someone ought to do something in circumstances where they lack the power. (The latter of the two ideas is clearly more general, except insofar as one may already be in the grip of the morality system's commitment to all oughts being obligations and all obligations being practical conclusions.) As such, Williams regards the slogan as untrue, and that is because he understands 'ought' in what he has identified as the everyday sense, so that it simply expresses the idea that there is a consideration that has a bearing on what one should do. This understanding of 'ought' is of course in line with the similarly everyday understanding of obligation he has explicitly invoked to contrast with the notion of obligation that is fundamental to the morality system. In the everyday usages of obligation or ought, it can be the case that I ought to get the shopping done, or that I have an obligation to get it done, even though, because it's pouring with rain out there, my (perfectly proper) practical conclusion is that I'll leave it until tomorrow. Practical conclusions are all-things-considered statements about what one should do. Williams wants to emphasize, by contrast, that statements of what one has an obligation to do, or what one ought to do, are often simply statements of considerations with a bearing on what one's practical conclusion should be. In its construction of morality as a special practical sphere, the morality system appropriates these words, and tends to fix them in their strongest possible sense, as expressions of *conclusions of* practical deliberation as opposed to *considerations in* practical deliberation.

At $\boxed{c} \mapsto$ Williams says it is a notoriously problematical question when it is in the agent's power to do something and when it isn't.

What are the two reasons he discusses for its being problematical?

The 'large and unnerving' theories he mentions are forms of causal determinism – the view that everything that happens is necessitated by what comes before. The reason determinism might be unnerving is that it can seem to pose a threat to free will. A classic form of the worry is that if everything that happens – including every act of human will, every practical decision we make – is causally necessitated by what brings it about, then what we *will* seems not to be free at all, and the human will comes to seem more 'like a weathervane on a well-oiled pivot in a changeable wind' which points in whichever direction it is blown.[2]

---

[2] Schopenhauer, Arthur, 'Prize Essay on the Freedom of the Will', excerpted in S. Guttenplan, J. Hornsby, and C. Janaway, *Reading Philosophy* (Blackwell, 2003), p. 187.

The second reason mentioned is simply that the idea of what it is in a person's power to do is very often open to interpretation, to say the least, and may sometimes even be indeterminate. If someone holds a gun to my head and tells me to put the cash in his sack, is it in my power to refuse? Well, yes and no. If someone was brought up to identify with a powerful code of gang loyalty and violence, with precious little outside influence upon his thinking, could he have thought differently from his peers? Well, yes and no.

The problematical nature of this question about what is and what is not in a person's power is a general problem, but Williams suggests that the morality system confronts it in peculiarly acute form, as the next feature of the morality system reveals.

The second feature of moral obligations (in the sense given by the morality system) is that ultimately they never conflict. He says this flows directly from the idea that the fulfilment of obligations as such is always in the agent's power, so long as one adds what is sometimes called the agglomeration principle.

> What is the agglomeration principle? Ask yourself how, if one combines this principle with the idea that a moral obligation to do an action entails that the action is in the agent's power, it follows that moral obligations never ultimately conflict.

The agglomeration principle simply says that multiple moral obligations automatically conjoin to form a single conjunctive obligation. If someone has a moral obligation to do X, and also a moral obligation to do Y, then these two obligations automatically conjoin to form an obligation to do X-and-Y. Given the assumption that it is necessarily in one's power to fulfil moral obligations (if it is not in one's power, then it's not a moral obligation after all), we can see how the morality system has the moral fabric neatly sewn up so that there cannot be conflicting obligations. In the morality system, two would-be conflicting obligations automatically generate a single conjunctive obligation which it is not in one's power to fulfil; therefore it is not an obligation at all. This is how the morality system carves up the moral conceptual space to ensure that there is no room for irresolvable moral dilemmas.

Once again, Williams contrasts the everyday sense of obligation with that generated in the morality system. In the everyday sense, moral obligations frequently come into conflict. That is the stock-in-trade of ethical deliberation. Balancing the different strengths and priorities of different obligations is what ethical deliberation *is*. In the morality system, by contrast, obligations cannot conflict, and balancing these priorities is construed as a matter of finding out what one's moral obligation is, and it is a defining feature of the morality system that there is always a do-able answer to this question. Thus the morality system ensures against the tragedy of unavoidable moral failure.

What do you think about the idea, here identified as part of the morality system, that there is no such thing as a moral obligation to do two practically inconsistent things, i.e. an obligation to do A and B where you cannot do both A and B? Do you agree with Williams that life can deliver intractable moral dilemmas, or do you agree with the opposing idea that morality, properly understood, spares us any such moral impasse?

The third feature of moral obligation that Williams picks out, at $\boxed{\text{d}}{\mapsto}$, is that it is inescapable. He describes this in terms of not being able to escape an obligation even if one would 'prefer not to be in this system or bound by its rules'. So the idea of inescapability relates to a lack of individual freedom to dissent from the moral rules generated by the morality system. Recall Kant's conception. He too is fundamentally concerned with freedom, but he constructs a reconciliation between the inescapability of moral obligation and the agent's freedom by sourcing morality's authority in the rules of rationality that are internal to the rational agent as such. Thus, for Kant, what may appear to human moral subjects as an externally imposed set of inescapable rules is really derived from an essential feature of the agent himself. The inescapability is in no sense institutional or societal, but is simply the inescapability of the authority of reason – not something any rational agent as such could dissent from. For Kant, then, freedom and the inescapability of moral obligation are reconciled in the all-important notion of autonomy: self-rule. By contrast, for Williams (whose scepticism about the role played by reason in the Kantian theory will become plainer as we read on), the inescapability of moral obligation remains implicitly threatening to the idea that the agent is free to dissent from whatever rules are generating the moral obligations. Remember the wry allusion to moral slavery in the chapter's sub-title.

Why do you think Williams says that blame is the characteristic reaction of the morality system? If blame is indeed its characteristic reaction, is there anything wrong in that?

We might count the blame-centredness of the morality system as its fourth feature. The reason blame is the characteristic moral sentiment is that if morality is centred on a species of obligation that is an inescapable and do-able obligation to perform (or refrain from) an action, then transgressing the obligation could hardly solicit anything less than blame, whether self-directed or other-directed. For how could one not be at fault in failing to fulfil such an obligation?

What does Williams mean when he says that the moral law is 'unequivocally just in its ideas of responsibility'?

In the morality system, blame is the definitive moral response, and one cannot be blamed for things one does unless they are done voluntarily. So there is a guarantee against a certain sort of bad luck – the bad moral luck of finding oneself responsible for deeds which were not, as described, voluntary. Think of Oedipus. He got married and got in a fight; but in doing so, he later discovers, he married his mother and killed his father. Under this latter description, he did not do these things voluntarily. Now, in the morality system, he is not blameworthy and the implication is that his moral copybook is not, or not really, blotted. There is justice in this, insofar as it was through no fault of his own that Oedipus did those terrible things. Williams expresses no reservation at this stage about the way the morality system guarantees justice in responsibility, and its concomitant conception of moral life as a luck-free practical sphere; but perhaps it is helpful to note that his general view of these matters is that it is absurd to say, as the morality system is inclined to do, that since Oedipus is not blameworthy, the terrible things he has done should just be written off, as if they had no ethical significance for him at all.[3] One way of thinking about this is to question whether blame should have quite such a monopoly on negative moral response.

According to the morality system, moral obligations present us with things we *must* (and can) do, so that self-blame, or remorse, is the first-personal response of agents within the system. This characteristic response is the first-personal aspect of the inescapability of moral obligation. And the third-personal aspect is that someone who fails to fulfil an obligation incurs blame even if they don't agree with the rules that generate the obligation. Williams goes on to suggest that if we put these two aspects together, then we arrive at the idea that moral obligations are, in Kant's term, categorical. However, we must take this point cautiously, for Williams's conception of inescapability is not the same as Kant's idea of the absolute authority of morals. On Kant's view there is simply no conceptual room for a rational agent as such dissenting from moral obligations, since the whole idea of a moral obligation, of duty, is constructed out of what a rational being as such can will. So if an agent were to dissent from the commands of morality, that could only be owing to some failure of rationality on his part. For Kant, categorical imperatives are categorical precisely because they apply to rational agents as such. So Williams's disagreement with Kant is not that he thinks moral dissent should be allowed and Kant does not. That would be a gross misrepresentation on all fronts. Rather, Williams is sceptical about the very idea of morality as a construction out of rational agency, and so of the whole Kantian enterprise. On Williams's conception, there is always room for rational dissent from any given moral obligation, because, contra Kant, there *is* no single, objectively correct moral system.

³ See Williams, *Shame and Necessity* (Berkeley and Los Angeles: University of California Press, 1993), ff. 70.

Next Williams asks, at $\boxed{e}\!\!\to$, how the morality system deals with actions that do not fulfil an obligation. These might be extraordinarily good actions that are above and beyond the call of duty (sometimes called supererogatory actions), or, on the smaller scale, they might be ethically good actions (a special kindness to a stranger, perhaps) that are, so to speak, less than morally required. He talks about the 'central, deontological, version of morality' and – deontological meaning duty-based – he has the Kantian system in mind. This version of morality, according to Williams, attempts to transform into acts of obligation all those good actions that we would ordinarily think of as either above or below the call of duty. He has already said that there is a special pressure in the morality system to represent all moral considerations as obligations. His example at $\boxed{f}\!\!\to$ explains why. It is an ethical commonplace that we regard someone as able to release herself from a promise, blamelessly, if there is sufficient cause to do so – i.e. if the thing she does instead is more important. Given the conception of obligation at work in the morality system, the only way she might be so released from her promise is if another obligation is seen to trump the original obligation (thereby dissolving it – once trumped, it is no longer an obligation). Thus the fifth feature of the morality system: only an obligation can beat an obligation.

Having given a critical characterization of the morality system's conception of obligation, Williams now launches his own positive characterization of obligation, conceived in the everyday manner, not as necessarily constituting a practical conclusion but as one kind of ethical consideration among others. He begins, at $\boxed{g}\!\!\to$, by introducing the simple notion of 'importance', or rather, two notions of importance.

> What are the two notions of importance Williams distinguishes here? Do you find his invocation of the idea of importance helpfully intuitive or unhelpfully vague?

He distinguishes a relative notion – one according to which something is important relative to a particular individual, or a particular set of interests, or a particular purpose. And he distinguishes a non-relative notion – one according to which something is unqualifiedly important. He suggests that this latter idea is not clearly understood, and specifically denies that it should be understood as important irrespective of human life and interests (it's not important 'to the universe'), and nor should it be understood in a majoritarian sense (it's not necessarily what *most* people find important), nor a strongly normative sense (it's not to be understood as what, in some independent sense, we *ought* to find important). So what is it, then? Williams is getting at an everyday distinction we all make between things that matter only because of some rather specific set of concerns (such as it's being important to Henry that he complete his stamp collection) and things that matter in a way that calls for no qualification. (Perhaps: freedom is, simply, important; art is, simply, important; love is, simply, important.)

> What is 'deliberative priority'? Why does Williams say, at ⬚h ↦, that questions of importance must be distinguished from questions of deliberative priority?

If you are deciding what to do – deliberating – and two considerations have a bearing on your decision, and you weight one of them more heavily than the other, then you are giving deliberative priority to that consideration. If, for instance, you are deciding whether to try and finish a piece of work before leaving to fetch a friend from the station, and you decide to leave your work unfinished in order to make sure you don't keep your friend waiting, then you have given deliberative priority to the consideration that you shouldn't keep your friend waiting.

It is tempting to assume that importance, and especially the non-relative kind, is straightforwardly in proportion to deliberative priority, so that the more important a consideration is the more it gains in deliberative priority. But the picture is not so simple, says Williams. First, there can be things of the utmost importance – advancing techniques of transplant surgery, political progress in the Middle East – that are deliberatively irrelevant to me, simply because virtually nothing I could do has any bearing on it. Indeed there are things of the utmost importance – evacuating the town before the tsunami reaches it – that can be deliberatively irrelevant all round because there is no agent or agency capable of doing it. Second, there is a 'deliberative division of labour'. This phrase refers to the fact that different people or groups have different deliberative jobs or roles, inasmuch as there are many deliberative conclusions whose propriety is role-specific. Thus there can be things I consider to be of the utmost importance but which it is not my place to do anything about. For example, I might think it crucially important that my friend's children should have been told by now about their parents' immanent divorce; but it is certainly not for me to tell them. Finally, if something is important – having friends, for instance – this idea would not in the ordinary run of things feature in one's deliberation. That is, if someone happens to be forming a new friendship, it would not ordinarily be a feature of her deliberations about whether to call them that she thinks to herself: 'Pick up the phone – it's important to have friends.' (She just thinks, 'Maybe she'd like to see a movie tonight … I'll call.') Things that are important often frame our deliberations, rather than feature in them.

By contrast, the ethical notion of obligation does create a direct connection between importance and deliberative priority, as Williams states at ⬚i ↦. His reason for saying this is that obligation is on the whole an exigent enough species of ethical consideration that it makes for reliability or predictability of how people are going to act. Now this kind of reliability is crucial when it relates to things that are, simply, important: personal security, respect for rights and so on. And so there can be a social ethical drift in the direction of ensuring reliability and social coordination about these fundamentally important things by instilling a habit in people such that they give these obligations a high deliberative priority, and sometimes an almost absolute priority. This can manifest itself in certain courses of action never even being entertained by the deliberating agent – for most of us, putting a stop to one's neighbour's late-night loud music by shooting him is not a thought that enters one's deliberations.

At $\boxed{j}\mapsto$, Williams specifically addresses the nature of conclusions of practical necessity: 'the conclusion not merely that one should do a certain thing, but that one *must*, and that one cannot do anything else'.

> Williams distinguishes two types of conclusion of practical necessity. What are they? Think about how they relate to Kant's distinction between hypothetical and categorical imperatives.

Once again, he distinguishes a relative notion from a non-relative notion. 'I *must* leave now if I'm not going to miss my train' as compared with an unconditional 'must' such as, perhaps, 'I *must* leave all this behind and devote myself to my art'. This example recalls a well-known example of Williams's own from an essay entitled 'Moral Luck' in a collection of the same name (see Further Reading) in which he imagines a painter, Gauguin (not quite the historical Gauguin, no doubt, but someone similarly placed), abandoning his family to pursue his art and indeed becoming, as it turns out, a great painter. The example illustrates his main point here: practical necessity is not a uniquely ethical phenomenon. Other sorts of consideration – for instance, a consideration rooted in what sort of a person one essentially is or wants to be, or what makes one's life worth living – can issue in a conclusion of practical necessity. In fact, given the right context, all manner of considerations might issue in such a practical necessity – in the list given by Williams at $\boxed{k}\mapsto$ we find even sheer self-assertion given as a possible source. Be careful not to misunderstand Williams here. He is not saying that if someone arrives at a conclusion to the effect that he must, as a matter of artistic self-assertion, say, abandon his family for a life of painting, that this magically renders his action ethically acceptable. Rather the point is the weaker one that, since ethical reasons must compete alongside other kinds of practical reason for deliberative priority, sometimes ethical reasons may lose. But the action may well remain an ethically bad one, even while it is intelligible from the agent's point of view as something which, for other reasons, he simply had to do. Contrary to the morality system, which tries to purify matters by casting moral reasons as obligations that are bound to override other sorts of practical reason, Williams's view is that there is no such thing as a moral reason in that inflated sense; rather, there are ethical reasons, and they are just one kind of practical reason.

> What do you think about Williams's idea that the sorts of reasons we would ordinarily call moral reasons (but he prefers to call ethical reasons) are not overriding – that is, they do not automatically trump other sorts of practical reason? How do you construe the example of someone like Gauguin?

Even when practical necessity does stem from ethical considerations, Williams argues that it need not signal an obligation, for obligation is associated with what others may expect from one, and blame one for failing to do. Someone can judge that he must do something, even while he makes that judgement of no one else – perhaps because he recognizes that the practical conclusion is dependent on things that are peculiar to him (he may be uniquely placed to do the thing envisaged, perhaps because of special skills, or particular commitments – he may be, for instance, the only trained fire-fighter among the employees who have evacuated the office building, as one of their number is spotted trapped in the burning building).

At ⎰I⎱↦, Williams compares Kant's conception of how practical necessity relates to morality: Kant conceived practical necessity as being unique to morality. More particularly, he conceived it as utterly unconditional on desire, whereas Williams has argued that certain sorts of desire can issue in practical necessity for a given individual. A crucial difference in their conceptions of practical necessity is really that Kant was after a particular sort of practical necessity for morality, namely one which applied to the agent irrespective of absolutely all contingencies about him, however basic or entrenched those contingencies might be. Kant's conception of moral authority requires a transcendence of the individual so that the moral law applies to the agent not qua individual at all but qua rational being. By contrast, Williams's conception of practical necessity grows out of observing that an experience of practical necessity can be had by an individual agent precisely because of what makes him the individual that he is – his particular commitments and projects, the shape of his particular life. Whereas Kant's starting point is the search for an a priori foundation for moral deliberation, Williams regards that ambition, with all due respect, as an enterprise in moralistic fantasy. The crucial boundary for Williams when it comes to identifying the source of practical necessity is between those desires and related states that 'the agent merely happens to have' and those that are in some measure essential to who he is and what makes his life worth living. For Kant, by contrast, all desires are on a par, and, given his foundationalist ambition for morality, all are equally irrelevant to anything that could count as moral deliberation. Desire-like states are either non-starters because they manifestly fail to be universal; or, if they are universal, they still won't do as a moral motive, since they can at best be contingently universal, and so cannot deliver the characteristic practical necessitation of morality.

At ⎰m⎱↦, Williams moves to the question of the ideal of purity that is distinctive of the morality system. The ideal of purity is inherent in its hiving off moral considerations as a special, autonomous set of practical considerations. But it is also a positive ideal in itself, and here Williams comes to address the issue of luck head-on. The naturally uneven distribution of beauty, ability, skill, charm, and so on, may be far from just, but merely in virtue of the fact that one belongs to a species of rational being, one is in control of one's moral merit. Everyone has equal opportunity to be morally good, no matter what personal attributes you may have, no matter how the consequences of your actions happen to turn out, and no matter what deeds you (like Oedipus) may involuntarily do. Moral worth is a matter of acting on the proper motive, and, as Kant presents it, that is in the power of all of us.

> Williams contrasts this ideal of purity and justice in morals with the moral outlook of orthodox Christianity. What is this contrast? Do you think there are other aspects of Christian thinking which are, however, reflected in the morality system?

The aspect of Christianity that he highlights in order to bring out the contrast is that Christianity does not put salvation in the individual's control; salvation is a matter of God's love, and God's love is not geared to men's efforts and merits in any straightforward way. We might say that the morality system, and Kant's system in particular, renders morality a strict moral meritocracy, whereas, interestingly, the Christian doctrine of grace is simply not about moral merit.

Ultimately, Williams's argument with the morality system is that it misrepresents the fundamental nature of ethical life by trying to abstract it away from all other forms of motivation, and to anchor it in something that transcends what should be seen as the real source of moral reasons: the individual agent and those deep-going, essential 'contingencies' of desire and practical commitment that determine who one distinctively is.

6

Boundaries of Moral Philosophy

Introduction to the Problem

Any selection of significant moral philosophical texts, however partial, cannot help but seem to represent the canon in some sense. And so it is important to include texts that problematize the canon, that question the assumptions of the tradition. The two pieces, from Martha Nussbaum and Raimond Gaita, each draw critical attention to the boundaries of traditional moral philosophy, and the boundaries to moral thinking that are drawn in traditional moral philosophy; and each points to ways in which those boundaries are false, or inadequate, or both. If we are reading and reflecting on moral philosophy, we should not forget to interrogate it according to its own standards and according to a conception of what moral philosophy, at its best, could and should be like. It seems a reasonable suggestion that moral philosophy should have something to say to the person who has a deep interest in moral life and its relations to other aspects of human understanding. And yet so much of moral philosophy is, for some readers at least, a signal disappointment in this respect. We should ask ourselves why this is. Part of the explanation is perhaps that the philosophical urge in many other subject areas (philosophy of mind, or language, for instance) is never with the particular but only with the general, and a concern to achieve maximal generality is a definitive mark of English-language philosophy. But perhaps this is an unhelpful trajectory in ethics. Perhaps a concern with the particular is an irreducible characteristic of moral understanding, so that the urge to generate moral *theory* – some set of suitably general moral principles – may be at odds with achieving satisfying accounts of moral understanding. It may be that such accounts call for something that is not traditionally, but perfectly well could be, a normal feature of moral philosophy: the close attention to the particulars of moral experience.

One hopes that this final pair of texts are together indicative that moral philosophy can indeed become increasingly satisfying to someone with a deep interest in moral life. But in the meantime, the tensions within moral philosophy – tensions between the philosopher's urge for a general theory and (what should be equally) the philosopher's urge to do justice to the perhaps irreducibly particular complexities of moral life – are themselves profoundly interesting. The following two texts play out those tensions in different ways, one by questioning the borders of moral philosophy and literature as they are traditionally conceived, and the other by vindicating the role of remorse in delineating what can count as morally wrong, thereby relegating moral theory to second place when it comes to the identification of right and wrong.

Introduction to Nussbaum

Martha Craven Nussbaum was born in New York in 1947. She taught philosophy and classics at Harvard in the 1970s and early 1980s, then moved to Brown University. Currently Ernst Freund Distinguished Service Professor of Law and Ethics at the University of Chicago, she also holds appointments in the Divinity School and in the Departments of Philosophy and Classics. A specialist in Aristotle, her work also ranges across political philosophy and ethics, and she has also contributed to feminist philosophy, writing in particular on the gendered nature of philosophical understandings of emotion, on sexual objectification and on universal justice for women. One of the most prominent and prolific philosophers of her generation, her work is well known throughout the humanities. She has also done much to apply philosophical thinking about human capabilities and justice in an internationalist context, serving from 1986–93 as a research advisor at the World Institute for Development Economics Research, Helsinki, which is part of the United Nations University.

Martha Nussbaum, *Love's Knowledge: Essays on Philosophy and Literature* (extracts from essay 4, 'Flawed Crystals: James's *The Golden Bowl* and Literature as Moral Philosophy')

At the centre, the bed of crystalline Love was dedicated to her name most fittingly. The man who had cut the crystal for her couch and her observance had divined her nature unerringly: Love *should* be of

crystal – transparent and translucent. ... Its roundness inside betokens
Love's Simplicity: Simplicity is most fitting for love, which must have
no corners, that is, no Cunning or Treachery.

Gottfried von Strassburg, Tristan.

No dogs, bicycles, or tricycles allowed in this garden at any time *by
order*. The gardeners are required to conduct from the garden anyone
infringing these rules.

Sign in the garden of Cadogan Square, London, 1980

I

She wants, this woman, to have a flawless life. She says to her good
friend Fanny Assingham, 'I want a happiness without a hole in it big
enough for you to poke in your finger. ... The golden bowl as it *was*
to have been. ... The bowl with all our happiness in it. The bowl
without the crack' (II.216–17)[1] – signalling in this way to us, who
know the properties of this remarkable flawed object, that she wishes
her life to be (unlike the bowl) a pure and perfect crystal, completely
without crack or seam, both precious and safely hard.

Two features of Maggie Verver's moral life, in the first half of this
novel, strike us as salient. One is this assiduous aspiration to perfection, especially moral perfection. The other is the exclusive intensity
of her love for her father, the oddness of her marriage to the Prince,
which, far from effecting the usual reordering of the commitments
and obligations of childhood, has permitted her to gratify, to an
extraordinary degree, her 'wish to remain, intensely, the same pas-
sionate little daughter she had always been' (I.395). This wish to be
without flaw and this desire to remain her father's daughter – we suspect that they must be somehow connected. And yet the nature of the
connection is not altogether obvious, especially since it is far from
obvious that this refusal to move from father to husband is a perfect
way of living for an adult woman. But I believe that a connection, and
a deep one, will emerge if we scrutinize more closely the particular
nature of Maggie's moral aspiration. This will be a route into the
novel, by which we can begin to appreciate the ways in which James
 is working here with questions about moral ambition, moralism, and
the nature of our worldly relation to value. (Since it is in connection

---

[1]   All page numbers are cited from *The Golden Bowl*, New York Edition (New York: Charles
Scribner's Sons, 1909). Prefaces to other works are cited from James. *The Art of the Novel*
(New York, 1970), hereafter *AN*. On the fact that this passage comes from the end rather than
the beginning of the novel, see p. 279 below.

with its exploration of these elements of experience that I wish to make, on behalf of this novel, the claim that it is philosophical or makes an important contribution to moral philosophy, it will serve at the same time to broach these further questions.)

Maggie, then, wants to be as good as possible; and when she says this, it is evidently moral goodness that is uppermost in her thoughts. If we ask more closely about what, for her, constitutes moral perfection, we find that the central idea is one of never doing a wrong, never breaking a rule, never hurting. 'Maggie had never in her life,' her father reflects, 'been wrong for more than three minutes' (I.236). The 'note of the felt need of not working harm' (II.64), the 'superstition of not "hurting"' (I.160) – these are the concerns pressed urgently by her 'quite heroic little sense of justice' (I.395) in every situation of choice. It does not surprise us that her husband should compare her, in thought, to a Roman *matrona*, bearing 'the transmitted images of rather neutral and negative propriety that made up, in his long line, the average of wifehood and motherhood' (I.322). What sharply sets her apart from this sternly upright figure is, above all, the intensity, the note of real fear, with which she insists on the claims of guiltlessness. In a revealing moment, she compares the requirements of morality (and especially its prohibition of certain bad acts) to the 'water-tight' insides of an ocean liner: 'Water-tight – the biggest compartment of all? Why it's the best cabin and the main deck and the engine-room and the steward's pantry! It's the ship itself – it's the whole line. It's the captain's table and all one's luggage – one's reading for the trip' (I.15). Morality and its rules of not hurting constitute for her a safe world in which to live and voyage, protected against nameless dangers. If ever a breach were made in the walls of that vessel, if even one seam should give way – but she does not dare to imagine that. She avoids it. She sits in the liner (perhaps the same vessel that Fanny refers to later as 'Mr. Verver's boat' [I.267]) and reads only what the captain, or father, has provided for the trip.

So, surrounded by her innocence, she goes about straining to keep herself right, to make her life a flawless crystal bowl holding, as far as pleasures go, 'nothing one was obliged to recognize, but innocent pleasures, pleasures without penalties' (I.11). The novel is dense with images for this splendid aspiration: images of crystal, of roundness, of childhood – and above all, references to the happy innocence which was, as the Prince says, 'the state of our primitive parents before the Fall' (I.335).[2]

---

[2] The Prince is here referring to the anomalous innocence to which he and Charlotte are forced to pretend because of the innocence of the other pair. References to the Edenic condition of the Ververs are striking throughout, and too frequent to enumerate. (For only a few examples, in addition to I.335 and II.367, discussed in the text, see I.78, 187, 309, 385, 393–95.)

As innocent as these of any knowledge of evil, either for doing or for seeing, they live, she and her father Adam, sheltered by the immaculate white walls and the placid gardens of 'monotonous Eaton Square' (I.333), a place which is the appropriate embodiment of Maggie's Edenic longing:[3] 'They knew, it might have appeared in these lights, absolutely nothing on earth worth speaking of – whether beautifully or cynically; and they would perhaps sometimes be a little less trying if they would only once for all peacefully admit that knowledge wasn't one of their needs and that they were in fact constitutionally inaccessible to it. They were good children, bless their hearts, and the children of good children' (I.333–4). In this passage, as in Maggie's speech about the steamer, we have a sense that bulwarks of ignorance are being erected against some threat that presses in from the world; that knowledge of some truth is not simply absent, but is being actively refused for the sake of beautitude. (For Adam's *daughter* was not born in Eden; and the 'children of good children' must have, in virtue of being this, some connection with original sin.)

Maggie has reached a time in her life at which we might expect her to notice a difficulty attaching to her ideal. She has, specifically, married. She has undertaken to become a woman and to move from her father's home into a husband's. This time might be expected to be a time of conflicting obligations. For the daughter of so exacting a father, a daughter who, moreover, has served for most of her childhood and adolescence as her father's sole travelling companion, friend, and partner, it might be expected to be a time of a painful breaking away from past attachments and commitments. To become a separate woman in her own right and the Prince's wife, this woman, it is clear, will have to give pain. Even if, as Fanny says, natural attachments 'may be intense and yet not prevent other intensities' (I.395), the nature of this particular blood relation, as deep as any marriage,

---

[3]   Eaton Square, structurally solid, immaculately white, and 'synonymous for respectability' even before James's time (Susan Jenkins, *Landlords of London* [London, 1975] 82), represents, for the pair, a retreat from worldly complication. 'The "world", by still another beautiful perversity of their chance, included Portland Place without including to anything like the same extent Eaton Square' (I.320). It should be noticed, too, that Maggie at first attempts, by interior decoration, to make Portland Place as well embody her moral ambition: 'she stood there circled about and furnished forth, as always, in a manner that testified to her perfect little personal processes. It had ever been her sign that she was for all occasions *found* ready, without loose ends or exposed accessories or unremoved superfluities: a suggestion of the swept and garnished, in her whole splendid yet thereby more or less encumbered and embroidered setting that reflected her small still passion for order and symmetry, for objects with their backs to the walls, and spoke even of some probable reference in her American blood to dusting and polishing New England grandmothers' (II.152).

surely makes claims that would block other, complicating loves.[4] But Maggie's conscience so shrinks from the guilt of rendered pain that she cannot bear at all to embark on this job of separation. Her resourceful imagination therefore discovers that in every conflict of loves or of values, one can, by the right sort of effort, reach an allegedly guiltless consistency and harmony – even 'that ideal consistency on which her moral comfort almost at any time depended'. What is this strategy? 'To remain consistent', we are told, 'she had always been capable of cutting down more or less her prior term' (II.6). This image from syllogistic logic means, I suppose, that a promising way to resolve a conflict of obligations is always to rewrite the major premise of the practical syllogism so that the prior term no longer covers the entire extension of the middle term. Instead of 'all B are A', we will now have, at most, 'some B are A'. By this device Maggie can cause a potentially troublesome value term no longer to apply in the given situation. She preserves her comfort by preserving her consistency; she preserves her consistency by 'simplifying' her world and even her character, as the Prince observes (I.322). In the case at hand, she solves the apparent conflict of marital love with filial duty by 'cutting back' the claims of marriage, marrying in such a way that she can still remain her father's 'undivided' (I.323).

b→ So in a funny way, what began as the noble idea of failing in no duty and cherishing every value ends, consistently pushed through, in an enterprise that cuts back, cuts down, alters values to fit the claims of consistency. Any claim that seems capable of conflicting with her primary duty to her father – a duty which to this good daughter looks identical with morality itself – can be allowed to have validity only insofar as it accords with his requirements, consents, as she and her father say, to be 'round' rather than angular, harmonious rather than discordant.[5] She and her father are, she imagines, in a boat together, sailing away from 'luxuriant complications' (II.255).

c→ Maggie's attachment to moral simplicity brings with it some disturbing consequences. The first is, plainly, an avoidance or suppression of her own adult sexuality. If she allows herself to mature and to experience marriage fully, then she opens herself immediately to complication and to the possibility of a break. She and her father will no

---

[4] Compare Sigmund Freud. *Three Essays on Sexuality* (1905). *Standard Edition of the Complete Psychological Works of Sigmund Freud*, trans. and ed. J. Strachey (London, 1953–72) VII. 207–43.

[5] See I.135–8, especially: 'No visibility of transition showed, no violence of accommodation, in retrospect, emerged' (I.135); 'Oh if he *had* been angular! – who could say what might *then* have happened' (I.137). Adam associates the Prince's 'roundness' with the claim that 'for living with, you're a pure and perfect crystal' (I.138).

longer be 'undivided'. Therefore Maggie, as she ostensibly matures, has cultivated, increasingly, an androgynous and even an ascetic persona. 'Extraordinarily *clear* ... in her prettiness' (I.9), she is even described as 'prim'. Her father recalls that 'when once she had been told before him, familiarly, that she resembled a nun, she had replied that she was delighted to hear it and would certainly try to' (I.188). Later she is compared to 'some holy image in a procession'; her character is said by Fanny to be like 'that little silver cross you once showed me, blest by the Holy Father, that you always wear, out of sight next your skin' (II.112). This deliberate suppression of her womanliness is evidently promoted by her father, who associates womanliness with weakness, the absence of judgement, and the inability to give genuine companionship, and who, on the other hand, thinks of his daughter as his first companion in his spiritual adventures. He is an intellectual and artistic pioneer, a Cortez discovering a new world. When he asks himself whether his wife might have accompanied him in this adventure, he comes quickly to a conclusion that rules out the womanly (or at least women of his own class) altogether: 'No companion of Cortez had presumably been a real lady: Mr. Verver allowed that historic fact to determine his inference' (I.143).

To become a 'real lady' is, then, to abandon her father, to wound him by ceasing to be his companion in all things. It is, I think, this moral claim, and not merely some vague girlish fear, that leads Maggie, even in marriage with a man to whom she is deeply attracted, so to repress her womanly responses that Fanny can confidently and, we feel, correctly assert that she has never really 'had' the Prince (I.384).[6] This link is confirmed by James's subtle use of water imagery in connection with both sexual passion and moral conflict or complication – frequently the two of these together. We have already noticed Maggie's 'water-tight' steamer, secured against a harm or a violation, and Mr Verver's boat, which sails safely away from complication. What we can now point out is that the first image is closely joined by Maggie herself to an admission that she does not respond to her husband's 'particular self'; in the second case, the complications from which Maggie imagines father and daughter sailing away are 'husbands and wives' who had 'made the air too tropical' (II.255). Maggie even asks herself at this point, 'Why ... couldn't they always live, so

---

[6] See I.398; where Fanny says of Adam, ' "But the whole point is just that two years of Charlotte are what he hasn't really – or what you may call undividedly – had," ' and Bob responds, 'Any more than Maggie by your theory, eh, has "really or undividedly," had four of the Prince? It takes all she hasn't had ... to account for the innocence that in her too so leaves us in admiration.'

far as they lived together, in a boat? She felt in her face with the question the breath of a possibility that soothed her; they needed only *know* each other henceforth in the unmarried relation.' Sexuality is seen and feared as a ground of conflict, a threat against the moral safety of not harming. Maggie's fear of water expresses the link between these two refusals – just as, in the passage in which the Prince and Charlotte renew their relationship, imagery of flooding (linked with a picture of breaking through or out of a perfect circle) indicates at once both their mutual sexual response and their acceptance of moral guilt: 'Then of a sudden, through this tightened circle, as at the issue of a narrow strait into the sea beyond, everything broke up, broke down, gave way, melted and mingled. Their lips sought their lips, their pressure their response and their response their pressure; with a violence that had sighed itself the next moment to the longest and deepest of stillnesses, they passionately sealed their pledge' (I.312).[7] This willingness to burst out of the tight circle of harmony, to risk the ocean, is what we know Maggie has so far lacked. In the case of her father's parallel avoidance both of moral guilt and of a full sexual life, we are told in no uncertain terms that the consequence has been physical impotence with his new wife.[8] With Maggie this is less clear and perhaps less important; whatever takes place physically, we are clear that there is a failure, on the level of imagination and emotion, to respond as a separate adult woman to her husband's own separate sexual presence. She is still intact in her innocence; nothing is damaged. 'She had been able to marry without breaking, as she liked to put it, with her past' (II.5).[9]

Another consequence of Maggie's innocence is, plainly, an inability in any area of her life to see values, including persons, emerge as

[7] Both Leon Edel in his biography (*The Master* [New York, 1971], 222–3) and Stephen Spender in his essay on the novel have suggested that this passage indicates a new acceptance, on the part of James himself, of the fact of physical intimacy. Spender writes that we see in the author 'a person who, profoundly with his whole being, after overcoming great inhibition, has accepted the *idea* of people loving' (quoted in Edel, pp. 222–3).

[8] See I.307, where Charlotte says that she knows now that she and Adam never will have any children and asserts positively that it is not her fault. (I assume that she could be so positive at this date only if impotence or unwillingness on his part, and not sterility, were the reason.)

[9] Compare Freud, *Three Essays*, 227: 'At every stage in the course of development through which all human beings ought by rights to pass, a certain number are held back; so there are some who have never got over their parents' authority and have withdrawn their affection from them either very incompletely or not at all. They are mostly girls, who, to the delight of their parents, have persisted in all their childish love far beyond puberty. It is most instructive to find that it is precisely these girls who in their later marriage lack the capacity to give their husbands what is due to them; they make cold wives and remain sexually anaesthetic.'

distinct ends in their own right. In every case they are rounded, accommodated, not recognized insofar as their claims collide with other claims. But this is plainly a way of viewing persons – those recalcitrant, inveterately 'angular' objects – that leads to a certain neglect. First, there is the neglect of what Maggie calls her husband's 'unknown quantity, [his] particular self' (I.9). She even tells him, 'You're not perhaps absolutely unique' (I.12). And in the famous image of the pagoda at the beginning of Part II she betrays for the first time a curiosity about her situation, of which the Prince is so prominent a part. She desires for the first time to peer inside this odd, towerlike object which for so long has oddly occupied a place at the centre of her garden, and into which 'no door appeared to give access from her convenient garden-level' (II.4). It is no wonder that at this point she begins to see, too, that her moral imagination is rather like an unsorted storeroom, full of 'confused objects', 'a mess of vain things, congruous, incongruous', tossed in, in a heap, and shut behind a locked door. 'So it was that she had been getting things out of the way' (II.14).

And it is not only personal qualitative uniqueness that goes into Maggie's storeroom; it is also, we need to add, personal *separateness*, the value of each person and each end as a distinct item generating its own claims. In the romance of Tristan, whose praise of love's crystalline simplicity James very likely had in view,[10] the lovers' cultivation of simplicity makes them blind to the way in which each commitment and each value is separate from and liable to conflict with each other; in the same way, Maggie sees only roundness where in real life there is angularity, and therefore misses the distinct claims of each particular value. This is, strikingly, true even of her love for her father, as we see from a brief, proleptic scene early in the novel. Returning from church, Maggie finds her father besieged by Mrs Rance, an irritating woman who wants to marry him. For the first time Maggie perceives that her own marriage *has* begun to entail for Adam the pain of abandonment and of harassment from would-be companions. And strangely, this idea suddenly gives her, also for the first time, a sense

---

[10]   The golden bowl itself recalls a bowl given by George I to a newborn child of the Lamb family, which much impressed James on a visit to Sussex in 1902 (see Edel, p. 209). There are also, doubtless, allusions to Ecclesiastes 12:6–7 ('or ever the silver cord be loosed, or the golden bowl be broken, … then shall the dust return to the earth as it was: and the spirit shall return unto God who gave it'), and the Blake's 'Can wisdom be kept in a silver rod, / Or love in a golden bowl?' But the fact that the bowl is a flawed crystal, and the repeated allusions to the perfect simplicity of crystal elsewhere, are not explained by any of these allusions, and we may very well have an allusion to the well-known symbolism of this great love legend. (For other aspects of the bowl's complex symbolism, see Quentin Anderson's *The American Henry James* (New Brunswick, N.J., 1957).)

of her father as a separate person: 'He was on her mind, he was even in a manner on her hands – as a distinct thing, that is, from being, where he had always been, merely deep in her heart and in her life; too deep down, as it were, to be disengaged, contrasted or opposed: in short objectively presented' (I.155). Moral objectivity about the value of a person (or, presumably, any other source of moral claims) requires, evidently, the ability to see that item as distinct from other items; this in turn requires the ability to see it not as a deep part of an innocent harmony but as a value that can be contrasted or opposed to others, whose demands can potentially conflict with other demands. In making her father's law normative for a world of harmlessness, Maggie has, ironically, failed to see *him*. It is not until much later that she really takes this in; her next move here is to resolve the conflict and restore the 'harmony' by giving him Charlotte as a wife. But because of this scene, *we* are aware of her manoeuvres as self-deceptive and false. Knowledge of a good, that is to say a value, in the world requires, we see, knowledge of evil, that is to say of the possibility of conflict, disorder, the contingent necessity of breaking or harming. Without eating this fruit she is just a child, ignorant of the value of the good as well.

[d]→ We are now in a position to appreciate one of the oddest and most striking features of James's portrait of this idealistic pair of Americans: the inveterate tendency of both father and daughter to assimilate people, in their imagination and deliberation, to fine *objects d'art*. This matter is given considerable emphasis in James's design. One of the most striking incursions of the authorial voice into a narrative told, for the most part, through the consciousness of one or another of its characters begins, 'Nothing perhaps might affect us as queerer, had we time to look into it, than this application of the same measure of value to such different pieces of property as old Persian carpets, say, and new human acquisitions' (I.196). And such a strange way of valuing is present too in our very first glimpse of Maggie, where she speaks of her husband as 'a rarity, an object of beauty, an object of price. ... You're what they call a *morceau de musée*' (I.12). We are, of course, invited to take the time ourselves to look into this odd matter.

We soon realize that this propensity for the aestheticization of persons does not precisely indicate that the Ververs neglect the moral, or reduce the moral to the aesthetic. Indeed, it is agreed all around that they are distinguished for their keen *moral* sense, even for their strict moralism. It is rather that the peculiar nature of their moral aim, with its extreme emphasis on flawless living and, because of this, on consistency and harmony, is best supported by a view of persons that tends to assimilate their properties to certain salient properties of works of art. Works of art are precious objects, object of high value. And yet it is a remarkable feature of our attention to works of art that it appears to spread itself round smoothly and harmoniously. I can, visiting a museum, survey many fine objects with appropriate awe and tenderness. I can devote myself now to one, now to another, without the sense that the objects make conflicting claims against my love and care. If one day I spend my entire museum visit gazing at Turners, I have not incurred a guilt against the Blakes in the next room; nor have I failed in a duty toward Bartok by my loving attention to Hindemith. To live with works of art is to live in a world enormously rich in value, without a deep risk of infidelity, disloyalty, or any conflict which might lead to these. It is the Ververs' brilliantly resourceful idea that the moral life, too, can be flawless and innocent of violation, while remaining full of value, if only persons can be made to resemble aesthetic objects, things to be displayed in a gallery for innocent attention. Closely linked with Mr Verver's aestheticization of Charlotte is a wish 'for some idea, lurking in the vast freshness of the night, at the breath of which disparities would submit to fusion' (I.205–6). This idea – that he should marry Charlotte so as to restore the general harmony – comes to him during the very moment at which he sees the precious Damascene tiles 'successively, and oh so tenderly, unmuffled and revealed', until they 'lay there at last in their full harmony and their venerable splendor' (I.215). It is surely the splendid order and harmony of these aesthetic objects (each tile lies uncompetitively side by side with its neighbours; the demands of tender attention to all can be faithfully met) which Mr Verver covets for his human life; and coveting it, he turns Charlotte, by marriage, into the finest piece of all. For Maggie as well, the wonderful idea is that a husband who resembles a 'fine piece' can be packed and unpacked, stored and brought out for show – or, if he should become too 'big', be sent to American City to be 'buried' (I.14); in none of these circumstances will its presence place a strain on the deliberation of the collector or spoil the harmony of the museum, or life, which testifies to his rare powers of perception.[11]

In short, then, we have begun with a noble and venerable moral ideal – not just the fancy of a childish girl, but a picture of personal conduct and personal rightness that has very deep roots in the moral tradition of our entire culture. (It is not fortuitous that this combination

---

[11]   It is instructive to examine the many places in the novel where a person is praised with the aesthetically linked word 'splendid'. It usually emerges that to call a human being that is to refuse that person a properly human tenderness and care.

of moralism and excessive simplicity is attributed to the American characters in this novel – nor that these Americans should be as resourceful in technical deliberation as they are naive in emotional response.) We are shown that this ideal, followed out to its strictest conclusion, generates an extraordinary blindness to value and ends by subordinating the particular claim of each commitment and love to the claims of harmony. And that *is*, we see, the fancy of a childish girl. It does not work on its own terms, since it does wrong to persons and commits acts of blindness and cruelty. (It is not inappropriate that Maggie and her father, as well as the other pair, are, in effect, charged with disloyalty and adultery [see I.304] – for each has been unfaithful to the commitments involved in making a marriage just because of this childlike unwillingness to break away or to experience guilt.) And it is morally objectionable in that it commits the holder to a systematic neglect of certain features of persons – namely, both their separateness and their qualitative uniqueness – on which their specific personal value might be thought to rest. The richness of the novel's moral vision lies in the way in which it both shows us the splendor of a rigorous moralism (for this simple vision attracts not only the Americans but to some extent every major character in the novel) and at the same time erodes our confidence in this ideal by displaying the guilt involved in such innocence. There is, as Maggie later says, an 'awful mixture in things' (II.292).

e→ The world of *The Golden Bowl* is a fallen world – a world, that is, in which innocence cannot be and is not safely preserved, a world where values and loves are so pervasively in tension one with another that there is no safe human expectation of a perfect fidelity to all throughout a life. [...] In this world our first choice as adults is the choice to pursue our personal goals at the expense of a separation from and a break with the parent. And we cannot ever count on the fact that our love of a husband will not require the spiritual death of a best friend and mentor, that fidelity to a wife will not require cruelty to a former lover. There are better and worse choices, naturally, within this tangled world; but it is childlike to refuse to see that it *is* in this way tangled, for this is a feature of our situation as creatures with values operating in the world of nature. [...]

I am claiming, then, that this novel works out a secular analogue of the idea of original sin by showing a human being's relation to value in the world to be, fundamentally and of contingent necessity, one of imperfect fidelity and therefore of guilt; by showing us ourselves as precious, valuing beings who, under the strains imposed by the intertwining of our routes to value in the world, become cracked and flawed. Guilt toward value is here, if not literally a priori, still a feature of our humanness which attaches to us as a structural feature of our situation in nature and in the family,[12] prior to the specific choices and failures that we enter upon in a particular life. The Prince says about crystal. 'Its beauty is its *being* crystal. But its hardness is certainly its safety.' On this analogy, human beings, like the golden bowl, are beautiful but not safe: they have ideals, but they split. Charlotte's question about the bowl was. 'If it's so precious, how comes it to be cheap?' The answer to this question is the story of four human lives.

This novel, I have indicated, is about the development of a woman. To be a woman, to give herself to her husband, Maggie will need to come to see herself as something cracked, imperfect, unsafe, a vessel with a hole through which water may pass, a steamer compartment no longer tightly sealed. Later, as her perception is shifting, she will in fact see herself as a house not perfectly closed against the elements: 'She saw round about her, through the chinks of the shutters, the hard glare of nature' (II.303). And in the world of nature, what Maggie sees is the suffering of Charlotte, caused by her act. Her guilt has entered her vision.

[f]→ The second half of the novel is the story of Maggie's initiation into knowledge of her fallen world. Beginning to *live* (see I.385–6) is, for her, beginning to see that meaningful commitment to a love in the world can require the sacrifice of one's own moral purity. To regain her husband she must damage Charlotte. We are fully aware, as is she, that her cruelty and dishonesty to Charlotte are in no way purified or effaced by the fact of Charlotte's own offense. Her love, unlike the ideal of the Tristanic lover, must live on cunning and treachery; it requires the breaking of moral rules and a departure from the comfortable garden.

It would be an important and fascinating task to trace the details of this development: the way, for example, in which exposure to conflict and a womanly exposure to sexuality are linked, here as before, in the imagery of water, as Maggie the passenger becomes a swimmer;[13] the

[12] One might ask whether to show that certain strains inhere in the structure of the family as we know it is in any way to show that they are an essential feature of human life. This question is nowhere more courageously pressed than in the *Republic*, where it is indeed argued that the most troublesome and pervasive of our moral conflicts have their roots in the family and could be eliminated by eliminating the family. But Plato is also aware that this would involve making human beings, especially with respect to their attachments and emotions, radically different from anything that we have known.

[13] See, for example, II.42–3, II.263; compare the descriptions of Fanny at I.365–79. It is worth noting that during the period in which Maggie is 'beginning to live' in the human world, her images for herself are frequently these images, linked as they are with birth or the wish to be born. See Freud, *The Interpretation of Dreams* (1900), *Standard Edition* V, chap. 6, sect. E.

way she comes to see that the value of persons and of objects is partially constituted by the risk they bring of pain and opposition – that 'any deep-seated passion has its pangs as well as its joys, and that we are made by its aches and anxieties most richly conscious of it' (II.7); the way in which the departure from Eden brings with it the possibility of certain moral emotions which were unknown in that garden – among them shame, jealousy, tenderness, and respect; the way in which, from having seen only clear, splendid objects, Maggie learns, inhabiting a human world, to be a 'mistress of shades' (II.142), a reader of nuance and complexity. (There are no books in Eden.)[14]

But although we do not have space to go into all of this, what we now must notice is that these new dimensions of perception and response begin to amount, strangely, for us and for Maggie, as things go on, not so much to a way of living with imperfection as to a new way of getting at perfection. Maggie, still as exigent and idealistic as ever, discovers a way of remaining a splendidly pure and safe object *within* this fallen world, 'as hard ... as a little pointed diamond' (II.145). (The alert reader will have noticed that the quotation with which this paper began came not from the novel's early chapters or later reflections on them, but from a very late point, at which Maggie is already deliberating in the newer and riskier way.) We might describe the new ideal this way: See clearly and with high intelligence. Respond with the vibrant sympathy of a vividly active imagination. If there are conflicts, face them squarely and with keen perception. Choose as well as you can for overt action, but at every moment remember the more comprehensive duties of the imagination and emotions. If love of your husband requires hurting and lying to Charlotte, then do these cruel things, making the better choice. But never cease, all the while, to be richly conscious of Charlotte's pain and to bear, in imagination and feeling, the full burden of your guilt as the cause of that pain. If life is a tragedy (see II.311–12), see that; respond to that fact with pity for others and fear for yourself. Never for a moment close your eyes or dull your feelings. The ideal is summarized by James in his preface to *The Princess Casamassima* as one of 'being finely aware and richly responsible'; it is nowhere more fittingly and fully embodied than in the long passage of deliberation in which Maggie, picturing vividly Charlotte's silent suffering, decides to urge her husband to speak to

---

[14] I have found illuminating, in this connection, the reading of the first chapters of Genesis given in Andrew Martin, 'The Genesis of Ignorance: Nescience and Omniscience in the Garden of Eden,' *Philosophy and Literature* 5 (1981) 3–20.

Charlotte once more before her departure (II.327–31). Here we feel that Maggie's keen sensitivity to the values of love and friendship, which she herself is violating, redeems and transfigures the cruelty of her act. If she acts badly of necessity, at least she takes upon herself the conscious guilt for that badness and, by her sense of guilt, shows herself as a person to whom badness is odious. It is not surprising that Maggie repeatedly imagines herself as a sacrificial figure who bears the pain and guilt of the situation through the fine responsibility of her consciousness. This idea of bearing guilt for love's sake is evidently the source of the comparisons of Maggie to the scapegoat of ancient Greek religion, who saves the community by bearing its pollution (II.234), and also to Christ, who took upon himself the sins of the world (II.112). The difference in her case is that she assumes this world's burden of sin not by going into exile or dying but by sinning, and by seeing that she is sinning, and by bearing, for love, her own imperfection.

But as the end approaches, we are troubled by our sense that this is, after all, a new way of being innocent. We are troubled by Maggie's comparison of herself to a diamond, more angular than the original crystal, but even more safely hard.[15] We note that she is still fond of the language of moral absolutes: ' "consummate" was [a] term she privately applied' (II.359). She has not so much altered her moral categories as rearranged the items to which she attaches these favoured terms; not so much accepted evil in herself as seen a new way to be (internally) safely innocent. We have been put on our guard against projects of safety and projects of perfection, so we wonder whether Maggie's new ideal has itself a crack in it.

And now, as we reflect in this way, it should strike us that in fact, according to the last scene of the novel, Maggie has not yet, as she approaches the final parting with Charlotte and her father and the final confrontation with Amerigo, eaten the fruit of the tree of knowledge of good and evil. It is still hanging before her, just before the end, 'the golden fruit that had shone from afar' (II.367). So the new moral ideal cannot really have been the fruit of that eating, and Maggie, until the very end, is still in some significant sense an innocent, though more responsive and more womanly than before.

---

[15]   Compare Adam's use of the diamond as an image of the angularity which Amerigo allegedly lacks: 'I can see them all from here – each of them sticking out by itself – all the architectural cut diamonds that would have scratched one's softer sides. One would have been scratched by diamonds – doubtless the neatest way if one was to be scratched at all – but one would have been reduced to a hash' (I.138).

What is, then, Maggie's innocent failure of recognition, and what can we discover in the final scene that will explain to us why here, and only here, James presents her as falling from purity? We notice, in her last encounter with Adam and Charlotte, some significant signals. Aesthetic images for persons reappear and multiply. There is talk of the 'human furniture required aesthetically by such a scene' (II.360); there is talk of the emptiness of a house with 'half of its best things removed' (II.362). There is, above all, a marked aestheticization of Charlotte as 'incomparable', 'too splendid'. We are forced to ask why, at this point of triumph for Maggie's new ideal rightness, she should reimport the techniques of the old innocence – why, after so deeply responding to Charlotte's solitude and pain, and after urging Amerigo to do the same, she should suddenly retreat behind these old refusals. An answer begins to emerge along with the question; we begin to sense the discovery for which James is preparing us.

Amerigo has refused Charlotte not only his love, but also his response and his vision. He refuses to see her pain; he allows it to remain at a distance, receiving her as 'Royalty' rather than as a woman who has arranged her life around her passion for him. What we now begin to see is that Maggie was wrong to think that it could, should be otherwise. The demands of his love for Maggie will not, in fact, allow the moral luxury of clear sight and generous response. To love one woman adequately he cannot always be tormented by a consciousness of the other. He must, then, of necessity banish the other, wronging her not only, like Maggie, in act, but also in the depths of his imagination and his vision. The demands of the new ideal of seeing are not always compatible with an adequate fulfillment of each of our commitments, for some loves are exclusive and demand a blindness in other quarters. Instead of being 'finely aware and richly responsible' we may, in fact, have to become, as lovers, grossly insensitive and careless with respect to other, incompatible claims. The mere fact of being deeply engaged forces a blindness. The moment at which Maggie finally tastes the 'golden fruit' is such a moment: on both sides, obtuseness feeds the triumph of love.

> 'Isn't she too splendid?' she simply said, offering it to explain and to finish.
> 'Oh, splendid!' With which he came over to her.
> 'That's our help, you see,' she added – to point further her moral.
> It kept him before her therefore, taking in – or trying to – what she so wonderfully gave. He tried, too clearly, to please

her – to meet her in her own way; but with the result only that, close to her, her face kept before him, his hands holding her shoulders, his whole act enclosing her, he presently echoed: '"See"? I see nothing but *you*'. And the truth of it had, with this force, after a moment, so strangely lighted his eyes that as for pity and dread of them she buried her own in his breast. (II.368–9)

The Prince, then, sees nothing but Maggie. And Maggie, seeing this singleness of vision, reacts to her sight of Amerigo as to a tragedy – with 'pity and dread'. For she sees, in truth, that he *does* see only her, that she and he together have brought about, within his imagination, an extinction of vision and a failure of response; and that this has happened of tragic necessity because of the requirements of his commitment to her. Long ago, Maggie did not see that choice among competing values could ever be tragic. Then she saw that it could be tragic, but thought that a heroine of tragedy could still avoid tragedy inwardly by being richly responsible to everything in intellect and feeling. Now she sees in her husband the genuine, unredeemed article, a 'hero' violating love for the sake of love, purified by no inner sympathy, no note of higher consciousness.

But at this moment, with the 'golden fruit' of knowledge hanging there before her, she discovers, too, that she cannot gaze on this tragedy like the perfectly responsive and responsible spectator, seeing and feeling for everyone, and still have the knowledge of love for which she has sacrificed. Aristotle argued that tragedy brings illumination concerning values: through the 'pity and dread' inspired by tragic events, we learn about what matters to us, and we are clarified. Maggie, in the last sentence of the novel, recognizes that the keen vision and acknowledgement of the good tragic spectator are themselves values which can, in the world of nature, collide with other values. To see all, to be present to all, requires of the spectator a narrowness of love; to surrender to love requires an infidelity of the soul's eyes. To look will be to judge him; to judge him is to fall short of the fullness of his passion. '"Thank goodness, then," said Charlotte, "that if there *be* a crack we know it!"' (I.119). Here Maggie sees beyond her, seeing that the gifts of love require a gentleness that goes beyond, and covers, knowledge.

So she makes for him the last and greatest sacrifice of all. She gives him her purity of vision, her diamond hardness – as he had given up, for her, his vision of Charlotte's humanity. Once he had, long before, asked Fanny Assingham to give him her eyes, meaning to lend him the higher keenness of her American moral sense (I.30). Now his American wife gives him her eyes in fact, burying her own vision, therefore her perfect rightness, in his body.[16]

And does one, as Charlotte asked, make a present of an object which contains, to one's knowledge, a flaw? To that Maggie herself has had, in the deeper moments of her connoisseurship, an answer: 'The infirmity of art was the candour of affection, the grossness of pedigree the refinement of sympathy; the ugliest objects in fact as a general thing were the bravest, the tenderest mementos, and, as such, figured in glass cases apart, worthy doubtless of the home, but not worthy of the temple – dedicated to the grimacing, not to the clear-faced, gods' (II.156).

[h]→ What are we to say about this? Is there, then, a moral ideal in this novel, or isn't there? Do the insights of the prefaces and of Part II stand or fall? I want to say that they stand, that there is an ideal here. It is not altogether undermined: it is still precious. It is only shown to be, like everything human, imperfect. (And perhaps, as the passage just mentioned suggests, this flaw in it is partly constitutive of its specifically human value and beauty.) The end of the novel does not tell us that it is pointless to become 'finely aware and richly responsible'; it only warns us against turning this norm into a new form of watertight purity by showing us that a deep love may sometimes require an infidelity against even this adult spiritual standard.

Well, how do we know? When are we to pursue this ideal and when to let it go? How much is a deep love worth, and under what circumstances is it worth a blinding? What boundaries are we to draw? What priorities can we fix? These, I take it, are the little girl's questions, resurfacing now, again, at yet another level – as they will resurface so long as the nature of little girls is still the same. She wants to be told ahead of time exactly what's right and when. She wants to know exactly how much she loves this person, and exactly what choices this entails. To counter her insistent demand, James repeatedly, in the second half of the novel, holds up to us a different picture: that of an actress who finds, suddenly, that her script is not written in advance and that she must 'quite heroically' improvise her role. 'Preparation and practice had come but a short way; her part opened out, and she invented from moment to moment what to say and to do' (II.33). The final understanding to which his criticism of little girls transports us

---

[16] The moment is prepared earlier by another refusal of vision that is, like this one, an expression of gentleness that opens the way for love: 'She sank to her knees with her arm on the ledge of her window-seat, where she blinded her eyes from the full glare of seeing that his idea could only be to wait, whatever might come, at her side. It was to her buried face that she thus, for a long time, felt him draw nearest' (II.294).

is that *this* is what adult deliberation is and should be. And there's no safety in that, no safety at all.

II

Suppose that this novel does explore, as I claim, significant aspects of human moral experience. Why, it may still be asked, do we need a text like this one for our work on these issues? Why, as people with an interest in understanding and self-understanding, couldn't we derive everything we require from a text that stated and argued for these conclusions about human beings plainly and simply, without the complications of character and conversation, without the stylistic and structural complexities of the literary – not to mention the particular obliquities, ambiguities, and parentheses of this particular literary text? Why do I wish to enter on behalf of this text the claim that it is philosophical? And even should this claim be granted, why should we believe it to be a major or irreplaceable work of moral philosophy, whose place could not be fully filled by texts which we are accustomed to call philosophical?

There are really two questions here. One is a particular question about the claim of this particular novel; another is a more general question about the philosophical importance of literary works generally – that is, of works which share with this work certain general features by virtue of which they are commonly classified and studied apart from admitted philosophical works. I shall not really attempt to answer the second question here, insofar as it ranges beyond the first. Among the particular features of this text on which I shall stake its claim to philosophical importance, some are, indeed, shared with other related novels and with tragic dramas; others are peculiarly its own, or belong to it in a particularly high degree. I therefore shall speak only about *The Golden Bowl* and James's later style; I leave to the reader the job of exploring the wider consequences of what I shall say for our conventional distinction between philosophy and literature.

First, to prevent confusion, we must have some rough story about what moral philosophy and the job of moral philosophy are – for on some accounts of these things, particularly the Kantian account, this text obviously falls entirely outside of moral philosophy in virtue of the empirical and contingent character of its content. We would like to find some way of characterizing the aims of moral philosophy that would be generally enough agreed not to prejudice the answer to our question about this text, and yet specific enough to give us some purchase on our question. I propose, therefore, that we begin with the very simple Aristotelian idea that ethics is the search for a specification of the good life for a human being. This is a study whose aim, as Aristotle insists, is not just theoretical understanding but also practice. (We study not just for the sake of learning but also to see our 'target' and ourselves more clearly, so that we can ourselves live and act better.) Nor can the theoretical aims of this study be accomplished in isolation from the practical aspect, for the working-through of the alternative theoretical conceptions is itself a Socratic process, which demands the active engagement of the interlocutor's own moral intuitions and responses.[17] The aim of the study will be to produce an intelligent ordering of the 'appearances' – the experiences and sayings of human agents and choosers. It cannot, then, in any way be cut off from the study of the empirical and social conditions of human life; indeed, ethics, in Aristotle's conception, is a part of the social study of human beings.

I choose this conception of moral inquiry not only because I find it appealing and broadly correct, not only because I hope that it will be sufficiently inclusive to command wide agreement, but also because James describes his conception of his own authorial task in language which brings him into intimate connection with the Aristotelian enterprise. In the preface to *The Princess Casamassima,* he describes his end as the production of an 'intelligent report' of human experience, that is, of 'our apprehension and our measure of what happens to us as social creatures' (*AN* 64–5). We can then hope to be assessing James's text against the background of a conception of moral writing that is at once powerful and one to which he himself lays claim.

I can here do no more than to sketch out the very general lines along which I would like to argue the case for *The Golden Bowl,* but I hope that the programmatic character of these remarks will prove suggestive rather than frustrating. The first claim concerns the moral content of this text, as I have elucidated it in Part I: the second centres on the nature of the moral abilities involved in reading and interpreting it. (This does not, as I hope will soon become evident, really amount to any claim that one can sever this novel's form from its content.)

---

[17]   Compare the remarks about the Socratic nature of moral theory in John Rawls, *A Theory of Justice* (Cambridge, Mass., 1971), 46–53. Rawls traces elements of this view back through Sidgwick to Aristotle. I have discussed Aristotle's view in 'Saving Aristotle's Appearances', in *Language and Logos,* ed. M. Schofield and M. Nussbaum (Cambridge, 1982); *Fragility,* ch. 8; and also in *Fragility* (Cambridge: Cambridge University Press, 2001), ch. 1, 'Perceptive Equilibrium', and 'Introduction', [...] to *Love's Knowledge: Essays in Philosophy and Literature* (New York/ Oxford: Oxford University Press, 1990).

First, then, the claims of this text concerning value and imperfection are views whose plausibility and importance are difficult to assess without the sustained exploration of particular lives that a text such as this one makes possible. The claim that our loves and commitments are so related that infidelity and failure of response are more or less inevitable features even of the best examples of loving is a claim for which a philosophical text would have a hard time mounting direct argument. It is only when, as here, we study the loves and attentions of a finely responsive mind such as Maggie's, through all the contingent complexities of a tangled human life, that the force of these ideas begins to make itself felt. When we have before us a consciousness who responds well and keenly, and when we see that even for such a consciousness the golden bowl is broken – then we have something like a persuasive argument that these features hold of human life in general. It is not only, then, the novel's capacity to explore the length and breadth of a life, but the combination of this exploratory power with the presence of a character who will count as a high case of the human response to value, that creates the telling argument. James tells us emphatically that the moral claims of his texts depend centrally on the presence inside them of such high characters, both agents and interpreters of their own lives, whose readings of life we will count as high exemplars of our own. In the preface to *The Princess Casamassima*, he writes of his choice of a hero: 'The person capable of feeling in the given case more than another of what is to be felt for it, and so serving in the highest degree to *record* it dramatically and objectively, is the only sort of person on whom we can count not to betray, to cheapen or, as we say, give away the value and beauty of the thing. By so much as the affair matters *for* some such individual, by so much do we get the best there is of it' (*AN* 67).

Here we see James deftly, as often, drawing together the good person with the good character, the good reader in life with the good reader inside a text: and both of these in turn suggest parallel norms of response and vision for the reader *of* this character and this text, who must be a moral being of the appropriate sort or else he (or she) will clearly cheapen the value of the text. Last of all in this assembled group of consciousnesses, and behind them all, stands, James makes clear, the author, whose responsibility it all ultimately is, and whose conscious testimony will either reveal the value of life or by neglect cheapen it. The author's struggle to express life's value and also its mystery is, in this preface, closely coupled with and likened to the task of the character who must respond to the confusions of his world; and the author, of course, is the one from whom the character's struggle

and sense of life must flow. Of the author he now goes on to write: 'If
you haven't, for fiction, the root of the matter in you, haven't the
sense of life and the penetrating imagination, you are a fool in the
very presence of the revealed and assured; but ... if you *are* so armed
you are not really helpless, not without your resource, even before
mysteries abysmal' (*AN* 78). Similarly, at the end of the preface to
The Golden Bowl, he speaks of the author as striving toward a high
sort of moral responsibility for the works which are his 'acts', striving
with 'his active sense of life' (I.xvii), which is 'the silver clue to the
whole labyrinth of his consciousness', so to express the 'general adventure' of that intelligence that a new reading, a renewed confrontation
with the completed act or text, will leave no room for 'mere gaping
contrition' (I.xxv).

We appear to have moved by now far beyond our immediate point
and into the labyrinth of James's complex conception of his authorial
task. But it is, in fact, not possible to speak about the moral view
revealed within this text without speaking at the same time of the created text, which exemplifies and expresses the responses of an imagination that means to care for and to put itself there for us. 'Art',
James writes, 'is nothing if not exemplary', 'care ... nothing if not
active' (I.xxv), and the 'example' in *The Golden Bowl* is, of course,
not merely the adventures of the consciousness of one or another
character, as our emphasis heretofore may have suggested. It is the
entire text, revealed as the imaginative effort of a human character
who displays himself here as the sort of character who reads lives and
texts so as not to cheapen their value. I claim that the views uncovered
in this text derive their power from the way in which they emerge as
the ruminations of such a high and fine mind concerning the tangled
mysteries of these imaginary lives. And we could hardly begin to see
whether such views were or were not exemplary for us if this mind
simply stated its conclusions flatly, if it did not unfold before us
the richness of its reflection, allowing us to follow and to share its
adventures.

k⟩   It is a further fact about the views of this text that they are views
very seldom put forward and seriously examined in works of moral
philosophy. And this, I claim, is no accident. Any view of deliberation
that holds that it is, first and foremost, a matter of intuitive perception and improvisatory response, where a fixed antecedent ordering
or ranking among values is to be taken as a sign of immaturity rather
than of excellence; any view that holds that it is the job of the adult
agent to approach a complex situation responsively, with keen vision
and alert feelings, prepared, if need be, to alter his or her prima facie
conception of the good in the light of the new experience, is likely to

clash with certain classical aims and assertions of moral philosophy, which has usually claimed to make progress on our behalf precisely by extricating us from this bewilderment in the face of the present moment, and by setting us up in a watertight system of rules or a watertight procedure of calculation which will be able to settle troublesome cases, in effect, before the fact. Philosophers who have defended the primacy of intuitive perception are few. And when they have appeared, they have naturally also concluded – as does, for example, Aristotle – that moral theory cannot be a form of scientific knowledge that orders the 'matter of the practical' into an elegant antecedent system; and they have also naturally turned to works of literature, as Aristotle turns to tragic drama, for illumination concerning practical excellence. In fact, Aristotle makes it very clear that his own writing provides at most a 'sketch' or 'outline' of the good life, whose content must be given by experience, and whose central claims can be clarified only by appeal to life and to works of literature.[18]

To show forth the force and truth of the Aristotelian claim that 'the decision rests with perception', we need, then – either side by side with a philosophical 'outline' or inside it – texts which display to us the complexity, the indeterminacy, the sheer *difficulty* of moral choice, and which show us, as this text does concerning Maggie Verver, the childishness, the refusal of life involved in fixing everything in advance according to some system of inviolable rules. This task cannot be easily accomplished by texts which speak in universal terms – for one of the difficulties of deliberation stressed by this view is that of grasping the uniqueness of the new particular. Nor can it easily be done by texts which speak with the hardness or plainness which moral philosophy has traditionally chosen for its style – for how can this style at all convey the way in which the 'matter of the practical' appears before the agent in all of its bewildering complexity, without its morally salient features stamped on its face? And how, without conveying this, can it convey the active adventure of the deliberative intelligence, the 'yearnings of thought and excursions of sympathy' (II.330) that make up much of our actual moral life?[19]

---

[18] On the 'sketch' and its relation to particular intuitive judgements, see 'Discernment'. *Fragility*, chs 8 and 10. For some further remarks about literary storytelling as an expansion of experience, see *Fragility*, ch. 6. A picture of deliberation closely related to the one sketched here is developed in David Wiggins. 'Deliberation and Practical Reason', *Proceedings of the Aristotelian Society* NS 76 (1975–76), 29–51.

[19] There are obvious connections between these thoughts and the line of argument pursued in Iris Murdoch's *The Sovereignty of Good* (London, 1970), whose view of the moral importance of imaginative work I discuss in *Fragility*, ch. 2.

Finally, without a presentation of the mystery, conflict, and riskiness of the lived deliberative situation, it will be hard for philosophy to convey the peculiar value and beauty of choosing humanly well – for we have suggested that the flawed and unclear object has its own, and not simply a lower, sort of beauty. James himself expresses this point, again in the preface to *The Princess Casamassima*: 'It seems probable that if we were never bewildered there would never be a story to tell about us; we should partake of the superior nature of the all-knowing immortals whose annals are dreadfully dull so long as flurried humans are not, for the positive relief of bored Olympians, mixed up with them' (*AN* 63–4). It is this idea that human deliberation is constantly an *adventure* of the personality, undertaken against terrific odds and among frightening mysteries, *and* that this is, in fact, the source of much of its beauty and richness, that texts written in a traditional philosophical style have the most insuperable difficulty conveying to us. If our moral lives are 'stories' in which mystery and risk play a central and a valuable role, then it may well seem that the 'intelligent report' of those lives requires the abilities and techniques of the teller of stories. (And in this way we might come to see James not so much as a novelist-by-profession who, because that was his profession, expressed in that form his moral vision, as an intelligent maker of a moral vision who embodied it in novels because only in that form could he fully and fittingly express it.)

These remarks suggest, then, that there are candidates for moral truth which the plainness of traditional moral philosophy lacks the power to express, and which *The Golden Bowl* expresses wonderfully. Insofar as the goal of moral philosophy is to give us understanding of the human good through a scrutiny of alternative conceptions of the good, this text and others like it would then appear to be important parts of this philosophy. But we said at the beginning of this section that the aim of moral philosophy was not simply theoretical understanding, but also something connected with practice – meaning by this that the philosophical study of the human good is inseparable from, cannot be conducted in isolation from, a Socratic working-through of the interlocutor's or reader's own moral intuitions that will leave this person clearer about his or her own moral aims.[20] What

[20] If one is persuaded that a sharp distinction is to be made between moral theory and moral education, the following remarks can be taken as remarks about the importance of this text for moral education. Since, however, the conception of moral philosophy with which I am working makes philosophy's specification of the good an outgrowth of an educational, Socratic interchange between text and reader, who actively judges how well the text accounts for his or her ethical experience, I shall speak as though the activity of the reader is pertinent to moral philosophy. On 'moral' versus 'ethical', and on 'philosophy' versus 'theory', see 'Perceptive Equilibrium', n. 2, this volume.

we must now take into account, then, is the activity and response of the reader of this text – an activity to which James makes frequent and emphatic reference, both by direct remarks about what 'we', or some concerned observer, or someone whose attention to the character qualifies the character's isolation (I.125) might find to say and to feel about these happenings; and also by the inclusion within the text of two characters, the Assinghams (Fanny alone among the characters is referred to as 'our friend' [II.162]), whose function, like that of the Greek tragic chorus, seems to be that of concerned interpretation of the events to which they bear witness. (The connection between this imaginary reader and the imagination of the responsible author is suggested at several points and brought out most strikingly in the preface, whose main theme is the author's rereading of his own created text.) Our question must be, What sort of activity on the reader's part will best fulfill the aims of the Socratic assessment process?

[1]→   What I now want to suggest is that the adventure of the reader of this novel, like the adventure of the intelligent characters inside it, involves valuable aspects of human moral experience that are not tapped by traditional books of moral philosophy; in this way as well it would be necessary for the completion of the enterprise of working through all of our moral intuitions. For this novel calls upon and also develops our ability to confront mystery with the cognitive engagement of both thought and feeling. To work through these sentences and these chapters is to become involved in an activity of exploration and unraveling that uses abilities, especially abilities of emotion and imagination, rarely tapped by philosophical texts.[21] But these abilities have, at the very least, a good claim to be regarded as important parts of the moral assessment process. In his preface James speaks of a reading of his novel as 'the very record and mirror of the general adventure of one's intelligence' (I.xix). If traditional philosophical texts do not record this whole adventure, call upon all of the abilities that are engaged in it, this would be a good reason to think that a Socratic enterprise requires texts like this one for its completion.

We have spoken so far as if the ideal reader of this text were like the 'ideal' Maggie Verver of the novel's second part. He or she would, then, be someone keenly alive in thought and feeling to every nuance of the situation, actively seeing and caring for all the parties concerned – and therefore safely right in the perfection of his or her attention. But we

---

[21]   The interpenetration of imagination, reflection, and feeling in deliberation is revealingly characterized (and called upon) throughout the novel; this, on further examination, emerges as one of its most fascinating contributions. I discuss these issues further, with reference to Proust, in 'Fictions of the Soul'.

know already that this 'ideal' is not the work's entire story about human practical wisdom. We know that where there is great love in one direction there may also be, in another direction, a tragically necessary blindness. We now want to know whether this feature of our moral life also finds its place in the author's way of being responsible to his created story and in the reader's way of responding to his text. In other words, does the text itself acknowledge the flawed nature of the consciousness that produced it and elicit from us in turn, as readers, an acknowledgment of our own imperfection?

I want to claim that it does, in two ways. First, with this text, as perhaps with few others in English literature, we are struck at every point by the incompleteness and inadequacy of our own attention. We notice the way we are inclined to miss things, to pass over things, to leave out certain interpretative possibilities while pursuing others. This consciousness of our own flaws and blind spots (created in the first place by the sheer difficulty of James's later style) is heightened by Fanny's regular self-criticism, her ongoing revision of her previous, defective 'readings'. It is nourished, too, by the frequent reminders of the author-reader's 'we' that our concern has its limits. Phrases such as 'at the moment we are concerned with him' (I.3), 'at the particular instant of our being again concerned with her' (I.245), 'had we time to look into it', 'which we have just found in our path' (I.163) recall to us the fact that our path is only one path and that we cannot humanly follow all paths through these tangled lives at all times. The authorial voice also reminds us that, even when we do attend, our attention, like all human attention, is interested and interpretative. We are told that such-and-such is 'the main interest … for us' (I.326) in these events, and we work through an account of 'these gropings and fittings of his conscience and his experience, that we have attempted to set in order here' (I.319). In all these moments, the author places himself humanly within the world of his text and links us to himself as limited and human adventurers.

It is the explicit design of this novel that this should be so. For James tells us in his preface that he has elected to avoid 'the mere muffled majesty of irresponsible "authorship"' and to become a responsible (and, we suspect, therefore guilty) agent in the midst of his work. 'It's not,' he continues, 'that the muffled majesty of authorship doesn't here *ostensibly* reign; but I catch myself again shaking it off and disavowing the pretence of it while I get down into the arena and do my best to live and breathe and rub shoulders and converse with the persons engaged in the struggle' (I.vi) – persons whom he soon describes as 'the more or less bleeding participants'. James here implicitly criticizes a tradition in the English novel for having created, in the authorial voice, a persona who is not humanly finite and who therefore does not show us a way to the understanding of our own finitude.[22] *The Golden Bowl* looks, then, like an attempt to move the novel itself out of the Eden of pure intelligent responsibility.

Central to this task, and of at least as much importance for it as the scattered first-person remarks, is the fact that the intelligence animating this text, in virtue of its choice to engage itself with and, we might say, to care for one or another of the characters, has left beyond itself and, therefore, us certain deep mysteries into which our adventuring consciousness has no access. As we carefully follow and respond to Maggie, seeing this world through her intelligent eyes, we hardly notice that we ourselves are rapidly becoming as distant from Charlotte, and as blind to the inner life of her pain, as Maggie herself. It is sometimes said by critics that the second part of this novel shows Charlotte to be a morally superficial character with an impoverished inner life. It would be more accurate, and more in keeping with the announced spirit of James's design, to say that it is not so much Charlotte who is revealed as superficial; it is Maggie, and therefore we, who are revealed as superficial and impoverished with respect to Charlotte. Charlotte and her pain are, at the end, not revealed but hidden.[23] Our active care for Maggie and our acceptance of the invitation to see as Maggie sees have brought upon us (upon the 'we' composed of author and reader) a blindness with respect to this part of the moral world. (The second and last time we do get a direct feeling for the inner life of this woman, James stresses the oddness of the event by calling this 'the particular instant of our being again concerned with her' [I.245].) James tells us that our responsive attention, when we choose to bestow it, 'qualifies' the 'isolation' of his characters (I.125) – much as in life, our solitary separateness is qualified, though never removed, by the fact of another person's care. Charlotte, lost to our attention, becomes at the end our pagoda: a 'splendid' object with its 'affirmed presence' (II.356), 'throned' in our midst (II.358) – and here James significantly adds, 'as who should say'. As who, indeed,

---

[22] It is plain from other writings of James that George Eliot is a primary target.
[23] James's notebooks show that the novel was begun with the tentative title *Charlotte* (see Edel, p. 572). This essay was also begun, long ago, as an essay about Charlotte. It appears to be a confirmation of the claims advanced here that the paper's original aim of focusing attention on Charlotte was frustrated by the ubiquity of the author/reader's care and concern for Maggie, who more or less inevitably 'took over'. Could this have been James's experience with his own creation? Or did he think of giving a title that would point us to the central importance of the novel's silences, just as its actual title points us to the flaws in human response that produce these silences?

should say. For into that isolation and pain and silence our intelligent conversation and response do not enter. No door appears to give access from the convenient garden level. The 'great decorated surface' remains 'consistently impenetrable and inscrutable' (II.4).

So, as readers, with the author as our guide and accomplice, we eat the golden fruit. With pity and dread we bury our eyes.[24]

Commentary on Nussbaum

Nussbaum's essay principally incorporates an exploration of the moral themes developed in Henry James's novel, *The Golden Bowl*. There are two epigraphs prefacing her essay, one from the medieval German courtly romance, *Tristan*, written in the thirteenth century by Gottfried von Strassburg, which tells the story of Tristan and Isolde; and another, taken from a sign in Cadogan Square, London, the city in which *The Golden Bowl* is set. The first – and Nussbaum believes James is likely to have had this source in mind – expresses a romantic ideal of Love as like a true and transparent crystal, an ideal which James transfers to the moral realm in the consciousness of one of his four central characters, Maggie Verver. The second reflects a certain background attitude towards proper conduct as thoroughly rule-bound, an attitude which supports the crystal moral ideal and which Nussbaum finds subtly critiqued in James's novel. We shall increasingly appreciate the moral philosophical significance of these themes as Nussbaum's text unfolds.

Maggie Verver is the only child of an enormously rich American financier and art collector, Adam Verver. She is to be married to the Italian (and impoverished) Prince Amerigo. We begin with Maggie's proclamation to her friend Fanny Assingham that she wants a flawless happiness, a happiness which – unlike the beautiful but cracked golden bowl of James's title – remains perfect. (The title refers to an exquisite bowl which the Prince – when out shopping for a wedding present for Maggie with his former amour, Charlotte Stant – finds and rejects on the grounds that it must contain a hidden flaw, so low is the price. The bowl is painted in gold, and is claimed by the shopkeeper to be made out of one complete crystal. Much later, Maggie is to purchase the

---

[24] I owe thanks to Daniel Brudney, Stanley Cavell, Arnold Davidson. Guy Sircello, and Susan Wolf for their valuable criticisms of an earlier draft of this paper; and especially to Richard Wollheim and Patrick Gardiner, who commented on the paper at the American Philosophical Association, Pacific Division, and the Oxford Philosophical Society, respectively. I am especially grateful to David Wiggins for showing me the parts of London in which this novel is set, helping me to learn something about their history, and, in general, for giving me a sense of 'the fashion after which the prodigious city ... does on occasion meet half-way those forms of intelligence of it that *it* recognizes' (*The Golden Bowl*, I.xii).

bowl, and her doing so triggers a turning point in the story and in her own moral outlook.) This aspiration to a life in which nothing of value is cracked or broken may explain Maggie's failure, in her marriage to the Prince, to break her primary loyalty of affection to her father. Already we see how the ideal of flawlessness can cause trouble, how the will to conserve a certain undivided daughterly love can stall the advance of marital love – further, the preoccupation with conserving existing relationships may actively disguise the damage thereby done to newly forming ones.

The novel is intensely focused on the relationships of four central characters: Maggie; her father, Adam Verver; the Prince; and Charlotte. Maggie, concerned for her father and innocent of Charlotte's former relationship with the Prince, persuades her father to propose to Charlotte. But, subsequently, Maggie and her father's intense relationship leaves both spouses out in the cold, and they come together to renew their former relations, now adulterously. Maggie comes to suspect the adultery – partly through her purchase of the selfsame golden bowl from the shopkeeper who had witnessed the Prince and Charlotte's intimate conversation when they visited his shop together – and finally manipulates things to salvage both marriages, getting her father to leave London and take Charlotte away to America.

At $\boxed{a}\!\!\rightarrow$ Nussbaum effectively announces the chief claim she aims to make in her essay: that James's novel makes an important contribution to moral philosophy.

> How would you expect moral philosophy to relate to fiction? Do you think of these two sorts of writing as having similar or quite different aims? What role do you see the imagination as playing in each?

Typically, in works of moral philosophy, fiction enters in only as illustration. Literature figures, if at all, as a store of examples – a scenario that neatly constitutes a tragic dilemma, perhaps; or a character who is a thoroughgoing amoralist. Moreover, the use that moral philosophers typically make of such illustrations tends to be driven by a hope for the kind of clarity that requires a certain simplification, or shutting down of ambiguity; for the business of moral theory generally calls for examples merely to assist the argument by being, precisely, unambiguous and philosophically uncontroversial. (If it's meant to be an example of a dilemma, it should be a dilemma on anyone's reckoning; if it's meant to be an example of an injustice, then it's no use if it won't strike just about everyone as manifestly unjust.) Moral philosophical writing does not have to put illustrations only to that purpose, but the standard discipline of philosophical argumentation – which aims at the sort of persuasion that comes from establishing agreement and then drawing an inference that would not have been so readily assented to before the progress of the argument – pressurizes moral philosophical writing into that relationship with example, including literary example. By contrast, Nussbaum is already suggesting that the relation of James's novel to moral philosophy is by no means as a stock of potential examples to be used in the service of some pre-established conclusion. There is probably nothing in this novel whose moral status is straightforward and closed down to alternative interpretations. Nussbaum's thesis is remarkable because, far from presenting the novel as something outside moral philosophy which can be broken up and its parts put to new use in the service of a moral philosophical argument, she suggests instead, of James's novel at least, that 'it is philosophical', that it in some part *constitutes* a piece of moral philosophy, albeit embedded in the novelistic, rather than the argumentative, form.

> At ⓑ→ Nussbaum summarizes the problem with Maggie Verver's perfectionist moral ideal of failing in no duty and causing no pain. What do you understand to be the problem with this ideal?

The primary trouble is that the ideal is impossible. One cannot live life never 'breaking' anything, because living is a dynamic business and relationships must be responsive to change. Maggie's ideal leads her to experience the prospect of transferring her primary loyalty and affection from father to husband as a matter of causing pain to her father, of damaging him and her relationship to him. But since she is marrying, and wants also to see that prospect as something that will hurt no one and leave her guiltless, she is led into psychological subterfuge. She tells herself, perhaps, that she can do both, that marrying does not require her to change her relationship to her father in any way. We are told that she is artful at adjusting her moral beliefs and commitments so that they can retain a semblance of consistency, even when this involves a certain self-deception. There are two things wrong with Maggie's moral ideal: it is impossible; and the effort to sustain it therefore encourages dishonest moral thinking.

> What are the 'disturbing consequences' of Maggie's attachment to her ideal of moral simplicity or 'innocence' that Nussbaum discusses from ⓒ→?

The attempt to cause no break with her father leads Maggie to repress her adult sexuality. Her relationship to Adam Verver is essentially that of a young daughter, and so the effort to preserve it brings a certain preservation of girlishness. In the effort 'to marry without breaking, as she liked to put it, with her past' Maggie resists full commitment to her marriage, and this includes sexual commitment, whether that resistance is to be thought of as actual or only imaginative.

This is connected with the second consequence: that she is closed off to the *particularity* of other persons. Her repression of sexual connection with her husband is a form of closedness to the particular person that he is. But her incapacity to recognize the particularity of others is more general than this, and stems ultimately from her fear of the collision of values. To recognize persons as distinct ends in their own right is to recognize that they can have conflicting claims on one (as is the case with the claims that father and husband both effectively make on her). But it is a definitive feature of Maggie's moral outlook that if one gets things right then one reconciles competing values so that they are not ultimately conflicting. Her ideal of moral perfection or 'innocence', then, involves a fantasy of ultimate moral harmony. Along with this incapacity, Nussbaum suggests, Maggie is also closed off to the *separateness* of individual persons. This idea does not differ much, in this context, from the idea that Maggie fails to appreciate the particularity of persons. But the recognition of the separateness of persons is a precondition of recognizing their particularity: you can't have particular characteristics as an individual unless you are already seen as an individual, separate from others. Nussbaum's suggestion here is that James depicts Maggie as someone whose aspiration to avoid hurting anyone leads her to fail to see persons – even those she knows best and is most loyal to – as distinct beings with distinctive particular characteristics and so with potentially conflicting claims on her.

> At [d]⟶ Nussbaum discusses Maggie and (her father) Adam Verver's shared tendency to assimilate people to fine art objects. What is the significance of this tendency?

The aestheticization of persons by Maggie and her father is understood, on Nussbaum's reading, as a corollary of Maggie's moral ideal of innocence, for the value of *objets d'art* does not typically lead to any conflict. Maggie could love two paintings equally without being disloyal or breaking ties with either. The Ververs know how to appreciate fine objects, and this ethos of the aesthetic is transferred in Maggie's moral consciousness to all that is valuable, most notably, people. This transfer serves the ideal of moral innocence, but covertly does violence to the separateness and the particularity of the very people she so keenly aspires to avoid damaging or compromising in any way.

> At [e]⟶ Nussbaum describes the world of *The Golden Bowl* as a 'fallen world'. How so?

Nussbaum's interpretive thesis that this novel works out a secular analogue to the idea of original sin (and the references to father and daughter's Edenic world reveal it as no accident that Maggie's father is named Adam) brings out the central theme of the inevitably cracked or flawed nature of human value, life and love. But the impetus of the novel is no lament; on the contrary, as we shall see, it is a story of progress through certain styles of moral knowledge – a progress that ends with the seemingly forbidden but nonetheless necessary and life-affirming knowledge of the ever-present risk of conflict between values and, ultimately, between different moral ideals. That human life is so fundamentally compromised by the disunity of values defines our world, and this is what Nussbaum means when she talks of our relation to value being imperfect as a matter of 'contingent necessity'. That there is a disharmony of values is not given a priori, but it is such a fundamental feature of the human condition that it is, in a constrained sense, necessary. It is *humanly* necessary that there is the ever-present possibility of conflict between different values, and so there is a certain implicit guilt running through moral life. (One might speculate, however, that this particular kind of guilt belongs specifically to the moral ideal of innocence that Maggie is to move away from. It may be that, once free of that problematic ideal, there need be no such feeling of guilt, for may we not hope to achieve a more coherent, and so more psychologically relaxed, accommodation to our compromised relation to the good?)

The second stage of Maggie's progress of moral sentiments, and moral ideals, comes at [f]→, where Nussbaum begins to discuss Maggie's resolve to seize the situation with both hands and bring about the separation of her husband and Charlotte by manipulating people where necessary – most notably, Charlotte, to whom she is never open about her knowledge of the adultery, and whose fate she seals by persuading Adam Verver to take his wife away to America. Maggie's moral outlook at this stage requires her to take full responsibility for the pain she causes, and to remain (in James's phrase from another novel) 'finely aware and richly responsible' in relation to her actions.

Nussbaum swiftly suggests, at [g]→, that James intends us to be suspicious of this new moral outlook too. What is the suspicion here?

The suspicion is that in this new moral ideal of clear-eyed responsibility, Maggie has surreptitiously found a new model of moral perfection to achieve. It affords a different, more dirty-handed moral innocence, but a moral innocence for all that. Things get broken in Maggie's new moral universe, but everything is accounted for, the inventory is kept up to date and fully in view. By contrast, living out choices of value may sometimes require a partial moral blindness, an insensibility to the suffering of certain others, and so a failure to keep a complete moral account of things. The practical realization of Maggie and the Prince's love requires them precisely to turn their eyes away from Charlotte's suffering, and to see only each other. Sometimes the pursuit of one value requires the abandonment of another. There can be no perfectionist redemption in moral choice. Imperfection runs through moral life like the flaw in the golden bowl.

How, according to Nussbaum, are we to understand the relations between the three moral outlooks that Maggie passes through in this novel? Do you agree with the emergent conception of moral life as more like improvisation than adherence to moral rules? Can that conception be squared with the idea that there is such a thing as moral principle?

At ⌊h⌉→ Nussbaum addresses this issue. On the one hand, there is assuredly a narrative and philosophical progress through three different stages of moral maturity here. And yet we must resist thinking that the final stage – of acquiescence to the unredeemed nature of our relation to moral conflict and moral choice – represents 'the right answer' to the question of what our moral outlook should be. Some priority must inevitably be given to it, but the final acknowledgement that the flaw in our relation to value must sometimes remain hidden, so that we cannot take any clear-eyed responsibility for it, is itself only one part of a rich conception of our relation to value. There remains a place too for Maggie's former ideals of innocence. On Nussbaum's reading, the ideals of innocence are not refuted by the novel, but rather explored and revealed as flawed. Yet, like the golden bowl, they are no less beautiful for all that. What James depicts for us in this novel – depiction being the novelist's form of argumentation – is the flawed beauty of different, eminently recognizable, moral ideals, and the impossibility of questions of value being settled in advance. What he shows us, and it is a philosophical thesis, is that our moral predicament is that of the protagonist who must improvise her role responsively to the situations and relations in which life places her. Our world is not like Cadogan Square garden, where all is governed by pre-set rules; how to live one's life cannot be settled in advance, and the choices one makes may do damage that one cannot keep in moral view.

With the exploration of the moral ideas in the novel complete, Nussbaum moves, in section II, to make her case for the view that James's novel is, among other things, a work of moral philosophy.

At ⌊i⌉→ Nussbaum asks two closely related questions. What are they, and how does she answer them?

She poses the question why she wants to claim that *The Golden Bowl* is philosophical, and, more generally, how far this claim might be made of novels more generally. But her focus will be on *The Golden Bowl* in particular. She begins to answer her question(s) first by fixing on a characterization of moral philosophy that she regards as sufficiently general not to rule her claim out of court from the start, and uncontroversial enough to make the claim worth substantiating. She fixes on the Aristotelian conception, which represents moral philosophy as 'the search for a specification of the good life for a human being' where this is understood to encompass not only theory but practice; that is, it aims to achieve not only an augmented moral theoretical understanding but also a better practical idea of how to live our lives well. Furthermore, this conception of moral philosophy fits with James's own idea of moral writing.

Her case rests on two things: the moral content of James's text, as she has already elucidated it; and her argument that the techniques of reading and interpreting it (and perhaps reading and interpreting at least some other novels with sufficiently complex moral content) are themselves techniques of moral understanding. In respect of the first, the key point is that the moral content of the novel – chiefly, though not exclusively, Maggie's progress through different moral outlooks – could not be depicted except through a detailed narrative presentation of the particularities of character, circumstance and relationships. Through Maggie's fine sensibility we are given 'something like a persuasive argument' that her moral discoveries (even if she never articulates them as such) have a certain general force. Nussbaum's phrase 'something like a persuasive argument' is very telling here, because the way a novel 'argues' is on the whole by narrative depiction, a kind of showing. That is a very different method from philosophy, which generally aims above all at the explicit articulation of whatever is the main moral philosophical point. Through narrative depiction, certain general moral insights of a philosophical nature can be implied persuasively – perhaps more persuasively than in an argument – and this suggests that there may be moral philosophical insights which can only be conveyed in narrative, by telling a story. But narrative is a resource that philosophy generally deprives itself of, perhaps more so than necessary.

> What is the significance, for Nussbaum's argument, of the fact that James ensures he has a central character who is both agent and excellent interpreter of her own life?

At ⊠ j ⊠→, Nussbaum explains that James sees an alignment between the art of interpreting life and the art of interpreting narrative texts, and she finds this highly suggestive of her thesis that there are 'parallel norms of response and vision' in the two interpretive contexts. But, further, it connects with the thought already mentioned, that James's text is somehow managing to venture into moral territory that moral philosophy rarely visits. As she makes explicit at ⊠ k ⊠→, this is no accident. Much of traditional moral philosophy – moral theory – is precisely geared to the aspiration to fix everything (or most of it) in advance by establishing general principles of moral judgement and conduct. The anti-theoretical idea that some significant part of moral life requires the antithesis of this aspiration, requires precisely an openness to new detail, and an improvisatory stance on the part of the agent-interpreter, comes as something of a shock to traditional moral philosophy. (Think about the a prioristic aspirations of Kant's text, and the role of the illustrations there. Agential improvisation might be seen as precisely what he sets out to save us from, by founding a procedure for moral decision-making for which nothing more than our basic rationality is sufficient.) It is tempting also to say – as is first implied by Nussbaum's use of the term 'watertight' in connection with traditional moral philosophy's aim – that moral philosophy is here character-ized as stuck in one of Maggie Verver's stages of moral innocence. The desire to establish a set of inviolable moral rules comes to seem, in the light of Nussbaum's reading of James's text, an enterprise in a certain fantasy of moral perfection and innocence, one that is driven by a 'refusal of life' in its fear of the kind of responsibility imposed by improvisation.

> How far, and in what ways, do you think moral philosophy can expand and diversify to make more room for the improvisatory aspect of moral thinking?

This may make it sound as if traditional moral philosophical writing can expand its styles and ambitions and become less innocent in the manner of Maggie Verver. But Nussbaum is in a certain way more pessimistic than this about the ability of moral philosophy as we know it to embrace improvisa-tion and the beauty of systemic moral flaw: she ventures the idea that James is 'a maker of a moral vision who embodied it in novels because only in that form could he fully and fittingly express it'. Her vision is rather that a radically expanded category of 'moral philosophy' should include the novel (or, at least, novels like James's). This is, in the first instance, a point about the moral content of the novel. But, given that the aim of moral philosophy is not only theoretical understanding but also practical education of how-ever indirect a kind, we now confront the question of what it is about the process of reading and interpreting such a novel that brings 'a Socratic working-through of the ... reader's own moral intuitions that will leave this person clearer about his or her own moral aims'. Here Nussbaum's suggestion (at 1⊦→) is that the reader of a novel like James's has an adven-ture that is parallel to the moral adventure of the relevant character(s) in the text, in that it exercises abilities of imagination and emotion that are essential to moral perception.

> Allowing that there are many styles of argumentation, how far do you think it is definitive of philosophy that it is explicitly argumentative? While we may appreciate the moral philosophical content of novels like James's, and the moral enlightenment they can (perhaps uniquely) bring by presenting us with a narrative containing certain moral patterns for us to discern and reflect upon, might we not still be shy of the conclusion that such a novel *constitutes* a piece of moral philosophy, simply on the grounds that it does not proceed by presenting reasons for and against certain conclusions?

Another important feature of James's message about moral perception was that sometimes our relation to value – particularly in our personal relationships – demands a certain failure of moral perception, a blindness to the suffering of others. Accordingly, Nussbaum now asks whether this aspect of moral life finds an analogue in the author's creation of a novel and the reader's interpretive activity. She argues in the affirmative on two counts. First, the reader is repeatedly made aware of the partiality of her attention: there is, simply, the difficulty of James's inspissated style; and his many reminders of such-and-such being, for the moment, the focus of attention for the 'we' that is the author–reader pair; and this in turn reminds one too that even as we may be paying our best and fullest attention to some character or other, that attention is bound to be shaped by interpretive bias and interest.

Second, James's authorial stance is not that of the omniscient author he is critical of in the English novel, but rather that of someone who creates a narrative in which he can rub shoulders with the characters somewhat (as his frequent explicitations of where 'our' attention is currently directed attest). He, as author, self-consciously engages us, the reader, in his roving partial vision. The upshot is that as the author–reader duo increasingly engages in Maggie's point of view, we become blind to the off-the-page suffering of Charlotte, just as Maggie and Amerigo do. Making moral meaning can be a matter of obliterating other moral meanings, just as making life choices can be a matter of breaking with alternative values, cutting oneself off from the concerns of certain other people. As we see or pursue one thing with finely responsible sensitivity, we may have to turn our backs on another. This aspect of the human relation to value – this potentially tragic flaw that runs through moral life, and which surely only renders it more rather than less beautiful – is what narrative may be uniquely qualified to teach us.

Introduction to Gaita

Raimond Gaita was born in Germany in 1946, and was educated in Victoria, Australia, before coming to the UK as a doctoral student. He first taught at the University of Kent at Canterbury, before moving to King's College London. He now divides his time between the UK and Australia, holding two appointments, as Professor of Moral Philosophy at KCL and as Foundation Professor of Philosophy at the Australian Catholic University. He has written in political philosophy, the philosophy of mind, and on Wittgenstein, though his main philosophical focus is on ethics. He has published both for an academic readership and also for readers outside the academy, most notably perhaps, a prize-winning memoir about his father. His book, *Good and Evil: An Absolute Conception*, from which this reading is excerpted, explores the nature of good and evil, and argues for the centrality of remorse to moral understanding. In doing so it develops a powerful critique of traditional moral philosophy.

Raimond Gaita, *Good and Evil: An Absolute Conception* (extracts from Ch. 4, 'Remorse and Its Lessons')

[...]

[In] a television series called *The World at War*, a Dutch woman was interviewed in an episode on the Nazi concentration camps. She had given shelter to three Jews fleeing the Nazis, but after some days she asked them to leave because she was involved in a plot to assassinate Hitler and judged that it would be at risk if she were caught sheltering Jews. Within days of leaving her house the three were murdered in a concentration camp. She said Hitler had made a murderess of her, that she hated him for many things but most of all for that.

I shall not quarrel with her judgement of what she had done – that it made a murderess of her – although I understand why many would. Any argument over her response would need to judge the significance of the differences between what she did and those deeds that inform our sense of the seriousness of murder. In one clear sense she was not a murderess. No court would judge her to be that. Indeed, she did nothing that would bring her before a court. Perhaps more significantly, no one could seriously say to her, nor even of her, that she was, morally speaking, a murderess. Not even the relatives of the three who were murdered by the Nazis could say that. How, then, can I say that I do not quarrel with her judgement?

She did not, I believe, judge herself as she did in ignorance of what I have acknowledged. Nonetheless, her sense of the seriousness of what she did is captured in her judgement on herself. The Jews were hunted by those who would murder them in the spirit of ridding the world of vermin. They needed shelter but she refused it. Many others did the same. But as I said, the significance of these and other things remains to be judged.

a ⟶   In judging their significance we should not give undue weight to the fact that she is not to be blamed for what she did. People can do morally terrible things yet not be blameable for them, or not, at any rate, in a way commensurate with their terribleness. In *that* sense they are not *accountable* for what they did. No one can point a finger and hold them to account. They cannot be *accused*. It would be wrong to infer that they are not morally responsible for what they did, meaning, that they should not feel remorse for what they did and that our relation to them cannot be conditioned by a moral description of

Editors' note: The original footnotes have been renumbered as parts of the text have been omitted.

what they did. Those who believe this often appeal to a sharp contrast between the psychological and the moral. With that contrast in mind they say that they understand why the Dutchwoman should feel terrible, that it is natural, perhaps even morally good that she feels terrible, but she should not feel remorse for what she did because it is irrational to feel remorse for an act for which one cannot (rationally) be blamed.[1]

'Blame' is a word with many connotations and it is sometimes used in a general way to mean no more than 'to hold responsible'. The chorus held Oedipus responsible for his unintentional deeds for which he showed remorse. It did so through the quality of its pity for him, for the evildoer he had unwittingly become. To hold someone responsible in this sense means to hold them, to fix them, in a lucid response to the significance of what they did. It means that the moral significance of what they did must not be evaded, neither by them nor by us, but it does not, thereby, mean that we find fault with them, that we can accuse them, or that we find them culpable. Those are all specific and different human acts (different kinds of holding responsible) and are therefore liable to moral appraisal and criticism even when the person to whom they are a response is uncontroversially a wrongdoer. They are species of the genus 'to hold responsible', but there is no act which is merely that.

[b]→ The tendency to connect moral responsibility too tightly to culpability has led to a moralistic distortion in much contemporary discussion of moral responsibility. Those who, in certain circumstances, rightly refuse to blame someone, occasionally fall into a sentimental social and psychological determinism in order to justify what they take to be the logical corollary of their refusal to blame, namely, the refusal to apply moral descriptions. Those who rightly react to the sentimentality and to the suspect determinism often fall into an unpleasant moralism that is supported by an implausible voluntarism in order to justify their sense that moral descriptions are appropriate. The idea that a person who judges that someone has done evil (logically) must blame him in a sense which conflicts with pitying him appears to be, at least partly, a rationalization of our apparently natural, but unsavoury disposition to point fingers at one another disguised as moral theory

---

[1] The matter is sometimes discussed in relation to Oedipus. It is clear in Sophocles' play that Oedipus feels remorse when he discovers that he murdered his father and married his mother. Yet he did both unintentionally and because of non-culpable ignorance. To be sure, the chorus does not blame him: it pities him, but it pities him for what he has morally become. There are many who would say that if he acted in non-culpable ignorance, then remorse is rationally inappropriate. But if we ask why that should be so, I know of no answer which does not, in the end, beg the question about the connection between responsibility and blame.

or conceptual analysis. It leads to an unnecessary sense of conflict between pity and moral judgement and is responsible for the unedifying tone of much of the contemporary discussion of the relation between crime and social circumstances.

A serious conception of responsibility need not be connected so tightly with conditions of culpability. We can say that *a person is morally responsible for what may claim her and us in one of the many forms of serious and lucid moral response*. It is common and natural to think that a critical assessment of such a response requires a critical assessment of its object, independently of the response itself. (How else are we to assess whether responses are appropriate or rational?) However, *what* can claim us in serious moral response need not, at all levels, be establishable independently of what is revealed to us by authentic and authoritative response.

Ways of responding, like intuitions, are not self-authenticating if that means that they are beyond critical scrutiny. But it does not follow that we have, *at all levels*, independent critical access to their objects. [...] [I]t is important even here to note and to describe, more accurately than philosophers generally do, how contrary to the appearances such a thought is. One way of responding is often judged in the light of another, and what needs more accurate description is the critical grammar that determines our sense of the authority with which one thing shows up another as being, perhaps, sentimental or self-indulgent. The quality of the Dutchwoman's response teaches me what its proper object can be, and so what a serious relation to it can be. That is why I call it authoritative. She was not sentimental or morbid or self-dramatizing. Of course, I can only make such judgements because of what can be said of the kind of thing she did independently of the character of her response to it. But I came to see the moral significance of what she did in the light of her response – a response that is naturally characterized as remorse.

$\boxed{c}\!\!\rightarrow$ When Kant said that even in the presence of Jesus he would need to step back and turn inwards to listen to the deliverance of Reason, he was partly right and partly wrong.[2] He was right insofar as he wished to stress that the acknowledgement of Jesus could not be a blind response, but he was wrong to think that insofar as we responded because we were moved, then to that extent we responded blindly. He was right insofar as he thought that lucidity required one to be obedient to the critical grammar of *thought* (Reason), but he was wrong to believe that that critical grammar is conditioned by an a priori conception of

---

[2]   Immanuel Kant, *The Groundwork of the Metaphysic of Morals*, trans. H. J. Paton (London: Hutchinson, 1958), p. 294.

what it is to think well and what it is to think badly which necessarily excluded feeling as something extraneous to it. Aristotle was closer to the truth when he said that if we want to know what justice is then we should turn to the example of the just man – but we must have eyes to see.[3] For Aristotle, *the education of feeling and character was an epistemic condition of right judgement on what could only be disclosed in authoritative example.* It is common to read Plato as being closer to Kant on this matter, as saying that all examples need to be judged according to a standard independently of them and which is revealed to Reason purified of feeling. Yet it is possible to read him as having said first what I have attributed to Aristotle, with the addition [...] that ethical understanding is possible only in the light of the form of the Good.

d→   I want to concentrate on something else the Dutchwoman said. She said she hated Hitler for many things but most of all for making a murderess of her. From one perspective – an external perspective on the terrible evil and suffering of that time – her reaction may seem inappropriate to the relative insignificance of what she had done. Surely (it might be said) she had better reasons to hate Hitler than any that connected him with what she did. Indeed, someone might say that in the face of all the evil and suffering of that time, it was indecent of her to place her own guilty suffering as being so important. In reply she might say that there is a sense in which she does not *place* her suffering at all, that, if anything, it placed her. To make clear what I mean by that, I shall (to begin with) consider two critically sympathetic responses to her sense of the weight of her guilt.

First, someone who appreciated that our reaction to evil done is different from our reaction to evil suffered and who realized that her guilty suffering in recognition of what she had become plays a different role in her life from her suffering over the loss of her own family, might suggest that she gain a perspective on her guilt by placing it in relation to the many mass murderers of the time. That would be appropriate, however, only if she failed to distinguish in an important way between what she did and what they did. The fact that she said that she hated Hitler most because he had made a murderess of her, together with the facts mentioned earlier, is no reason to think that she did. She might be thankful that her guilt is not greater than it is, but that leaves her guilt and her suffering recognition of it exactly as it was.

Secondly, someone might note that her guilt is necessarily personal and that it is natural to what is both personal and painful that it is not

---

[3] Aristotle, *Nicomachean Ethics*, trans. W. D. Ross, Book 6, chapters 8–12.

overwhelmed by knowledge of the suffering of others. A spectator's horror at the suffering of another person is easily overwhelmed when she sees the sufferings of countless others, to the point where she is likely to lose any sense of their individuality. Her own suffering is not like that. No matter how many die and suffer around her, her own severe pain will not leave her to merge into an indeterminate sense of horror. Our sufferings, provided they are severe enough, stick with us.

Remorse, too, sticks with us, although corrupt forms of it merge readily enough into a sense of common guilt, where all are guilty and so none is. But it sticks with us in a way radically different from other forms of suffering. Someone who is true to her remorse will always reject, as inappropriate, consolation that is based on her recognition of the guilt of others. Any other kind of suffering (except perhaps the kind Simone Weil called 'affliction'[4]) may be consoled when we see it in the light of the suffering of others.

Isak Dinesen said that all 'sorrows can be borne if you put them into a story or tell a story about them'.[5] That is not true of the sufferings of the guilty, if they are true to their recognition of themselves as guilty. Although we may all suffer in recognition of what we have become in becoming evildoers, we cannot look on this as part of our common lot or our common condition in the way that we do when we accept our mortality or our vulnerability to misfortune. The capacity to say 'we' – we mortals, we who have suffered together – not merely enumeratively but in fellowship, consoles. 'We of this family', 'we of this nation', 'we who have been left behind' when said at a funeral, are examples of the 'we' of fellowship. It is always possible for the consoling 'we' of fellowship to revert to the merely enumerative 'we', and with severe suffering there is characteristically an oscillation between the two. It is sometimes said that we are always alone in our grief and when we die, to protest that there is something illusory in a sense of fellowship in such instances. Whatever truth there may be in that, it is not that there is never genuine and uncorrupt consolation to be found in the capacity to speak in fellowship with those who grieve as we do and with all who must die as we must. But there can be only corrupt consolation in the knowledge that others are guilty as we are.

The Dutchwoman spoke personally, but not as she would had she said, 'I hate Hitler most because he murdered my family.' The 'I' that

---

[4] Simone Weil, 'The Love of God and Affliction', in *On Science, Necessity and the Love of God* (London: Oxford University Press, 1968).
[5] Isak Dinesen, quoted in Hannah Arendt, *The Human Condition* (Chicago: University of Chicago Press, 1958).

answers in remorse to the recognition of guilt is not the 'I' that naturally and properly partners the 'we' of fellowship. Those who, in remorse, suffer in guilty recognition of what they have become are radically singular, and for that reason remorse is a kind of dying to the world.

'World' is a difficult word, especially in philosophy. I mean by it here what we mean when we say the world has become lost to those who are self-absorbed, as may happen to someone who is self-absorbed in the fear of her impending death. We mean that she cannot speak out of a sense of fellowship that is conditioned by unselfcentred and sympathetic responsiveness to others. The 'world' in this sense is a common world, and its kind of commonness is marked by the 'we' of fellowship. The radically and continuously self-absorbed lose, but are not thereby lost to, the common world. Only an enumerative use of 'we' may come out of self-absorption of this kind.

Remorse, because it is a kind of dying to the world, can be mistaken for self-absorption and its kind of dying to the world. But remorse is not self-absorption. It is, amongst other things, a form of the recognition of the reality of others – those we have wronged. Corrupt forms of remorse *are* a form of self-absorption. Then the 'I' of self-absorption becomes a false semblance of the radically singular 'I' who is discovered in genuine remorse. I call genuine remorse a kind of dying to the world because it is the discovery of a dimension of ourselves that cannot enter into common and consoling fellowship with others. That is why I said the Dutchwoman did not *place* her guilt. It could not be placed by any story we might tell of our common sufferings. Nor could she be asked to gain a perspective on it by comparing it with what others had done and suffered.

When we hear of the sufferings of others, when we become alive to the reality of others in their suffering, we often say that it enabled us to place our own suffering in proper perspective. That is partly because our self-absorption competed with the recognition of the reality of others, and therefore with the recognition of the perspective within which we can place our own pain. Remorse, however, does not compete with the recognition of reality. On the contrary, it is a form of the recognition of reality. Therefore, when the Dutchwoman said that she hated Hitler most for making a murderess of her, she was not, despite the comparative expression, vulnerable to the rebuke that her moral sense of that period would be more edifying if she hated Hitler most for the millions of human beings he murdered. That rebuke would have point only if she cared too little for what others had suffered, as would be the case if her remorse were a form of self-absorption, for it is a mark of the self-absorbed that they care too little for others. But she cannot be accused of moral self-indulgence, of caring too little for the suffering of others, merely because she said that she hated Hitler most for making a murderess of her.

Guilt and remorse (which I take at least often to be the suffering recognition and acknowledgement of one's guilt) as I have been speaking of them are not psychological phenomena. The notion of the psychological is obscure, but I take it to refer to facts about our common and individual natures. Fear, anger and jealousy are examples of psychological phenomena, as are neurotic or corrupt guilt feelings. They can be compared and discussed, and this comparison and discussion is not only an expression of common human fellowship, but a condition of it. Its consoling power is the basis of psychotherapy. If moral psychology is the study of the relevance to the nature of morality of facts of our common human nature as they might enter a sense of human fellowship, then guilt and remorse, as I have characterized them, are beyond its scope.

What I have said about the consoling comparability of psychological phenomena is also true of many moral phenomena. It is true of the virtues and vices because their character is conditioned and limited by an empirical understanding of human possibilities. It may be a proper rebuke against moral haughtiness and *hubris* to remind someone who judges their failings of character too harshly that she is only human, meaning that she should gain a perspective on her failings by remembering she is not alone in such failings. Aristotle rightly noted that there are sufferings beyond any human capacity to endure and he thereby set an empirically conditioned limit to accusations of cowardice. If even Achilles could tremble in fear, if even the bravest of heroes could be broken by fear, then that may be proper consolation to others in a similar situation. Similar things could be said in relation to the other virtues because of the relation of virtue to character. Our virtues and vices reveal what kind of human beings we are, and therefore judgements in their name are necessarily relative, under pain of *hubris*, to what is humanly possible.

It is different with guilt. It should be no consolation if what we did was also done by the best of people. That is not pride because remorse does not focus on what kind of person we are. Its focus is on what we have become only because we have become wrongdoers. [...]

Reflection on remorse might prompt someone to speak of the 'special authority' or the 'special dignity' of the ethical. It might prompt someone to speak of the ethical as something *sui generis*, and even of it as something otherworldly, irreducible to a humanist understanding of it.

I hope that I have shown how misconceived is the modern tendency to be suspicious of remorse. (It might be thought to be more accurate to say that the suspicion is of guilt and feelings of guilt, but I am – oversimplifying a little – treating guilt feeling as remorse which is itself the pained recognition of the significance of our guilt, guilt being the *condition* of one who is a wrongdoer.) In one of the most fundamental ways possible the modern hostility to guilt and guilt feelings threatens a proper understanding of good and evil, and a proper sense of our humanity and of the independent reality of others.

The reasons for the hostility to remorse are various, ranging from a reductive functionalism about value, that focuses on the superficial thought that guilt serves no purpose (why should it?), to the most high-minded of them, which scorns remorse as a form of self-indulgence at the expense of a proper concern for the victim of our wrongdoing. There are, to be sure, almost infinitely many corruptions of remorse, and some may be, as Iris Murdoch says, the subtlest and most seductive of moral corruptions, but they are corruptions.[6] Remorse as I have described it is an awakened sense of the reality of another. It is time for me to begin to explain what I mean by that. [...]

 It is strange, and sometimes it is mysterious, that other people can affect us as deeply as they do. Our sense of the reality of other people is connected with their power to affect us in ways we cannot fathom, as that is revealed in the fact that our lives seem empty when we lose those we love or, in a different way, in the destructive nature of certain dependencies. Although we often cannot fathom this power, we accept it as part of human life: if we are plunged into grief or despair because of it, we may hope that time will heal our suffering and that life will reassert itself in us. It is not so with guilt. Time, working alone, is denied the right to heal guilty suffering, if the suffering is lucid. What may heal it is as strange as the suffering itself – repentance, atonement, forgiveness, punishment. We are so familiar with this that we have lost a sense of its mystery.

We are perfectly familiar with the fact that a person might commit suicide because she became a murderer, even if she murdered a total stranger whose death would otherwise mean nothing to her and who was, if measured according to those qualities which are relevant to self-esteem, utterly worthless. We might condemn suicide like that as confused and as the expression of a corrupt rather than a lucid remorse, but we find it perfectly intelligible. The fact that we do is part of our conception of the gravity of murder and of what another human being may mean to us. Any account of the seriousness of

---

[6] Iris Murdoch, *The Sovereignty of Good* (London: Routledge & Kegan Paul, 1970).

murder that does not give prominence to the way the murderer becomes haunted by his victim will be inadequate to the way remorse is an awakening to the terribleness of what was done. [...] Many moral theories are inadequate in exactly that way. They would say that the murderer discovers in her remorse how terrible it is to become someone who broke a certain principle or rule. The absurdity of that cannot be ameliorated unless the concrete individual who was murdered assumes the kind of prominence I tried to convey by saying that a murderer is, in her remorse, haunted by her victim. [...] A certain sense of her victim's individuality is internal to a murderer's understanding of the moral significance of what she did, and that it is part of what it is to be aware of the reality of another human being.

The power of human beings to affect one another in ways they cannot fathom is partly constitutive of that sense of individuality which we express when we say that human beings are unique and irreplaceable. [...] Our need of certain other human beings is partly constitutive of a certain sense of their preciousness and of their reality, but it is also, in some of its forms, destructive of it. That is why the need human beings have for one another has been a target for a familiar kind of moralism which fails to recognize that our sense of the independent reality of another human being, the acknowledgement of which is said (by the moralist) to be threatened by need of that human being, is itself conditioned by the terrible effect that the loss of a human being may have on us. Something similar is true of remorse. Remorse is a recognition of the reality of another through the shock of wronging her, just as grief is a recognition of the reality of another through the shock of losing her. Both are liable to egocentric corruptions. Our dependencies, even at their best, tread a fine line between awakening a sense of the reality of another and submerging that sense in one of the many forms of egocentric absorption. Exactly the same is true of remorse. But the egocentricity is not merely a feature of the corruption, it is its central feature. Love must sometimes find its expression in grief, and our sense of the reality of other human beings must sometimes find its expression in remorse.

There are two common, natural and related misunderstandings of remorse which are often thought to follow from the fact that the importance the victim assumes to the one who has wronged him, and who acknowledges that wrong in remorse, depends entirely on the wrongdoer's sense that she has wronged her victim. The first is that remorse teaches us nothing about the nature of our sense of what it is to wrong another because it is conceptually recessive in relation to it. The second is that the recognition that we have wronged someone is best revealed in reparation, and that is where we should locate a proper sense of the seriousness of what we did. Reparation rather than remorse is expressive of what it is to take another seriously. These misconceptions underlie the modern objection to remorse as a form of self-indulgence.

I shall take the second point first. Remorse and reparation are not exclusive of each other, and without a serious concern with reparation, where it is possible, remorse would be corrupt. Reparation for what, though? The obvious answer is that it is for the wrong we have done. But how should we understand that?

Bernard Williams discusses an example in which a lorry driver, through no fault of his own, runs over and kills a child.[7] He points out that the driver will feel quite differently from a spectator, even if the spectator was in the cabin with him. His regret will be of a different kind – the kind for which it matters that *he* did it. Williams calls this 'agent-regret' and brings out the difference between regret *simpliciter* and agent-regret by suggesting that if the lorry driver's sense that he owed something to the child's parents could be satisfied by an insurance payout, then his regret would not be agent-regret. The point is not so much that there are some sufferings that cannot be relieved by money. It is that some regrets are directed not only to what we did or to its effects, but also at the fact that *we* did it. Williams speaks of agent-regret rather than remorse, partly because he thinks that remorse can rationally be directed only on to voluntary actions, and partly because his discussion is an expression of a long-standing suspicion of morality which goes through many phases and which I will discuss again later. But Williams's excellent point about the insurance money brings out that reparation is not directed only at the natural effects of what we did. The point which emerges from my discussion of the Dutchwoman (though it is not Williams's and does not follow from his) is that when remorse is appropriate, reparation is a response to a sense of what we did and what our victims suffered, both of which are *sui generis*.

h⟶   The point has often been made, particularly in discussions of consequentialism, that ethical concern is not merely with the effects of *what* we did but also with the fact that *we* did it.[8] Of course, we can no more do philosophy by italics than we can by shouting it, but an important distinction has been invoked and needs to be clarified. Part of what is intended is that human beings with normal projects and interests cannot see themselves as replaceable units in a system of

---

[7]   Bernard Williams, 'Moral Luck', in *Moral Luck* (Cambridge: Cambridge University Press, 1981).
[8]   See, for example, 'War and Massacre' or 'Ruthlessness in Public Life', in Thomas Nagel, *Mortal Questions* (Cambridge: Cambridge University Press, 1979).

cause and effects, and that morality cannot require this of them. It is, therefore, wrong to say that we should concern ourselves with *what* we did rather than with the fact that *we* did it, partly because, in some cases, that *we* did it is internal to the character of *what we did* and, as we shall see, to what the victim suffered. Consequentialists have not merely an inadequate sense of evil done: they have an inadequate sense of evil suffered.

To say emphatically that certain philosophers have an inadequate sense of evil *done* is not to say that they have an inadequate sense of agency, not anyhow if that suggests that they require an improved, but morally neutral, philosophy of action. It is the expression of an ethical perspective on action and of an ethically conditioned sense of individuality. Williams's example was not, of course, an example of evil done. Indeed, it was part of his point that the interesting contrast is not between remorse and regret but between regret and agent-regret. That is part of his attack on a Kantian kind of dualism between morality and everything else. Or, perhaps more accurately, on a sense of dualism, which he thinks is most clearly represented in Kant, between what he (Kant) takes morality to be and everything else. Williams would say, I think, that in ethical contexts the emphatic sense of 'done' has been assimilated to the contrast between remorse and regret, whereas it is, in fact, conditioned by the contrast between regret and agent-regret. Up to a point he is right, but the relatively bare notion of agent-regret is clearly inadequate to the kind of remorse I have been describing. Moreover, there is good reason to believe that remorse is not rationally dependent on a sense of culpability. Remorse is not, as Williams takes it to be, rationally appropriate only for voluntary actions, and the contrast between the personal and the impersonal that is implied by remorse is different from that implied by the distinction between regret and agent-regret. The 'I' that is acknowledged in a serious response of agent-regret is not the radically singular 'I' that is discovered in remorse.

The other and more direct objection to what I have been arguing was that remorse is a reaction to an independently intelligible conception of wrongdoing and is a psychological state structured by it. The main reason for this claim is that (leaving neurotic cases aside) we cannot feel remorse unless we judge that we did wrong. That is true, but it does not entail that remorse and our sense of wrongdoing cannot be conceptually interdependent. Wittgenstein said that pity was a form of the conviction that another was in pain. He meant, I think, that our natural dispositions to pity are one of the determinants of our concept of pain.[9] Whatever is to be said for that, it would be

---

[9]   Ludwig Wittgenstein, *Philosophical Investigations* (Oxford: Basil Blackwell, 1963), Part 1, §287.

naive to think that we could show it to be wrong simply by pointing out that we pity someone *because* we see that she is in pain.

We can see the point more clearly if we consider an example discussed by Peter Singer. He asks whether there is a moral difference between 'going over to India and shooting a few peasants' and failing to give money to Oxfam.[10] He knows that most people think there is a serious difference but he wonders whether they should. After some discussion of the moral difference between acts and omissions, he concludes that the judgement that it would be *murder* (or something morally the same as murder) not to send money to Oxfam is too harsh, but he then goes on to say: 'an ethic which put saving all one possibly can on the same footing as not killing would be an ethic for saints or heroes [but this should] not lead us to assume that the alternative must be an ethic which makes it obligatory not to kill but puts us under no obligation to save anyone. There are positions in between these extremes.'[11] He says that after ruing the fact that it is quite difficult to avoid killing people (by acts of omission). I therefore take him as at least seriously inviting us to consider that a saint may properly judge himself to be a murderer (multiple murderer, indeed) merely because he forgot to send his monthly subscription to Oxfam.

A person who says that he knows what evil he has done by 'going over to India and shooting a few peasants', yet who shows no grievous remorse, is someone who understands neither what he is saying nor what he did. A person who says that *he is as one who did this* because he failed to give money to Oxfam, but who showed no grievous remorse, does not understand what he is saying either. But if he should feel such remorse as does someone who had murdered people, then he would need to do more than philosophize about acts and omissions to convince us he was not insane. In the absence of an appropriate, morally intelligible, possibility of remorse, the expression 'morally the same as', in 'failing to give money to Oxfam is morally the same as "shooting a few peasants"', idles. But that, I think, is not an entirely philosophical judgement. It is the judgement of one who speaks out of a certain conception of moral value which philosophy cannot underwrite as the 'right' conception, and in the light of which what Singer says is not so much false as it is frivolous – which is not to say that national or personal omissions in relation to those who are starving cannot be seen in a morally serious light. On the contrary, it is because they can that I say what Singer says is frivolous.

10   Peter Singer, *Practical Ethics* (Cambridge: Cambridge University Press, 1979), p. 162.
11   Ibid., p. 167.

I am not arguing that if we do not feel remorse for some action then that action (or omission) cannot properly be said to be evil. It is perfectly proper to say that an action is evil although none of us feels, or would feel, remorse for doing it. Singer wishes to say that an action may be morally wrong even though our capacity to recognize it outstrips our morally reactive emotional capacities to keep in step with that recognition. He will say that it is principally a matter for psychology to explain why that is so, and he will say that it is because of the true deliverances of 'cognition' or 'reason' that we progress morally, rather than because of our sluggish and conservative affective life. He will say that recognition of the truth can outrun our capacity to cope with that recognition, and that philosophers, especially, should not encourage the idea that an emotional reaction to a judgement or practice may discredit an *argument* for it.

I would deny none of this *understood in a certain way*. It is, after all, no more than the edifying rhetoric of a familiar kind of philosophical self-congratulation. My argument was not that since we do not feel remorse we need not or ought not to feel it, but rather, that if we find the claim that we ought to, or that we might, morally unintelligible in connection with a kind of action, then we cannot find intelligible the claim that such an action was evil. That is not to deny that our sense of which actions are an intelligible object of remorse might change (as it did with some who justified slavery) and that an action might, indeed, be evil though we did not find it an intelligible object of remorse. *However, that our sense of what is a morally intelligible object of remorse can change is not a reason for saying that what we judge to be evil can, and in some cases 'rationally' should, outrun it.* Yet that is what is often suggested, and it is made to seem more plausible by contrasting our 'pre-reflective intuitions' with the deliverances of reason. I have not been speaking of our 'intuitions', and the 'claims of Reason' cannot outrun what we find intelligible.

Singer would not be very interested in remorse. No consequentialists are, and I am not now suggesting that they should be. He is concerned with what he (mis)takes to be Reason's deliverances on what we ought (morally) to do, and I do not now wish to say that he should not be. I am concerned only to argue that a certain conception of remorse is internal, partly grammatically constitutive of a certain conception of what it is for something to be morally right or wrong and what it is for a concern to be a moral concern. For consequentialists, remorse, although perhaps psychologically ineliminable and so consequentially significant, is conceptually, at best, peripheral to a right understanding of the nature of morality, which is, for them, essentially given by our manifold consequential relations to species of natural evil. By way of contrast, when Socrates said it was better to suffer evil than to do it and that the evildoer was necessarily 'miserable and pitiable', he was urging an understanding of the nature of good and evil for which a recognition of the kind of harm an evildoer had done himself, only and necessarily because he was an evildoer, was conceptually necessary. I take the harm to be what is revealed to the pained recognition that is remorse. Socrates would not judge consequentialism to be a misunderstanding of good and evil or a mistaken theorizing of it: he would judge it to be no understanding of good and evil at all.

Suppose that we go to Singer's room to find him about to hang himself from the rafters. We ask him why he is doing this and he says that he cannot live with the multiple murderer he became when he failed to renew his bank order to Oxfam. We would not conclude that he was a saint whereas poor Fred, who hanged himself only last week after 'going off to India and shooting a few peasants', was morally rather ordinary. The example is absurd, and that is my point. We do not believe that someone could kill himself because he judged himself to be a murderer because he failed to renew his banker's order to Oxfam, no matter what philosophical beliefs we credit him with, unless we judge him to be unhinged. And to say that a person could believe something only if he were unhinged is one way of finding it unintelligible that we ought to believe it under pain of irrationality.

[...]

☐j⟶ If we judge someone to be unhinged then we cannot think of him as being seriously remorseful. Remorse requires a sober collectedness, or perhaps, more accurately, it aspires to it as a perfection belonging to its nature. A person who is unhinged cannot be responsive to the demands of remorse, and someone who cannot be responsive to its demands cannot be in remorse, for to be in remorse is to be in disciplined obedience to its requirements. That is one way of understanding the idea that the mad cannot know what they do: they lack the kind of inner unity to be responsive to the claims of morality. Moral understanding requires a kind of integration (a kind of integrity) of a moral subject who is more substantial than merely a rational agent.

Moral understanding requires that those who would claim to have it should be serious respondents to morality's demands. Someone who cannot be responsive to morality's demands is one for whom morality has no reality. The 'reality' of moral value is inseparable from the reality of it as a claim on us, and serious responsiveness to that claim is internal to the recognition of its reality.

[...]

Commentary on Gaita

The chapter begins with a Dutch woman's remark about the murder in a Nazi concentration camp of three Jews to whom she had briefly given shelter, but had judged she should send away. The way she sees it, Hitler made a murderess of her. Gaita makes the point that even though, clearly, no court would deem her a murderess, the lucidity and moral seriousness of her understanding of what she did, and of what it made her, is revealed in her remark. This prompts a discussion of the scope of blame and its relation to moral responsibility, which begins at a ↦.

Clearly the Dutch woman did nothing she could be blamed for, and a typical reaction in moral philosophy would be to infer that she therefore is in no way morally responsible for the deaths that her action facilitated, and that if she feels any remorse, then, while that may be understandable at the level of psychology, it is strictly speaking inappropriate, even irrational. Gaita criticizes this response, arguing that someone's being non-culpable does not entail that they are not responsible, or that they should not feel remorse. That this is so is revealed by the fact that in relation to a wrongdoer we may quite properly hold them responsible for what they have blamelessly done, where holding them responsible means fixing them 'in a lucid response to the significance of what they did'. (Gaita mentions the plight of Oedipus – recall our previous discussion of this in relation to Bernard Williams's critique of the 'morality system'.)

Why does Gaita say, at b ↦, that the tendency to connect moral responsibility too tightly to culpability has led to a moralistic distortion?

The claim is that the failure to recognize other forms of moral responsibility besides culpability can lead to one or other of the following mistakes. Those concerned to apply some social understanding to the phenomenon of wrongdoing are led into a kind of social determinism that underplays freedom and effectively lets the culprit off the moral hook; and, in turn, this undue moral neutrality can inspire those who are concerned to apply a moral vocabulary to exaggerate the element of choice so that they wind up espousing an 'implausible voluntarism' that depicts everyone as simply free to choose what they do. This latter mistake contains the moralistic distortion, and crucially what makes it moralistic is that it enjoins a finger-wagging style of blame – a style of blame that is incompatible with pity for the evildoer.

Gaita then offers a broader, serious conception of moral responsibility, such that responsibility covers whatever 'may claim [the agent] and us in one of the many forms of serious and lucid moral response'. That is, if someone does something (voluntarily or otherwise) which can sustain a serious moral response, then she is responsible for what she has done. One might find this conception of responsibility question-begging, because the question *what* can indeed claim us in serious moral response is precisely what is up for grabs. But this circularity need not be troubling, for we manifestly are able to make sound judgements about what is and what isn't a serious moral response – this is what Gaita has in mind when he alludes (using a Wittgensteinian term) to the 'critical grammar' of moral response. That grammar governs what we properly judge to be an authentic moral response as opposed to, say, a sentimental or cowardly or self-indulgent one. Far from its being the case that there is a wholly separate moral fact which we grasp and by reference to which we then judge the appropriateness of others' responses, there is typically an interdependence between the objects of moral response and the response itself: the authenticity of the Dutch woman's response can teach one the moral significance of what she is responding to. One can learn to see something one might have missed – the nature of her responsibility for what happened – by seeing it through her eyes.

> At [c]⟶ Gaita says that Kant's remark – that even in the presence of Jesus he would need to step back and turn inwards to listen to the deliverances of Reason – is partly right and partly wrong. Explain Kant's remark, and Gaita's points of agreement and disagreement with it.

Kant's point is that, since the authority of morality is absolute, it cannot come from anything external to the agent, for an external authority can command one's obedience only contingently – faith can be lost; an agent's rationality cannot. Gaita can agree that the authority of moral thinking is that of human reasoning in the broad – 'the critical grammar of *thought*' – but he endorses an entirely non-Kantian conception of what that is. Kant's foundationalist ambition for morality meant he was interested only in *pure* reason – reasoning that is unconditioned, in particular, by any emotions. By contrast, Gaita's conception of moral judgement is fundamentally Aristotelian, so that emotional response is considered a proper part of moral reasoning, indeed an essential part of it.

At [d]⟶ we return to the Dutch woman and the second part of her remark, in which she says she hated Hitler most of all for making a murderess of her – something one might feel is at odds with a proper sense of the enormity of the horrors of the Holocaust. Gaita considers two responses. First, someone might try to alleviate her sense of guilt by inviting her to compare herself with the real mass murderers of the time. Gaita thinks this misses the point, since her feeling of guilt does not involve a mistake about whether she had become a murderess in the straightforward sense – obviously not, for she hasn't herself killed anyone. Her moral response is clear-eyed and her sense of guilt is about her proximal role in the causal chain that led to three murders. Relating her guilt to the far graver guilt of others leaves her own suffering just as it was. Second, he imagines someone pointing out that the Dutch woman's suffering is necessarily personal, and that it is typical of personal suffering that it cannot be alleviated or put in a first-personally different perspective by awareness of the suffering of others. But, for Gaita, this too misses the point somewhat. For what is sticking with the Dutch woman is not so much personal suffering as that specific kind of suffering that is remorse. Whereas other kinds of personal suffering can be consoled and alleviated by an awareness of the suffering of others, by a solidarity with them, guilty suffering or remorse (the feeling of guilt that is properly focused on the harmed party) can never be consoled in this way. Both responses miss the point by failing to appreciate the radical solitude of remorse. Gaita brings out the point by contrasting the 'we' of fellowship – one that consoles and brings solidarity – with the 'we' of mere enumeration. The guilty can only have the 'we' of enumeration, and there is no (non-corrupt) consolation in that. It is precisely the lucidity and seriousness of the Dutch woman's response that deprives her of consolation vis-à-vis either attempt to put her feeling of guilt into a different perspective.

> **Why does Gaita describe remorse as 'a kind of dying to the world'?**

The 'world' here relates to the 'we' of human fellowship. Remorse seals off any possibility of fellowship in guilt. Self-absorption too is a dying to the world in this sense, but remorse – non-corrupt remorse – is precisely not a form of self-absorption (though remorse can become corrupt through self-absorption). On the contrary, remorse is about others; it involves 'the recognition of the reality of others', specifically the reality of their pain caused by the wrong we have done them. The Dutch woman's remark expressed her clear-eyed remorse, her recognition of the murders she had played a causal role in bringing about, a pained recognition of the reality of the lives lost. Gaita does not choose to put the point quite this way, but on his conception remorse is an emotion with cognitive content – it is a feeling that can tell one about the world, about moral reality.

> **What does he mean by saying, at $\boxed{e}\rightarrow$, that guilt and remorse are not psychological phenomena?**

He is using the notion of the psychological somewhat narrowly to mean psychological phenomena which, if shared, make way for fellowship and solidarity, and so perhaps consolation. Anger, fear and jealousy are examples given; but remorse (the feeling of guilt that is focused on the harmed party) does not fit into this pattern, for there can be no consolation in sharing it. There is no therapy for the pained grasp of one's own wrongdoing. This makes the guilt-feeling that is remorse very distinctive, even among moral emotions, for Gaita points out that other moral emotions do open onto fellowship. The realization, for instance, that one is not alone in falling short of a certain level of courage may well comfort one and stop one beating oneself up about it. Not so with guilt: remorse shared is not remorse halved, for it cannot half the harm one has done. This distinctive feature of remorse is what prompts Gaita to reflect on how someone might talk quite aptly of the 'special authority' or 'special dignity' of the ethical. A lucid perception of one's own wrongdoing brings a sense of existential isolation, and of the ultimate solitude of one's lived accountability. On Gaita's view, a failure to see the centrality of remorse in moral life threatens a proper understanding of our relation to value. He detects a modern hostility to remorse, which may take various forms, ranging from the idea that it is an unhelpful negative emotion that serves no purpose, or the idea that it is a form of self-indulgence that detracts from a proper attention to the victim of wrongdoing. But Gaita regards these as misperceptions.

At $\boxed{f}$→ Gaita elaborates more on the nature of remorse. What, on his view, are its main features? Do you agree with his characterization?

We have already discussed the radical solitude of remorse – the unavailability of fellowship in remorse. Remorse sticks to one as a lone individual, and one must deal with it, perhaps recover from it, by other means than through the therapy of fellowship. What about time? Time heals most things, but not remorse: it may be half-forgotten, but in itself remorse will remain unchanged by the mere passage of time. The mystery of the phenomenon of remorse, of guilty suffering, is reflected in the mystery of what can bring recovery: repentance, atonement, forgiveness, punishment.

This mystery is a function of the unfathomable nature of the effects that other people can have on us. Grief in bereavement is one example of this, and remorse is another. If we consider how readily intelligible we find it that someone who has murdered another might kill herself for what she has done, then we remember how readily we grasp the mystery of the importance of other people. And yet moral philosophy tends not, on the whole, to help us articulate this mystery. We find ourselves talking instead about the wrong involved in breaking a moral rule or principle, or violating another rational agency. A murderer's grasp of the moral significance of what she has done entails a realization of the reality of the human being whose life she has extinguished. That realization is the mark of remorse, and in the case of a murder, possibly a remorse powerful enough to explain something as dreadful as the murderer taking her own life.

At $\boxed{g}$→ Gaita describes two common misconceptions relating to remorse. What are they? And why, according to his argument, are they misunderstandings?

The first is that remorse cannot be fundamental in moral understanding because remorse is just a feeling one has as a result of achieving proper moral understanding of a wrong one has done. Remorse, on this view, does not teach us anything about what we have done. The second is that, by contrast, the way we learn about our own wrongdoing is through reparation, and so it is in making reparations that we express what it is to take others morally seriously. Together these encourage the idea that remorse is a kind of moral self-indulgence.

In respect of this second point, about reparation, Gaita, emphasizes the importance of reparation and its close relation to remorse by acknowledging that remorse without a willingness to make reparations where possible would be a corrupt remorse. But the person who is indeed willing to make reparations will already need a sense of *what* they are making reparations for. (And so making reparations cannot be independent of feeling remorse.) He invokes an example from Bernard Williams, in which a lorry driver, through no fault of his own, runs over and kills a child. Williams uses the example to characterize the distinctively first-personal kind of regret that is, from the agent's point of view, regret for 'something *I* have done'. Williams calls this 'agent-regret'. Gaita explains the point by saying that 'some regrets are directed not only to what we did or to its effects, but also at the fact that *we* did it'. And he suggests, in relation to Williams's example, that the two things reparation is a response to are *sui generis*. That is to say, neither the sense of what one has done, nor of what our victims have suffered, can be reduced to something else; each is a basic moment of moral awareness. They are twin features of remorse; and so the point is reinforced, that remorse is not reducible to reparation.

At |h|-> Gaita develops his response to the previous point in relation to consequentialism: the style of moral theory that identifies moral rightness and wrongness exclusively in the goodness or badness of actions' consequences. The particular conception of goodness varies with the particular consequentialist theory: it might be happiness, as in the case of utilitarianism (see the extract from J. S. Mill in chapter 1); or else it might be well-being, or preference satisfaction, and so on. The critical thought in relation to consequentialism here is that consequentialist theories, as such, give no moral significance to the fact that, from the agent's point of view, '*I* did it', except insofar as that fact itself has certain morally relevant consequences. The only thing that has moral significance is the states of affairs that are brought about by actions under moral consideration. It typically matters morally that it was *me* who brought about certain bad consequences (think of Williams's lorry driver), but this kind of moral mattering doesn't register in the basic consequentialist framework. That this first-personal aspect of morality is missing in consequentialist thinking is what leads Gaita to say that consequentialists have an inadequate sense of evil done (it can matter, from the agent's point of view, that it was *she* who caused all this suffering) and an inadequate sense of evil suffered (it can matter, from the point of view of those wronged, that their suffering was caused by *her* – that it was she who did it is a proper part of the wrong that they suffer).

Gaita and Williams are agreed that agent-regret captures a crucial aspect of moral significance, but Gaita differs over how it relates to remorse. Whereas

Williams restricts remorse to voluntary actions (so the poor lorry driver would quite properly feel agent-regret, but would be rationally spared remorse), Gaita sees no reason to restrict remorse in this way. On the other hand, he does not want to assimilate remorse to the broad category of agent-regret, not least because agent-regret does not necessarily impose the radical solitude that is characteristic of remorse.

Gaita now turns, at ⟨i⟩↦, to the first of the two misconceptions of remorse he flagged at ⟨g⟩↦: that remorse is a response to an independent moral understanding of our wrongdoing. Gaita's point is that there may be an interdependence between moral understanding and remorse, so that while it may be granted that one does not feel remorseful without moral understanding of what one is remorseful for, it may remain equally true that one does not have real moral understanding in the absence of the proper remorse. Remorse is an integral part of moral understanding.

He supports this point by considering a discussion by Peter Singer, a utilitarian, of the moral difference between committing a multiple murder and failing to give money to Oxfam with the result that the same number of people die. Singer is of course trying to induce in his readers a troubled sense of the moral gravity of failing, by omission, to save even very distant lives. He does this by inviting us to consider that, at least for a moral saint, the two cases might be relevantly similar: failing to prevent distant deaths might be, for a saint, morally akin to murder. But Gaita argues that the whole idea of assimilating the two cases, even for a saint, is morally absurd. No one who grasps the evil of murder, and uses that word ingenuously and seriously, would ever suggest that forgetting to send one's cheque to Oxfam could possibly approximate to the same thing. And if someone who had forgotten to send his cheque did really believe that these things were relevantly similar, then he would be stricken with remorse (but more on this in a moment). That is why Gaita finds Singer's theoretical suggestion 'frivolous' – the relation of the wealthy, well-fed people of the world to those who live under poverty and hunger is a morally serious issue, and Singer's morally hysterical suggestion that failure to help can be seen, at least from the point of view of the moral saint, as relevantly similar to murder signally fails to address the real moral responsibility of those who can afford to help distant others but don't.

Gaita's point is not that it's impossible that something should be evil even while we do not feel remorse for it. Not at all. The point is rather that it makes no sense to call something evil (for instance, to call it murder) if it is unintelligible to us that someone might feel an appropriate remorse for it. We might express this by saying that there is a conceptual connection between remorse and evil. That conceptual connection is part of 'the critical grammar' of moral thinking, to invoke Gaita's Wittgensteinian phrase: it is in a certain sense 'ungrammatical' to talk about something as evil unless it makes sense that someone should feel remorse for it. If a moral theory – purportedly delivering the 'claims of Reason' – tells us otherwise, then there is something wrong with the theory, something wrong with the moral reasoning it employs. That is what Gaita means when he asserts that 'the "claims of Reason" cannot outrun what we find intelligible'.

> Why does Gaita say, at ☐ ↦, that 'if we judge someone to be unhinged then we cannot think of him as being seriously remorseful'?

Earlier, it was said that if someone did believe that by omitting to send his cheque to Oxfam he had done something even remotely morally akin to mass murder, then he would be stricken with remorse. But it emerges as part of Gaita's argument that this is impossible: if we did find someone ready to hang himself from the rafters of his study because he'd forgotten to send off his usual cheque to Oxfam, then we could not possibly make sense of this as a lucid moral reaction – such a man would be unhinged. This is not a further point; rather it satirically illustrates Gaita's main point against the style of moral philosophy he finds exemplified by Singer: that the conditions under which it makes sense to feel remorse set the boundaries of what can count as wrongdoing, the boundaries, that is, of evil. Thus we see that Gaita's conception of remorse and its role in moral life is the central example of a more general point he is making about what moral phenomena can be real, as opposed to illusory or mistaken. Note that he is not concerned with the boundaries of moral reality in the empiricist sense explored by Mackie. Rather, the notion of moral reality at work here is akin to that contained in Nagel's normative realism, where the notion of the reality of values flows from our attempts to make critical sense of the appearances of values – the appearances that survive the requisite critical scrutiny are real. Gaita's meta-ethical question, like Nagel's, is one that arises within the practice of moral understanding, though Gaita expresses this in rather different terms, as a question about the boundaries of what is morally intelligible. His argument is that the boundaries of intelligible remorse set the boundaries of wrongdoing. Putting the point in its most general form, we might say that morality's claim on moral sensibility sets the boundaries of moral reality.

> Do you think there is a role for the sort of moral thought experiment Singer introduces in expanding our capacity for remorse? If remorse and moral intelligibility change and develop over time, perhaps such stretched examples can serve a morally progressive purpose?

Further Reading

Chapter 1: Goodness

Feldman, F. (1997). *Utilitarianism, Hedonism, and Desert* (Cambridge: Cambridge University Press).

Foot, P. (2001). *Natural Goodness* (Oxford: Oxford University Press).

Griffin, J. (1986). *Well-Being* (Oxford: Oxford University Press).

McDowell, J. (1980). 'The Role of *Eudaimonia* in Aristotle's Ethics', in *Essays on Aristotle's Ethics*, edited by Amelie Rorty (Berkeley, CA: University of California Press); also published in McDowell's collection of essays, *Mind, Value and Reality* (Cambridge, MA: Harvard University Press, 1998).

Scheffler, S. (1985). 'Agent-Centred Restrictions, Rationality, and the Virtues', *Mind* 94: 409–19.

Smart, J. J. C. and Williams, B. (1973). *Utilitarianism: For and Against* (Cambridge: Cambridge University Press).

Williams, B. and Moore, A. (2006). *Ethics and the Limits of Philosophy* (London: Routledge).

Chapter 2: Justice

Annas, J. (1981). *An Introduction to Plato's Republic* (Oxford: Oxford University Press).

Daniels, N. (ed.) (1974). *Reading Rawls: Critical Studies of* A Theory of Justice (New York: Basic Books); among other things, read the well-known essay by H. L. A. Hart.

Fine, G. (ed.) (1999). *Plato 2: Ethics, Politics, Religion, and the Soul* (Oxford: Oxford University Press); see especially the essays by Dahl and Irwin.

Freeman, S. (ed.) (2003). *Cambridge Companion to Rawls* (Cambridge: Cambridge University Press); see especially the contributions by Nagel, O'Neill, Nussbaum and Scanlon, as well as an extensive bibliography listing books and articles that respond to Rawls.

Kraut, R. (ed.) (1997). *Plato's Republic: Critical Essays* (Lanham, MD: Rowman and Littlefield); this is another useful collection of essays.

Pappas, N. (1995). *Plato and the Republic* (London: Routledge); this is introductory but very useful.

Vlastos, G. (ed) (1971). *Plato: A Collection of Critical Essays, II: Ethics, Politics, and Philosophy of Art and Religion* (New York: Doubleday and Company); see especially the essays by Sachs and Demos.

Chapter 3: Reasons for Action

Dancy, J. (2000). *Moral Reasons* (Oxford: Oxford University Press).

Foot, P. (1978). 'Morality as a System of Hypothetical Imperatives', in her collection *Virtues and Vices* (Oxford: Blackwell).

Parfit, D. (1997). 'Reasons and Motivation', *Proceedings of the Aristotelian Society*, Supplementary Volume 71: 99–130.

Pettit, P. (1987). 'Humeans, Anti-Humeans, and Motivation', *Mind* 96: 530–3.

Smith, M. (1987). 'The Humean Theory of Motivation', *Mind* 96: 36–61.

Stroud, B. (1981). *Hume*. (London: Routledge).

Svavarsdóttir, S. (1999). 'Moral Cognitivism and Motivation', *Philosophical Review* 108: 161–219.

Williams, B. (1981). 'Internal and External Reasons', in his collection *Moral Luck*. (Cambridge: Cambridge University Press).

Chapter 4: Subjectivism and Objectivism

Benn, P. (1998). *Ethics* (London: UCL Press), ch. 2, esp. pp. 40–2.

Brink, D. (1989). *Moral Realism and The Foundations of Ethics* (Cambridge: Cambridge University Press), chs 1 and 2.

Dancy, J. (1993). *Moral Reasons* (Oxford: Blackwell), ch. 1.

Harman, G. (1977). *The Nature of Morality: An Introduction to Ethics* (New York: Oxford University Press), ch. 1; reprinted as 'Ethics and Observation', essay 6, in Geoffrey Sayre-McCord (ed.), *Essays on Moral Realism* (Cornell: Cornell University Press, 1988).

Miller, A. (2003). *An Introduction to Contemporary Metaethics* (Cambridge: Polity), ch. 6.

Platts, M. (1979).'Moral Reality', essay 12, in Geoffrey Sayre-McCord (ed.); originally published as ch. 10 of Platts, *Ways of Meaning* (London: Routledge and Kegan Paul).

Smith, M. (1993). 'Objectivity and Moral Realism: On the Significance of the Phenomenology of Moral Experience', in J. Haldane and C. Wright (eds), *Reality, Representation, and Projection* (Oxford: Oxford University Press).

Williams, B. (1985). 'Ethics and the Fabric of the World', in Ted Honderich (ed.), *Morality and Objectivity* (London: Routledge & Kegan Paul); reprinted in Williams's *Making Sense of Humanity and Other Philosophical Papers 1982–1993* (Cambridge: Cambridge University Press, 1995).

Chapter 5: Morality and Obligation

Chappell, T. (2006). 'Bernard Williams', *Stanford Encyclopedia of Philosophy* (Feb. 2006), <http://plato.standford.edu/entries/williams-bernard>.

Hollis, M. (1995). 'The Shape of A Life', in J. E. J. Altham and Ross Harrison (eds), *World, Mind, and Ethics: Essays on the Ethical Philosophy of Bernard Williams* (Cambridge: Cambridge University Press).

Jenkins, M. (2006). *Bernard Williams* (Chesham, Bucks: Acumen), ch. 4.

Korsgaard, C. (1996). *Creating the Kingdom of Ends* (Cambridge: Cambridge University Press), esp. chs 2, 3 and 4.

Korsgaard, C. (1997). 'Introduction', *Groundwork of the Metaphysics of Morals*, trans. and ed. Mary Gregor (Cambridge: Cambridge University Press).

Louden, R. B. (2007). 'The Critique of the Morality System', in Alan Thomas (ed.), *Bernard Williams* (Cambridge: Cambridge University Press).

Moore, A. (2003). *Noble in Reason, Infinite in Faculty: Themes and Variations in Kant's Moral and Religious Philosophy* (Abingdon: Routledge), 'First Theme: Morality'.

O'Neill, O. (1989). *Constructions of Reason* (Cambridge: Cambridge University Press), esp. chs 5 and 7.

O'Neill, O. (1991). 'Kantian Ethics', ch.14 in P. Singer (ed.), *A Companion to Ethics* (Oxford: Blackwell).

Taylor, C. (1995). 'A Most Peculiar Institution', in J. E. J. Altham and Ross Harrison (eds), *World, Mind, and Ethics: Essays on the Ethical Philosophy of Bernard Williams* (Cambridge: Cambridge University Press).

Williams, B. (1981). 'Moral Luck' and 'Persons, Character, and Morality', in *Moral Luck. Philosophical Papers 1973–1980* (Cambridge: Cambridge University Press).

Chapter 6: Boundaries of Moral Philosophy

Crary, A. (2007). *Beyond Moral Judgement* (Cambridge, MA: Harvard University Press), esp. ch. 4.

Diamond, C. (1991). 'Missing the Adventure: Reply to Martha Nussbaum', in *The Realistic Spirit: Wittgenstein, Philosophy, and the Mind* (Cambridge, MA/London: MIT Press).

Gaita, R. (2000). *A Common Humanity: Thinking About Love, Truth and Justice* (London: Routledge; first published 1998).

Nussbaum, M. (1986). *The Fragility of Goodness: Luck and Ethics in Greek Tragedy and Philosophy* (Cambridge: Cambridge University Press), ch. 1.

Nussbaum, M. (1990). '"Finely Aware and Richly Responsible": Literature and the Moral Imagination', and 'Perceptive Equilibrium: Literary Theory and Ethical

Theory', in *Love's Knowledge: Essays on Philosophy and Literature* (Oxford and New York: Oxford University Press).

Raphael, D. D. (1983). 'Can Literature be Moral Philosophy?', *New Literary History* 15/1 (Autumn): 1–12.

Singer, P. (1979). *Practical Ethics* (Cambridge: Cambridge University Press).

Index

Printed and bound by CPI Group (UK) Ltd, Croydon, CR0 4YY

24/08/2023

08104433-0001